Ben Jonson and Possessive Authorship

What is the history of authorship, of invention, of intellectual property? In this book, Joseph Loewenstein describes the fragmentary and eruptive emergence of a key phase of the bibliographical ego, a specifically Early Modern form of authorial identification with printed writing. In the work of many playwrights and non-dramatic writers – and especially in the work of Ben Jonson – that identification is tinged, remarkably, with possessiveness. This book examines the emergence of possessive authorship within a complex industrial and cultural field. It traces the prehistory of modern copyright both within the monopolistic practices of London's acting troupes and its Stationers' Company *and* within a Renaissance cultural heritage. Under the pressures of modern competition, a tradition of literary, artistic, and technological imitation began to fissure, unleashing jealous accusations of plagiarism and ingenious new fantasies of intellectual privacy. Perhaps no one was more creatively attuned to this momentous transformation in Early Modern intellectual life than Ben Jonson.

Joseph Loewenstein is Professor of English Literature at Washington University, St Louis, Missouri. He is author of *Responsive Readings: Versions of Echo in Pastoral, Epic, and the Jonsonian Masque* (Yale, 1984); *The Author's Due: Printing and the Prehistory of Copyright* (Chicago, 2002); editor of *The Staple of News* for the *Cambridge Edition of the Works of Ben Jonson* (forthcoming); and a general editor of the Oxford Edition of the *Complete Works of Edmund Spenser* (forthcoming).

Cambridge Studies in Renaissance Literature and Culture

General Editor
STEPHEN ORGEL
Jackson Eli Reynolds Professor of Humanities, Stanford University

Since the 1970s there has been a broad and vital reinterpretation of the nature of literary texts, a move away from formalism to a sense of literature as an aspect of social, economic, political and cultural history. While the earliest New Historicist work was criticized for a narrow and anecdotal view of history, it also served as an important stimulus for post-structuralist, feminist, Marxist and psychoanalytical work, which in turn has increasingly informed and redirected it. Recent writing on the nature of representation, the historical construction of gender and of the concept of identity itself, on theatre as a political and economic phenomenon and on the ideologies of art generally, reveals the breadth of the field. Cambridge Studies in Renaissance Literature and Culture is designed to offer historically oriented studies of Renaissance literature and theatre which make use of the insights afforded by theoretical perspectives. The view of history envisioned is above all a view of our own history, a reading of the Renaissance for and from our own time.

Recent titles include

A complete list of books in the series is given at the end of the volume.

From the Stationers' Register (liber D, f. 115), partial record of one of the largest transfers of copyrights on record prior to the establishment of statutory copyright. This transfer from 1626 shifts rights in a number of books, including the text of Jonson's *Every Man In His Humour*, from Thomas Snodham to William Stansby.

Ben Jonson and Possessive Authorship

Joseph Loewenstein

CAMBRIDGE
UNIVERSITY PRESS

CAMBRIDGE UNIVERSITY PRESS
Cambridge, New York, Melbourne, Madrid, Cape Town, Singapore, São Paulo

Cambridge University Press
The Edinburgh Building, Cambridge CB2 8RU, UK

Published in the United States of America by Cambridge University Press, New York

www.cambridge.org
Information on this title: www.cambridge.org/9780521812177

First published 2002
This digitally printed version 2007

A catalogue record for this publication is available from the British Library

Library of Congress Cataloguing in Publication data

Loewenstein, Joseph, 1952–

Ben Jonson and possessive authorship / Joseph Loewenstein.

    p.   cm. – (Cambridge studies in Renaissance literature and culture: 43)

Includes bibliographical references and index.

ISBN 0 521 81217 8 hardback

1. Jonson, Ben, 1573?–1637 – Authorship. 2. Authorship – Economic aspects –
England – History – 17th century. 3. Authors and publishers – England –
History – 17th century. 4. Intellectual property – England – History – 17th century.
5. Literature publishing – England – History – 17th century. 6. Copyright –
England – History – 17th century. 7. England – Intellectual life – 17th century.
8. Imitation in literature. 9. Renaissance – England. I. Title. II. Series.

PR2636 .L69 2002 822′.3 – dc21   2001052959

ISBN 978-0-521-81217-7 hardback
ISBN 978-0-521-03818-8 paperback

. . . Meum Theatrum . . .

Contents

Illustrations

Frontispiece: from the Stationers' Register (liber D, f. 115),
partial record of one of the largest transfers of copyrights
on record prior to the establishment of statutory copyright. This
transfer from 1626 shifts rights in a number of books, including
the text of Jonson's *Every Man In His Humour*, from Thomas
Snodham to William Stansby.
(Reproduced by permission of the Worshipful Company of
Stationers, photograph by Geremy Butler)   *page* iv

Acknowledgments

At the outset of this particular book, it seems ironic and superfluous to dwell on how much of it is the work of others. ("Mine own and not mine own," Helena puts it in a very different context.) This book concerns itself with the complex contingencies – the institutions, the intellectual forbears, the friends, the materials and machines – that enabled one writer to specify a body of writing as his own (and so to know himself and so to puzzle over having written). I remain enough under Jonson's influence to resist the materialist temptation to acknowledge the fan-fold paper, the archaic keyboard, and the unsupported operating system and word-processing programs (though it's not clear to me that we can expect tenderness from objects if we deny them our gratitude), but it will be a pleasure to specify the other contingencies of "my own" writing.

Institutions. Research for this book was supported by grants from the Exxon Education Foundation, the National Endowment for the Humanities, the American Council of Learned Societies, and the Graduate School of Arts and Sciences at Washington University. I received useful feedback from audiences including the Renaissance Seminar of the University of Chicago, the English Department at the University of Notre Dame, the Group for Early Modern Culture Studies, the conference on Early Modern Habits of Reading at the Huntington Library, the Early Modern Dissertation Group at Washington University, the Editorial Board of the *Cambridge Edition of the Complete Works of Ben Jonson*, and from readers for *ELH*, *Renaissance Drama*, and, of course, Cambridge University Press. The common rooms in the English Department at Washington University, the Newberry Library, the Warburg Institute, and the National Humanities Center provided invaluable havens.

Portions of this book are based on articles first appearing in *ELH* (published by The Johns Hopkins University Press) and *Renaissance Drama* (published by Northwestern University Press), and on essays for Jennifer Brady and W. H. Herendeen's *Ben Jonson's 1616 Folio* and Laurie E. Maguire and Thomas L. Berger's *Textual Formations and Reformations* (both published by the University of Delaware Press).

Forbears. I had the good fortune to study with three great teachers of Jonson, John Hollander, Tom Greene, and Ted Tayler: this is not their sort of work, but it was written with them very much in mind. For some reason, the New Bibliographers, and particularly A. W. Pollard, W. W. Greg, E. K. Chambers, and (less widely recognized) Evelyn Albright and Leo Kirschbaum, have been much condescended to of late: I hope this book indicates how much remains to be learned from them – as from those of their modern students and critics on whom I've relied here: Peter Blayney, David Gants, Don McKenzie, and Paul Werstine, among others.

Friends. At the early stages of this work, it was nurtured along in conversations with Albert Ascoli, Leonard Barkan, Michael Baxandall, Margaret Ferguson, Steve Justice, and Mary Beth Rose. Somewhere in mid-project, Jonathan Dollimore and Alan Sinfield challenged me to untangle my argument. And all along, my colleagues at Washington University – especially from Wayne Fields, Naomi Lebowitz, John Morris, George Pepe, Dan Shea, and Steven Zwicker – offered needling and cheer to distract me from my research and writing and to herd me back to it; all along, too, conversation with Richard Halpern, Jon Haynes, Rosemary Kegl, and Chris Kendrick was an occasional, bracing necessity. Theresa Everline, Christiane Auston, and Chris D'Addario have checked references, edited, saved me from some inanities, and asked questions that reminded me why this work might be worth pursuing.

Lynne Tatlock has been this book's most complex and determining contingency; it is therefore hers.

1   An introduction to bibliographical biography

> One thing I must answer before it bee objected; 'tis this: When these Comedies
> and Tragedies were presented on the Stage, the Actours omitted some Scenes
> and Passages (with the Authour's consent) as occasion led them; and when
> private friends desir'd a Copy, they then (and justly too) transcribed what
> they Acted. But now you have both All that was Acted, and all that was
> not; even the perfect full Originalls without the least mutilation; So that were
> the Authours living, (and sure they can never dye) they themselves would
> challenge neither more nor lesse then what is here published; this Volume
> being now so complete and finish'd, that the Reader must expect no further
> Alterations.
>
> (Humphrey Moseley, letter prefatory to the *Works* of Beaumont and Fletcher, 1647)

What is the history of authorship, of invention, of mental making?

The author's challenge

A history of literature able to rewrite itself as a sociology of symbolic forms, a history
of cultural conventions, should perhaps finally find a role and a dignity in the context of
a total history of society. (Franco Moretti, *Signs Taken for Wonders*)[1]

This book investigates what I take to be a central moment in the early cultural history of English intellectual property, the larger narrative of which
I offer in a related volume, *The Author's Due: Printing and the Prehistory
of Copyright*.[2] My goal in the present study is to describe the fragmentary
and eruptive emergence of what I have elsewhere called the bibliographical
ego, a specifically Early Modern form of authorial identification with printed
writing.[3] Although the sense that a printed book is proper to a writing self
is conditioned by a variety of institutions and habits, my particular concern
here is to show that this sense of the proper-ness of books was conditioned
by the ways in which writing was reproduced and sold, and especially by the

[1] Trans. Susan Fischer, David Forgacs, and David Miller (London: Verso, 1983), 19.
[2] Chicago: University of Chicago Press, 2002.
[3] "The Script in the Marketplace," *Representations*, 12 (Winter 1985), 101–14.

ways in which printed books were made the objects of monopolistic competition. In the Early Modern period, this proper-ness of books is shaped, even
determined, by the ways in which quasi-proprietary claims were asserted by
the possessors of manuscript copies, by printers, by publishers, and by authors. And although individual authors might experience this connectedness
idiosyncratically, we may speak of the cumulative effect of such experiences,
which was to transform authorship into a form of public agency increasingly
distinguished by possessiveness. I want to add immediately that this is not a
determination that operates in a single direction: the new possessiveness of
authorship in turn transformed the commercial practices within the book trade,
adjusted the public debate on liberty of the press and, eventually, changed the
legislative activities of Parliament. The transformation in the way authors understood themselves – as producers and (in Mark Rose's nice phrase) as owners –
conditioned the political struggles that lead to the legal institution of intellectual
property.[4] *Jonson and Possessive Authorship* describes the literary, theatrical,
and book-producing milieu in which a distinctive, though by no means ec-
centric bibliographic ego developed, an ego shaped by prevailing proprietary
practices and shaping those that would come after. I hope that this goes a way
towards realizing Moretti's hope for a history of literature that can "perhaps
finally find a role and a dignity in the context of a total history of society."
To discover how Jonson experienced his own writing as it was variously circulated and why he experienced it that way, to compare Jonson's experience
to Heywood's, Shakespeare's, Daniel's, and others', is not only to advance the
work of literary biography, but also to discover both a central effect and a central
cause of the development of English (and, thence, Anglo-American) intellectual
property.[5]

Jonsonian authorship appears in the following pages, then, as recovery and invention, effect and cause. The first two chapters sketch the proprietary structures
that shaped Tudor and Stuart theatrical practices, advancing and refashioning an
inquiry initiated early in the twentieth century by those scholars who founded
modern bibliography and modern theater history – Pollard, Greg, Albright,

---

[4] Mark Rose, *Authors and Owners: The Invention of Copyright* (Cambridge, Mass.: Harvard
University Press, 1993). For the various ways in which authorial self-understanding shapes legal
developments, see the last four chapters of *The Author's Due*.

[5] While, in many of the following pages, emphasis falls on Jonson's experience of print, it is im-
portant to remember that Jonson's non-dramatic works, as well as his masques, seem to have had
a fairly wide circulation in manuscript. While Harold Love (*Scribal Publication in Seventeenth-
Century England* [Oxford: Clarendon, 1993]), Arthur F. Marotti (*Manuscript, Print, and the
English Renaissance Lyric* [Ithaca: Cornell University Press, 1995]), and Jonathan Goldberg
(*Writing Matter: From the Hands of the English Renaissance* [Stanford: Stanford University
Press, 1990]) have variously attempted to reconstruct a generalized Early Modern scribal imag-
inary, the reconstruction of an individual author's experience of manuscription has not been
attempted. My contribution to such a reconstruction may be found below, in the reading of
"Inviting a Friend to Supper" and in the discussion of Martial's influence on the development of
Jonson's bibliographic ego.

Simpson, and Chambers. These chapters describe the competitive milieu in which such practical artists as Shakespeare, Heywood, Greene, and Jonson worked, the milieu that shaped their sense of what theatrical work and dramatic Works were and could be. They aim to reveal the shifting and stiffening boundaries that emerged in London's competitive theatrical culture, boundaries between theater and press, between authors and actors, and, most important, between imitation and plagiarism. These analyses prepare for the more concentrated discussion of Jonsonian authorship offered in the second half of the book, a discussion that is designed not only to indicate (as others have) the remarkable *degree* of Jonsonian intellectual possessiveness, but to specify the *shape* of that possessiveness – as is necessary for any serious understanding of Jonson's place in the history of intellectual property. At the center of this book, in chapters 3 and 4, the reader will find an economic and intellectual history of the Name of the Author.

It may be useful to summarize here the larger economic and political history of English intellectual property in which the literary history of possessive authorship unfolds.[6] This larger history leads from an evolving set of proto-legal institutions of intellectual property that predate the invention of printing and proceeds to the passage of the Statute of Anne of 1710, known to most legal historians as the first copyright statute. This history was powerfully shaped by monopolistic practices within London's Stationers' Company during the two centuries that saw that unusually powerful company succumb to the general weakening of the English craft guilds, organizations that were rendered factionalized and unstable by burgeoning claims of capital. To quote an observation made in *The Author's Due*:

The changes in industrial organization characteristic of Early Modern economic practice can be seen with particular clarity in the early history of the book trade: it is exemplary. In fact, the book trade led some of those transformations: it *was* exemplary. That is, the book trade is both a significant instance and a significant agent in the transition from feudalism to capitalism. In effect, then, an account of the late renaissance reader is significantly an account of the early capitalist consumer; the history of printing is a history of early capitalist industry; the book is quintessentially a modern commodity and the author in some ways quite an unexceptional laborer. Therefore, the intellectual, political, and commercial competitions that, I will argue, produce modern intellectual property as we know it are vividly engaged in struggles central to the construction of post-feudal reality.

Copyright could be said to have developed out of the regulatory mechanisms that most immediately constrained Elizabethan printing: the exclusion of non-stationers, and non-Londoners from printing by means of the Stationers' Charter of 1557, the licensing "system," the system of "registration" or stationers'

---

[6] Much of the following summary is quoted from the analyses in *The Author's Due*.

copyright, and the printing patent.[7] It might be more accurate to say, however, that copyright developed out of struggles to elaborate or transform these regulatory mechanisms.

Although there may have been some sort of licensing system in the second decade of the sixteenth century, Henrician licensing as we know it seems to have developed out of the ecclesiastical proscription of particular books during the mid-1520s.[8] Licensing is the subject of repeated royal proclamations from the 1530s forward and the system was subject to various modifications in procedural detail. It is important to realize that Tudor censorship constrains both authors and stationers – with stationers including publishers, printers and booksellers. It is perhaps as common to see a stationer suffering for the publication of seditious or heretical works as to see authors so suffering; indeed, the language of those Tudor royal proclamations and Star Chamber rulings that promulgate licensing is aimed specifically at the book trade and not at authors (or at readers), whose activities were not constrained by *special* forms of legislation.

Licensing, which constrained the printing industry from without, was complemented by an internal institution, "entrance," the institution from which modern copyright is the direct descendant.[9] In order to control competitive pressures within the printing industry, the Stationers' Company developed a

---

[7] The account of stationers' copyright, the printing privilege, license, and the larger mechanism of constraint, the London Stationers' near-monopoly on English printing implies several other forms of constraint: illiteracy (which inhibited demand), market inefficiency (which immeasurably, but certainly led to misguided production), and apprenticeship and similar mechanisms (which limited productive capacity).

[8] In *Burned Books*, 2 vols. (New York: Columbia University Press, 1932), Ripley Gillett asserts that Henry made his first direct attempt to regulate the press in 1526, but the 1526 proclamation that Gillett attributes to Henry was in fact issued by the Archbishop of Canterbury; *Burned Books*, I:20. John B. Gleason suggests that a system for scrutinizing religious books printed in England may have existed as early as the first decade of the sixteenth century; "The Earliest Evidence for Ecclesiastical Censorship of Printed Books in England," *The Library*, series 6, 4 (1982), 135–41. For a careful account of the origins and practice of early Tudor censorship, see Cyndia Susan Clegg, *Press Censorship in Elizabethan England* (Cambridge: Cambridge University Press, 1997), 25–54. Her great contribution to the study of the early English press has been to show the incoherence of Elizabethan censorship and so to demonstrate how poorly the notion of hegemonic discursive control sorts with the factual record.

On ecclesiastical censorship in the 1520s, see A. W. Reed, "The Regulation of the Book Trade Before the Proclamation of 1538," *Transactions of the Bibliographical Society*, 15 (1918), 157–84 and D. M. Loades, "The Press Under the Early Tudors: A Study in Censorship and Sedition," *Transactions of the Cambridge Bibliographical Society* 4 (1964), 29–50. And see also Rudolph Hirsch, "Pre-Reformation Censorship of Printed Books," *The Library Chronicle* (University of Pennsylvania), 21 (1955), 100–05.

[9] A. W. Pollard, "The Regulation of the Book Trade in the Sixteenth Century," *The Library*, series 3, 7 (1916), 18–43; M. A. Shaaber, "The Meaning of Imprint in Early Printed Books," *The Library*, series 4, 24 (1943), 120–41; W. W. Greg, "Entrance, License, and Publication," *The Library*, series 4, 25 (1944), 1–22, and *Some Aspects and Problems of London Publishing Between 1550 and 1650* (Oxford: Clarendon, 1956); and Leo Kirschbaum, vigorously contesting Shaaber's argument, "Author's Copyright in England Before 1640," *Papers of the Bibliographical Society of America*, 40 (1946), 43–80.

system whereby individual members could secure an exclusive right to market a given text – to print it or to have it printed, to distribute the printed text, to sell it or to have it sold. A guild member submitted a MS, the so-called "copy," to the guild leadership, and paid a registration fee; upon his doing so, the text was usually "licensed to him" or "entered to his copy" in the company Register.[10] It was not always so registered: from the somewhat casual nature of the convention of actual registration ensued a number of disputes concerning what procedure was necessary and sufficient to secure copy; more will be said of this in the next chapter. One can say securely, however, that a stationer's exclusive right to market a manuscript was not originally seen as the sort of personal property right which we associate with modern copyright; it was a privilege conferred by the guild on one of its members, part of an imperfect, but not ineffective system by which the guild sought to preserve internal order.[11] Licensing served the crown as a mechanism of ideological control, safeguarding England from sedition or heresy; entry served the guild as a mechanism of economic control, safeguarding the stationers from internal hostilities and profit-shrinking competition.[12]

But the crown had more particular interests than those of ideological control and the guild had broader concerns than those of mere internal stability and prosperity. That it was normal company policy to enter only copies which had been approved by a reputable licensing authority is implied by occasional entries in the Stationers' Register indicating exceptional and grudging registration: copies "tolerated unto" their owners and those to be printed "at the peril" of the registrant.[13] The draft ordinances drawn up for the Company in 1559

[10] In *Shakespeare and the Stationers* (Columbus: Ohio State University Press, 1955), 34–37, Kirschbaum offers a brief but useful survey of the various formulae used in the Registers to record entrance and suggests an intelligible drift in the valence of entrance discernible in the various locutions. See also Clegg, *Press Censorship*, 15–18.

[11] On these matters, L. R. Patterson's *Copyright in Historical Perspective* (Nashville: Vanderbilt University Press, 1968) is particularly useful, though his narrative of the development of sixteenth-century regulatory mechanisms has some notable gaps. See also A. Renouard, *Traité des droits d'auteurs dans la littérature, les sciences, et les beaux-arts*, 2 vols. (Paris, 1838); Henri Lemaitre, *Histoire du dépôt légal* (Paris, 1910); Royce Frederick Whale, *Copyright: Evolution, Theory and Practice* (London, 1971). For a more general introduction to jurisprudential issues, see M. J. Kaplan, *An Unhurried View of Copyright* (New York, 1967).

[12] A terminological *caveat*: throughout this book, unless otherwise noted, I use "ideology" and "ideological" in a limited sense, to refer not to the deep structure of historical experience, a semantic substrate to which individual historical agents usually have no conscious access, but to the strategic orthodoxies that those in power seek consciously to impose on others.

[13] The first of the "tolerated" entries – they are usually entries for ballads – dates from May 1580. (This comes – not coincidentally – only a few months after the publication of Stubbs' *Gaping Gulf* for which two stationers were convicted of slander and sentenced to lose their right hands; only one of the two was pardoned.) The remarkable entry "at peril" dates from November 1583, though an entry from May 7, 1582 shows a similar scruple: the latter reads, "*Edward white* Receaved of him for printinge a booke of phisicke called *the pathwaie to health for the poore* Translated and gathered by PETER LEVENS And the said *Edward* hathe undertaken to beare

(but probably never approved), suggest that the Company intended to conduct, or to continue conducting, its own blanket scrutiny of all manuscripts to be printed.[14] The guild eventually assumed some of the responsibility for licensing, so that by the seventies entrance can usually be assumed to entail license. More important than guild participation in censorious regulation, though, is the fact that the crown frequently involved itself intimately in the regulation of competition. It did so by granting printing patents to favored stationers, following an older model of privileged printing which had long flourished in continental Europe: the patent constitutes the fourth of the major English regulatory institutions.[15] English printing privileges were remarkably broad grants, and very lucrative ones, whereby certain stationers gained control of whole classes of publication: law books, for example, or service books; music, or the official primer.[16]

That these regulatory mechanisms constitute a complex suite of constraints on publishing has some general theoretical consequence. To allege an interrelation between mercantilist protectionism and censorship – to trace press licensing, for example, not only to efforts to secure religious orthodoxy but also to monopolistic policies designed to encourage industrial development – is to challenge the Foucauldian truism that penal regulation of discursive practices has precedence over economic ones. In *The Author's Due* I argue that monopolistic competition and its discontents do more to condition the rise of intellectual property than do censorship and its critics. This is intended not to discredit the importance of ideological regulation as a stimulus to authorial self-consciousness, but merely to assign that stimulus its appropriate historical place.

Early in *The Author's Due*, I discuss a labor dispute that erupted within the Stationers' Company in the late 1570s. This episode has general historical interest, since it brings to the surface a trade instability that will persist to the end of the seventeenth century and thereby guarantees that the book trade continued to present itself as a problem in need of solution: the Statute of Anne was one of many such solutions. But this printers' revolt has a more particular interest as well, since it specifies one of the regulatory mechanisms as an irritant to internal trade relations. The printers manifest their discontent, first, by petitioning against printing patents and, then, in the early 1580s, by infringing

and discharge all troubles that maie arise for the printinge thereof... 12d" (Edward Arber, *A Transcript of the Registers of the Company of the Stationers of London, 1554–1640 A.D.*, 5 vols. [London and Birmingham, 1875–94], II:411).

[14] "Every boke or thinge to be allowed by the stationers before yt be prynted" (Arber, *Transcript*, I:350). The language of the register is, however, ambiguous, and this "allowance" may simply be that guild sanction, regulating competition, which is implied by entrance.

[15] For an account of Venetian printing privileges see chapter 3 of *The Author's Due*.

[16] A list of privileges extant in 1582 may be found in Arber, *Transcript*, I:115–16 and 144; a similar list may also be found at II:775–76. The history of English industrial privilege is taken up in the fourth chapter of *The Author's Due*.

some of the more important ones – among them the Psalter, the Primer, and the Grammar. These patents were tremendously lucrative engines of capital formation and, in the long run, devastatingly disruptive to guild fellowship. The Elizabethan rights of copy could not cohere, just as the fragile internal stability of a self-regulated guild economy could not endure, under the disruptive pressure exerted by royal privileges.

The Privy Council intervened to quell the unrest and in 1586, the Star Chamber issued a decree that strengthened the power of the company masters to police the trade and to ward off competition from without. The most important institutional effect of the revolt against the printing patent is that, in the short term, stationers' copyright, the right conferred by entry, was consolidated, while the risks of failure to register also increased somewhat. But monopolistic practices within the book trade continued to be as irritating as they were important in the years when the likes of Jonson and Shakespeare began their writing careers, years in which new monopolistic practices ramified throughout the English economy and were subjected to stringent criticism. A literary history that can "perhaps find a role . . . in the context of a total history of society" may begin by probing the relationship between the growth of English monopolies and the rise of intellectual property.

Thomas Coryat, Samuel Daniel, and George Wither enter the "total history of society" as authors who found ways to perform functions normally performed by stationers exclusively. Daniel, the first English author to supervise the publication of a collected *Works*, is of particular importance in the history of possessive authorship. A non-stationer, but a patentee, he secured an unprecedented degree of monopolistic protection for several of his other books, while his long-term alliance with the stationer, Simon Waterson, enabled him to control the resistance of the Stationers' Company to his infringements on their customary prerogatives. George Wither also secured extraordinary publishing privileges, but was hardly so fortunate in his relations with the Stationers' Company, and largely because he managed to intrude upon some of the company's most valuable privileges. He made himself a particularly articulate adversary of the stationers' monopolies. Since he was himself the beneficiary of such a grant, he exempted printing patents from his criticism, but mounted an attack on stationers' copyright as a misappropriation of what Wither asserts to be authorial rights.

Wither's assertion is ground-breaking, although the anti-monopolism is not: the chapter also investigates the development of this important idiom of seventeenth-century politics. The problem of monopolies became an important concern of the last Elizabethan parliaments and Bacon's presence in those sessions guaranteed that the concept of monopoly itself should be subjected to careful analysis, an analysis that developed into a reflection on inventiveness as such. But since anti-monopolist sentiment was expressed in any number of forums in late sixteenth-century England, I devote some attention to Sir John Harington's strange Erasmi-Rabelaisian pamphlet, *The Metamorphosis of A-Jax*, at once a contribution to the history of indoor plumbing and to the late Elizabethan critique of monopoly and invention.

Late in *The Author's Due*, the question of censorship, so long deferred, is resumed as part of a sustained discussion of Milton's *Areopagitica* and censorship here takes its place among the other regulatory determinants of authorship and intellectual property. *Areopagitica* has long been accorded an important place in the historiography of English book culture, and particularly in that Whiggish historiography that makes freedom of expression into the central problem in literary history. My purpose is to situate the treatise in the history of intellectual property by rendering as precisely as possible just what properness to authors Milton attributes to books. To some extent, my account wrests Milton from his traditional place of honor in the historiography of individual liberty and replaces him in a somewhat less honorable – but somewhat more interesting – history of possessive individualism. The next chapter, which continues the political history of licensing through to the early eighteenth century, also continues the work of "replacing" Milton in the history of English Book culture: the Whig Milton of the late seventeenth century turns out to be most important as a figure around whom those who wished to abridge the power of the stationers would rally. The Statute of Anne turns out to be a device for hobbling the stationers; it purges the work of ideological regulation of the trade protectionism which had shadowed it since the first half of the sixteenth century. By the turn of the eighteenth century the Milton of *Areopagitica* and, more important, the Milton of *Eikonoklastes* had emerged as a hero of authorial property, and he would remain so in the legal tradition that made modern sense of the Statute of Anne by discovering beneath it – inventing in opposition to its terms – a "natural" authorial copyright that commodifies thought itself.

This is the larger historical argument to which the pages that follow contribute. *Jonson and Possessive Authorship* offers an account of the imaginative culture that conditions, say, a Witherian sense of authorial prerogatives, a Haringtonian hostility to intellectual protectionism, and a Miltonic sense of the uncanny vitality of the printed book under a regime of suspicion; it is an institutional history of various distinctively Early Modern authorial affects. Earlier literary historians have attempted sociological explanations for the sudden rise of authorial self-promotion around the middle of Elizabeth's reign. My purpose in this book is to situate this "author-campaign" within the quickening (and mutually interfering) economies of book trade and theater. The possibility of authorial participation in these early economies transforms the way authors present themselves – on stage and on the page – and accelerates the decay of literary patronage. A variety of authors figure in this discussion of the economics of authorship – Sidney and Heywood, Shakespeare and Brome – but, as

L. C. Knights shrewdly observed more than half a century ago, it was Jonson who was most excruciatingly alert to the competitive economic milieu of writing, in which actors, theater owners, stationers, and authors collaborate and compete. Knights' Jonson is a critic of this milieu; the pages that follow detail his vexed and compromising engagement therein: Jonson's reactionary creativity makes him almost unrivalled as both chronicler and agent of modern authorial practice. But I have also sought to disturb the conventions of literary historiography, at least occasionally, by remembering that there are other "agents of discourse" who determine the evolution of intellectual property and even the evolution of authorship. In *The Author's Due*, a number of stationers – John Wolfe, Christopher Barker, Simon Waterson, John Twyn, and Jacob Tonson – appear as determining figures in literary and legal history. Here in *Jonson and Possessive Authorship*, several others join their ranks – William Ponsonby, George Eld, Walter Burre, and William Stansby – for they make an inestimable contribution to the sociology of Early Modern symbolic forms, the history of cultural conventions.

Still, authorship is my focus here, and its determining conditions are various. An account of the origins of authorial "investment" in both the theater (and its constituent institutions) and the printed book (and the industrial structures that support it) would necessarily be partial were it to ignore the influence of received ideas concerning authorship. Chapters 3 and 4 below recall a crucial antique contribution to the history of intellectual possessiveness, the development of a discourse of plagiarism, and examine its revival in and around the work of Ben Jonson. My goal in these pages is to examine an occasion at which the economic conditions of writing, and the technological determinants of printing crucially interact with a very specific revival in intellectual culture; we might think of it as a moment at which the Renaissance provides a conceptual map of modern practice, at which the Early Modern comes to know itself as a Renaissance.

Towards authorial fantasy

In 1604 John Baylie entered and Simon Stafford printed *The View of France*, apparently annoying its author, Robert Dallington. He complained of the unauthorized publication in his prefatory letter to the new and very slightly expanded edition issued within a few months by Thomas Creede:

Gentlemen, The Marte is open for writing: & this towne at this time more ful of such Novelties then ever was Franckfort, though more for the Printers gaine, then the Authors credit, or benefit of us the Readers.

The letter marks the deliquescence of what might be called literary feudalism, for it shows us the customary structures of patronage exploded by the market in printed books. We now say "market," but this is perhaps inaccurate; for Dallington it is a permanent fair, which registers the transitional moment, the moment when politics gives way to economics as fundamental social determinant: "this towne . . . more ful of such Novelties then ever was Franckfort." A modern market, then, a constant explosion, with concomitant burstings-open of old intimacies: Stafford has "exposed that to publicke view, which I had destined to perpetuall privacie." The spectacular idiom of the travel writer makes Dallington himself a violator of privacies and thus not so very different from Stafford. Dallington may have a dim sense of this: the title page of the revised edition, *A Method for travell. Shewed by Taking The view of France*, suggests an attempt to mute the spectacular character of his undertaking by placing viewing under the supervision of method. Dallington is working within the conventions of prefatory *apologiae*, no doubt, but his modesty has an unconventional pitch:

> This discourse was written long since, when the now Lord *Secretarie* was then Lord Embassador (*quem honoris causa nomino*) & intended for the private use of an honourable gentleman: you may therefore pardon those passages which have lesse coherence with these times, for that the face of thinges is much altered in France.

Writing and, especially, printing fix texts indiscriminately, rendering them mimetically "incoherent" and dislocating them from those private milieux in which, Dallington urges, they have true utility. This mournful sense of social disruption and of representational lapse – fallings-off regularly exposed and lamented in Elizabethan social satire – marks, as I said, the end of literary feudalism, but Dallington imagines the market as a terminal blow to authorship (though the next decades and centuries expose the groundlessness of such fears). He feigns a personal collapse: "As it was out of my power to call in the booke: so it is out of my will to correct it." The press is regulated, books are licensed and proofs corrected, but Dallington protests that authorial intention has been made impertinent to such regulation.

Knowing that "it was out of my power to call in the booke," Dallington did some next best thing, though it is difficult to reconstruct from the bibliographical evidence just how he proceeded. The title page of *A Method for travell* indicates that the book was printed by Thomas Creede, but that is almost certainly not true. Creede had printed a new title page, Dallington's prefatory letter, "To All Gentlemen That have Travelled," from which I have been quoting, and Dallington's brief essay, "A method for travell," which defensively subordinates the travel book to a larger project, the promulgation of a theory of travel. But that seems to have been all that Creede printed; the rest of the book was made up by binding in the unsold sheets of Stafford's edition of the *View of Fraunce*. This much is clear. What is not clear is how Creede acquired Stafford's pages – whether he (or Dallington) purchased them at wholesale prices from booksellers, or from Stafford (though there is little reason to suppose that Stafford kept a large stock of the book on hand) – nor is it clear whether he did any *more* than acquire the unsold copies of the *View*, as, for example, arranging for a more-or-less formal transfer of stationers' copyright in the work. The Stationers' Register contains nothing to shed light on the case, which is made somewhat more confused by Dallington's own account:

As it was out of my power to call in the booke: so it is out of my will to correct it: not holding it worthy the paines of a re-view, much lesse the charge of a re-impression. I have onely taken it from the Godfathers and Nurses this publisher had bespoken (being now almost seaven yeares olde and past the Nurse) and put him to schoole to your favourable entertainment.

There is a great deal to be said of the frequency with which Early Modern authors personify printed books: figures of books as persons abused, misused, or in need of discipline often reflect simultaneously on censorship, on the relation between the editorial labor and that of press-correction, and even on the proper-ness of authors and books.[17] Dallington's figures are only gently disciplinary. Maintaining the imagery of enforced incoherence, Dallington presents the book as a youth infantilized by the book trade and describes himself as having restored the youth to the instructive and maturing social institution of an urbane readership. These imaginings obscure the actual commercial negotiations entailed by the "new" edition. Dallington can hardly wish away the agency of the press, of course, and when he waives any serious engagement in trade matters – "not holding it worthy the paines of a re-view, much lesse the charge of a re-impression" – his detachment is clearly partial. One way to interpret Dallington's absolute construction is to take it that the author *might* have been called upon to finance a corrected edition, although that would have been a fairly exceptional proceeding, but the syntax untethers the exceptional, and lets the idea of the author's commercial engagement with the book float free, as fantasy.[18] Language production, epitomized in figuration, is pitted against book production, epitomized in trade relations: "I have onely taken it from the Godfathers and Nurses this publisher had bespoken." We shall not know who paid for this "taking from," whether Dallington or Creede, nor shall we know what was taken – printed sheets or those sheets together with an abstract right: Dallington closes the Stationers' Register as he puts the book to school. The willful obscuring of the material production of the book is Dallington's jealous counterstrike against the press.

---

[17] See the discussion of *Areopagitica* in *The Author's Due*, pp. 171–91 and my "Personal Material: Jonson and Book-burning," *Re-presenting Ben Jonson: Text, History, Performance*, ed. Martin Butler (Houndmills: Macmillan Press, 1999), 93–113.

[18] On publishing by authors, see chapter 4 of *The Author's Due*.

Over what is he fussing and fighting? Over the very nature of the book. Is it to be (1) a material object or commodity, (2) a tributary gift, the sign and site of a complex socio-cultural relationship, or (3) the material signifier of "ideas" proper to their author? The personification resists the first conception, but the three conceptions are intertwined and Dallington is unable fully to set one against another; his personification fails to clarify. So the letter stumbles at the end, the referential function of his figures collapsing: the book has been taken from the publisher's godfathers and nurses and consigned to the tutelage of its readers, "of whome he may learne to speake better French, and to knowe the French better. Desiring as tender parents doe (because he is of a soft nature, and quickly snibd,) that you use him gentlie." It is fruitless to try to determine what is meant by describing the book as instructed by its readers: scholarship seems to shade here towards wardship, implying the most richly subjectifying discipline, the book stringently socialized. Of course, the figure is not analytic, but fantastic. In his effort to free the book from its place in a network of commercial relations, Dallington confers upon it an inordinately and incomprehensibly labile sociality. We could say, in summary, that he has responded to the mart for writing with a prefatory letter that is much too personal.

Cultural historiography may seek to reconstruct the ponderable, the range of possible thoughts and conceivable actions available at a given historical moment, but the outlines of the ponderable are not the only proper object of historical reconstruction; there are good reasons to wish to reconstruct the fantasies made possible by the knowledge, the conditions, the full *habitus* of the past. Dallington's prefatory letter is abuzz with fantasies – that books are personal, that a market in books is insignificant and may be forgotten, that conversational or epistolary or, at least, manuscriptive intimacies may be restored to writing within a modern culture of the printed book, that the gentlemen to whom an author might write in a printed epistle are distinguishable from the consumers who might buy a book, and – a final and more bluntly contrafactual fantasy – that it might be *in* an author's power as author (rather than as nobleman) to call in a book, as if an author were a kind of intimate censor. These deserve to be understood as determinate fantasies. Since such fantasies are both historical products and historical motives, an attempt to "account for" such fantasies seems an entirely appropriate extension of normal historiographic practice.[19] This book takes up two complementary problems: how the institutional structure of the book trade determines authorial fantasy and how such determinate fantasy manifests its motive power. How and how far. Jonsonian authorial fantasy cannot be exhaustively explained as a function of institutional history – it is idiosyncratic, but not capriciously so, and my purpose here is to account for

---

[19] The attempt is not, of course, unprecedented; an influential recent antecedent may be found in Giles Deleuze and Felix Guattari, *A Thousand Plateaus: Capitalism and Schizophrenia*, trans. B. Massumi, 2 vols. (Minneapolis: University of Minnesota, 1987).

many of the idiosyncrasies – nor (of course) does authorial fantasy, however willful, prescribe the destiny of proprietary practice.

If the sense of *semantic* rupture between sender and receiver is as old as language, the sense of *social* rupture between sender and receiver is as old as writing – the press did not invent it. For example, the poet who writes "*Voi ch'ascoltate in rime sparse il suono / di quei sospiri ond'io nudriva 'l core*" testifies not only to that interminable work of semantic reconstruction endemic to language, but also to the labors of recovery inevitable within a manuscript culture, labors made at once piquant and harsh as systematic textual scholarship invents itself.[20] When Petrarch goes on to refer to his "*vario stile*," in the fifth line of this sonnet, he is not merely boasting of his range, he is lamenting the fact that inscriptions, by their very scribal nature, are doomed to mimetic variance. These gaps, or variances, however endemic to writing *per se*, sustain themselves on the casual and manifold variances of manuscript dissemination, the brute mechanisms intervening between inscription and its vagrant dispersals. Petrarch's philological "vaneggiar" anticipates Dallington's plaintive fantasy. It more closely anticipates Chaucer's more low-mimetic complaint:

> Adam scriveyn, if ever it thee bifalle
> Boece or Troylus for to wryten newe,
> Under thy long lokkes thou most have the scalle,
> But after my making thou wryte more trewe;
> So ofte a-daye I mot thy werk renewee,
> It to correcte and eek to rubbe and scrape;
> And al is thorugh thy negligence and rape.[21]

Noting the texts traduced – "Boece" (Chaucer's translation of a late-antique treatise) and "Troylus" (a "translation" of a "late-antique" tragedy) – we can see that the complaint against manuscript transmission is specifically aroused and authorized by early Renaissance philology, with its broad dismay about textual variability. Of course, the complaint is also personal; Chaucer curses his scribe, not scribal culture. (That there is something primal – Adamic – about the scribe he curses does not render the lapse abstract or impersonal.) Chaucer's complaint and Petrarch's plaintive self-display provide useful contrasts to Dallington's protest; Dallington is in a tradition that includes Petrarch and Chaucer, but his complaint is *impressive* and not *inscriptional*. But this is far too general a characterization: the novelty of Dallington's complaint against dissemination, its specificity to print culture, has to do with the coherent institutional character of the book trade he opposes. Impressive book culture is regular, impersonal, and abstract; it is a market phenomenon. The same may be

[20] *Petrarch's Lyric Poems: The* Rime sparse *and Other Lyrics* by Robert M. Durling (Cambridge, Mass.: Harvard University Press, 1976), 37.
[21] *The Works of Geoffrey Chaucer*, ed. F. N. Robinson (Boston: Houghton Mifflin, 1957), 534.

said of the bibliographical ego, the fantasies it hosts: Dallington's fantasy is a market phenomenon.[22]

The press enters cultural history as an extension of manuscript: early typography, for example, aims to reproduce handwriting. The evolution towards mass production, however, quickly disrupted the affiliation of printing with manuscript: the capital logic of mass production forced the development of broad and efficient distribution networks; the new scale at which dissemination operated forced the development of a censorship oriented toward the book rather than the writer; and, in England, the idiosyncratic history of guilds generated a book trade with highly developed monopolistic prerogatives. Together these developments created a book trade marked by an early dislocation from scribal disseminative traditions, an extreme rupture between the writing hand and the printing press. The alterity of the press expresses itself in Dallington's reactionary fantasy of authorship. But there is a good deal more to say about how this fantasy was conditioned. I want to propose that mass production, book censorship, and highly regulated marketing of books motivate Dallington's fantasies, but that the Elizabethan theater stimulated the *release* of those fantasies.

---

[22] On the *ethos* of early-modern market phenomena, see Jean Christophe Agnew, *Worlds Apart: The Market and The Theater in Anglo-American Thought, 1550–1750* (Cambridge: Cambridge University Press, 1986), 40–56.

2 Community properties

The spectacle ... is no more than the economy developing itself for itself.

Guy Debord, *Society of the Spectacle*[1]

Returning from Parnassus

The regulation of the early Tudor press and the regulation of the Tudor stage begin to share a history in the 1540s.[2] Several years into the Henrician campaign to constrain religious discussion and control access to the English Bible, "an act for the advancement of true religion" was promulgated to suppress such false doctrine as might be promoted, not only by subversive sermons, "but allso by printed bokes, prynted balades, playes, rymes, songes, and other fantasies."[3] The list may be slightly formulaic, a way of exhausting the field of discourse, and not strong evidence of specific royal concern over the power of dramatic performance to stir up an unlettered populace.[4] Edward's proclamation of 1551,

---

[1] *Society of the Spectacle and Other Films* (London: Rebel Press, 1992), 65.

[2] Muriel Bradbrook asserts that "as early as 1533 interludes on controversial matters had been forbidden" (*The Rise of the Common Player* [Cambridge: Harvard University Press, 1962], 31), despite Virginia Gildersleeve's convincing argument that this proscription is a "ghost" that originates with Warton's *History of English Poetry* (*Government Regulation of the Elizabethan Drama* [New York: Columbia University Press, 1908], 5). Gildersleeve does assemble some instances in which individual early Tudor performances provoked specific repressive responses. Repression of non-liveried professional performers – as opposed to repression of controversial performance – has a distinguishable history, associated with the general Henrician alarm over vagabondage.

[3] 34 and 35 Henry VIII, cap. 1, 1543. The act is not entirely prohibitive in character, acknowledging as it does that the imagination can serve orthodoxy as well as heterodoxy: "it shalbe lawfull to all and everye p[er]sone and p[er]sones, to set foorth songes, plaies and enterludes, to be used and exercysed within this Realme and other kinges Domynions, for the rebuking and reproching of vices and the setting foorth of vertue: so allwaies the saide songes, playes or enterludes meddle not with interpretacions of Scripture, contrarye to the doctryne set foorth or to be sett foorth by the Kinges Majestie."

[4] A 1546 proclamation specifically concerned with heretical theological works and unauthorized Bible translations uses a portion of this list – "the King's majesty straightly chargeth and commandeth ... that from henceforth no printer do print any manner of English book, ballad, or play, but he put his name to the same" (Paul H. Hughes and James F. Larkin, *Tudor Royal Proclamations*, 3 vols. (New Haven: Yale University Press, 1964–69), *Volume I: The Early Tudors*, 272). The phrasing suggests little more than the redundancies of legalese.

15

on the other hand, certainly *was* an attempt to secure absolute control of the discursive field to the crown, but it treats dramatic performance as a threat at once singular and analogous to that of the printed book: after a long exordium and a set of rules governing vagabonds, the proclamation takes a censorious turn –

And for because divers printers, booksellers, and players of interludes, without consideration or regard to the quiet of the realm, do print, sell, and play whatsoever any light and fantastical head listeth to invent and devise, whereby many inconveniences hath and daily do arise . . . his highness therefore straightly chargeth and commandeth that from henceforth no printer or other person do print nor sell within this realm or any other his majesty's dominions any matter in the English tongue . . . unless the same be first allowed by his majesty or his Privy Council, upon pain of imprisonment without bail or mainprize and further fine at his majesty's pleasure. Nor that any common players or other persons upon like pains do play in the English tongue any manner interlude, play, or matter without they have special license to show for the same in writing under his majesty's sign, or signed by six of his highness' Privy Council.[5]

The statute indicates that the drama had established itself as a significant constituent of English polemical culture, for like the press, it could now claim the censor's notice.[6]

The induction of book and play into a regime of licensing had national and institutional consequences. This is easy to trace in the case of the book, for the complementary pursuits of ideological and industrial regulation had made the book trade the engine of English cultural centralization. The stationers' national monopoly in book production, formalized at mid-century, was the crucial mechanism of this centralization and it facilitates and naturalizes the plan which the Bishop of London set forth in 1583 in a letter to the Lord Treasurer; he seeks to install an exclusively Londonish culture, easily susceptible to constant supervision:

hearinge . . . that of late there were presses sette uppe in secret Corners and a purpose to sett uppe other presses in places remote from the citie, and from The ordinarie serche of the wardens and personnes skilfull and of the officers attendinge the Comission before

---

[5] Hughes and Larkin, *Tudor Royal Proclamations*, I:371. This conjunction recurs in a Marian edict of August 18, 1553 – the third proclamation of her reign – which enjoins the queen's subjects "neither . . . to print any books, matter, ballad, rhyme, interlude, process, or treatise nor to play any interlude except they have her grace's special license in writing for the same" (Hughes and Larkin, *Tudor Royal Proclamations*, II:6–7).

[6] E. K. Chambers' summary of the history of play-licensing in London, the documentary history of which begins in the late 1540s, remains useful: it "really turns upon an attempt of the Corporation, goaded by the preachers, to convert their power of regulating plays into a power of suppressing plays, as the ultimate result of which even the power of regulation was lost to them, and the central government, acting through the Privy Council and the system of patents, with the Master of the Revels as a licenser, took the supervision of the stage into its own hands" *The Elizabethan Stage*, 4 vols. (Oxford: Clarendon, 1923), I:277. David Bevington surveys the polemical engagement of Tudor drama in *Tudor Drama and Politics* (Cambridge: Harvard, 1968).

whome theis matters Commonlie be disclosed . . . I gave order to the wardens of the
Stacioners to make serche and to staie suche presses and printinge stuffe.

Dramatic performance "in places remote from the citie" was brought under
similar central control somewhat earlier, as town councils in the 1560s and
1570s delivered up play books for perusal and correction to archbishops, bish-
ops and their representatives, to members of Her Majesties Commission for
Ecclesiastical Causes in the North. Thus, during the middle decades of the
century, as print gained in influence and the London stationers secured their
dominion over the English market in printed books, provincial playing of
interludes was frequently suppressed and the acting of local mystery plays
was steadily curtailed, so that by 1575, the year in which the elder Burbage
opened the Theater, the old Cycle was given its last performance at Chester.[7]
The prevailing pattern is the replacement of indigenous theatrical activity by
performances by centrally licensed, visiting professionals.[8] By 1616, the Lord
Chamberlain would enlist local magistrates to support his centralized management of a professional theatrical culture which had replaced the indigenous and
usually amateur culture, quashed in the middle of Elizabeth's reign:

Whereas Thomas Swynnerton and Martin Slaughter beinge two of the Queenes Majesties
company of Playors havinge sepa[ra]ted themselves from their said Company, have
each of them taken forth a severall exemplification or duplicate of his majesties Letters
patente to the whole Company and by vertue therof they severally in two Companies with
vagabonds and such like idle p[er]sons, have and doe use and exercise the quallitie of
playinge in div[er]se places of this Realme to the great abuse and wronge of his Majesties
Subjects in generall and contrary to the true intent and meaninge of his Majestie to the
said Company.[9]

Irregular duplication: those who recall the idiom of Christopher Barker, a privileged stationer outraged at the disorderly printing of the 1570s and 80s will find

---

[7] Bradbrook, *The Rise of the Common Player*, 32. The suppression of the Chester Cycle was
followed in 1576 with prohibitions of the religious dramas at Wakefield and York; the Coventry
plays were banned in 1581; see Glynne Wickham, *The Medieval Theatre*, 3rd edn. (Cambridge:
Cambridge University Press, 1987), 221 and *Early English Stages, 1300–1660*, 3 vols. (London:
Routledge, 1959–72) I:114–16. Unlicensed companies continued to play in the provinces during
the reign of Elizabeth, but they remained vulnerable to arrest and punishment for vagrancy – although some occasionally performed under the auspices of municipal authorities (and, Chambers
notes, an exceptional company quartered in Bristol performed after 1613 under a patent from
Queen Anne; *ES*, I:304). The trend, all told, is towards royal control of the stage and away from
local independence; for the regulatory history, see Gildersleeve, *Government Regulation*, 26–34
and Wickham, *Early English Stages*, vol. II, pt. I, 47–8. On the breakdown of the provincial
dramatic tradition, see Wickham, *Early English Stages*, 141–42; a fuller account may be found
in Harold C. Gardiner, S. J., *Mysteries' End: An Investigation of the Last Days of the Medieval
Religious Stage, Yale Studies in English*, 103 (New Haven: Yale University Press, 1946).
[8] Gardiner, *Mysteries' End*, 91–3.
[9] John Tucker Murray, *English Dramatic Companies*, 2 vols. (Boston: Houghton Mifflin, 1916),
II, 343.

these accents familiar.[10] Pembroke goes on to cite William Perry for having similarly sharked up a troupe to travel under the name of the Children of the King's Revels, Gilbert Reason for mustering a troupe touring as the Prince's Men, and Charles Marshall, Humphrey Jeffes, and William Parr for touring with others as the Prince Palatine's Company.[11] All were to have the exemplifications of their patents confiscated and were summoned to appear at Whitehall. The custom of touring with slight companies was being exaggerated to the point that the corporate identity of the patentee came under stress. ("O, pardon!" they might have said facetiously, "since in a crooked figure may / Attest in little place a million": it was the fate and *business* of theatrical representation to put identities under stress and, specifically, to mistake, distort, and develop the precise subject of monopoly protection.) The actors are called back from their secret corners and diverse (or "little") places, restored to their strictly licensed companies and so bound into a now national culture.

London thereby achieved a large measure of discursive hegemony; the provinces had been effectively "provincialized." But the centralization of English government and of its economic life underwrites not only a centralization of cultural life but also a destabilization of social and discursive norms: henceforth social and cultural life in England operates under the sway of *fashion*, a febrile sensitivity to mode, itself felt to be temporary and obtrusively insubstantial.[12] Although the press was a powerful instrument of cultural centralization, far more powerful in this respect than ever the stage could be, the latter emerged as the greatest exponent of fashion, of London's fashionableness.[13] What the press produces, the theater renders spectacular.[14]

Most of the processes just sketched – the assistance of the press in both the decay of patronage and the centralization of English cultural life, the regulatory yoking-together of London's press and London's stage, the constitution of the theatre as a privileged site of scandal – are variously documented in that casually brilliant sequence of university skits, the Parnassus Plays of 1598, 1599, and 1601.[15] G. K. Hunter offered a crucial analysis of the urbanization of English

---

[10] On Barker, see chapter 2 of *The Author's Due.*

[11] Murray, *English Dramatic Companies*, II, 343–44.

[12] On "the unifying and disintegrative aspects of [Tudor] fashion," see Richard Halpern, *The Poetics of Primitive Accumulation* (Ithaca: Cornell University Press, 1991), 38–45.

[13] On the stage as exponent of fashion, see Jonathan Haynes, *The Social Relations of Jonson's Theater* (Cambridge: Cambridge University Press, 1992).

[14] Indeed, one of the ways of expressing the enormity of the press was to mark its achievements as theatrical. Take, for example, that famous assault on ecclesiastical polity, the Marprelate controversy. Although the Marprelate controversy is essentially a print phenomenon, one of the episcopal writers would single out the coarse idiom of Marprelate polemic as quintessentially theatrical: "the stage is brought into the church; and vices make play of church matters" (Chambers, *ES*, I:294).

[15] I cite these plays from the edition of J. B. Leishman, *The Three Parnassus Plays* (London: Nicholson, 1949); I here accept his argument for the dating of these plays.

literary culture in his great study of John Lyly, describing the adaptation of a humanist intelligentsia to balked political ambition – for Hunter, the efflorescent literature of the Elizabethan eighties and nineties is a "literature of frustration" – but Hunter's analysis is substantially anticipated in the anonymous work of this Cambridge trilogy, which furnishes a fascinating report on literary sociology at the end of the reign of Elizabeth.[16] The trilogy charts cultural urbanization, above all. *The Pilgrimage to Parnassus* initiates the trilogy with a pedestrian satiric tour of literary culture, one which pits dissolute anti-intellectualism, puritanical anti-humanism, and chic literary eroticism against the rigors of humanist scholarship. The threats to serious scholarly commitment are crowned in the fifth act, however, by the entrance of Ingenioso, a rollicking, pragmatic University Wit, possibly modelled on Thomas Nash. His brief against Parnassus, the university, is simply that

Parnassus is out of silver pitifullie, pitifullie . . . I, after manie years studie, havinge almoste brought my braine into a consumption, looking still, when I should meete with some good Mæcenas, that liberallie would rewarde my desertes, I fed soe long upon hope, till I had almoste starved . . . Goe to Parnassus? Alas, Apollo is banckroute, there is nothing but silver wordes & golden phrases for a man. (lines 575–621)

This disrupts the logic of the play, which has concerned itself with *distractions* from scholarship, and not with threats to the very cultural status of scholarship. Ingenioso not only anticipates the Hunter thesis, he also prepares for the new departures of the next two plays of the trilogy.

The First Part of the Return from Parnassus finds the protagonists, Studioso and Philomusus, leaving Parnassus; they encounter Ingenioso at the urban threshold

What? Philomusus and Studioso? Have noe hungrie schools swallowde youe up before this time? Yts merie y faith when *vacui viatores* meete. As for my state, I am not put to my shiftes; for I wante shiftes of shirtes, bandes, and all thinges els, yet I remaine thrise humblie & most affectionatlie bounde to the right honorable printing house for my poore shiftes of apparell. (lines 148–54)

A new patron, but untender: instead of the customary bonds represented by livery, we have the occasional bonds of debt (the language of clientage – of humble affection – is parodic, registering and protesting the affective vacuum of capitalist relations of production). Ingenioso straddles a patronage system and a new market economy in printed books.[17] He figures writing as usurious

---

[16] *John Lyly: The Humanist as Courtier* (Cambridge: Harvard University Press, 1962), 1–35.

[17] This between-ness is defining for Ingenioso. In the first play, Ingenioso is leaving Parnassus when the two heroes, Philomusus and Studioso, are arriving; in *The First Returne*, when the heroes are about to leave Parnassus, he arrives, having given up on London. When his attempt to find a Maecenas in the vicinity of Parnassus fails, he resolves upon a return to London. He is always on the rebound, always lives, in his terms, by his *shifts*.

lending – "for the husbanding of my witt, I put it out to interest, and make it returne twoo Phamphlets a weeke" (lines 201–2) – and so associates literary activity with the most "progressive" sector of the economy, yet his most recent piece of pamphleteering is an attempt to secure personal patronage, an attempt to use the press to shore up clientage: "It pleased my witt yesternight to make water, and to use this goutie patron in steed of a urinall, whome I make the subject and content of my whole speache" (lines 214–17). For his pains, Ingenioso receives a mere two groats from his "Maecenas." As the Parnassus of patronage crumbles, Ingenioso ushers his charges into the modernity of a loosely conceived social space which might best be described as "literary London."

Literary London is a deeply competitive milieu: the Parnassus plays continue to hold scholarly attention largely because of the satiric assaults on contemporary authors that can be found in the latter plays of the trilogy.[18] Indeed, censure is the consuming center of *The Second Returne*, the last play of the trilogy, a shrewd evocation of the kind of infighting endemic to an articulate but uprooted class.[19] After the prologue, Ingenioso enters reading Juvenal, admiring his "jerking hand." But this is not a specifically scribal satiric culture: its determination by print is marked by the entrance of Judicio – not, surprisingly, some sort of neoclassical arbiter, but a press corrector. Judicio joins in the general cultural project of censure, but with the special dolor of the weary wage laborer: "Would it not grieve any good spirritt to sit a whole moneth nitting over a lousy beggarly Pamphlet, and like a needy Phisitian to stand whole yeares tooting and tumbling the filth that falleth from so many draughty inventions as daily swarme in our printing house?" (lines 142–46). The meeting of Ingenioso and Judicio immediately provokes them to an extended survey of the literary scene, the characterizations of the poets included in Anthony Munday's anthology, *Belvedere, or the Garden of the Muses*, Spenser, Constable, Lodge, Daniel Watson, Drayton, Davies, Locke, Hudson, Marston, Marlowe, Jonson, Shakespeare, Churchyard, and Nashe; of the others anthologized there, Judicio remarks, in the smudged language which seems to be the signature of his trade, they "write as men go to stoole, for needes, and when they write, they write as a boare pisses, now and then drop a pamphlet." Ingenioso is more charitable: "*Durum telum necessitas.* Good fayth, they do as I do, exchange words for mony" (lines 324–28).

This gesture of demystification may be facile, but it keeps our attention focused on an especially modern literary market – "they do as I do, exchange

[18] Not all the literary judgments are dismissive; see the *Second Part*, lines 202–319.

[19] That competition *defines* literary London for the University Wits may be gathered not only from the habit of censure in the play, but from its allusions to the feud between the satirists Marston and Hall, to the feud within the London theatrical scene specifically dramatized in *Poetaster* and *Satiromastix* and to that more generalized competition between a successful romantic idiom associated with Shakespeare and a successful academic idiom associated with Jonson.

words for mony: I have some traffique this day with *Danter*, about a little booke which I have made, the name of it is a Catalogue of *Cambrige* Cuckolds" – and the scene ends with Ingenioso rushing off to haggle with Danter over the price the disreputable printer has offered for this salacious book. Danter was an excellent choice, for he was a real printer and a notoriously irregular one. He is remembered by bibliographers for his piratical printing of the *Romeo and Juliet* first quarto, but his contemporaries no doubt knew him as one of several printers who had pirated the *Grammar* in the early eighties and printed Roman Catholic devotional texts in the nineties. His ties to Thomas Nashe no doubt helped to earn him his place in this literary satire, but the character has emblematic force as well. Danter reminds us that, in the 1590s, the quest for a stable literary culture was an industrial matter.[20]

The career of Ingenioso traces that quest to brilliant failure. Precocious in his early repudiation of the university, Ingenioso dances along an economic faultline: in hock to an unnamed printer, he had attempted the good old path of clientage; when Patron proves niggardly – he has spent all his ready cash on expensive purgatives – Ingenioso resolves to return to London and there, once again, to "live by the printinge house." We next find him in a new relationship of clientage, one clearly marked as modern and debased, another instance of a perceived breakdown in patronage. Indeed, the relationship might as well have been lifted from one of Jonson's plays: Ingenioso becomes a syco-phant to Gullio, a braggart of military and literary pretentions.[21] Ingenioso's *ingenium* gives way to literary cony-catching, as he makes it his hectic business to flatter Gullio's taste (its pedestrian conventionality apparently signified by his special fondness for the plays of Shakespeare) and to ghost-write sonnets for him. This deflated clientage is short-lived, however, and Ingenioso is again thrown back on pamphleteering for the popular press. The first two plays of the trilogy thus sharply punctuate each of Ingenioso's several "shifts": a new economic arrangement is attempted, its failure performed, and the necessity of

---

[20] Sidney had offered a much differently inflected version of Ingenioso's cultural analysis. For Sidney poetry suffers, not by a decay of patronage, but by a deliquescence of military activity: "Poesy...like Venus (but to better purpose) had rather be troubled in the net with Mars than enjoy the homely quiet of Vulcan: so serves it for a piece of reason why they [i.e., poets] are less grateful to idle England, which now can scarce endure the pain of a pen. Upon this necessarily followeth, that base men with servile wits undertake it, who think it enough if they can be rewarded of the printer"; *Defense of Poesy*, ed. J. A. van Dorsten (London: Oxford University Press, 1966), 62. This represents cultural history as an undialectical class event, the replacement of an imagined feudal corps of soldier–poets (dimly adumbrated in Puttenham's "courtly makers," Wyatt and Surrey) by a servile class, yet the novel "reward of the printer" disrupts and complicates Sidney's historiography. What Sidney begins as an indictment of Elizabethan pacifism ends up as a grumble against industrial determinations of literary culture.

[21] Although this portion of the plot might have been lifted from Jonson, but might equally have been lifted, like the social relations of Jonsonian comedy, from life: Leishman argues that both this episode in Ingenioso's career and the earlier encounter with Patron are closely modelled on phases of Nashe's life; *The Parnassus Plays*, 75–78.

yet another arrangement is announced. In the last play of the trilogy, although the careers of Ingenioso's fellow alumni, Studioso and Philomusus, are still rendered punctually, the treatment of Ingenioso's career grows blurred – he spends a large portion of his time drinking with Furor Poeticus and Phantasma – as if to suggest that he can no longer hope for a stable place in the literary economy. Like the *Defence of Poesie*, the *Second Return* is concerned with the "place" of a poesy dislocated by the deterioration of servile relations: Sidney relocates poesy "in theory"; the satirist's version of this dislocated elsewhere is the tavern or, perhaps, the stupor.

Significantly, at precisely this juncture, at which literary clientage seems so unsteady as to produce the compensatory delusion of a purely Phantastic literary society, the theatrical culture of London is brought on stage. If the Parnassus plays have been offering a materialist pilgrimage through the transitional literary economy of England, the itinerary has led from a Parnassan university through a devastated landscape of clientage and a printed metropolis, and now beyond: late in the play, Studioso and Philomusus offer their services to Kemp and Burbage; a few scenes later, Ingenioso announces that "writts are out for me, to apprehend mee for my playes, and now I am bound for the Ile of doggs . . . Farewell, *mea si quid vota valebunt*" (*Second Return*, 2064–68). Ingenioso departs for one of the most notorious theatrical loci of the London stage: *The Isle of Dogs*, a dramatic satire by Nashe, Jonson, and perhaps some others, had been staged in July of 1597, and was thought sufficiently "seditious and sclanderous" that the Privy Council, usually disposed to protect the theater, acceded to long-standing pressures from the City government and commanded the cessation of theatrical activity in London and the razing of London's playhouses.[22]

Once again, stage and press are conjoined beneath the gaze of the early Tudor censor. Here at the end of the century we can glimpse the nervous relationship that had developed between the two media, a relationship partly fostered by censorship. The 1597 crackdown on playing, the result of a confluence of old municipal anti-theatrical zeal and court hostility to unregulated topical representation, produced a temporary self-restraint within the theatrical community. This moment of theatrical caution was fairly brief – by autumn it was clear that London's stages were *not* to be razed and by February the Privy Council

---

[22] I take the quotation from a letter of the Privy Council, dated August 15, 1597, calling for an investigation of how the play came to be written and performed (Chambers, *ES*, IV, 323). The play is not named in this letter, nor is it named in the July 28 Order, calling for a moratorium on playing in the London area and the "plucking down" of London's stages, but Henslowe's indication (*Henslowe's Diary, Edited with Supplementary Material, Introduction, and Notes*, eds. R. A. Foakes and R. T. Rickert [Cambridge: Cambridge University Press, 1961], 240) that *The Isle of Dogs* was the immediate provocation for the restraint on playing has never to my knowledge been questioned. Wickham gives a detailed account of the July Order and its implications in *Early English Stages*, II, part ii, 9–29; for a judicious reflection on the 1597 crackdown, see Janet Clare, "*Art Made Tongue-Tied by Authority": Elizabethan and Jacobean Dramatic Censorship* (Manchester: Manchester University Press, 1990), 51–55.

and the City aldermen had roughed out regulations that would limit theatrical performance in London but would maintain sufficient theatrical activity to satisfy the recreational needs of Elizabeth and her court.[23] Still, the actors proceeded cautiously, and the year of cautious theatrical suspense had reciprocal effects on the press: although satire had been a fashionable idiom for at least a decade, output began to escalate in 1598, perhaps in response to the relative quiescence of *theatrical* satire.[24] And so, a see-saw, a resonating cultural system: disturbed by this flurry of satiric printing, Richard Bancroft, Bishop of London, and John Whitgift, Archbishop of Canterbury stiffened the licensing procedures in order to curtail the publication of satiric *books*. On June 1, 1599, Whitgift and Bancroft commanded that several notorious printed satires be burnt, and proscribed the future printing of satires or epigrams. Predictably, the theaters simply took over as the principle medium of satiric expression (and, it might be added, thereby became the site of that sometimes hilarious and often deeply intelligent public competition over comical satire sustained by Marston, Dekker, Jonson, Shakespeare, and others). A watershed: at the end of the century, and under the influence of a various regulatory regime, the press and the stage discover each other as competitors. The dramatic text is crucial to the development of intellectual property at this juncture precisely because it is the focus of so many vectors of competitive interest – more, in most instances, than non-dramatic texts. It is therefore the proper center of concern in this and the following three chapters.

Comedies for commodities

Indeed M. *Kempe* you are very famous, but that's as well for [your] workes in print as your parts in que" (Philomusus in *The Second Part of the Return from Parnassus*, lines 1796–7)

Censorship, having constrained the circulation of representations, had significantly spurred monopolistic tendencies within the disseminative economy. But

---

[23] The follow-up letter from the Privy Council to the Master of the Revels and the Justices of the Peace of Middlesex and Surrey is explicit: "licence hath bin graunted unto two companies of stage players retayned unto us, the Lord Admyral and Lord Chamberlain, to use and practise stage playes, whereby they might be the better enhabled and prepared to shew such plaies before her Majestie as they shalbe required at tymes meete and accustomed, to which ende they have bin cheefelie licensed and tollerated as aforesaid" (Chambers, *ES*, IV, 325). This letter, which was meant to quash the activities of "a third company who of late (as wee are informed) have by waie of intrusion used likewise to play," follows ten days on a revision of the act for punishment of vagabonds in which the licensing of provincial playing was withdrawn from local Justices of the Peace; see C. W. Wallace, "Shakspere and the Blackfriars," *Century Magazine*, 80 (1910), 744–45.

[24] On satire in the late 1590s, see J. B. Leishman's introduction to *The Parnassus Plays*, particularly pp. 42–45; on the entry of satiric books during this period, see G. B. Harrison, "Books and Readers, 1599–1603," *The Library*, series 4, 14 (1933–34), 13–15.

the ban on printing satire and the closing of public theaters were not the sole inhibitions on the free circulation of representation. We must now consider other evidence of competition *between* the press and the stage and treat of the various means devised by players and stationers to control public access to dramatic texts. The historiography of this control has been an area of scholarly contest for nearly a century, and I cannot hope to resolve the scholarly debates on copyright, stage-right, ownership of scripts, or the nature of copy-texts for dramatic publishing – all matters of central concern to editors of Early Modern drama. Myriad tendrils of possessiveness entangle these dramatic texts, and so far historical bibliographers have not managed to see a logic in the tangle. Still, I do think it possible to discover in the bibliographic data evidence of important general developments in the economy of playbooks.

Thomas Heywood's *If You Know Not Me, You Know No Bodie* was first performed *c.* 1605. In a prologue for a Caroline revival of the play (*c.* 1632), Heywood suggests that the original production had been particularly well-received –

> as well perform'd at first,
> Grac't and frequented, for the cradle age,
> Did throng the Seates, the Boxes, and the Stage

– and that it was quickly published in response to this popularity –

> So much; that some by Stenography drew
> The plot: put it in print: (scarce one word trew:)
> And in that lamenesse it hath limp't . . .[25]

This prologue has often been quoted, for it raises a number of bibliographic questions: were the printed texts of many plays based on such reported copy? what does Heywood mean by "Stenography"? what features of the early printed texts seem to betray "stenographic" copy?[26] It has also raised some more skeptical questions: does Heywood believe what he says here or is he simply giving us a special version of the common disclaimer of intention to publish? why lodge a protest against inaccurate publication decades after that publication? None of these questions admits of secure answer, yet the prologue is revealing nonetheless. Interrogating what have come to be known as the "moral rights"

---

[25] *The Dramatic Works Of Thomas Heywood*, 6 vols. (London: G. Pearson, 1874), I:191.

[26] This poem was already central to various debates about the bibliography of Elizabethan drama as early as 1934, when G. N. Giordano-Orsini referred to it as "often-quoted"; see his "Thomas Heywood's Play on *The Troubles of Queen Elizabeth*," *The Library* ser. 4, 14 (1933–34), 313. Giordano-Orsini makes a convincing argument for memorial reconstruction and not stenography. One can watch Greg changing his mind on the subject by comparing "The Function of Bibliography in Literary Criticism Illustrated in a Study of the Text of *King Lear*," *Collected Papers*, ed. J. C. Maxwell (Oxford: Clarendon Press, 1966), 289–90 and *The Shakespeare First Folio* (Oxford: Clarendon, 1955), 379–81.

of artists, their continuing right to regulate the consumption of their works even after an original has been sold, Heywood's prologue points to a nexus of competition not yet mentioned here, the competition between press and playwright for "creative control" of the dramatic text. Heywood seems to assume that his audience will neither be scandalized nor even surprised by the existence of such competition.

> And in that lamenesse it hath limp't so long,
> The Author now to vindicate that wrong
> Hath tooke the paines, upright upon its feete
> To teach it walke, so please you sit, and see't.

The competition to which these lines attest was hardly strenuous: the late quartos of this play do not improve on the earlier ones, so Heywood either made no effort to displace the "limping" first editions or could not prevail upon any stationer to do so. Rather, Heywood seems to allege the corruption of the printed text merely as a way of puffing the performance. Still, two important features of early modern English culture may be discerned here: first, that press and stage compete, however genially, and second that the author's post-originative endorsement – we might call it an "editorial signature" – is useful as an instrument of that competition. The two features are, in fact, related: competition between media develops, energizes, shapes the Author's authority by producing editorial signature. This chapter and the one which follows, will pursue the hypothesis.[27]

It was variously understood that the theater had made a special contribution to the destabilization of authorship. If hindsight enables us clearly to recognize such destabilization as an important first stage in the process by which authorship was converted into a new form of economic agency, contemporary intuitions were sometimes prescient. Consider Thomas Dekker's witty commentary on the cultural marketplace:

The theater is your Poets Royal Exchange, upon which their Muses, (that are now turned to Merchants,) meeting, barter away that light commodity of words for a lighter ware then words, *Plaudites*, and the *breath* of the great *Beast*; which (like the threatnings of two Cowards) vanish all into air. *Plaiers* and their *Factors*, who put away the stuffe, and make the best of it they possibly can (as indeed tis their parts so to doe) your Gallant,

---

[27] A related, but very different hypothesis is offered by Peter Stallybrass and Allon White in *The Politics and Poetics of Transgression* (Ithaca: Cornell University Press, 1986), who propose that "the symbolic domain of 'authorship' was produced *over against* the popular, as embodied in the ... popular drama" (61); I am proposing that there are important ways in which possessive authorship develops within popularity, but on the borders between popular media, and that this is an economic development. I hope here to advance the important adjustments of the Stallybrass–White thesis begun by Alan Farmer and Zachary Lesser in "Vile Arts: The Marketing of English Printed Drama, 1512–1660," *Research Opportunities in Renaissance Drama* 39 (2000), 82.

your Courtier, and your Capten had wont to be the soundest paymasters; and I thinke
are still the surest chapmen.[28]

The old *topos* of the immateriality of words is given economic inflection in
the fashionable sphere of London cultural life. The commonplace has suddenly
acquired ironic force; Dekker is startled to find not only that words have social
force, but that that force is valuable. The mimetic has become a stuff, poetry
has become property. Of course, this is presented as an authorial fantasy, like
Dallington's, a self-conscious elaboration of a contrafactual idea – that the
semiotic relation between playwright and audience is an economic relation, an
exchange in which the players are no more than the author's agents. Dekker
knows that the semiotic relation is incongruous with the economic one: how
could he not? His insistence on the odd coinage of plaudits and breath, the ironic
and figurative energy of these sentences, is founded in an acquisitive fantasy of
what *could* be "your Poets" proper place in the theatrical economy. The fantasy
emerges, that is, from the startled resentment of the laborer within a rapidly
evolving industry who has recognized that he does not control the means of
production.

It will be useful here to recall – there is no need to recapitulate – the work of
Jean-Christophe Agnew on how richly the recently established public theaters
in London expressed the experience of an only somewhat-less-recently established market economy.[29] But the theater did more than mediate the market;
it participated in it (and, of course, as an engine of fashion, it also helped to
elaborate it). Dekker knows – how could he not? – that, in 1609, the mart is open
for plays. In the same year, this same figurative vocabulary was put to slightly
different use in the printed foreword to *Troilus and Cressida* (Q1, second state):

A never writer, to an ever reader. Newes.

Eternall reader, you have heere a new play, never stal'd with the Stage, never clapper-
clawd with the palmes of the vulger, and yet passing full of the palme comicall; for it is
a birth of your braine, that never under-tooke any thing commicall, vainely: And were
but the vaine names of commedies changde for the titles of Commodities, or of Playes
for Pleas; you should see all those grand censors, that now stile them such vanities,
flock to them for the maine grace of their gravities: especially this authors Commedies,
that are so fram'd to the life, that they serve for the most common Commentaries, of
all the actions of our lives, shewing such a dexteritie, and power of witte, that the most
displeased with Playes, are pleased with his Commedies.

The quarto *Troilus and Cressida* seems to have been set up with a conventional
title page, one that advertises the book as the record of a performance, in this
case "As it was acted by the Kings Majesties servants at the Globe." But there

---

[28] *The Gull's Hornbook, The Non-Dramatic Works of Thomas Dekker*, Alexander B. Grosart, ed.,
5 vols., *The Huth Library* (London: Hazell, Watson, and Viney, 1885), 2:246–47.
[29] *Worlds Apart*, particularly Prologue and chapters 2 and 3.

is another state of this title page in which no mention is made of a performance –
it is usually supposed that performance at the Globe was hindered or deferred,
perhaps by plague or by censorious intervention or, voluntarily, by a decision
to perform the play in some more private and prestigious venue – and this state
of the title page, apparently the second, complements the preface.

This preface has been as much sifted for elementary bibliographic data as
Heywood's prologue to *If You Know Not Me* has been, but commentators have
been distracted from the exceptional semantic flurry of its few sentences. We
can, after all, find in the description of the play as born of the reader's brain
the nostalgic fantasy of an intimate patronage, a social situation of writing in
which the patron is so obviously involved in the poet's subsistence that he
becomes the poet's surrogate. The fantasy of the "never writer" reacts to the
public commercial theater as if it were the pre-eminent site in which poesy loses
its stable social base (a locus of dislocation, as it were) and makes the press the
site of a reconstruction of semiotic intimacy between sender and recipient.[30]
Although it apologizes for dramatic poetry, the preface condescends to the stage,
and it thereby sustains the same competition as that proposed by Heywood's
prologue – though the preface favors the press, whereas the prologue had favored
the stage.

Disdaining the anti-theatrical strictures of the "grand censors," the never-
writer suggests, in his play on the words "comedy" and "commodity," "play"
and "plea," that they would hold the theater in higher esteem if only it were to
advertise itself as "the entertainment business." The preface implies, that is, that
the attack on the theater is not really organized by the Platonic opposition of
fact and fiction, or by the related, Christian opposition of gravity and vanity, but
by a modern opposition of debased leisure and regulated commerce. Whatever
the tone of the never-writer's evasive voice, there is no misconstruing the fact
that the preface makes the encounter between press and stage into an occasion
for an insistent exposure of cultural economics, of literary property relations:

And beleeve this, that when hee [i.e., Shakespeare] is gone, and his Commedies out of
sale, you will scramble for them, and set up a new English Inquisition . . .

– the never-writer thus recognizes that connection between Inquisitorial interest
and commercial value which had been so important to the "mart" for both
writing and playing in the previous decade[31] –

---

[30] The phrase, "birth of *your* braine" is very likely a misprint for "birth of *that* braine" or, perhaps,
"birth of *his* braine" – the braine of that author whose plays are always serious. If so, the writing
reader is a *collective* fantasy, the casual collaborative product of a compositor, proofreader, and
reader.

[31] He scrambles the logical relation between censorship and value: whereas censorship causes
scarcity and inflated value, the never-writer imagines it as a means of coping with the effects of
scarcity.

... you will scramble for them, and set up a new English Inquisition. Take this for a warning, and at the perill of your pleasures losse, and Iudgements, refuse not, nor like this the lesse for not being sullied, with the smoaky breath of the multitude; but thanke fortune for the scape it hath made amongst you. Since by the grand possessors wills I beleeve you should have prayd for them rather than been prayd.

We are exhorted to approve not only of comedy but of the stationer's achievement in having wrested control of the dramatic text from those "grand possessors," the acting company. In these concluding lines, the never-writer admits what he has only been willing to advance in just, concedes what we have known all along, that comedies *are* commodities.

Hardly a shattering bit of materialist demystification, it could have been made at virtually any moment since, say, 1590. In 1592, those plays most popular on the stage were the focus of disorderly competition among stationers, for in that year Abel Jeffes printed *Arden of Feversham*, already registered to Edward White, and White avenged himself by printing Jeffes' *Spanish Tragedy*; the company fined both men, and confiscated their copies of both plays "to thuse of the poore of the companye."[32] Such infringements are not the sole sign of the stationers' heightened interest in dramatic publishing. There was a palpable increase in the rate of such publishing at the end of the sixteenth century.[33]

[32] *Records of the Court of the Stationers' Company, 1576 to 1602 – From Register B*, eds. W. W. Greg and E. Boswell (London: The Bibliographical Society, 1930), 44. This episode was the focus of a disagreement between Greg and Leo Kirschbaum, both of whom wrote several times on the episode. The key arguments may be found in Greg, "*The Spanish Tragedy* – A Leading Case?," *The Library*, ser. 4, 6 (1925), 47–56 (and reprinted, usefully annotated with second thoughts, in Greg, *Collected Papers*, 149–55), and Kirschbaum, "Is *The Spanish Tragedy* a Leading Case?," *JEGP*, 37 (1938). Jeffes had entered the play on October 6, 1592. However, by December 18 – and perhaps even before Jeffes had registered the play – Edward Allde had printed it, undated, for White: we have the *terminus ab quo* because the Stationers' Court considered Jeffes' complaint against White on that date. Greg and Kirschbaum agree that the play was almost certainly printed before White's undated edition, since the title page of that text advertises it as "Newly corrected and amended of such gross faults as passed in the first impression"; they agree, moreover, that "the first impression" was almost certainly Jeffes'. Their dispute concerns the force of the registration and the nature of White and Jeffes' rival claims. Greg believed that Jeffes' registration is an attempt to forestall White's edition or to challenge any subsequent claim that White might have made to printing rights in the work: he is arguing the binding force of registration. Kirschbaum holds that the first printing secured Jeffes' right, and that the subsequent registration was at once a protest and a formalization of a right that the Company would have recognized anyway (though perhaps would not have earnestly defended, since Jeffes was not in good odor with company officials). The stationers' adroit solution to the dispute was apparently to restore the rights of copy to the registrants, but to stipulate that White have the right to print the play for Jeffes. In 1599, Jeffes transferred his rights in the play to White.

[33] See Peter W. M. Blayney, "The Publication of Playbooks," in *A New History of Early English Drama*, ed. John D. Cox and David Scott Kastan (New York: Columbia University Press, 1997), 384–87. The tendency of Blayney's essay is to deny Pollard's thesis, which I am reasserting, of a competition between publishing and playing. Pollard's notion that the interests of actors and publishers are fundamentally hostile cannot survive Blayney's criticism; that hostility occasionally *was* manifest, and that nodes of tension developed in the relations of players and stationers, is the burden of this and the following chapter.

According to Greg's count, sixteen of the dramatic texts now extant from the reigns of Elizabeth and James were first printed in the decade between 1581 and 1590, 77 in the decade of 1591–1600, and 112 in 1601–10.[34] One of the truisms of historical bibliography is that dramatic texts were regarded by stationers as ephemeral productions, not worthy of painstaking workmanship, and the truth of that truism ought not to be denied. The question of workmanship aside, Greg's rather intricate tabulations suggest, on the contrary, that dramatic publishing – or at least the protection of publication rights in plays – slowly became more interesting to the book trade. He estimated that during the period from 1581 to 1640 the ratio of books entered to books published was on the order of 60 to 67 percent, probably closer to the smaller figure. Dramatic texts were entered at a slightly higher rate during this period, roughly 67.5 percent. In the two decades from 1591 to 1610, the percentages are just enough higher to signify: 70 percent and 74 percent respectively. Indeed, an accurate calculation of the overall ratio of entry to publication for dramatic works for 1581–1640 "should have been higher still," says Greg, "for the total [of works printed] is swollen by a number of publications issued elsewhere than in London, and also by certain private issues of masques and pageants, which seem not to have needed registration. Perhaps we should conclude that plays were rather more regularly entered than some other classes of works."[35] It thus appears that stationers were eager to secure their rights in plays. This is not difficult to understand, for the "permanent" theaters stimulated a market for printed drama in general, and the popularity of particular plays made it easy to identify marketable scripts, which minimized the small but appreciable capital risks involved in a print run.

As early as 1909, in *Shakespeare Folios and Quartos*, Pollard noted that the upsurge of dramatic publishing in the nineties had an irregular topology. He begins by noting that "in the eight years 1585–1592 only nine plays were entered for publication on the Stationers' Register." Then, "in the last of these years, 1592, the theatres were closed, owing first to riots and subsequently to the plague, from the end of June to December; but the players doubtless hoped for better times, and only three plays were entered." Pollard here assumes that "the players" both wished to control the release of plays to publishers, and successfully mustered such control. This remains, of course, to be proved. Still,

---

[34] "Entrance, Licence, and Publication," 6. Greg is working with the old STC, of course, but adjustments in dating in the revised STC hardly made an appreciable difference. Blayney has recently redone the count without changing the historical outline; see "The Publication of Playbooks," 384–96.

[35] *Ibid.* Greg goes on to note (p. 7) that the decades of highest productivity in dramatic publishing, 1591–1600, 1601–10, and 1631–40, also show the highest rates of entrance, 70 percent, 74 percent, and 69 percent, respectively. It will be recalled that the coincidence of a relatively high rate of entrance for Shakespeare's plays and a relatively high degree of interest in establishing "ideal" texts – the one a discovery of historical bibliographers, the other a motive of historical bibliography – led Pollard to propose a link between regular entrance and "goodness" of text.

it is difficult to resist the first steps in his explanation for the unprecedented outburst of dramatic publishing during the ensuing year. "In 1593, however, plague again broke out, and the theatres were closed for an even longer time, viz. from April to December, a period of nearly eight months. It is, therefore, very significant that a few months later we find a nearly similar period beginning (October 8, 1593 – July 20, 1594) [*sic*], during which no fewer than twenty-eight plays were entered on the Register."[36] He explains the next unusual upsurge in entrance again on grounds of inhibition of playing, so that, once again, we find the stage and the press in a relation at once competitive and complementary: "In the rest of 1596 and in the three years 1597–1599 we have only nine more entries, but in 1600 the number again rises suddenly to twenty-eight. The theatres were not closed that year because of the plague, but, apparently, there was trouble of another kind."[37] This new trouble was, of course, the Privy Council order of June 22 limiting performances to two public theaters and severely constraining the number of performances to be allowed at these two playhouses.[38] These are plausible explanations; they suggest that the "grand possessors" of playtexts were relatively successful at regulating the flow of scripts to the print market.[39]

This is not very surprising, if only because by the late 1590s the players and their managers had their own market in plays (parallel to the stationers' market for printable ones) and the habit of constrained circulation of scripts was well-established *within* the professional theater. In 1589 Edward Alleyn bought Richard Jones's share of a property that Jones had held jointly with Alleyn and his brother, John; according to Chambers, the Lord Admiral's Company was then dissolving – it would be reconstituted in recognizably independent form by 1594 – and Alleyn was preparing for a move to the Lord Strange's company.[40] In order to take his "stage properties" with him, he paid £37 Jones

---

[36] *Shakespeare Folios and Quartos: A Study in the Bibliography of Shakespeare's Plays* (London: Methuen, 1909), 9. Pollard must account for this time lag, of course, in order to make his explanation of the chronology credible, but he is not conspicuously successful when he suggests "the inference that . . . [the plays] were being sold by the players during the time that the theatres were closed and they were now being registered as they were got ready for publication" (*Ibid.*).

[37] Pollard, *Shakespeare Folios and Quartos*, 9–10.

[38] *Ibid.*, 9–10. We are dealing in hypotheses, of course, but Pollard's surmise, that the 1600 inhibition on playing scared the players into dumping plays onto the print market, provides a negative complement to Wickham's argument, that the *1597* strictures on theatrical activity were little more than nominal – and not, therefore, sufficient to have stimulated any similar dumping in 1597–98. For criticism of Pollard's argument here, see Blayney, "Publication of Playbooks," 386.

[39] Pollard's account of the flow was the historical cornerstone of his "optimistic" editorial theory of the Shakespeare texts. He argued that the only truly bad text was a pirated text and he construed the record of entrances as proof that only a minority of the plays entered for printing were pirated.

[40] Greg took the position that Alleyn was moving from the old Worcester's Men (which he supposes to have endured until this moment, despite the fact that no company performing under this name appears in the documentary record between 1584 and 1590) to the Admiral's company (*Henslowe's Diary*, 2 vols. [London: A. H. Bullen, 1904–08], ii:83). Chambers' view has prevailed, but Greg's hypothesis in no way unsettles my own argument here.

for "playinge apparalles playe Bookes, Instrumentes, and other commodities whatsoever."[41] Since the series is unqualified, unruffled by signs that it contains a category violation, it is tempting to suppose that "playe Bookes" denotes mere objects, *scripts*, one of the tools of an actor's trade. Yet analogous documents from a few years later suggest that the commodity thus transferred was of a more complex kind. In late 1600, after a brief retirement from the stage, Alleyn returned to the Admiral's Men, though not as a full sharer; between August 1601 and October 1602, his father-in-law, Phillip Henslowe, records several payments to Alleyn on behalf of the company for the purchase of a number of "plays" and "books" – these are Henslowe's terms. Alleyn sold most of these "books" for about £2.[42] Although this is considerably more than the market rate for either a manuscript copy or quarto text of a script – the mere object – it is about a third of the amount then being paid to playwrights for original scripts. Alleyn was probably selling promptbooks, which, uniquely, bore the marks of official license from the Master of the Revels. As crucial evidence of sanction, the promptbook guaranteed a rudimentary form of stage or performance right, the mark of ideological control being converted into something like an intellectual property right. This possession (more complex than "grand") was edging towards that abstract yet livelier post-romantic status that we refer to when we speak of "works of literature."

It's worth noting that ownership of this commodity was not always communal: Alleyn, after all, purchased Jones's share in his playbooks (and costumes and props) and became their sole and personal possessor. Similarly, just before Martin Slaughter left the Admiral's Company in the summer of 1598, he sold the company five "boocks" for £8.[43] Again, this is too much to pay for a mere physical book; like Alleyn, Slaughter seems to have owned the promptbook and all the utility that might be associated with it. Wallace supposes that Slaughter was the company book-keeper and claimed right of sale by possession, but Henslowe would never have acquiesced in such an extortionate purchase if he were purchasing only an annotated text.[44] Yet Wallace's instinctive association of the sale with the physical book is well-judged, for the performance right associated with the promptbook seems to have remained closely associated with the physical being of the promptbook. As long as Slaughter remained a member of the company, and the promptbook remained in their midst – like a costume or a

---

[41] *Henslowe's Diary*, ed. Foakes and Rickert, 273.

[42] His colleague, Martin Slaughter, sold several plays to Henslowe in the spring of 1598, plays that the company had already performed. It seems that Slaughter had acquired "creative control" of these plays, but only relinquished them at this juncture, at a moment, apparently, when Henslowe seemed to be attempting to clear his title in performance rights.

[43] The purchase unfolded in two stages: Slaughter was paid £7 on May 16, when he turned over four of the five books, and another 20*s*, when he delivered *Alexander and Lodowick*.

[44] C. W. Wallace, "The Swan Theatre and the Earl of Pembroke's Servants," *Englische Studien* 43 (1911), 376 n. 3.

prop – the performance right was treated as a community property: prior to the sale, no special payments were made to him on the occasion of performances of these plays. Only his departure, and the prospect of the removal of the "boocks," produced the heightened values associated with those books. Thus, although this sale cannot be specified to the physical book nor to the "work" that may be abstracted from it, as long as the book of a play was relatively scarce, the existence of the "work" would remained a kind of secret, closely tethered to the rare copy.[45]

This will seem to press the questions of the location and shape of property towards a precision impertinent to normal professional practice: we seldom inquire into, seldom know what constitutes the means of production at any given moment. But events hedging Slaughter's departure had in fact pressed the point. A month or so earlier, Henslowe financed Thomas Downton's suit in the Queen's Bench against Slaughter for what amounted to theft of a playbook: Downton had lost the book in December of 1597 and Slaughter had found it (although it is difficult not to put both these verbs in scare quotes).[46] Having refused to turn the book over to Downton, Slaughter instead sold it to an unnamed party on March 1. Downton put the value of the lost play at £13/3s/8d and sued for £30 in damages; the court awarded £10/10s. An Elizabethan legal claim is as unreliable an index of value as a modern one would be, and we would be much aided if we knew whether the lost book were unique, whether it were a licensed promptbook of a play already performed, but the amount of the award is certainly higher than the cost of a scribal transcript. Moreover, the court would not have heard the suit were it simply a matter of the theft of a manuscript. We have here a suit for theft of intellectual property, though it were not explicitly recognized as such.

Such properties detached themselves only very slowly from the physical playbooks, infringement only slowly becoming discriminable from theft. But that theater professionals distinguished such rights from property in physical

---

[45] It may be that property relations, at least within Henslowe's company, were shifting at this time. On December 10, 1602, Henslowe paid 40s to Robert Shaw, one of the actors in the Admiral's Company, to acquire *The Four Sons of Aymon* for the company. This looks like a straightforward purchase, although this time the actor-seller was not leaving the company, but Shaw's own signed receipt stipulates that the transaction was a kind of lease on the play, "which booke if it be not playd by the company of the fortune nor noe other company by my lea<ve> I doe then bynd my selfe by theis presentes to repay the sayd some of forty shillinges upon the delivery of my booke att Cristmas next ... 1603"; Foakes and Rickert, *Henslowe's Diary*, 208 and 211.

[46] Wallace refers to the suit in "The Swan Theatre and the Earl of Pembroke's Servants," 382–83; see also Harold Newcomb Hillebrand, *The Child Actors: A Chapter in Elizabethan Stage History, University of Illinois Studies in Language and Literature*, 11 (1926), 224, n. 1. The summary of the case may be found in *Placita Coram Rege*, roll 1351, Trinity Term, 40 Eliz., part 2, m.830b. Slater had left the Admiral's company on July 18, 1597, according to Henslowe's notes (*Diary*, f. 27^v); Henslowe lent Downton and Gabriel Spencer 30s to carry forward the suit (f. 39) in March; Slater sold plays to the company that May (f. 45^v) and, as he had in the mid-nineties Henslowe loaned him money again in 1604 (f. 129^v).

books by the beginning of the seventeenth century cannot be doubted. On or around 1604, the Children of the Revels performed a play called "*Jeronimo*," probably the play printed by Pavier in 1605 and probably part of the repertory of the King's Men.[47] We can be fairly certain because the King's Men retaliated with a performance of *The Malcontent*, which had been written for the Revels Children; an Induction composed by Webster for the performance by the King's Company makes much of the reciprocal infringement:

S L Y : . . . I would know how you came by this play?
C O N D E L L : Faith sir the booke was lost, and because twas pittie so good a play should
    be lost, we found it, and play it.
S L Y : I wonder you would play it, another company having interest in it?
C O N D E L L : Why not Malevole in folio with us, as Jeronimo in Decimo sexto with
    them.[48]

The exchange ends with a quip implying that competition between acting companies is a mock-meta-theatrical reflection on revenge tragedy: "They taught us a name for our play," says Condell, "wee call it *One for another*." The exchange could hardly be wittier. Condell (whom Shakespeareans know above all as the Shakespeare Folio's great defender against infringing dissemination) urges that stage right is simply a matter of having one's hands on a script: "we found it, and play it"; finder's keepers. It is an argument that Sly knows to be specious, for he recognizes a performance right, however inchoate, detached from the material book – and Webster plainly expects the ready assent of his audience to Sly's position. Having acquired a manuscript, an acting company thenceforth expected to maintain an exclusive right to a play – a convention from which the technicality of, say, an individual actor's private property in a play would be a special variance. And there may be more to be gleaned from these lines: Condell's joke about the relative size of boy-actors and adult performers – as decimo-sexto to folio – is quite off-handed, no doubt, but it is surely revealing that an exchange about competition between acting companies is mediated by language coming from the book trade, a War of the Theaters figured as a Battle of the Books.[49]

The evidence provided by this induction jostles that of the *Troilus* preface, though that may not be obvious at this point. The induction suggests that some

[47] This is presumably *not* Kyd's *Spanish Tragedy*, on which the King's troupe had no conceivable claim; see Chambers' observations in *ES*, 2:50–51 and 3:396.

[48] John Marston, *The Malcontent*, ed. M. L. Wine, *Regents Renaissance Drama Series* (Lincoln: University of Nebraska Press, 1964), Induction, lines 70–77.

[49] Later the players experimented with newly formal and newly rigorous means of protecting stage-right. In 1627, the King's Men paid Sir Henry Herbert £5 to bar the Red Bull Company from performing Shakespeare's plays; in 1639, the Lord Chamberlain intervened to protect the repertory of Beeston's Boys from rival performance. For more on how scripts figure in competition between companies, see Roslyn L. Knutson, "The Repertory," *A New History of Early English Drama*, 469–72 and 476–77.

form of performance rights had emerged within the theatrical economy and Alleyn's latter sales contract suggests that such rights had been given commercial reification within that economy. The *Troilus* preface, moreover, depends for its piquancy on the implication that printing the play seems to violate just such rights as Alleyn had bought and sold, or violates rights *like* those which Alleyn had bought and sold. Yet the *Troilus* preface only *figures* printing as transgression, yet surely the preface may be taken as evidence that the stationers involved in the edition, George Eld, Thomas Walleys, and Richard Bonion, believed that printing the play could not be actionable – else why draw attention to the transgression? We may infer from Webster's induction that limited performance rights were recognized as a convention guaranteeing order among theater professionals; we may infer from Alleyn's sales that those rights were developing independent and identifiable commercial value among theater professionals. The specificity to that industry, analogous to the specificity of stationers' copyright, is quite unsurprising. But the *Troilus* preface suggests a novelty. The never-writer worries over the idea that stage right might somehow overlap copyright, although the possibility is not fully feared.

It will be best to suggest the range of possible constructions to be placed on this evidence. First, the stationers might have been wrong: the printing might indeed have been actionable. Second, the stationers might have been bold: the printing might have been taken as a test of, or challenge to, the rights of the bold possessors. Third, if actors like Alleyn or his company possessed only performance rights, not a more general set of rights to control the dissemination and consumption of dramatic fiction, then the printing could not be construed as a genuine transgression. Before going on to further constructions, it may be appropriate to tease out subsets of this third. We might suppose that the owners of performance rights were not interested in more extensive control, that they cared only to secure themselves from competition from rival troupes – in which case the *Troilus* preface is merely droll – or we might suppose that the possessors aspired to even grander possession, and that they lamented the possession of a property right so severely circumscribed – in which case the *Troilus* preface is rather more heavily exultant. The latter seems to be closest to the truth, but that truth is surely molar: in turn-of-the-century London the various proprietary interests hovering round a script were in various and fluctuant states of reification. To print a play in which an acting company had *some* rights recognized by *some* other groups – by some other acting companies, some playwrights, some courtiers, some stationers – might have seemed an activity of uncertain consequences, consequences worth risking or testing; printing a play might seem actionable to some, improper to others, provoking, harmless, irrelevant to still others. Once we have sifted the evidence concerning the emergent property rights in Elizabethan and Jacobean plays, it will be difficult to resist this fourth construction – that the competition between the press and the stage yielded the sort of uneven development specific to emergency.

I have instanced the *Troilus* preface not only to probe the competition between the press and the stage, but also to keep open the question of how the playwright functioned within that competition. It will be noticed that the author is introduced along a logical fault line in the argument of this preface. Certainly, the logic of the *Troilus* preface is strangely skewed, for by some rhetorical sleight-of-hand the superiority of Shakespeare's plays to those of others is made to function as a rationale for discrediting the claims of the grand possessors: as Shakespeare is to be preferred to other playwrights, so is the press to be preferred to the theater. The analogy is off. That is, the preface associates the author with an anti-theatrical press – perhaps because both produce legible words, as the grand possessors do not – but the never-writer never specifies this, or any other, grounds for the association. We can understand the logical lapse as a function of the jurisdictional confusion produced by the competition between actors and stationers. Members of the Stationers' Company had long been accustomed to trade regulation, but the monopolistic practices of the acting companies, albeit less elaborate, raised questions about the breadth of the stationers' jurisdiction in matters of intellectual property: how, wondered the never-writer, could proprietary claims from outside the regulatory regime of the press be frustrated? What was called for here was some higher, or at least extrinsic, authority. In this tight spot, the never-writer makes his shallow and illogical appeal to the excellence of the author. His excellence, not his rights: a discourse of authorial property had yet to be elaborated. The prestige of the author – legally irrelevant, but rhetorically potent – does duty for rights yet to be invented; the impressive *enargia* of the preface is calculated to mask or perhaps to even up the practical mismatch between the diffuse charisma of creativity and the narrow, stubborn claims of property.

This makes only a small contribution to the proof of my earlier hypothesis, that competition between the press and the stage works to produce editorial signature, the Author's authority. The *Troilus* preface hardly invents a way of talking about authorial property, but it does show that, in the face of new forms of dissemination, the book trade might need to propound such a discourse. To sell books, the press needs authorial prestige; to maintain a monopolistic edge, the press might need, would need, an author who has his claims.

Border disputes

But I have raced ahead of my argument. In order to trace the emergence of authorial rights in plays it will be necessary to describe the border between the theater and the press. This will require that we return to the research program of the New Bibliographers. They were consistently concerned with articulating the unfolding competition at that contentious border, a competition that demanded that emergence.

It is a commonplace of dramatic historiography to focus on the outcast status of the Elizabethan player and on the threatening marginality of the theater, but the case can be overstated and can so obscure the privileges that hedged the stage. It is certainly true that the early Tudors curtailed the freedom of strolling companies, and thereby forced some of them out of business and drove others to seek noble patronage. But this campaign bespeaks a desire to stabilize the populace and control vagabondage; it was by no means conceived primarily as a statute for controlling a threat represented as specific to the theater.[50] The regulation of vagabondage contributed not only to the geographical stabilization of the theater – the erection, in fairly rapid succession, of the Theatre, the Curtain, and the unnamed playhouse in Newington – but also to its professionalization and to the regularization of its *social* position.[51] Bradbrook's formulation of the situation of players within the Tudor regulatory milieu thus strikes a sensible balance:

Under the protective shield of their lord's badge, invoking a declining, obsolescent form of service, which was in their case sometimes little better than a legal fiction, the players established themselves as purveyors of a commodity for which the general public was prepared regularly to put down its cash ... Players aspired to the condition of merchants and citizens; to attain it they masqueraded as members of the gentlemanly profession of serving men. By their enemies, they were constantly confounded with rogues and vagabonds, thieves and cheaters who lived at Fortune's alms. It was the men to whose condition they aspired who provided the strongest opposition.[52]

This latter specification cannot be over-emphasized, since it reminds us that at the end of the sixteenth century the social center of Elizabethan anti-theatricality was neither royal nor aristocratic (and, moreover that this anti-theatricality was not a competition for control of ideological *state* apparatuses). Noblemen found it an agreeable augmentation to their own magnificence to bestow liveries on talented companies, while the cavil of City merchants and City fathers made patronage a rather grander gesture.[53]

When, early in her reign, Elizabeth began to take on the drama as one of the crucial objects of ideological regulation, she attempted to make aristocratic patrons part of a dual regulatory regime. In a proclamation of May 1559 she established licensing by the magistracy – "within any city or town corporate by

[50] The often-cited parliamentary "Acte for the punishment of Vacabondes" (1572) was designed to control itinerant workers of all sorts – peddlars and tinkers as well as bearwards and players; see Bradbrook, *The Rise of the Common Player*, 37.
[51] *Ibid.*, 37–38.   [52] *Ibid.*, 39–40.
[53] 1572 was a banner year for efforts at coding and stabilizing the population: in this the same year as the act against vagabondage, the queen issued a proclamation (Hughes and Larkin, *Tudor Royal Proclamations*, II:350) devised to discipline the wearing of livery. Those fraudulently passing themselves off as retainers and those unlawfully keeping retainers were equally admonished.

the mayor or other chief officers of the same, and within any shire by such as shall be lieutenants for the Queen's majesty in the same shire" – but she also designated the aristocracy as a regulatory *class* – "her majesty giveth special charge to her nobility and gentlemen, as they profess to obey and regard her majesty, to take good order in this behalf with their servants being players, that this her majesty's commandment may be duly kept and obeyed."[54] This should alert us to the contradictory status of Elizabethan theatrical practice within the regulatory regime, a version of the contradictions that Bradbrook describes in slightly different terms. On the one hand, ideological regulation promoted the formation of relatively stable theatrical companies in semi-permanent locations and so conduced to the constitution of the troupe as firm; on the other hand, ideological regulation worked to maintain acting companies within the archaic economic sphere of patronage. An important latency within the theatrical economy, noble patronage had an instrumental function in the players' competition with the stationers.[55]

The letter of August 7, 1641 from Robert, Earl of Essex, to the leaders of the Stationers' Company must be a crucial document in any attempt at reconstructing how that competition unfolded. Essex, who had become the Lord Chamberlain two weeks earlier, informed the company wardens that "the players which are his Majesty's"

have addressed them selves unto mee as formerly to my predecessors in office, complaining that some Printers are about to Print & publish some of their Playes which hitherto they have beene usually restrained from by the Authority of the Lord Chamberlain. Their Request seems both just and reasonable, as onely tending to preserve them Masters of their proper Goods, which in Justice ought not to bee made common for another mannes profitt to their disadvantage. Upon this ground therfore I am induced to require your care (as formerly my Predecessors have done) that noe Playes belonging to them bee put in Print without their knowledge & consent.

With this letter Essex furnished a list of some sixty plays that he wished to protect.

If any of those Playes shall bee offered to the Presse under another name then is in the List expressed, I shall desire your care that they may not bee defrauded by that meanes but that they may bee made acquainted with it, before they bee recorded in your hall & soe have Oportunity to shew their right unto them.[56]

---

54 Hughes and Larkin, *Tudor Royal Proclamations*, II:115–16. Ideological classification takes over as the primary mark of social structure in this proclamation: plays "wherein either matters of religion or of the governance of the estate of the commonwealth shall be handled or treated" were designated "no meet matters to be written or treated upon but by men of authority, learning, and wisdom, nor to be handled before any audience but of grave and discreet persons."

55 On actors' status as retainers, see Richard Dutton, *Mastering the Revels* (Iowa City: University of Iowa Press, 1991), 25–28.

56 *Malone Society Collections*, I:4–5 (1911), 367–8, transcribed from the Lord Chamberlain's Warrant Books (PRO, LC 5, 96).

Written after a generation of court masquing had renewed court patronage and secured court involvement in the workings of the London theater, this letter comes long after the attack on "the grand possessors" in the foreward to the quarto *Troilus and Cressida*, confidently asserting a very different conception of property. Of course, this constitutes no evidence of a decisive shift; indeed, the letter refers to a continuous tradition of interventions by various Lords Chamberlain on behalf of the players seeking to control publications rights in dramatic texts.[57] In 1637, Philip Herbert, Earl of Pembroke and Montgomery and Robert Devereux's predecessor as Lord Chamberlain, wrote to the stationers to remind them that his brother, the *previous* Lord Chamberlain (from December 1615 to August 1626), had commanded "the stay of any further impression of any of the playes or interludes of his majesties servants without their consents" and to reassert the stipulation of consent as a prerequisite to publication, "which is a course that can be hurtfull unto none but such as are about unjustly to peravayle themselves of others' goods."[58] Malone cites a 1619 letter in the same vein from William Herbert to the stationers barring the printing of the King's Men's plays "without some of their consent."[59] William and Philip, those "incomparable paire of brethren" to whom Shakespeare's fellow-sharers in the King's Men dedicated the folio collection of his plays, seem to have been great supporters of the company's efforts to stave off unwanted printing of plays.

When did such interventions begin? Further regress is possible, though it brings this inquiry to what was once the most vexed intersection of dramatic and bibliographic historiography.[60] An entry in the Stationers' Register for

---

[57] It is noteworthy, moreover, that this tradition of intervention grounded the Lord Chamberlain's authority over theatrical property at the time of the Restoration, when the then Lord Chamberlain distributed performance rights in Shakespeare's plays between the two reconstituted acting companies.

[58] *The Plays and Poems of William Shakespeare* (The Third Variorum), ed. James Boswell and Edmond Malone, 21 vols. (London: F. C. and J. Rivington, 1821), III:160–61.

[59] Cited in Chambers, *William Shakespeare: A Study of Facts and Problems*, 2 vols. (Oxford: Clarendon, 1930), 1:136. The letter is no longer preserved, but the gist of the letter was recorded by the stationers' clerk in their Court Book C under the heading of "Decrees and Ordinances": "that no playes that his Majesties players do play shalbe printed without the consent of somme of them" (*Records of the Court of the Stationers' Company, 1602–1640*, ed. W. A. Jackson [London: The Bibliographical Society, 1957], 110). Kirschbaum plausibly argues that the immediate impetus for the Lord Chamberlain's intervention in 1619 was the surreptitious publication of the Pavier quartos; his argument is pitched against Chambers' claims that the Lord Chamberlain's letter was sent before or during the printing of the Pavier quartos. This was, however, a moment in which the King's Men seemed generally interested in securing a regulatory hedge around their enterprises, having applied for and received a new patent for playing in London, apparently a redundancy, save insofar as it specified their right to play at the Blackfriars.

[60] For an excellent survey of both the evidence and the history of conjectures concerning staying entries, see the New Variorum edition of *As You Like It*, ed. Richard Knowles (New York: Modern Language Association, 1977), 353–64. Fleay's early reflections on these entries still repay attention; see *Life and Works of Shakespeare* (London: Nimmo, 1886), 40 and 140.

July 22, 1598 records an early intervention by the then Lord Chamberlain, Henry Carey:

James Roberts. Entred for his copie under the handes of bothe the wardens, a booke of the Marchaunt of Venyce or otherwise called the Jewe of Venyce Provided that yt bee not prynted by the said James Robertes or anye other whatsoever without lycence first had from the Right honorable the lord Chamberlen.[61]

Although this was an unusual entry, it was by no means the first instance of provisional entrance in the Stationers' Register. The Star Chamber Decree of 1586 had increased the importance of both entrance and license. In subsequent years the wardens frequently stipulated that the entrance of a given text was provisional, contingent upon that text having been officially licensed. Whereas prior to 1586 the wardens had often acted confidently as licensing agents, the Star Chamber Decree appears to have shaken that confidence – indeed during the next fifty or so years company officials seem to have become steadily more reluctant to enter unlicensed books. But it is not so easy to situate the provisional entrance to James Roberts within this tradition, for the Lord Chamberlain was not one of the usual press licensers – although he could, of course, be regarded as a member of a regulatory class. Moreover, it was to the Lord Chamberlain that the Master of the Revels, who was charged with licensing plays for the stage, was accountable, and it may be that under some unusual circumstances the normal procedures of press licensing were displaced by an extraordinary elaboration of stage licensing.[62] Or it may be that the Lord Chamberlain was simply interested in inhibiting publication of "his" company's plays, as later Lords Chamberlain would be.

Roberts has long been thought the key to the mystery. Possessed of a privilege for all printing of playbills, he was enmeshed in theatrical business, and this entrance may have been his way of assisting the players in their struggle against the depredations of the stationers: by thus registering the play, and requiring the unusual approval of the Lord Chamberlain, he could have been helping them to erect a bar to publication. It was once a bibliographical orthodoxy that this obstacle was sought because the company or someone in the company (or, more specifically, Shakespeare) objected to the printing of bad texts of their plays in recent years – the bad quartos of 2 and 3 Henry VI in 1594 and 1595 (the latter an octavo, really), of Romeo and Juliet and Richard III (1597). Yet we have no contemporary evidence that zeal for textual fidelity (to whatever exemplar) stands behind the stay, though protests, like Dallington's, against garbled first editions are a staple of arguments for second ones during the period.

[61] Arber, Transcript, III:122.
[62] Subsequent Masters of the Revels would assert their authority over the printing of plays – between 1607 and 1615 Sir George Buc or his deputy licensed all plays for the press and Henry Herbert resumed the practice between 1628 and 1637.

It has also been proposed that those who had easy access to a printed text would have little incentive to attend a theatrical performance, but again there is no evidence to confirm or disconfirm this hypothesis. That the players wished to inhibit rival performance of these plays, whether in London or in the provinces, by making playtexts difficult to come by seems more plausible to me, but here, too, evidence is lacking.[63] There is also evidence, but from the 1630s, that the acting companies sometimes commissioned scribal copying of their plays for use as presentation copies; that such a practice would have been thwarted by the ready availability of printed texts may be the particular motive for their appeals that the Lords Chamberlain help them maintain their control of printing – but whether the company was already trying to maintain exclusive control of scribal copying as early as the end of Elizabeth's reign must remain a matter of speculation.[64]

On behalf of arguments that Roberts was assisting the players (whatever might have been their interest in inhibiting publication), it can be said that such cooperative maneuvering is not without parallel. On March 1, 1596, Thomas Dawson, one of the company wardens, entered five books on behalf of Hugh Astley, a draper who had been publishing and selling books for several years, for which favor Dawson secured the printing, though Astley was to own the copies (Arber, III, 60).[65] Roberts himself seems to have assisted another draper, Richard Smith, by entering books in his own name that he would later print for Smith, who provided the capital for the enterprise.[66] Of course these entries were preliminary to *publication*; but one can also point to the assistance of stationers in assisting outsiders in *inhibiting* publication. Henslowe records the loan of 40*s* to Robert Shaw on March 18, 1600, "to geve unto the printer to staye the printing of patient grisell."[67] If the analogy holds in the case of *The Merchant of Venice*, the players may be supposed to have been marshalling every available means of controlling publication by enlisting the supervention of both the Lord Chamberlain and a friendly stationer.

On the other hand, the stationer may not have been so very friendly: Roberts may have exploited his frequent contacts with the players to acquire an authorized copy that he then presented for entrance at Stationers' Hall, in which case the stay on this registration may evidence the wardens' caution at the prospect

[63] But cf. Blayney, who finds all these particular traditional assertions unpersuasive; "Publication of Playbooks," 386. In the absence of decisive evidence, he is reluctant to advance any hypothesis concerning Roberts' motives (387).

[64] See Greg, "Prompt Copies, Private Transcripts, and The 'Playhouse Scrivener'," *The Library*, ser. 4, vol. 6 (1926), 148–56, F. P. Wilson, "Ralph Crane, Scrivener to the King's Players," *The Library*, ser. 4, vol. 7 (1927), 194–215, and Love, *Scribal Publication*, 65–66.

[65] For examples of similar surrogate entrance, see Gerald D. Johnson, "The Stationers Versus the Drapers: Control of the Press in the Late Sixteenth Century," *The Library*, ser. 6, 10 (1988), 8.

[66] Sidney Thomas, "Richard Smith: 'Foreign to the Company'," *The Library*, ser. 5, 3 (1948), 186–92.

[67] Foakes and Rickert, *Henslowe's Diary*, 132.

of a dubious registration, or of the players' direct intervention to forestall the printing of a pirated text. Yet whether Roberts were the players' agent or the players' adversary, this registration indicates an attempt at some level to transfer to the Chamberlain's Men monopolistic protections proper to the Stationers' Company. In either case, moreover, it is the authority of the Lord Chamberlain that serves to disrupt the customary regulatory structures of the Stationers' Company on behalf of the actors. To put it more precisely, a tradition of aristocratic patronage of theatrical activity has disturbed older proprietary conventions and stimulated new ones.[68]

It will be helpful to probe the "stayed" entries somewhat further in order to gauge the competitive practices that adumbrated property in dramatic texts. It must be admitted, again, that the evidence is inadequate for a full reconstruction of the players' efforts to appropriate the stationers' monopolistic devices. The central documents for even a partial reconstruction – besides the Roberts entry of *The Merchant of Venice* – are two notes on the second of two unnumbered leaves at the begining of the Stationers' Register C.[69] Between August 1596 and May of 1615, the clerks of the company used these leaves for miscellaneous memoranda, most of them records of contingent or deferred registrations. Here is the first of the two crucial notes:

> my lord chamberlens menns plaies Entred
>   viz

27 may 1600
To master   A moral of clothe breches and velvet hose
Robertes

27 may
To hym   Allarum to London

These memoranda take the normal form for entrance of copy; they are abnormal simply by virtue of the fact that they are recorded *here* and not in a customary location in the Register. Although the surrounding entries were added after these of May 1600, the documentary context suggests that the entrances to Roberts

---

[68] More potent and more general patronage would be forthcoming from the crown in April of 1604, when James' Privy Council instructed the magistracy of London, Middlesex, and Surrey to "permitt and suffer the three Companies of Plaiers to the King, Queene, and Prince publicklie to Exercise ther Plaies in their severall and usuall howses"; in July, Parliament reconfigured the Elizabethan Act for control of vagabondage, withdrawing the aristocratic privilege of "personally" protecting acting companies. (Wickham offers the terse gloss, "James' intention is quite clear: actors act by his authority or not at all"; *Early English Stages*, vol. 2, pt. 1, 105.) The crown here enables a small number of Londonish acting companies to consolidate their position as cultural monopolists. The limitation on competition made it possible for a company like the Chamberlain's Men to perform not only for large audiences paying low admissions fees at the Globe, but also to secure an audience willing to pay much higher entrance fees for the small number of seats at the Blackfriars'.

[69] For a full description of these pages, see Kirschbaum, "Is *The Spanish Tragedy* a Leading Case?," 185–86.

are contingent ones, similar to that of two years earlier, for most of the other entries on these pages are for texts still requiring proof of license, and many of the books thus contingently entered treat of politically volatile subjects.[70] The contingency of the entries to Roberts is not, however, simply a matter of inference: elsewhere in the Register "Clothe breches and velvet hose" is entered to Roberts with the provision "that he is not to putt it in prynte Without further and better Aucthority" (May 27; Arber III:161) and "Allarum to London" entered to him "provided that yt be not printed without further Aucthoritie" (May 29, Arber III:161). Again, Roberts is involved in the contingent registration of a Chamberlain's Men's play, which is put into a kind of regulatory limbo by the registration. We still cannot tell whether Roberts is working with the players or is being inhibited from working against them.

The next, and adjacent, notation on these leaves somewhat compounds the mystery. It again concerns plays in the repertory of the Chamberlain's Men:

> 4. Augusti
>
> As you like yt. a booke
> Henry the ffift. a booke
> Every man in his humour. a booke   to be staied
> The commedie of muche A doo about
> nothing. a booke

The intended force of this entrance has long been debated. Even the meaning of its adjacency to the memoranda of May 27 is uncertain: it may be fortuitous, though this is unlikely. It *almost* certainly indicates that this entry was made in the same year, 1600, in which the May entry was made; it may also concern the common association with the Chamberlain's Men; or it may involve the more specific circumstance that it is *Roberts* – the dubious Roberts? – who has again presented some play texts for registration. If adjacency marks these four plays out for association with the earlier contingent entrances to Roberts, the force of the association is still uncertain: the new memorandum may have been contrived to reserve future publication rights to Roberts (a stay, that is, *for* him), or to bar him from publishing these plays, a bar erected in contradistinction to the earlier grant of publication rights for "A moral of clothe breches" and "Allarum to London."[71] After all, the entry may record an official determination to block

---

[70] Several of the entries on these leaves note that the registration fee has not been paid, an indication that the Company intends to withhold official sanction for publication. This is not the only place in the Registers in which contingent entries were recorded; they may be found scattered throughout the Registers. The preliminary leaves in Register C are distinctive as a place where the Clerk had *gathered* several such entries.

[71] The bibliographical literature does not contain this latter hypothesis, though it seems quite plausible. Roberts may even be supposed to have presented all six texts for entrance at more or

publication indefinitely – that is, it may not be even a contingent registration, which would explain why no particular stationer's name is associated with the entry.

One way of assessing the intended force of this memorandum is to consider its actual effect. The record suggests that, if the stay was intended as a permanent bar, it was remarkably ineffectual. To be sure, *As You Like It* was not printed before the publication of the Shakespeare Folio, but *Every Man In* was entered to Cuthbert Burby and Walter Burre on August 14 and Burre had it printed in 1601, *Much Ado* was also duly entered on August 23 and printed soon thereafter, and *Henry V* was printed before the year was out (though its official history is a bit more complicated than that of the other plays in these two memoranda). At any rate, the stay was quite temporary.[72] These instances are consistent with the publication history of several other books registered as "stayed" during the period, although a large degree of variation must be conceded in these matters.[73] In a pattern that resembles that for *Every Man In* and *Much Ado*, *Patient Grisell* was entered unconditionally to Burby on March 28, 1600, ten days after Henslowe loaned Shaw money to stay its printing; it departs from the pattern in that the play was not printed until 1603 – by Henry Rocket, Burby's apprentice. *The Merchant of Venice*, the first of Roberts' contingent entrances, remained unprinted for two years; yet it may well be worth noting that on October 28, 1600, the play was entered again, this time to Thomas Heyes "by

less the same time. Two could have been approved immediately; the four latter plays may have provoked some uncertainty; later, after some investigation, it could have been determined that *they* should not be entered to Roberts. The May license may be supposed to have been contingent or non-contingent; the August stay may be supposed to have been temporary or permanent. What is important to this hypothesis is simply that the two notations were contrastive.

[72] The play was printed (late?) in 1600 by Thomas Creede for Millington and Busby, yet in an entry dated August 14, 1600, the play was listed among several "thinges formerlye printed and sett over to . . . Thomas Pavyer." Pavier seems to have maintained some claim to the copy – in 1602 the play was again printed, this time for Pavier – yet the key figure in these transactions appears to have been Creede (who, having printed Q1 for Millington and Busby, printed it two years later, for Pavier). Creede had entered *The Famous Victories* in 1594 – it was one of several plays from the repertory of the Queen's Men that found their way into print as the company disintegrated under the pressure of competition and plague – and his continued association with the quarto printing of *Henry V* has suggested to many scholars that he claimed a continuing interest in Shakespeare's play based on his 1594 entrance of the earlier Henry V play. The transfer to Pavier may well be a device for recording in the Register that the play, having already been allowed, was invulnerable to the stay. But it may just as easily be an acquiescence to the stay. Thus Creede, having claimed rights to the Chamberlain's Men's *Henry V* on the dubious basis of his prior printing of the Admiral's Men's *The Famous Victories* is barred from printing it, but an accommodation is made: if he will relinquish his claim by a formal transfer to Pavier of rights in *Henry V*, he can reserve the right to print the play for whoever is authorized to pay the production costs.

[73] Andrew S. Cairncross collects several such contingent registrations, entries that forestall printing until a company warden or some censoring authority would agree to put his hand to the entrance, or until competing claims to copy could be investigated; "Shakespeare and the 'Staying Entries'." *Shakespeare in the Southwest: Some New Directions*, ed. T. J. Stafford (El Paso: Texas Western University Press, 1969), 80–93.

Consent of Master Robertes" and Roberts printed the play for Heyes before the year was out.[74] So we may well be dealing with very different kinds of inhibition: the Roberts stay on *The Merchant of Venice* intended to forestall publication, and successful; the Henslowe stay on *Patient Grisell* intended similarly, but unsuccessful; etc. Of course, it may be that the memorandum of August 1600 was intended by the recording clerk merely as a reminder that these books needed careful scrutiny before they were entered, perhaps because the Lord Chamberlain's company was making difficulties about the printing of "their" plays.[75] And in an argument that has had perhaps too little influence on this still unsettled debate, Kirschbaum supposed that the memorandum accommodates both the actors and the stationers: it serves the actors by inhibiting any entries of which they did not approve, yet it in no way compromises the principle that registration itself was a privilege proper only to stationers. This would explain why three of the four plays were printed in relatively short order – *As You Like It* becomes the anomalous case: the players were not permitted simply to block publication but they were allowed to designate the stationers to whom the plays would be assigned, provided they made such designation quickly.[76]

Although the precise arrangements that led to and followed from the staying registrations may never be discovered, it is clear that the late nineties saw not only a diffuse competition between stationers and players for control of the satiric mode but also some quite specific instances of competition for control of dramatic publishing, a border skirmish between rival trades of very different organizational structure. Roberts would register *Troilus and Cressida* early in 1603 and it was not printed; it was re-registered, but without indication of

---

[74] It will be noticed that Roberts seems to have preserved some claim on *The Merchant of Venice*; it may then be objected, against the hypothesis that Roberts had anything to do with the plays stayed in August 1600, that he seems to have preserved no obvious claim to *them*. As a weak counter to this objection, it might be observed that Roberts seems to have preserved no claim on the plays registered contingently to him in May 1600.

[75] C. J. Sisson is even more skeptical of claims for the extraordinary significance of the August 1600 notations. Near the end of his provocative essay on "The Laws of Elizabethan Copyright: the Stationers' View" (*The Library* ser. 5, vol. 15 [1960], 8–20), he makes the salutary distinction between the staying of an entry and the staying of publication (19) and (like Kirschbaum before him) supposes that the 1600 stays are stays of entry.

[76] Kirschbaum places the emphasis slightly differently and his formulation bears quoting: "This entry simply means that none of the four plays is to be entered without the Lord Chamberlain's men's consent, but it must have been made clear to the acting company that this mere notice would not suffice and that they must have the plays regularly entered in order to prevent stealing," *Shakespeare and the Stationers*, 213. The greatest difficulty in Kirschbaum's argument involves explaining why *As You Like It* was neither registered nor printed in the proximate aftermath of the stay. He supposes, as Chambers had, that the stationers allowed Creede control of *Henry V* on the grounds of his 1594 registration of *The Famous Victories*, but presses the point farther: conjecturing that the stay had been motivated by a rumor that the actors were about to lose a single, popular, but unidentified play, he concludes that Creede's 1600 printing of *Henry V* dispelled the mystery. "The players now knowing which one of their four plays stayed on August 4 had been stolen, they would no longer think it necessary to sell *As You Like It* to a stationer in order to avoid the surreptitious printing of this play" (216).

transfer, six years later and printed soon thereafter. Its prefatory epistle describes the publication as a victory against possessiveness: the spruce bad faith of this claim should now be clear.

Whereas the defenses that London's players mustered to protect their newly – and incompletely – reified property have an improvised feel, the stationers were accustomed to such challenges. They had made it quite literally their business to assist the various authorities engaged in ideological regulation, but dissident publishing inevitably challenged trade regularities. As Unwin famously observed, "No other company ever attained the degree of monopoly as that which the State thought it expedient to confer on the Stationers", yet because the stationers' monopoly seemed, after all, to conflict with the commercial privilege traditionally accorded to all free men of London, the right to buy and sell any sort of good, the Stationers were obliged to combat steady intrusions on their monopoly from at least the mid-seventies forward.[77] Christopher Barker, who eventually became one of the most zealous defenders of stationers' prerogatives, had apprenticed and taken his freedom as a draper, but he began registering books for printing in 1569, acquired lucrative printing patents in 1573 and 1577, and only in 1578 shifted his affiliation from the drapers to the stationers. Gerald Johnson has documented the steady growth in the number of drapers – like Hugh Astley – who engaged in book-selling: "an alarming increase," he tells us, "as the early book-selling drapers indentured apprentices, trained them as stationers, and then freed them as drapers."[78] Thus the struggle

---

[77] George Unwin, *The Gilds and Companies of London* (London: George Allen and Unwin, 1938), 261. From the mid-eighties on, there was also competition from Cambridge, which had an old, unexploited, but perfectly lawful printing patent; Oxford joined the challenge in 1632. On the early years of the Stationers' long-standing struggle with the university printers, see Cyprian Blagden, *The Stationers' Company: A History, 1403–1959* (London: Allen and Unwin, 1960), 101–06, and John Johnson and Strickland Gibson, *Print and Privilege at Oxford to the Year 1700, Proceedings and Papers of the Oxford Bibliographical Society*, 7 (1946), 5–7 and 18–23. The Stationers' Court Book records a variety of efforts to enforce their monopoly. In August 1597, for example, a typefounder, Benjamin Simpson, was put under bonds not to cast any new founts "without first advertysinge the master & wardens thereof in wrytinge and the names of the parties that shall have them, before he delyver them out of his handes" (Greg and Boswell, *Records of the Court*, 58). Court Book C bears traces of an attempt to restrain a Dutch printer, Richard Skilders, who had set up shop in Middlesborough.

[78] Johnson, "The Stationers Versus the Drapers," 6. Johnson offers an account of twelve drapers who were translated in 1600 from the Drapers' to the Stationers' Company, five of whom had served their apprenticeships with drapers who had been engaged in book-selling for a quarter of a century. (In 1578 Christopher Barker had applied for a similar translation from the Drapers', this a year *after* he had been appointed Queen's Printer.) So common was the industrial "poaching" that Barker's suit to the Drapers' Court for transfer to the stationers was determined only after "Dyvers Booke sellers of our Company" had been consulted; his translation was allowed on the condition that he promise "to shewe what ffriendshippe he myght Lawfully Doe to those of our Company as Contynue booke sellers" (Johnson, "The Stationers," 5–6). Johnson speaks of the stationers' alarm, but there was alarm on both sides: the records of the Drapers' Court attest that "there are diverse freemen of this fellowship greately vexed hyndred and troubled by other Companies whose trade they exercise" (7) – the general language is mere tact, for the context makes it clear that the Stationers' Company was the chief source of "vexation."

between the players and the stationers has its place in a growing tradition of challenge to the stationers' monopoly.[79] The challenge to monopoly by grant of privilege that had arisen in the late seventies yielded, at the end of the century, to practices that challenge or compromise the monopoly by registration.[80]

Such challenges naturally confer increasing definition on customary monopolistic practices. Thus, by 1619, the King's Printer, John Bill, could argue that "entry in the hall booke is the commun and strongest assurance that Stationers have, for all their copies. which is the greatest parte of their Estates."[81] But this was already perceived as the case in the late nineties, by which time entry for outsiders clearly presented itself as a problem to those on the Court of Assistants.[82] In January of 1598, the Company developed rules designed to curb "diverse abuses [that] have been Committed, by sundry persons of this Companye in procuringe of Copies and Bookes to be entred and alowed unto them and then pryntinge the same for suche persons as be not of this Company."[83] In fact, this ordinance articulates a policy that had been asserted earlier in the decade. Dawson's 1596 registrations for the draper, Astley, were cancelled five weeks later by order of the Stationers' Court; Dawson managed to reserve the printing rights of all but one of the books he had entered for Astley (the exception had been found to be another man's copy), with some of his profits from the venture to be donated to the poor of the company; four years later Astley translated

[79] The site of struggle shifted a bit over time, from the monopoly in bookselling – the early issue in the border feud with the drapers – to jurisdiction over apprenticeship – the later issue in the feud with the drapers (as also with continental workmen living in London) – to the right to publish without any constraints other than those of normal licensing and of intra-corporate regulation – the issue in the border dispute with the players. And not only with the players: one month after Warden Dawson entered five books on behalf of the draper, Hugh Astley, the Stationers' Court disallowed the entry, diverting a substantial portion of the interest in these books to the poor of the company (Arber, *Transcript*, III:60). On the problem with alien bookbinders taking apprentices, see Arber, *Transcript*, III:40–2.

[80] Challenges to patents did not end, however. Simon Stafford, originally a draper, had fallen afoul of the stationers by infringing the patent in the ABC. Cyril Bathurst Judge reconstructs Stafford's attempt to circumvent the stationers' regulations by securing the direct protection of the Archbishop of Canterbury, the Lord Mayor, and the Court of Aldermen for his printing ventures (*Elizabethan Book Pirates* [Cambridge: Cambridge University Press, 1934], Chapter 6) in 1596–97. But the stationers pressed their case against Stafford, raiding his home in March 1598; Stafford responded with a warrant against the wardens for forcible entry and theft, to which the stationers responded with a complaint to the Star Chamber. After protracted inquiry, the case ended with Stafford's translation to the Stationers' Company.

[81] Arber, *Transcript*, III:39–40; cited in Johnson, "The Stationers," 7. Bill was trying to clear his title to Fulke's *Answer to the Rhemish Testament*.

[82] Greg offers a few instances of such "screen" entrances in "Entrance, License and Publication," 20. It is not merely coincidental that, in July of 1595, the clerk of the Stationers' Company began to record entrances in a volume, Liber C, reserved exclusively for that purpose.

[83] Greg and Boswell, *Records*, 59. The rule was thought sufficiently important that it was recorded with a memorandum that it was to be regularly read aloud to the company on quarter days. That the trade was carefully trying to calibrate its claim on this monopoly may be gleaned from the fact that this regulation was instituted on the same day as was a strict new set of price controls – a regulation which was also to be read aloud on quarter days.

his freedom from the Drapers' to the Stationers', whereupon his claim to these titles was recognized by a new entry.

The quashing of Astley's claim in 1596 seems not to have been isolated, for in July of 1596 the friction between the drapers and the stationers provoked an inquiry from the Court of Aldermen, who apparently supported the stationers' claims.[84] For the next four years, the competing claims of drapers and stationers were contested in a variety of venues, the Custom of the City pitted against the 1563 Statute of Artificers, according to which artisans were to apprentice in the trade they intended to practice, as well as against the rights conferred by the Stationers' Charter and by the Star Chamber Decree of 1586. The translation of twelve drapers to the Stationers' Company in May of 1600 signals the industrial victory of the stationers. During the same period a more muted and diffuse contest over rights of entrance and publication took place between the Stationers and the Lord Chamberlain's Men. The results in both cases are comparable. At roughly the same time that the competing drapers were translated and so brought within the regulatory purview of the stationers, a small logjam in the print dissemination of plays that had been performed by the Chamberlain's Men was broken: in the space of a few months, *Every Man in His Humour*, *The Merchant of Venice*, *Henry V*, and *Much Ado About Nothing* were printed. Of the stayed plays, only *A Moral of Cloth Breeches* did *not* see print. It seems that the players had less success in asserting their industrial claims at this point than did the drapers.

Subsequent assertions in a later regime were sometimes more successful and this is at least partly because the players were more consistently abetted by the interventions of the Lords Chamberlain and their agents.[85] More registrations seem to have been stayed, possibly on behalf of acting companies.[86] But the players tried out new devices for controlling the flow of plays to the press, in various attempts to secure possessive grandeur. The sharers who founded the

[84] Johnson, "The Stationers," 9–10.
[85] Some such assertions were far less successful, however. With the closing of the theatres came a hiatus in opportunities for the players to assert their rights and for their patrons to support such assertions, and many stationers benefitted. Scripts passed from authors directly to stationers without any theatrical intermediary, and acting companies surrendered manuscripts that they might otherwise have tried to hoard. When the reopening of the theaters became likely, acting companies scrambled for scripts. In a letter to Henry Herbert, Humphrey Moseley reveals that the companies of the Red Bull, the Cockpit, and Whitefriars had all sought his scripts, but that he had remained unwilling: "neither did I ever consent directly or indirectly, that hee or any others should act any playes that doe belong to mee, without my knowledge and consent had and procured" (cited in Alfred Harbage, "Elizabethan-Restoration Palimpsest," *MLR* 35 [1940], 291).
[86] Fredson Bowers argued that the condition in the 1605 registration to Rocket of Dekker and Webster's *Westward Ho*, "provided that he get further authoritie before it be printed," was added in specific response to company pressures; he alleges that the entry was subsequently vacated for the same reasons (*On Editing Shakespeare and the Elizabethan Dramatists* [Philadelphia: University of Pennsylvania Press, 1955], 17–18).

King's Revels children's company in 1608 made covenants to keep the company property intact –

> if . . . any apparrell, bookes, or any other goods or commodities shalbe conveyed or taken awaye by any of the said parties without the consent and allowance of the residue of his fellow sharers, and the same exceedinge the value of twoe shillinges, That then he or they soe offendinge shall forfeite and loose all such benefitt, profitt, and comoditie as otherwise should arrise and growe unto him or them by their shares.

And they also agreed

> that noe man of the said Company shall at any tyme hereafter put into print, or cause to be put in print, any manner of playe booke now in use, or that hereafter shalbe sould unto them, upon the penaltie and forfeiture of ffortie pounds starlinge, or the losse of his place and share of all things amongst them.[87]

By 1609 the enterprise seems to have collapsed, and two of the chief sharers were suing each other. The opportunistic plaintiff was Martin Slaughter, during whose career, one can see from this vantage, various mechanisms for securing monopolistic competition were improvised and refined. Having retained rights to certain plays acted by the Admiral's Men while he was with the company, he sold them on his departure, but soon thereafter we find him insisting that all plays performed by the Children of the King's Revels be owned by the corporation.[88] Having so insisted on protecting rights of the unitary corporation, he ended his career on provincial tour leading one of two fragmentary companies each travelling under the same name, each carrying a copy of an exclusive patent granting the right to tour and perform. During most of his tenure with the Admiral's Men, Slaughter was one of the agents to whom Henslowe entrusted important financial arrangements, but he ended his career with the company in a lawsuit with a fellow member in which he is charged with having stolen a play. Slaughter's professional biography carries us across a period in which the corporate bodies like the Stationers' Company or the Admiral's Men or the syndicate controlling the Children of the King's Revels often mustered new economic protections in the face of threats both from outside their own industries and from within their own ranks.

Owing to the short life of the King's Revels Children, the attempt to secure its books from the stationers was unsuccessful. Several of this company's plays were eventually published, possibly after the collapse of the company; certainly,

---

[87] J. Greenstreet, *Transactions of the New Shakspere Society*, ser. 1, p. 3 (London: Kegan Paul, Trench, and Trübner, 1889), 275–6.

[88] The collapse of that company in 1608, if not engineered by Slaughter, certainly did not redound to his disadvantage: in a deposition in the 1609 Chancery suit brought by Slaughter (and alluded to below), George Androwes plausibly claims that he was lured into the syndicate with false promises, only to discover that the syndicate had already incurred large undisclosed debts. No record of the Court's decision survives, although relevant documents may be found in Greenstreet, *Transactions*, 269–84.

there is little evidence of protest from the sharers. Once the company was embroiled in the courts, for example, Thomas Archer printed *The Two Maids of Moreclacke*, printed it without registration.[89] This is the year in which the never-writer complained against the possessiveness of the King's Men, and the "Epistle to the Reader" of the *Two Maids of Moreclacke* adopts a cognate idiom. The author of this epistle, and of this fascinating play, was Robert Armin who informs his reader that the play is now being "acted by the boyes of the Revels, which perchaunce in part was sometime acted more naturally in the Citty," probably by the King's Men's in one of their first performances at Blackfriar's. An unspecified inhibition provokes a vague invidiousness: "I would have againe inacted *John* my selfe but *Tempora mutantur in illis*, & I cannot do as I would." There was Martin Slaughter to consider: if we suppose that his suit for £200, for breach of the unusually detailed and rigorous contract in defense of the King's Revels Children's property, had been mounted shortly after the King's Men's performance of Armin's play, that would surely have been enough to inhibit another performance. Whatever kept Armin from competing with the children, he was not inhibited from turning the play over to the printer.[90] The actor has contrived a role and a plot that suits his skills and temperament, but he cannot perform in the play he has written; in this extreme case of alienated labor, the press functions as an alternative medium of relatively free expression, and authorship a professional subjectivity slightly more unconstrained than the actor's professional agency. Armin returns us to the question of *authorial* position: it will be useful now to consider the emergence of editorial signature within the contested network of theatrical and bibliographic property. Because the artisans of stage and page compete so variously and so consistently it is hardly surprising that playwrights like Marston and Brome come to question their property in their plays and that Armin's fellows, such actor–playwrights as Shakespeare, Heywood, and Jonson should interrogate the possibility of that property with particular eloquence and force.

[89] On the other hand, he *was* fined for publication without entrance (Greg and Jackson, *Records*, 443), and there is a distant possibility that the fine arose because of a protest against publication from without the Stationers' Company.

[90] Markham and Machin's play for the Revels Children was published as early as 1608, but only Markham's name appears on the title page and that was withdrawn for the second and third issues of this edition. No specific legal bar to publication survives that would have inhibited Markham, Machin, or Armin; John Mason and Lording Barry, on the other hand, also wrote plays for the company, and they, as sharers, were under bonds to the syndicate: their plays for the King's Revels Children did not see print until 1610.

3   Upstart crows and other emergencies

The author at the border

The prolific Thomas Heywood seems to have been particularly sensitive to the tendrils of emergent proprietary interest and to the various strains to which they were subject, hence his tender sense of infringement when faced with such practices as "stenography." We get a more complex manifestation of this sense of infringement in Heywood's epistle prefatory to *The English Traveller*, which appeared a year later, in 1633:

> This *Tragi-Comedy* . . . comming accidentally to the *Presse*, and I having Intelligence thereof, thought it not fit that it should passe as *filius populi*, a Bastard without a Father to acknowledge it: True it is, that my Playes are not exposed unto the world in Volumes, to bear the title of *Workes*, (as others) one reason is, That many of them by shifting and change of Companies, have beene negligently lost, Others of them are still retained in the hands of some Actors, who thinke it against their peculiar profit to have them come in Print, and a third, That it never was any great ambition in me, to bee in this kind Volumniously read.

The passage provides important evidence, however late, that actors felt the press to be a threat to their profits. But the epistle has a good deal more to tell us: an obscure sense of infringement issues in unusual articulations of authorship. Heywood describes himself as paternal and responsible as the stationers are not, he seems himself as a writer for public performance and *not* for private reading; he discloses a tendency to jealous disdain for those like Daniel, Jonson, or Shakespeare, whose plays have been metamorphosed by the press into *Works* and whose very sense of dramaturgic identity, Heywood implies, has been consequently transformed, so that they now suffer under the paradoxical ambition "to be in this kind Volumniously read"; above all, he situates himself at a border between acting companies and the press, with his plays variously bastardized, neglected, and hoarded by the industrial practices on either side of the border. The figure of paternity is asserted against the fact of his impotent authority, inexplicitly proposing rights over printing that do not exist. As in Dallington's *View of France*, so here: proprietary authorship originates in figure, in fantasy.

The translator of Sallust and Ovid, and author of *Troia Britannica, History Concerning Women*, and *The Hierarchy of the Blessed Angels*, Heywood was by no means opposed to being volumniously read, yet long before the publications of *The English Traveller* he had developed a firm sense of the differences between writing for performance and writing for print. He felt those differences not so much as generic or modal imperatives – throughout his career Heywood was a remarkably irregular exponent of genre and mode – but more as a matter of business ethics. From the first he claimed this scruple as a distinction: "It hath been no custome in me of all other men (curteous Readers) to commit my playes to the presse," he announces in his preface to his play, *The Rape of Lucrece* (1608), "for though some have used a double sale of their labours, first to the Stage, and after to the Presse; For my owne part I here proclaime my selfe ever faithfull in the first, and never guilty of the last."[1] The protest is a trifle disingenuous. As a leading member of the Queen's Men, his interests were closely allied with those of the company, and if press publication would hurt their fortunes, it would hurt his. At any rate, he here anticipates a later prologue, that to *If You Know Not Me*, by claiming to be providing printer's copy, or assisting in its provision, as a way of thwarting misappropriation, perhaps by Stenography, perhaps by memorial reconstruction: "since some of my Playes have (unknowne to me, and without any of my direction) accidentally come into the Printers handes" – he may be referring to *If You Know Not Me*, to an early edition (now lost) of *The Four Prentices of London*, or to any of a number of anonymously printed plays now accepted as Heywood's –

and therefore so corrupt and mangled, copied onely by the eare) [*sic*] that I have beene as unable to know them, as ashamed to challenge them. This therefore I was the willinger to furnish out in his native habit: first being by consent, next because the rest have bene so wronged, in beeing publisht in such savage and ragged ornaments.[2]

If the phrase "by consent" were more explicit, we might determine whether it indicates that Heywood has been consulted about the edition or that the principals of the Queen's Men had, as a group, approved the publication, since this would tell us whether Heywood retains any rights distinct from those of the company with respect to publication. But Heywood is here clearly assenting to a derivative publication in print of a work allocated to the Queen's Men for their primary publication on the Red Bull stage. Once again, one can detect a sense of intellectual property tethered to the idea of the unique exemplar, the holograph.

---

[1] V:163.
[2] *Ibid.* Chambers, who was exceedingly conservative in attributing plays to Heywood, still grants that "of the twelve plays at most which appeared before 1619, the first seven were unauthorized issues" (*Elizabethan Stage*, III:338–39).

The double sales to which Heywood refers test a principle that Robert Greene had clearly transgressed in the early 1590s. In the *Defence of Conycatching*, the pseudonymous Cuthbert Conycatcher taxes Greene with violating an acting company's exclusive and enduring property in the scripts they acquire:

> What if I should prove you a *Conny-catcher*, Maister *R. G.* would it not make you blush at the matter?... Aske the Queens Players, if you sold them not *Orlando Furioso* for twenty Nobles, and when they were in the country, sold the same Play to the Lord Admirals men for as much more. Was not this plaine *conny-catching*, Maister *R. G*?[3]

Beneath the obvious difference between the two episodes – that the double sales against which Heywood protests are to two different sorts of "publisher" whereas Greene had sold to two different firms operating in the same medium – lies a more interesting difference. It is worth recurring to "Cuthbert Conycatcher's" railing charge against Greene's double-dealing:

> But I heare when this was objected, that you made this excuse: that there was no more faith to be held with Plaiers, than with them that valued faith at the price of a feather: for as they were *Comædians* to act, so the actions of their lives were *Cameleon* like, that they were uncertaine variable, time pleasers, men that measured honestie by profite, and that regarded their Authors not by desart but by necessitie of time.[4]

It is particularly telling that Cuthbert Conycatcher knows no plausible defense of Greene's behavior, and assumes that any reader will also find the behavior indefensible. Certainly the assailant imagines no "natural" authorial claim to enduring property in dramatic literature, else he would not have mounted this particular attack on Greene. Heywood's protest is less certain. What is at issue in the preface to *The Rape of Lucrece* is Heywood's sense of propriety. The double sale *unsettles* Heywood, since it violates the integrity of the artisanal object, manufactured for unconditional sale. Put this way, we can see that what disturbs Heywood, at bottom, is the press itself, the multiplication for sale of durable exempla. There is thus a flicker of the truly radical in Heywood. Many of Heywood's contemporaries were much haunted by the disintegrative function of theatrical impersonation, its collusion in the dispersal of human identity, yet Heywood is the genial apologist for theatricality; most of Heywood's contemporaries were enthusiasts of the press, that far greater engine of iteration and distribution, but Heywood is its genial opponent.[5]

---

[3] *The Life and Complete Works in Prose and Verse of Robert Greene*, ed. A. B. Grosart, 15 vols. (London, 1881–86), XI:75.

[4] *The Defence of Conny-Catching*, ed. G. B. Harrison, *The Bodley Head Quartos* X (London: John Lane, 1924), 37.

[5] An opponent, albeit opportunistically so. Heywood was a prolific writer for print and on occasion exploits its apparatuses for self-promotion (see the detail noted in Farmer and Lesser, "Vile Arts," 99–101).

Here at the border between stage and printed page, then, an ethics of authorial effort and trade is being worked out, and with it comes an emergent disturbance in the ontology of the letter. Such disturbances do not, of course, emerge only at this border, at the nexus of composition, performance, and printing of plays. They appear at various sites and moments in Early Modern culture, and were fostered by a variety of developments, all more or less dependent on the spread of printing: the proliferation of literacies, confessional and devotional transformations, the ostentatiously willed regulation of verbal style as a central practice of political and social elites. But the urban bookstall and the urban theater are noteworthy as sites of *rapid* commercial growth and we should not be surprised that this border should be a site of small but prophetic conceptual skirmishes: we have already observed the ways in which bookstall and theater served as engines of a fashion culture – a culture of experiment, caprice, obsolescence, fetishistic attention, and fierce connoisseurship – and we can observe the dynamic of fashion at the level of concept-formation as well.

Greene's double-dealing indicates that authors were beginning to wrest some new economic advantages from within the quickening market of the London stage in the early 1590s, while the double sales of those whom Heywood denigrates indicates a crucial elaboration of this new authorial economic power, for the competition between media promoted authorship as a new node of value. We can detect this promotion in other developments, but it will be best to point to the more obvious one, which is that speculative composition and piece work were no longer the exclusive forms of dramaturgic labor. Shakespeare's rise to a position as shareholder in the Globe consortium is the most famous instance of such a change in the conditions of authorial labor. Marston's case is similar: once one of Henslowe's stable of writers, he bought into the Queen's Revels syndicate in 1604. In the mid-thirties, the playwright Richard Brome was wooed away from his work with Prince Charles's Men to become a salaried employee, first, of the Queen Henrietta's Men at the Salisbury Court and, then, of Beeston's rival troupe based at the Cockpit.[6] In 1635 he contracted with the Queen's Men to provide three plays a year for 15s a week, plus profits from one early performance of each of the three plays, but plague disrupted the ensuing seasons; neither party made good on the terms of the contract in 1636 and Brome defected temporarily, writing at least one play for the Cockpit. Still, in 1637, when prospects for uninterrupted seasons seemed good, Brome again entered into negotiations with the Queen's Men, and, because Beeston had been trying to tempt him away, the terms of his second contract were even better – a salary of £1 a week this time, again in return for three plays a year, but with the added stipulations that this was to be an exclusive arrangement, with Brome providing plays for no other company (he had written one play for the Cockpit

---

[6] Ann Haaker, "The Plague, The Theater, and the Poet," *Renaissance Drama*, n.s. 1 (1968), 283–306.

in 1636) and with none of his plays to be printed without the permission of the company. He never signed the contract, though he drew the salary for at least a few weeks (for a year, the Queen's Men claimed) and in 1639, he finally went over to Beeston.

The competition for exclusive rights to Brome's output firms the commercial shape of creative personality, transformed it into a property and, in 1640, subjected it to legal inspection – for on February 12 of that year the Salisbury Court Theater filed a bill of complaint against Brome.[7] This competition seems to have given form to relationships that had already had some abiding, if informal standing in the theatrical economy.[8] Though no contract survives, John Fletcher seems to have had a similarly exclusive relation to King James' company. Bentley points out that, during the dozen or so years prior to Fletcher's death "none of his own plays or his collaborations ... can be shown to have been written for any other company, and the great majority are in the King's repertory of unprinted plays submitted to the Lord Chamberlain in 1641."[9] With Fletcher, we appear to have the same pattern as that stipulated in Brome's 1637 contract with the Queen's Men: exclusive composition for a single company and, thanks to regular interventions by the various Lords Chamberlain, a substantial bar to print publication. Massinger seems to have succeeded Fletcher as the King's Men's playwright, for after Fletcher's retirement Massinger can only be shown to have written once for any other company.[10] The acting company monopolizes the author.

Such exclusive association of individual playwrights with particular companies can be traced to late Elizabethan practice, and not only to Shakespeare's exclusive work for the Lord Chamberlain's-King's Men, from 1594 until his retirement. In 1598, when Henslowe was assisting in the reconstitution of the Admiral's Men, he loaned £2 to Henry Porter in earnest of the soon-to-be-completed *Two Merry Women of Abington*, "& for the Resayte of that money he gave me his faythfulle promysse that I shold have alle the boockes which he writte ether him sellfe or with any other." Three years later, Henslowe again made a loan on behalf of the company, £3 this time, "at the sealleynge of h Chettells band to writte for them."[11] The arrangement extends by analogy the quite common practice of binding actors, both sharers and hired men, to

---

[7] PRO Reg. 2/622; Brome's response of March 6 is numbered 723. Haacker transcribes substantial portions of the bills in the article cited above.

[8] Thus G. E. Bentley: "Since the [Salisbury Court] theatre was so conventional in its arrangements, it is probable that Richard Brome's two contracts in 1635 and 1638 were traditional and similar in their basic provisions to those of 'ordinary' playwrights for other major companies, at least in the reigns of James and Charles," *The Profession of Dramatist in Shakespeare's Time, 1590–1642* (Princeton: Princeton University Press, 1971), 112–13.

[9] *Ibid.*, 117.

[10] And Shirley apparently succeeded Massinger: he had written all but one of his plays for the Queen's Men between 1625 and 1637, then left for Ireland; upon his return, he wrote exclusively for King Charles' Men.

[11] Foakes and Rickert, *Henslowe's Diary*, 105 and 199.

particular companies for terms of various lengths. Such practices maintained the loose linkages of company, performance style, distinctive performers, and dramaturgic idiom that gave the theatrical "market" its coherence: the continuing and frequently exclusive association of particular playwrights with a given company helped to anchor the expectations of late Elizabethan, Jacobean, and Caroline audiences. That the sense of authorial property is quickened in the course of such cartellization is perhaps hinted by the trajectory of Heywood's career. His nervous intuitions of propriety and infringement were doubtless fostered by his early involvement with Henslowe's enterprises, both as an actor and as a playwright, for Henslowe seems to have been particularly ingenious at improvising new structures of obligation within his cartel. Heywood signed an agreement with Henslowe in 1598 to act exclusively with the Admiral's Men for a term of two years, and although there is no similar record of his having bound himself to exclusive work as a playwright, he seems to have written for no other company in the late nineties. His association with Henslowe continued even after he transferred to Worcester's Men, later the Queen's company, for Worcester's Men operated out of Henslowe's Rose and Henslowe provided many of the company with his usual combination of benevolent and usurious financial assistance. After his transfer Heywood wrote almost exclusively for the Worcester's / Queen's company, this not surprisingly, since he was one of the principals of the company.

Around 1614 he apparently stopped writing plays, or substantially reduced his dramatic output, and for just about a decade he devoted himself to non-dramatic poetry and to prose; in about 1624, Heywood returned to dramatic writing, providing plays for the two companies performing at the Phoenix under the management of his old colleague from the Worcester's Men, Christopher Beeston.[12] But his loyalties did not remain undivided, for sometime around the publication of *The English Traveller* Heywood began writing plays for the King's Men, usually in collaboration with Brome. This non-contractual labor would appear to revert to the piece-work of Greene's generation. The crucial difference lies in the fact that such writers as Heywood and Brome operate in a theatrical market in which new forms of monopoly had emerged and were emerging, some transient and others more permanent. To begin with what seems a transient form of protection, we can consider the play that was probably the first of the collaborations between Heywood and Brome. In the summer of 1634, when four women were brought to trial in London for witchcraft, Brome and Heywood hurried out a new play on the subject,

---

[12] There is some reason to suppose that Heywood also stopped performing sometime in the second decade of the century. Distance from theatrical affairs might therefore explain the difference between the Heywood of *The English Traveller* and the Heywood of *The Rape of Lucrece*: in the earlier text he is primarily concerned with the misappropriations of drama by the press, whereas in the latter he registers some displeasure with theatrical business as well, with the negligence of actors who have lost his scripts and even with those who now obstruct print publication, thinking "it against their peculiar profit."

The Late Lancashire Witches, for the King's Men. A rival company at the Salisbury Court had at the same time contrived a more efficient topical response, which was to spruce up an older play about the once notorious conjurer Doctor Lambe with more timely additions and to present it as *Doctor Lambe and the Witches*. The King's Men once again exploited their warm relations with the Lord Chamberlain's office, with a petition to Philip Herbert "complayning of intermingleing some passages of witches in old playes to the prejudice of their designed Comedy of the Lancashire witches, & desiring a prohibition of any other till theirs bee allowed & Acted."[13] Pembroke seems to have endorsed their request to the Revels Office, for the revisions to *Doctor Lambe and the Witches* were not licensed for four weeks, enough time, one supposes, for Heywood and Brome to finish their new play and for the King's Men to stage it.[14] Richard Dutton has alleged that by means of the special protection accorded the King's Men "the authorities ensured that an acceptable version of the story ... was the one that reached the stage"; although this may overestimate the degree of official assistance secured by the King's Men, the nature of the protection they garnered is certainly unusual, for in this instance a cluster of current events, a subject matter, became the object of a temporary monopoly.[15]

The King's Men were often assisted by the Lord Chamberlain and by those who answered to him, but such aid, sporadic and capricious, partakes of the merely improvised character of most Early Modern patronage, the benefits of which ramified quite unsystematically. We have already considered some of the other forms of the Lord Chamberlain's aid: three years after his assistance with

---

[13] *Malone Society Collections*, vol. 2, pt 3 (1931), 410.

[14] The play was ready for printing by October 28, when Benjamin Fisher entered the play in the Stationers' Register. The license for *Doctor Lambe and the Witches* may be found in *The Dramatic Records of Sir Henry Herbert*, ed. Joseph Quincy Adams (New York: Blom, 1964), 36.

[15] *Mastering the Revels*, 25. Monopolies specified to subject matter are not a novelty, having been common among patented stationers since the beginning of Elizabeth's reign; indeed, the second printing privilege on record was a late fifteenth-century Venetian monopoly in the historiography of the Venetian Republic (*The Author's Due*, chapter III). However, this protection seems to be less an extension of a monopolistic form originating in the book trade than an adaptation of a regulatory form proper to the Revels' Office. It was quite normal for Henry Herbert to forbid or carefully to constrain the performance of plays on volatile topical material: the proscription of certain topics (as opposed to the proscription of specified stances) was the fundamental mode of censorship, easy enough to adapt as a mechanism of patronage. Here, then, is one of the sporadic rapprochements between censorship and market regulation, a regulatory consolidation facilitated no doubt by the temporary concentration of the responsibilities for both stage and press licensing plays in Herbert's Revels Office.

It is worth remembering that, in the normal conduct of theatrical business, plot – comparable to subject matter, but not equivalent to it – was itself a commodity, distinguished from fully realized scripts. Authors often received advances based on the plot they pitched. In 1597 Jonson received such a payment for the plot of a tragedy; in the autumn of the following year Chapman was paid for having written two acts based on that plot.

The Late Lancashire Witches, Philip Herbert would make company permission a condition for the printing of all plays in the repertory of the King's Men. That the Herberts were willing to authorize such monopolies may not indicate decisive developments in intellectual property, but they supported a steady probing of proprietary possibilities: in effect, the commercial events themselves seem to inquire whether a firm can (temporarily) own a story, whether words declaimed before a paying audience could nonetheless be considered the property of the speakers.

These "questions", the interrogatives of commercial practice, were posed with increasing frequency from the last years of Elizabeth's reign forward, during decades that saw a striking efflorescence of the regulatory milieu. Beeston and his son, William, who succeeded him in 1638, were important agents of new attempts to steady and shape the theatrical marketplace. We have already observed the elder's efforts to monopolize Brome's talents in the mid-thirties, but this was not his sole contrivance: in 1639 Brome offered grudging praise for the son, "by whose care and directions this Stage [the Cockpit] is govern'd, who has for many yeares both in his father's dayes, and since directed Poets to write & Players to speak."[16] A few months earlier, William had appealed directly to the king for exclusive stage-right in a list of 45 plays and the Lord Chamberlain was duly charged with securing compliance. The plays had been in the repertory of the Queen Henrietta's Men, which the elder Beeston had disbanded early in 1637, this as part of a reorganization of the London theaters worked out under the close supervision of the Lord Chamberlain and the Master of the Revels.[17] According to Henry Herbert's record-book, "Mr. Beeston was commanded to make a company of boyes" at the Queen's Men's old theater, and his son wanted to confirm that the plays "doe all and every of them properly and of right belong to the said house, and consequently that they are all in his propriety."[18] We

---

[16] Epilogue to *The Court Beggar*, printed in *Five New Plays* (London, 1653); see Gerald Eades Bentley, *The Jacobean and Caroline Stage*, 7 vols. (Oxford: Oxford University Press, 1941–68), II:370–4 and III:4–5. Like Aleyn and Burbage before him, Beeston had augmented his position in various acting companies by the purchase of all sorts of property necessary to theatrical production – props, costumes, playbooks – by renting these properties to his fellows, and by lending them money. He seems also to have acquired some interest in the Cockpit Theater, though it is not clear whether his claim on the property was justified; see C. J. Sisson, "Notes on Early Stuart Stage History," *MLR* 37 (1942), 25–36 and Chambers, *Elizabethan Stage*, II:236–39.

[17] *Jacobean and Caroline Stage*, I:237.

[18] Evelyn May Albright, *Dramatic Publication in England, 1580–1640: A Study of Conditions Affecting Content and Form of Drama* (London: Oxford University Press, 1927), 231, quoting from Malone's *Variorum*, III:239–40 and 158. Inconclusively, but carefully, Albright discusses the issues surrounding the younger Beeston's maneuver; she does not observe that, since his father had formed the new company at the behest of the Lord Chamberlain or, at least, with his strong endorsement, Beeston had a claim on royal support in the murky business of establishing title to the plays.

Six of the old Queen's Men actually remained at the Cockpit but three members of the old company joined a minor troupe then playing at the Salisbury Court and so founded a new

are a long way from the jocular reference, in Webster's 1605 prologue to *The Malcontent*, to mutual infringements, the King's Men performing the Children of the Revels' play in amiable retaliation for the Children's performance of the King's Men's *Jeronimo*. Beeston's appeal to the king is far more earnest: competition for the stage rights in plays was strenuous, but there was no settled way of answering the questions of how such rights were to be known, where precisely they were vested, and by what conventions or mechanisms they had been so vested.

However various were the interrogatives of commercial practice, they clustered with increasing frequency around the persons and names of authors. A theater-goer might have made an effort to see Burbage, or to see what was being played at the Blackfriars; he or she might seek out a tragedy or a play that promises the frisson of topicality; moreover, a consumer might seek such pleasures on stage or on the page. But the record of contracts and protections suggest that acting companies, theater owners, and stationers had all observed that members of the public would occasionally – and with increasing frequency – extend themselves to attend performances of a play by Heywood or to purchase the printed texts of a play by "Shakespeare." One of the first explicit directives from the Lord Chamberlain's office, the letter from William Herbert in May of 1619 barring the printing of the King's Men's plays was almost certainly a reaction to Thomas Pavier's edition of a small collection of Shakespeare's plays, apparently in the process of being printed at the Jaggard press.[19] A great deal has been inferred from the Lord Chamberlain's letter – that a few of the King's Men were involved in preparations for the Shakespeare Folio at an early stage (and if so we might suppose that they had already begun to think of the printing of plays as an appropriate adjunct to their cartel) – but it also tells us something that we often take for granted – that the imprint of the author is a crucial element of the dramatic commodity. The players had always needed authors; now they needed authorship and they began to work steadily to enhance it.

The players had perhaps been involved in earlier stays of publication, but this one was preliminary to what must have been a far deeper involvement in the book trade than any they had experienced before. In the next few years, Heminges, Condell, perhaps Edward Knight, and others from the company must have performed a variety of editorial labors; as decisions were made about what should be included, their attention must have been caught by their

Queen's Men while five others went off to the King's Men: the younger manager wished to forestall the sort of dispute concerning the old company's property that dogged his father when Queen Anne's company broke up a decade and a half earlier; see C. J. Sisson, "Notes on Early Stuart Stage History," 25–36.
[19] Greg, *The Shakespeare First Folio*, 11–16.

publishing colleagues' efforts to accumulate the printing rights to those texts; and, indeed, their early assistance in undermining Pavier's collection was an important first step in facilitating the industrial arrangements for the Folio. This was hardly disinterested labor. The players brought their professional expertise and their claim on the Lord Chamberlain's good graces to bear on the production of a book that would monumentalize Shakespeare as *their* fellow and *his* plays as *theirs*: they were using print to increase their corporate prestige. Moreover, the King's Men seem to have learned a new trick. Having assisted the Folio syndicate as it transformed the mechanisms of stationers' copyright into a monopoly on the printing of Shakespeare's works, the King's Men soon sought to transform their own informal stage right into a monopoly on the playing of Shakespeare's work: in 1627, in a gesture nicely symmetrical to their 1619 appeal to the Lord Chamberlain for an inhibition of printing, they turned to his cousin, Henry Herbert, *de facto* Master of the Revels, to bar the Red Bull Company from performing any plays by Shakespeare.[20] The Folio would have made such performances particularly easy, but their work on the Folio had taught them how effectively monopoly could operate on the authorial form; what could be named as *his* could be more easily secured as theirs.

The entitled author

In a letter appended to Okes's edition of his *Apology for Actors* (1612), Heywood recalls the fate of *Troia Britannica* (1609) at the press of William Jaggard:

> To my approved good Friend,
> Mr. *Nicholas Okes*
> The infinite faults escaped in my booke of *Britaines Troy*, by the negligence of the Printer, as the misquotations, mistaking of sillables, misplacing halfe lines, coining of strange and never heard of words. These being without number, when I would have taken a particular account of the *Errata*, the Printer answered me, hee would not publish his owne disworkemanship, but rather let his owne fault lye upon the necke of the Author:

Note the science of retaliation: as Jaggard has appropriated and unflatteringly represented Heywood's text, so Heywood, exploiting the uncanny and slippery art of indirect discourse, appropriates and unflatteringly represents Jaggard's speech. He returns to Okes and flatters, albeit on behalf of his own "rights":

> and being fearfull that others of his quality, had beene of the same nature, and condition, and finding you on the contrary, so carefull, and industrious, so serious and laborious to

---

[20] *Dramatic Records of Sir Henry Herbert*, 64.

doe the Author all the rights of the presse, I could not choose but gratulate your honest indeavours with this short remembrance.

But Heywood is just getting underway. In the letter prefatory to his *Apology* Heywood indignantly distinguishes *his* sense of attributive proprieties from Jaggard's looser impression of authorship by directing our attention to another of Jaggard's books, *The Passionate Pilgrim Or Certaine Amorous Sonnets betweene Venus and Adonis, newly corrected and augmented. By W. Shakespeare*, the third edition of which appeared in 1612:

> Here likewise, I must necessarily insert a manifest injury done me in that worke, by taking the two Epistles of *Paris* to *Helen*, and *Helen* to *Paris*, and printing them in a lesse volume, under the name of another, which may put the world in opinion I might steale them from him; and hee to doe himselfe right, hath since published them in his owne name: but as I must acknowledge my lines not worthy his patronage, under whom he hath publist them, so the Author I know much offended with M. *Iaggard* (that altogether unknowne to him) presumed to make so bold with his name. These, and the like dishonesties I know you to be cleere of.

Heywood sharply distinguishes his use of authorial ascriptions, his use of "Heywood" or "Shakespeare", from Jaggard's. This is by no means opportunistic. Heywood had himself been scrupulous about acknowledging his inclusion of some slight lyrics by others in his 1608 *Rape of Lucrece*. Yet it might be argued in Jaggard's defense that a Jacobean stationer's "Shakespeare" might be very nearly generic. Jaggard's was the third edition of *The Passionate Pilgrime*, and if he had expanded on the earlier edition(s) by including poems from Heywood's *Troia Britannica*, this was hardly an unusual procedure: the second (?) edition of 1599, *The Passionate Pilgrime. By W. Shakespeare*, also published by Jaggard, includes poems now generally held to be by Marlowe, Raleigh, Barnfield, Griffin, Shakespeare and others.[21] If only five of the poems in *The Passionate Pilgrime* are now securely attributed to Shakespeare – three poems from *Love's Labors Lost* and two from *Sonnets* – four other sonnets treat of the dalliance of Venus and Adonis and five other poems adopt the "Venus and Adonis' stanza: they are thus "Shakespearean" or "Shakespearistic" if they are not Shakespeare's.[22] The innovation in the 1612 title page, *The Passionate*

---

[21] This seems to be the second edition: unique exemplars of two sheets from what would seem to be the first edition are bound into the Folger copy of the dated 1599 edition. No title page of this other edition survives. It should be observed here that other stationer–anthologists proceeded with greater, Heywoodian scruple: see the discussion of *England's Helicon* (1600) on p. 101 below.

[22] In *The Oxford Shakespeare* (Oxford: Clarendon Press, 1986), Stanley Wells and Gary Taylor include, but designate as doubtful attributions, nine other poems. For another attempt to place Heywood's epistle in the cultural history of intellectual property, see Max W. Thomas, "Eschewing Credit: Heywood, Shakespeare, and Plagiarism before Copyright," *New Literary History*, 31 (2000), 277–93.

Pilgrim Or Certaine Amorous Sonnets betweene Venus and Adonis, registers the tie-in.

What's in a name? The answer to this question was especially mobile at this moment in the history of book culture, as Heywood's attack on Jaggard suggests. Heywood anticipates current bibliographic norms in his claim that Shakespeare's name was over-extended in *The Passionate Pilgrim*, yet not many years earlier what now seems under-extension had been an acceptable norm. Thus *Venus and Adonis* (1593) and *The Rape of Lucrece* (1594) are not attributed to Shakespeare on their title pages, although Shakespeare's name subscribes the prominant dedicatory epistles of both works: these are the first works printed "over" Shakespeare's name and none would be attributed to him again until 1598, around which time we can speak of a palpable shift. When Valentine Simmes printed the second quarto of *Richard II* for Andrew Wise in that year, he changed the title page (see figure 1) from

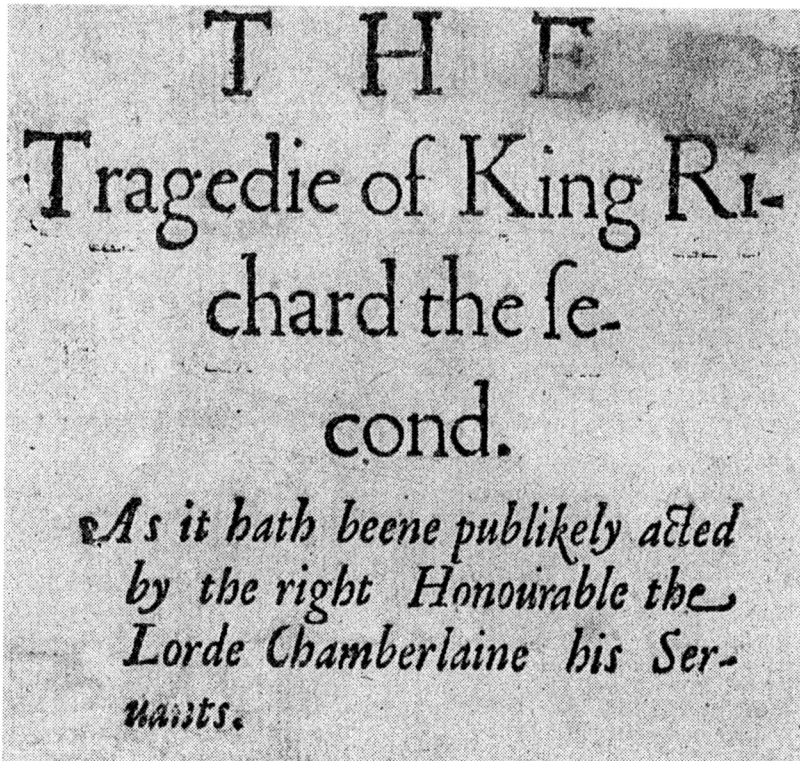

THE
Tragedie of King Richard the second.
As it hath beene publikely acted by the right Honourable the Lorde Chamberlaine his Seruants.

1 Title page of *The Tragedie of King Richard the Second*, Q1, 1597

to (see figure 2)

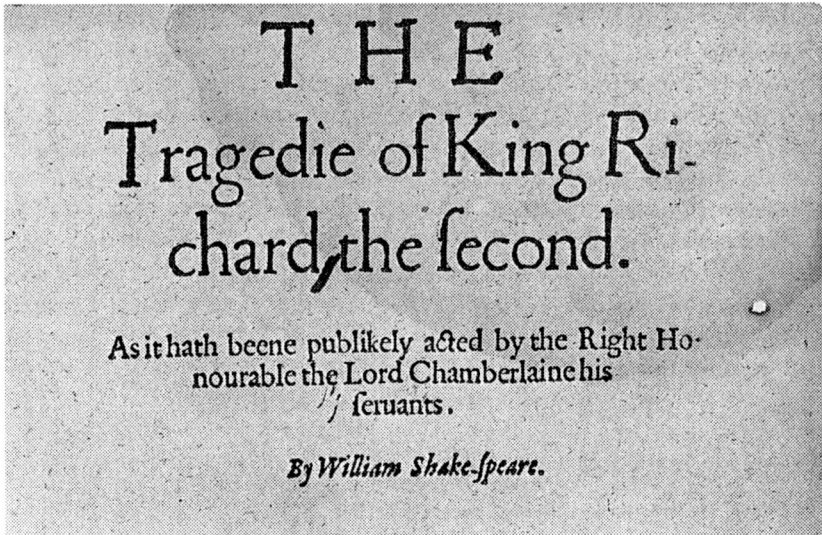

THE

Tragedie of King Ri-
chard,the second.

As it hath beene publikely acted by the Right Honourable the Lord Chamberlaine his
seruants.

By William Shake-speare.

2   Title page of *The Tragedie of King Richard the Second*, Q2, 1598

In the same year, Wise arranged that the title page of Q2 *Richard III* similarly depart from that of Q1, the name of the author supplementing the name of the acting company. These are novelties: the normal practice in early dramatic publication had been to identify plays by a reference on the title page either to the performing company alone or – a slightly less common alternative – to the venue of performance.[23] At the same time that the printing of plays began to accelerate a bit, the norm of authorial anonymity gave way.[24] 1594 is a breakthrough year for the attribution of printed plays: Marlowe's name appeared on the title pages of *Edward II*, *The Massacre at Paris*, and (with Nashe's)

[23] Shakespeare is unidentified on the title pages not only of the first quartos of *Richard II* and *Richard III* but also of *Titus Andronicus* (1594) and *Romeo and Juliet* (1597) – to say nothing of that of *The First Part of the Contention* (*2 Henry VI*; 1594) or the octavo of *Richard Duke of York* (*3 Henry VI*; 1595). A similarly slow-paced extension of the authorial name may be observed, outside the sphere of dramatic publication, in the case of Spenser, for which see both Patrick Cheney, *Spenser's Famous Flight: A Renaissance Idea of a Literary Career* (Toronto: University of Toronto Press, 1993) and my "Spenser's Retrography: Two Episodes in Post-Petrarchan Bibliography," *Spenser's Life and the Subject of Biography*, eds. Judith H. Anderson, Donald Cheney, and David A. Richardson (Amherst: University of Massachusetts Press, 1996), 99–130.

[24] In 1584 R. W. [Robert Wilson] is indicated as the author of *The Three Ladies of London*, in 1590, R. W. is again designated as the author of *The Three Lords and Ladies of London*, and in 1591, R. W. is designated as the author of *Tancred and Gismund*; Robert Wilmot's full name is given in the dedicatory epistle. In 1593, Peele's name appears at the end of the text of *Edward I*.

Dido, Queen of Carthage; Lodge and Greene are designated as the authors of *A Looking Glass for London* and Greene alone as the author of *Friar Bacon and Friar Bungay*.[25] The shift, the new weight given to dramatic authorship, is by no means decisive: after the Restoration, Pepys records his attendance at some fourteen plays without mentioning the name of the playwright; six of those plays were printed without attribution.

The attribution on the title pages of either the 1599 or the 1612 *Passionate Pilgrim* may be the effect of a stationer's confusion, of his unconcern, or of his shrewdness. The same must be said of the attribution of *The London Prodigall. / As it was plaide by the Kings Majesties Servants. / By William Shakespeare* (1605), which may or may not have been thus presented to capitalize on Shakespeare's reputation, but certainly that reputation was secure and valuable by this time.[26] It is impossible confidently to assess motives for the attribution of even *A Yorkshire Tragedy* (1608), for although it is Pavier's edition, and although Pavier would later willfully provide false imprints for his editions of Shakespeare plays, the attribution to "W. Shakespeare" may well be guileless. Pavier's 1608 entry of the play in the Stationers' Register also attributes it to "Wylliam Shakespere" and so anticipates the title page, and the Stationers' Register is not the usual site for intentional misattribution since attribution was unnecessary in the Register.[27] A burgeoning name: in 1591 the two-part *Troublesome Raign of John King of England* appeared anonymously;

---

[25] Daniel's name appeared on the title page of *Delia and Rosamond augmented / Cleopatra*, also printed in 1594. Of course, *Cleopatra*, which seems not to have been written for public performance, is not otherwise authenticated as having been performed at a given venue, on a given occasion, or by a given company. In the next four years, title pages would make attributions not only to these men, but also – and for the first time – to Peele, Chapman, Lyly (many of whose plays were then being issued in second editions) and finally to Shakespeare: in 1598, not only *Richard II*, but also *Love's Labors Lost* and *Richard III* appeared with authorial ascriptions.

For a systematic assessment of the history of title-page attributions of printed plays, see James P. Saeger and Christopher J. Fassler, "The London Professional Theater, 1576–1642: A Catalogue and Analysis of the Extant Printed Plays," *Research Opportunities in Renaissance Drama*, 34 (1995), 63–109. They give the powerfully significant overview of the trend between 1580 and 1660: a tripling of (extant) printed plays attributed to authors but not companies (from 20 percent to 60 percent) and the virtual collapse of attribution to acting companies without attribution to authors (from 60 percent to 5 percent).

[26] Very few have maintained that Creede (the printer) or Butter (the publisher) knew something that we do not and that the attribution is sound.

[27] Taylor is more confident, however: "the attribution to Shakespeare is probably, in this instance, deliberately dishonest" (Taylor and Wells, *et al.*, *William Shakespeare: A Textual Companion* [Oxford: Oxford University Press, 1987], 140). These are not the only early instances of overextensive Shakespearean namings, though others are less emphatic. In 1599, a commendatory poem by "W. S." was prefixed to Nicholas Breton's *The Will of Wit*; in 1602, *Thomas Lord Cromwell* was published, "as it hath been sundrie times publikely Acted by the Right Honorable the Lord Chamberlaine his Servaunts. Written by W. S."; the title page of *The Puritan* (1607) also gives a "W. S." as the author; and a small volume dated 1612, comprising a single elegy for William Peter of Whipton, was also attributed on its title page to "W. S." There is no need to multiply theories as to the warrant or motives of such attributions: the initials may refer slyly, or uncertainly, or irresponsibly, or cautiously, or ambiguously, to William Shakespeare,

in 1611 authorship – "by W. Sh." – was cautiously initiated; the title page of 1622 delivers the plays, finally, "written by W. Shakespeare." A name-brand for historical drama, linked and sequenced history plays, the matter of Henry, the stuff of Falstaff. And, if so, and if such naming be the stationers' norm, then in 1612 Jaggard is using just such a brand name for venereal poetry, for the matter of Adonis, evoking loose links between the bitternesses of the *Sonnets* of 1609 and the occasional, slack misogynies of *The Passionate Pilgrim*. Jaggard may have supposed the name, "Shakespeare," to be very nearly generic, a marker of "family resemblance" among poems and a source thereby of borrowed meanings and borrowed value – it should perhaps not go without saying that the borrowing of meanings and of value is one of the functions of the generic within the literary system; even the merely competent acquiring gilt by association. Heywood was attempting to thwart the generic use of names.

It appears that Heywood was not leading, but following a small backlash on behalf of attributive scruple. A few months after the appearance of *The Passionate Pilgrim*, Nicholas Ling published *England's Helicon*, to which he prefaced a letter "To the Reader, if indifferent," one of the key documents for the history of English authorship. Anticipating Heywood, Ling writes a preemptive apology – as if (this is entirely conjectural) the attributive miscellany of *The Passionate Pilgrim* had already elicited an outcry of some sort:

If any man hath beene defrauded of any thing by him composed, by another mans title put to the same, hee hath this benefit by this collection, freely to challenge his owne in publique, where els he might be robd of his proper due. No one thing beeing here placed by the Collector of the same under any mans name, eyther at large, or in letters, but as it was delivered by some especiall coppy comming to his handes. No one man, that shall take offence that his name is published to any invention of his, but he shall within the reading of a leafe or two, meete with another in reputation every way equal with himselfe, whose name hath beene before printed to his Poeme, which nowe taken away were more then theft: which may satisfie him that would faine seeme curious or be intreated for his fame.[28]

A language of property is being improvised here, poised between a courtly discourse of honor and a Citified discourse of criminal procedure. The precise social and economic value of attribution is unclear here – it is plainly undergoing

or to the non-dramatic poet William Smith (author of the sonnet sequence, *Chloris*), or to Wentworth Smith (a playwright who wrote for the Admiral's and for Worcester's company). Clearly, however, direct attribution to Shakespeare, or slant attribution to someone who might be Shakespeare, came into fashion in the late 1590s.

[28] *England's Helicon: 1600, 1614*, ed. Hyder Edward Rollins, 2 vols. (Cambridge: Harvard University Press, 1935), I:6. I follow Hebel, Bullen, and Rollins in attributing the letter, signed L.N., to Ling; see Rollins' ed., II:41–63.

a kind of figurative negotiation – but it is urgent enough: the published volume is fastidious about attribution, if not always accurate, and many of the attributions originally printed are corrected by cancel slips, some of them substituting "Ignoto" for the names of eminent poets.[29]

Of all the modern analyses on the function of attribution within mimetic commerce (by Foucault, Derrida, and others), Baudrillard's most usefully probes the issues raised by this strife between Heywood and Jaggard. In "Gesture and Signature," he treats of the signature in twentieth-century visual art, but in terms that may be cautiously applied to the case of Early Modern writing. Baudrillard observes that the signature transforms the work, converts it to "a model to which an extraordinary, differential value is brought by a visible sign": "the painted oeuvre becomes a cultural object by means of the signature."[30] We could say that the signature constitutes the modern *thing* as *objet d'art*. But Baudrillard does not say quite so much: he would have it that the signature "does not cause the work to be seen, but to be recognized and evaluated in a system of signs, and which . . . integrates it in a series, that of the works of the painter" (102), a description of acculturation that is curiously captive to the biographical. Again: "What does the signature indicate? The act of painting, the subject who paints" (102). This is to understand the work of art as Heywood does, and to refuse to understand it as does Jaggard, for whom attribution is a source of value and, thus, one act in the suite of actions that constitutes the work of art as such.[31] We could say that Baudrillard's analysis is produced by the likes of Heywood's, which sustains (but does not initiate) a long tradition of arguments and practices that ground the work of art not only in human artifaction but in human

[29] Percy Simpson, *Proof-Reading in the Sixteenth, Seventeenth, and Eighteenth Centuries* (London: Oxford, 1935), 21.

[30] Jean Baudrillard, *For a Critique of the Political Economy of the Sign*, intro. and trans., Charles Levin (St. Louis: Telos Press, 1981), 102–03.

[31] "To refuse": in his effort to insert signification within the analysis of productive forces (and so to rescue it from the status of the merely superstructural to which, he alleges, classical Marxism banished it), Baudrillard refuses a *preliminary* analytic capture of the authentic to an origin in market relations. Thus: "The social consensus, and beyond that, of course, all the subtle combinations of supply and demand play upon the signature. But one can see that this myth is not purely and simply an effect of commercial orchestration" (105). This is salutary; it would be especially salutary if analysis had indeed *seriously* examined signature as captive to an origin in market relations. He issues a similar caveat against technologism, and particularly McLuhanite technologism: "It is useless to argue that the forgery, the copy of the counterfeit are unacceptable today because photographic technique has disqualified 'photocopy' by hand. That sort of explanation is specious. Something else has changed: the conditions of signification of the oeuvre itself" (103). Technologist explanation is not *necessarily* specious, though Baudrillard gives a bracing redescription of the "field of causes" that might be mapped in the study of modern forgery. But the redescription is not a mapping: the analysis here reproduces a general weakness in classical Marxist historiography, to wit, the difficulty in accounting for historical change in any but structural terms. For a promising corrective, much indebted to Baudrillard, see Richard Halpern, "Breeding Capital," chapter 2 of *The Poetics of Primitive Accumulation*, 61–100.

autobiography. As he elaborates his analysis of the function of signature in modern art, Baudrillard implicitly acknowledges a distinction similar to the one that I am making, between an attribution that aims to grace a work with authorship and an attribution that guarantees particular authorship as the origin of a work:

> There is a conjunction of sign and name in the signature – a sign different from other signs in the painting, but homogeneous with them; a name different from the names of other painters but complicit in the same game. It is through this ambiguous conjunction of a subjective series (authenticity) and an objective series (code, social consensus, commercial value), through this inflected sign, that the system of consumption can operate. (105)

One can discern the structuralist paradigm operating within the description of the signature as inflected sign: Baudrillard's observation that the authenticated name participates in the objective code of modern art is modelled on the mutual participation of *parole* in *langue*, the one impossible without the other. But the objective code of Jaggard's art does not depend on authentication, although Heywood struggles to transform that code; authentication adds to a value already secured by the mere fact of attribution. Indeed, authentication is a cultural practice historically subsequent to attribution and produced from it.

If Jaggard supposed that Shakespeare's name was generic and not stipulative, it was, of course, convenient for him to do so (this is not, however, to gainsay the coherence, the cultural logic, of his attributive practice). But Heywood wishes to nip such supposition in the bud and it is convenient for him to do so, though he is remarkable – it is an index of his various alertness to the conditions of mimetic practice – in so fervently pursuing this end. He does so by bringing a criminal vocabulary to bear on the matter of attribution.[32] Figures of criminal misrepresentation, of forgery, are virtually exhausted *topoi* in erotic poetry, and are nearly as tired within the metadiscourse of poetics; in his attack on Jaggard, Heywood is in the difficult position of trying to revive the exhausted vocabulary of forgery, trying to make it stick, while maintaining a degree of urbane detachment (hence the claim that Jaggard has offended against Shakespeare by the over-extensive use of his name, and not against Heywood himself, by the under-extensive use of *his*). We encounter such rhetorical maneuvers – and they are never merely rhetorical – again and again, even during the prehistory of authorial copyright. Jaggard's crime here is the displacement of a condition of scarcity originating in the book trade – not enough anonymous or Shakespearean

[32] Heyward's figure had an effect, for Jaggard printed a new title-page for a second issue of the 1612 *Passionate Pilgrim*, this time with no authorial ascription. In *Plagiarism and Imitation During the English Renaissance* (Cambridge: Harvard, 1935), Harold Ogden White notes that Heywood had himself been scrupulous about acknowledging the inclusion of some slight lyrics by others in his 1608 *Rape of Lucrece*, 188.

poems to make up a volume – onto manuscription, a displacement that, according to Heywood, makes it seem that, out of an insufficiency of wit, either he or Shakespeare has been forced to plagiarize. At this juncture, the book trade peculiarly constitutes the press, a mere instrument of mechanical reproduction, as an instrument of automatic plagiarism.

The foisting of industrial scarcities onto the sphere of manuscription changed the nature of plagiarism; if nothing else, it sharpened the sense of its injuriousness. In his preface to the printed version of *The Brazen Age*, published in the year following the publication of the *Apology for Actors*, Heywood shows himself quite prickly on the subject, instancing

> a Pedant about this Towne, who, when all trades fail'd, turn'd *Pedagogue*, & once insinuating with me, borrowed fro[m] me certaine Translations of *Ovid*, as his three books *De Arte Amandi*, & two *De Remedio Amoris*, which since, his most brazen face hath most impudently challenged as his own, wherefore, I must needs proclaime it as far as *Ham*, where he now keeps schoole, *Hos ego versiculos feci tulit alter honores*, they were things which out of my juniority and want of judgement, I committed to the view of some private friends, but with no purpose of publishing, or further communicating them. Therfore I wold entreate that *Austin*, for so his name is, to acknowledge his wrong to me in shewing them, & his owne impudence, & ignorance in challenging them.

Of course, the need for such acknowledgment has been obviated: this letter publicizes Austin's crime. (The ceremony of his naming, a trick at once of syntax and typography, contributes to the authentication of "Heywood," the conversion of the attributed into the authentic.) If print made plagiarism a matter of mass culture, a more fully public issue than it could have been in most sectors of manuscript culture, it also made it possible to appeal to a large court of public opinion for adjudication, as Heywood does here. Austin has not been identified to my knowledge (though Heywood had no doubt made it easy enough for local contemporaries to identify him) nor has the precise nature of his offense been established, for no text of "Austin's" translations has been preserved. It is worth noting that Heywood does not specify that Austin *printed* Heywood's translations as "his." Print is not the sole medium for the putative misappropriation of manuscripts. A plagiarized text could have been circulated in manuscript to a circle of admirers or to potential patrons; it could have been used as a teaching text in Austin's classroom in Ham: plagiarism does not need the press.

The press was nonetheless an engine of plagiarism. To risk the obvious: printing is far more capital-intensive than manuscription (to say nothing of story-telling), and in order to promote literacy and encourage literary consumption the book trade had to find ways to foster a preference for written over oral transmission, a preference for fixed forms over variable ones. So title pages and letters to readers urge the mimetic fidelity of printed books, their formal clarity, their accuracy of transcription and, above all, their originality in order to distinguish printing in general and individual books in particular: such advertising is calculated to safeguard industrial capital. The idea of literary distinction, of bibliographic individuation, is no more a novelty than is the idea of plagiarism, to which it is linked; neither was invented by print culture. But the development of a literary culture of bourgeois connoisseurship and the heightening of sensitivity to practices that disrupt the canons of literary individuation derive a considerable charge from the material conditions of book production. (If the press was an engine of plagiarism, it was also the case that, by a reciprocal logic, it stimulated a new attention to the niceties of attribution.) The proliferation of regulatory practices designed to constrain the dissemination of written words betrays the impress of moveable type, but so do the new tonalities that affect discussions of literary imitation, so does the increase in allegations of plagiarism, and so does the emergence of writers like Heywood, writers who persistently complain of unwonted "injuries" to rights not yet clearly recognized and by no means enforceable at law.

The historical grammar of plagiarism

The conjunction of Heywood's poems and Shakespeare's name in Jaggard's *Passionate Pilgrim*, or of his poems in Austin's schoolroom, presents Heywood with problems in cultural grammar. Then as now, the possessive constructions – Shakespeare's name, Austin's schoolroom, Heywood's poems – are conventional notations for mobile economic and cultural relationships (far more mobile in Shakespeare's, Austin's, or Heywood's day than in ours), usages in which possessivenesses in various states of development are crudely scrawled. Heywood is in the uncomfortable position of all grammarians, attempting to enforce, and perhaps to impose, rules of proper usage upon intransigent dialects. Yet whereas the normal grammarian is defending an archaic code, Heywood is defending a cultural grammar of the genitive that emanates, as it were, from the future, a code of possession that had not yet been formulated. Of course, we must defer to the complexities of the situation, to the obvious historical and linguistic fact that some form of the authorial genitive had long existed, and often those forms were susceptible to careful analysis. Here, for example, is Bonaventure, in his commentary on Lombard's *Sentences*:

Some one may write the works of others (*aliena*), adding or changing nothing, and he is simply called a scribe. Some one may write the works of others, adding but not from his own work (*suo*), and he is called a compiler. Some one may write the works of both others and of himself, but with the works of others predominating, and his own added for support; and he is called a commentator, not an author. Some one may write both his own works and those of others, with his own predominating, and that of others added for confirmation, and such a writer should be called an author.[33]

The authorial genitive that Bonaventure employs is clearly far weaker than that which Heywood claims. An exclusive authorship utterly independent of "others" has no place in this taxonomy of the subjects of whom writing can be predicated; for Bonaventure, authorship lies on a continuum of writing practices and not in some distinct category. Although he writes after several decades of progress in the detection and prevention of forgery, the boundary that had been patrolled was primarily that between documents truly ancient and antiquated impostures, or between documents that had been duly sealed or witnessed and those that had not – and not between documents appropriately attached to a particular personal origin and those spuriously attached.[34] This is not to say that the sense of category violations in the use of the genitive of possession was inconceivable before some ostensible break-point of modernity.[35] In the *Praeperatio Evangelica*, Eusebius records the existence of a six-volume collection compiled by Latinus, the *Peri ton ouk idion Menandrou*, which Putnam

---

[33] *Commentarius in I. Librum Sententiarum*, preface, *Opera Omnia* (Quaracchi, 1883–1902) I:14b–15a.

[34] Giles Constable, "Forgery and Plagiarism in the Middle Ages," *Archiv für Diplomatik, Schriftgeschichte, Siegel und Wappenkunde*, 29 (1983), 12–14. Christopher Brooke gives the mid-ninth to the mid-twelfth century as the great period of medieval forgery, "but forgery was apparently at its most widespread, and a most characteristic part of the scene, in the first sixty years or so of the twelfth century," "Approaches to Medieval Forgery," in *Medieval Church and Society* (London: Sidgwick and Jackson, 1971), 103 (but see his caveat that "it may even be the accidents of survival which lead us to suppose the twelfth century to be its golden age," p. 115). See also Hubert Silvestre, "Le problème des faux au moyen âge," *Moyen Age*, 66 (1960), 362–66 and Hartmut Hoffmann, "Zur mittelalterlich Brieftechnik," *Spiegel der Geschichte. Festgabe für Max Braubach* (Münster: Aschendorff, 1964), 141–70. Perhaps the most important document in the history of the war against forgery is the bull of Innocent III providing an inventory of the techniques of forgery (Lib. 1, no. 349); *Reg. Innoc. III*, ed. O. Hageneder and A. Haidacher, 7 vols. (Graz-Köln: H. Böhlaus Nachf., 1964), I:520.

[35] In his attempt to distinguish different structures of possession governing sacred and secular writing, the Master in Robert of Bridlington's mid-twelfth-century *Dialogue* is plainly pressing against an opposing and settled (if unarticulated) climate of opinion. Encouraged by his Student to compile a commentary, the Master knows he is courting derision; "I should be declared a thief," he says. He takes cognizance of God's scorn for the prophets "who steal my words from one another" (*Jeremiah*, 23:30), but then argues that "the word of God belongs to those who obey it," a pious grammar of possession that he clearly recognizes as counter-intuitive, even within the community of Christian scholars; see Constable, "Forgery and Plagiarism," 32–33.
Of course, major instances of authorial self-assertion are customarily taken as definitive of some form of Renaissance, if not of modernity. The historiography of the "renaissance of the twelfth-century" recurs to the efflorescence of autobiography; Ernst R. Curtius speaks of "unadulterated pride of authorship" in this period, and instances the decline of anonymous textual dissemination (*European Literature and the Latin Middle Ages*, trans. Willard R. Trask [Princeton: Bollingen, 1953], 517); Meyer Schapiro finds that, after 1100, an increasing number of visual artists signed their works ("On the Aesthetic Attitude in Romanesque Art," *Romanesque Art* [New York: Braziller, 1977], 22, cited in Constable, "Forgery and Plagiarism," 31).

neatly renders *Passages in the Writings of Menander which are Not the Work of Menander*.[36] The wonderfully facetious title, which anticipates the tonalities that hover around modern plagiarism, presses the distinction between dissemination and origination (slightly less rigorously, "writing" and "work") far more strenuously than does Bonaventure's paragraph and precisely so that the use of the genitive may be policed.

It will perhaps be useful to pursue this regress a bit farther, since efforts at attributive rigor are by no means a *late* antique phenomenon, and do not originate with Eusebius. In the *De architectura*, Vitruvius records an anecdote that suggests something of the energies of Hellenistic attributive culture. One of the Ptolemies established literary contests at Alexandria in honor of Apollo and the Muses, activities conceived as complementary to the regular functions of the Museum and library. At the advice of the directors of the library, the king appointed Aristophanes the grammarian as one of the judges, a man "who read each book in the library systematically day by day with comprehensive ardor and diligence." The poetry competition was first:

When Aristophanes was asked his opinion, he voted that the first place should be given to the candidate who was least liked by the audience. When the king and all the company showed great indignation, he rose and obtained permission to speak. Amid a general silence, he informed them that only one of the competitors was really a poet [*docuit unum ex his eum esse poetam*]; the others recited borrowed work, whereas the judges were to deal with original compositions, not thefts [*oportere autem iudicantes non furta sed scripta probare*] . . . Relying upon his memory, Aristophanes produced a huge number of parchment rolls [*infinita volumina*] from certain bookcases, and comparing these with what had been recited he compelled the authors to confess they were thieves. The king then ordered that they be brought to trial for theft; they were sentenced and banished in disgrace [*Itaque rex jussit cum his agi furti, condemnatosque cum ignominia dimisit*], while Aristophanes was raised to high office and became librarian.[37]

This revealing story and others like it remind us of the importance of Ptolemaic Alexandria for the history of attribution. The Aristophanes of Vitruvius' anecdote began work at the Library at Alexandria at the very beginning of the second century before the Christian era, the heir to at least a century of dedicated scholarship undertaken first by Demetrios of Phaleron and then by Zenodotus, the latter who seems to have been the first serious textual critic of Homer. Alexandrian criticism might be described as a new science of authorship:

---

[36] *Praep. ev.*, X:3.12 (465d); G. H. Putnam gives the translation in *Writers and their Public in Ancient Times* (New York: Putnam, 1894), 69.

[37] Bk. VII, Preface, 4–6. I have quoted from the Loeb edition of Frank Granger (2 vols. [New York: G. P. Putnam, 1934], 67), but have made some slight adjustments in Granger's translation in order to secure as much precision as possible: for example, although his "plagaries" for Vitruvius' *furta* makes perfectly good sense, "plagiaries" is cognate with a Latin criminal term that would not be applied to intellectual appropriation for another century, hence my choice of the more general "thefts."

Zenodotus' successor, Callimachus compiled a full catalog of the library organized by author and, in the course of this task attempted to distinguish authentic from spurious works; his massive compilation, the *Pinakes*, is the great legacy of third-century Alexandria, and, although it is often described as the first major literary history, its central concern is with attribution, the secure attachment of author to work.[38] Aristophanes of Byzantium so sustains what seems to have been an Alexandrian attributive mania.[39] His *Parallels to Menander and a selection of the sources from which he stole* clearly evidences the same quite particular critical orientation as that recorded in Vitruvius' anecdote and possibly inspired the later work, more wittily titled, of Latinus.[40]

Whence the sustained concern with attributive accuracy? It was compelled to some extent by the cultural centrality of Homer. Fourth-century scholars had noticed the variability of the text of Homer and had occasionally surmised misattributions to Homer; the sense of textual variation would have been felt emphatically at a repository like the Alexandrian library. Because of the importance of Homer to elite education, alertness to textual differentia acquired social prestige, and fuelled the scholarly construction of "better" and "best" texts as well as the discrimination of legitimate texts from impostures. Callimachus and then Aristophanes generalized the socio-textual craft of Homeric criticism to bibliographic work on the entire Greek literary inheritance: the century thus saw a double development in textual analysis, from Homer to the literary corpus, from the claims of individual variants to the claims – we could call them "personal" claims – of whole works. The discriminatory disposition is evident in Aristophanes' literary canons, but we can also trace it at the level of minute editorial practice, for one of the consistent features of the Alexandrian school is an over-willingness to obelize, to exclude or to query a passage for a very large range of reasons.[41]

[38] In the *Pinakes*, Callimachus lists authors' names, controlling for ambiguities of naming by listing all pseudonyms together with an author's place of birth and the name of his father; he then enumerates each work attributed to the author, discusses its authenticity, notes the first words of each work and stipulates its precise length in lines; 231–32.

[39] Eusebius records the existence of a treatise on the literary thefts of Ephorus compiled by one Lysimachus, apparently an Alexandrian scholar of the 2nd century BC (*Prep. Ev.*, X:iii,467d). Philostratus of Alexandria (1st C. BC) appears to have constructed a history of Greek drama based on misappropriation. Putnam remarks that Philostrates "accused Sophocles of having pillaged Aeschylus, Aeschylus of having permitted himself to draw too much inspiration from Phrynichus, and, finally Phrynichus of having taken his material from the writers who preceded him," *Writers and Their Public*, 69–70.

[40] On Aristophanes' complex, and generally enthusiastic, engagement with Menander, see Rudolf Pfeiffer, *History of Classical Scholarship: From the Beginnings to the End of the Hellenistic Age* (Oxford: Clarendon, 1968), 190–91.

[41] I should note, however, that Aristophanes seems to have been more conservative in this regard than were his predecessors; see Pfeiffer, *History of Classical Scholarship*, 173–74. Strabo laments the poor quality of much Alexandrian book production (*Geography*, XIII.1.54), an

Vitruvius' anecdote has its historical ironies since Aristophanes' censure of "illegitimate" appropriation takes place in the context of a transplanted Greek institution – the public literary competition – sponsored by a monarch whose dynastic dream is to claim a foreign empire. Hardly specific to Ptolemaic Alexandria, a complex jealousy of Greece was a fact of cultural life for much of the Mediterranean. Certainly it was felt in Rome, and well before Vitruvius' time. One of the key terms in Latin poetics, *vertere*, though it was often used generally to designate the making of verses was used more specifically to designate the amalgamating conversion of Greek literary materials into Roman ones; it has georgic associations, since a *versus* is a furrow, but also carries the military meaning, *to rout*. Latin *version*, with its characteristic combination of admiration and aggression, was characterized above all as a hyperawareness of degrees of originality and derivation – as, for example, in Cicero's or Horace's instructions on the precise degree of freedom appropriate to translation.[42] The measurement of indebtedness reached an unprecedented degree of precision in the last century of the Republic, as Rome succeeded Alexandria as the center of Mediterranean intellectual culture, but a scrupulous attention to Rome's debts to Greek culture was palpable earlier, appearing first (in Livius Andronicus) and reasserting itself most persistently, among the dramatists. In prologues to five of his plays, Plautus is careful to indicate that he has written a *version* of a Greek original. Terence similarly specifies five of his own plays: in the prologue to the *Adelphoe* he boasts of having performed a word for word translation (1.11); he describes the *Phormio* as *newly* imported.[43] The Greco-Roman

interesting piece of evidence since it suggests that what also flourished in Alexandria was an elaborate culture of occasionally dismissive bibliographic connoisseurship; in the last book of the *Geography* he shows himself to be the heir of such scholarship by identifying two books on the Nile, one by Eudorus and the other by Ariston the Peripatetic philosopher, as virtually identical "except in the matter of arrangement . . . [I] compared the one work with the other, but which of the two men it was who appropriated to himself the other's work might be discovered at Ammon's temple!" This passage, from *Geography* (trans. Horace Leonard Jones, 8 vols. [London: W. Heinemann, 1917–32]), XVII.1.5, suggests that the compilation of parallel texts was a normal scholarly task, presumably designed to facilitate such comparison, for Strabo describes himself as obliged to perform the comparison himself "being in want of 'antigraphs' with which to make a comparison."

[42] *De finibus*, iii.15; *Ars Poetics*, 133; see Gordon Williams, *Change and Decline: Roman Literature in the Early Empire* (Berkeley: University of California Press, 1978), 102–08. For the analogous attitude expressed in the area of Roman political thought, see the words attributed to Caesar in Sallust: "our ancestors never lacked either good sense or courage, and no false pride ever prevented their adopting the institutions of others if they approved them" (quoted in Williams, p. 110, from *Catiline*, 51.37).

[43] The spirit of the prologue to the *Adelphoe* is entirely in keeping with Gilson's genial observation that "il y a dans le plagiat littéral une sorte de naïve honneté"; for his attempt at a taxonomy of plagiarism, see Gilson's lecture for the occasion of his induction into the Belgian Royal Academy, "La philosophie du plagiat," *Bulletin de la Classe des lettres et des sciences morales et politiques* 5:45 (1959), 558–72.

literary alloy seems never to have been un-self-conscious, and the declaration of debts was one of the *topoi* of Roman literary practice from as early as Livius Andronicus, who declares in the prologue to *Compitalia*: "I borrowed not only from him [i.e., from Menander] but even from Latin poets."[44] Imitation is no doubt a simple substrate of all cultural practice, but the historical discontinuities that interfered between the Roman imitator and the Greek object of imitation brought the substrate to the surface, not only rendering imitation itself visible, but compelling the practitioner to bear witness to the practice. The attributive prologue to *Compitalio* is a kind of deposition.

Which is to say that Roman version was not always felt to be innocent.[45] Indeed, Vitruvius tells his story of the Judgment of Aristophanes as part of a protest against what he regards as the improper appropriation of others' ideas, itself a prologue to an elaborate acknowledgment of his own intellectual debts. Not surprisingly, he begins his discussion by drawing attention to writing itself as a boon both to the scholar and to the thief – and one can cautiously say "thief" in this context, since despite the fact that Roman law does not recognize

The prologue to the *Adelphoe* suggests how contested was the genitive of possession in Terence's literary milieu. In lines 15–21 Terence parries the charge that he was assisted by others in composing his plays – Suetonius records as *non obscura* the rumor that Terence had help from Laelius and Scipio (*Vita Terenti*, III) – by taking pride in receiving the assistance of those who have assisted all of Rome in war, in business, and in leisure.

[44] Terence brings this self-consciousness to a remarkable degree of refinement in the prologue to the *Andria*, in which he gently denigrates Menander for having repeated the plot of *his Andria* in the *Perinthia* and congratulates himself for having *combined* the two plots – in professed imitation of the techniques of Naevius, Plautus and Ennius. A crucial theme for Roman cultural historiography well into the late Empire, indebtedness is central to Books III to VI of Macrobius' *Saturnalia*, which linger carefully over Virgil's debts to Homer and to Ennius. This theme is taken up, with heightened intensity, in Christian cultural historiography. Clement of Alexandria argues – and Eusebius quotes him – that the Greeks had stolen many principles of philosophy from Hebrew theology and to bolster the assertion insists that "they who so openly filch their own works one from another establish the fact that they are thieves, and betray, however unwillingly, that they are secretly appropriating to their own countrymen the truth borrowed from us"; he follows this with a thick catalogue of Greek plagiarists, a catalogue that Eusebius supplements; *Preparation for the Gospel*, trans. Edwin Hamilton Gifford, 2 vols. (Oxford: Clarendon, 1903; repr. Grand Rapids: Baker House, 1981), X.ii.462a (p. 492). For other observations by Clement on plagiarism, see V.xiv.89:1 and 140:1; VI.i–iv; and especially X.iii.

[45] Plautus does not appear to be conspicuously apologetic about his translations and adaptations from the Greek, but Caecilius Statius, whose career intervenes between his and that of Terence, apparently had a guiltier sense of literary relations. Only fragments of his plays survive, but many of his titles are identical with those of plays by Menander and he seems to have been criticized in much the same way as Aristophanes of Byzantium had criticized the poets of Alexandria. According to Aulus Gellius, whose comparative analysis of passages from Caecilius and of Menander anticipates Macrobius' discussion of Vergil's debts, Caecilus seems to have adopted an aggressive vein of self-defense, alleging that Menander's *Deisidaimon* was itself a transcription of Antiphanes's *Oionistes*. Thereafter, Terence will strike very much the same note, his prologues bristling with boasting self-defense. The appreciative analysis of literary indebtedness – like that of Aulus Gellius or Macrobius – thus seems to operate within a somewhat "Alexandrian" critical climate.

intellectual property as such, Vitruvius insists on a criminal vocabulary, even as he does in the tale of Aristophanes.[46] The Preface begins

Our predecessors, wisely and with advantage, proceeded by written records to hand down their ideas to after times, so that they should not perish . . . While, then, these men deserve our gratitude, on the other hand we must censure those who plunder their works and appropriate them to themselves; writers who do not depend upon their own ideas, but in their envy boast of other men's goods whom they have robbed with violence, should not only receive censure but punishment for their impious manner of life [*qui eorum scripta furantes pro suis praedicant, sunt vituperandi, quique non propriis cogitationibus scriptorum nituntur, sed invidis moribus aliena violantes gloriantur, non modo sunt reprehendendi, sed etiam, qui impio more vixerunt, poena condemnandi*]. (VII, Preface, 1, 3)

It should be noted that the distinction between appropriation of content and appropriation of expression goes unremarked here. That Vitruvius maps the field of intellectual property so carelessly, resorting to an anecdote about improperly attributed poems to illustrate unacknowledged borrowing of concept, principle, or technique, confirms what the surviving records of Roman law suggests – that the amorphous sense of *cogitationes propriae* had not been given the shape or definition that comes from serious and sustained legal test.[47] Still, evidence from this passage in Vitruvius and from a related one in Cicero suggests that a rule of literary ethics, albeit not a law of intellectual property, had taken shape: in his *Brutus*, Cicero imagines himself rebuking Ennius who, although disingenuously affecting a disdain for subjects that others have already treated, "*a Naevio vel sumpsisti multa, si fateris, vel, si negas, surripuisti*" (from Naevius have *taken* much [if you admit it] or [if you deny it] much have *stolen*; XIX.76). Despite the use of legal language, there is no legal model for such a distinction, in which the character of the imitative act, worthy or culpable, is determined by the author's acknowledgment of the imitation.

The "legalization" of imitation seems to be far more strenuously at issue in Martial's *Epigrams* which appear a century later, full of accusations of literary theft. A poem in the first book offers one of the most ingenious and influential of ancient inquiries into the cultural grammar of possession:

> Commendo tibi, Quintiane, nostros –
> nostros dicere si tamen libellos
> possum, quos recitat tuus poeta.

---

[46] It is no surprise to find this idiom anticipated in Cicero, whose imagination was profoundly criminological; see, for example, *De Finibus*, V.74 and *Brutus*, 76, for which, see below.

[47] Konrat Ziegler (*RE*, 40:1964) holds that, after Aristotle, a convention was established among scientific writers whereby borrowings from earlier scientific works were to be acknowledged and that this convention was not accepted among authors of imaginative texts. Vitruvius' anecdote seems to challenge the distinction that Ziegler alleges.

Quintianus, I commend you my little books – that is, however, if I can call them mine when your poet friend recites them.

Sarcasm seldom trivializes the *Epigrams*; here as elsewhere in Martial a shrewdness infuses the sting. In this case, the interrogative of lines two and three seems at first to be nothing more than a handsome slyness, but Martial opens it as a genuinely mysterious question by the metaphoric work that follows:

> si de servitio gravi queruntur,
> assertor venias satisque praestes
> et, cum se dominum vocabit ille,
> dicas esse meos manuque missos.

If they complain of harsh enslavement, come forward to claim their freedom and give bail as required. And when he calls himself their owner, say they are mine, discharged from my hand. [I.52.1–7][48]

A remarkable figure: the published poem as manumitted slave. It will require some parsing.

The most simple gloss would concern attribution. Since it was customary, if not quite compulsory, for manumitted slaves to take the *nomen* or both the *praenomen* and *nomen* of the man who had freed them, by manumission Martial hopefully figures a convention of enduring affiliation of poem to poet. The figure also reflects on the relation between two distinct states in the social ontology of Roman poems, both of which survive in modern texts, though the first sometimes evades critical notice. The *second* state of a poem, the poem "as published," has remained a central object of critical scrutiny, whereas the first, the poem "circulated in draft" is usually treated uneasily as part of a poem's *pre*-history, a datum for the literary biographer, though recent studies in Early Modern manuscript circulation may be changing the disposition of scholarly readers. Classicists, however, recognize the period in which a poem circulates among an ostensibly exclusive coterie of ostensibly friendly connoisseurs as an important phase in the social being of a poem, however difficult its reconstruction may be.[49] It is useful to remember here the habit enjoined on the aspiring poet by Horace in the *Ars Poetica*, that the poet withhold a manuscript from public circulation for nine years in the meantime seeking the advice of skilled critics: "*nescit vox missa reverti*," he warns; "that which has been uttered, cannot be recalled" (line 390). The Latin cognates of "edition" refer with some specificity to this moment of missive, a release that marks the end of a writer's control over a work and the beginning of the second, autonomous phase of its social

---

[48] I cite Martial from the Loeb edition of D. R. Shackleton Bailey, 3 vols. (Cambridge, Mass.: Harvard, 1993), but have slightly adjusted the translation.
[49] Raymond Starr, "The Circulation of Literary Texts in the Roman World," *Classical Quarterly*, 37 (1987), 213–23.

being.[50] Before this release the poem serves as a vector of intellectual and social intimacy, constituting or sustaining a circle of *cognoscenti*; afterwards – if all goes well – wider approval will redound to the poet's credit and will confirm the literary authority and exclusivity of the group within which it circulated before. The last poem in Horace's first book of *Epistles* heightens the social drama by giving us an animate book, eager to go on sale, and an author who condescends to this eagerness for edition: *fuge quo descendere gestis* (Off with you down to where you itch to go):

> contrectas ubi manibus sordescere volgi
> coeperis, aut tineas pasces taciturnus inertis
> aut fugies Uticam aut vinctus mitteris Ilerdam.

When you have been well thumbed by vulgar hands and begin to grow soiled, you will either in silence be food for vandal moths, or will run away to Utica, or be sent in bonds to Ilerda. (*Epistles*, I:20.11–13).[51]

The effect of these lines is to enhance the elegant security of the period of the poem's "private" life. *Odisti clavis et grata sigilla pudico* (you hate the keys and seals so dear to the modest): although Horace's poems were not, in fact, simply kept locked up in his *scrinia*, the vulgar poem regards coterie circulation as tantamount to such a confinement, obliging the poet to reiterate the warning of the *Ars Poetica*, "*Non erit emisso reditus tibi.*"

For Martial's figure of manumission charts the phases of literary ontology upon a straining grid of ambivalent law:

In many ancient societies everybody was more or less unfree. Greco-Roman society, by polarizing freedom and unfreedom with a sharpness rare in human history, provided itself with a sharper version than most societies of the puzzle: what is a slave? Is it a thing or is he a person? In Roman society and law this ambivalence is everywhere ... *Res mortales*, 'mortal objects', slaves are called at one place in the *Digest*.[52]

The ambivalence to which Crook refers is not much alleviated by manumission, for a freed slave was still tethered to his or her former master by strict bonds of customary and legal obligation; under Claudius, Nero, and their successors legal mechanisms were put in place to assist in the re-enslavement of undutiful freedmen.[53] Martial's poem is stiffened by this rigorous social context, by an

---

[50] The most useful study of edition remains B. A. van Groningen's "Εκδωσις," [ekdosis] ser. 4, 16 (1963), 1–17.

[51] H. Rushton Fairclough, ed. and trans., *Satires, Epistles, and Ars Poetica* (Cambridge, Mass.: Harvard University Press, 1961).

[52] John Crook, *Law and Life of Rome* (Ithaca: Cornell University Press, 1967), pp. 55–56; Crook is citing the *Digest*, 4.4.II.5. And see also Alan Watson, *Roman Slave Law* (Baltimore: The Johns Hopkins University Press, 1987), 46.

[53] Crook, 51–55 and Alan Watson, *The Law of Persons in the Later Roman Republic* (Oxford: Clarendon, 1967), 226–36.

awareness of just how precarious was a former slave's purchase on liberty: one body of *causae liberales* to which Martial's poem is especially indebted concerns claims that someone supposed free was in fact another's property. Martial insists that he has granted the books, properly his slaves, the freedom of edition, but Quintianus' friend claims that in fact the poems are his own, his own and still slaves – and because Roman law treated all claims to freedom skeptically and, therefore, a putative slave could only approach a court by means of an *assertor libertatis*, Martial asks that Quintianus take on himself that responsibility: *assertor venias satisque praestes*; step forth to assert their freedom and post their bail.[54]

The analogy between book and slave does a good deal more, of course, than to distinguish the phases of literary circulation, and to dramatize the distinction between those phases, more even than to suggest that poem be tethered to poet by the decencies of responsive indebtedness. The complex felicity of Martial's analogy has a great deal to do with the slave's confused status as person and thing, a confusion sometimes implied in filial and spousal subordination, but in no way as pronounced as in the subordination of servitude. For all their dependence on slavery, the Romans felt that the slave in a sense exceeded his legal status; in the figure of the slave Martial probes the unruly uncanniness of the literary artifact, its selfness cleaving to and from its thingdom.

Finally, of course, the comparison discloses (without systematically addressing) an unsettled instinct for property in the fruits of intellectual labor. The insecure attachment of writer and written, *nostros* and *libellos* is probed by analogy to the attachments of owner to slave and of owner to freedman: the frequent legal difficulty of demonstrating and securing property in slaves lends something of its gravity to the urbane mystery of literary practice, worries the problem of literary property into more serious existence. The tactics of possession become nearly as mysterious as are the objects of possessiveness. In the last lines of this epigram Martial presses the proprietary theme of the analogy of book and slave one stage farther and in so doing constitutes the poem as a *locus classicus* in the Western discourse of intellectual property. He charges the *assertor* to accuse the misappropriating poet:

---

[54] Martial's audience would have recognized the "freedom" conferred by edition as an informal manumission, *per epistulam*, perhaps, or *inter amicos*, a freedom that does not entail citizenship, but instead offers the mediate rights belonging to Junian Latins. Freedmen in such status were usually much encumbered by obligation to their former masters. Martial has found a legal analogue for the highly contingent independence of the literary work of art in its second phase of social being. On informal manumission, see Watson, *Roman Slave Law*, 30–34; of the the obligations due to a patron – succession, *operae*, and *obsequium* – the latter is most relevant, for which see Watson, *The Law of Persons*, 39–40. Watson's most systematic exposition of how freedom was to be proven against claims of enslavement may be found in *The Law of Persons*, 218–25.

> et, cum dominum vocabit ille,
> dicas esse meos manuque missos.
> hoc si terque quaterque clamitaris,
> impones plagiario pudorem.

And when he calls himself their owner, say they are mine, discharged from my hand.
If you shout this three or four times, you will make the plagiarist ashamed of himself.
(I:52.6–9)

As we have seen, Martial is by no means the first to describe an imitation that
derogates its source, not the first to speak of falsely attributed texts as stolen
property, *furta*. But here, in the course of elaborating his analogy, Martial does
seem to have invented a new term. The thief of book-slaves is a kidnapper,
plagiarius. Kidnapping is one of the crimes that principally provoked conflict
about the status of slaves: they were covered, as persons, under the *lex Fabia
de plagiariis*, but as things, their misappropriation could be treated as a theft.
Thus, *plagiario pudorem*: the kidnapper will be *ashamed*, not guilty, the book
now not only a person but also merely a thing, the misappropriation merely
improper. This figurative use of the legal term apparently did not become part
of the vocabulary of commonplace Latin metaphors – conditions were not right
for the establishment of a permanent analytic vocabulary, much less a regular
legal or institutional reification, of the social, personal, or commercial aspects
of the intellectual artifact.

Thanks to Renaissance scholars, however, the term survived, although it
failed to thrive semantically: as the study of Roman law lapsed from the main-
stream of European intellectual life in the eighteenth century, the semantic
substrate of the term was lost; as intellectual property found legal reification,
"plagiarism" was no longer recognized as a figure of appreciable cunning and
force. It was still thus recognizable, however, when Valla used the term, possibly for the first time since the fall of Rome, in the preface to the second book
of his great treatise on Latin stylistics, the *Elegantiae*. Martial's poem is clearly
on his mind when he reports on those who have tried and failed to take credit
for Valla's own philological discoveries.

The lessons themselves disclose who is their proper possessor [*Sed res ipsa deprehendet,
cuius domini vere sit haec possessio*]. When, out of friendship, I began reading a book
by one of these people, with him present, I discovered some things of my own; I thus
learned what had been stolen from me without my knowledge . . . I was perturbed and
I said to the man, "I recognize this little lesson [*hanc elegantiam*]. I claim it as my
own chattel and I can have you up on charges under the law of kidnapping" [*mancipium
meum affero, teque plagiaria lege convenire possum*]. Reddening, he laughed it off with a
witticism, saying that it was appropriate to behave this way among friends. My response
was that this was not behavior, but misbehavior. "When you steal my laurels for having
been the first to have worked out this subject [*tu huius rei, in qua ipse laboravi, palma
semel occupaveris*], you will leave me with nothing." He responded even more wittily

that I would be a bad parent if I were to cast the children, whom I had born and raised, out from my dwellings; that he had taken them into his own home out of pity and for the sake of our friendship and was raising them as his own.[55]

Valla's is a slighter, less sustained handling of the figure than Martial's, though adroit in its own way. Like Martial, Valla not only asserts rights of property but also, and at the same time, figuratively animates the property. The unnamed interlocutor catches the animation, sustaining it in his alternative figure of the *elegantiae* as Valla's children, but he misses the neo-Martiallian vocabulary. He misses more than that. Though *mancipium* can designate any formally alienable property, the only such property governed by the *lex Fabia de plagiariis* are slaves: in the antiquarian arc of a learned sentence, litigious Rome itself quickens.

Figures that vivify oral or written compositions are very ancient, and serve a large variety of persuasive purposes, but they appear with extraordinary frequency when the pressures of patronage, commerce, or ideological regulation force questions of an author's relations to his or her works.[56] Under this pressure, the relation of author to work appears again and again as a relation between persons – person*ification* serving as a rhetorical instrument of person*alization*. It clearly functions this way in Martial, who frequently recurs to the device with sly gusto as he does, for example, in the very next poem in the *Epigrams*:

> Una est in nostris tua, Fidentine, libellis
> pagina, sed certa domini signata figura
> quae tua traducit manifesto carmina furto.

There is *one* page of yours, Fidentinus, in our little book, but stamped with the certain features of its owner, and it betrays your *Poems* as a manifest theft.[57]

– not quite a personification, since *signata figura* straddles the border between the represented and the real, persona and person, but by the end of the poem, Fidentinus' book is a full-fledged legal agent, animate and perversely autonomous:

> indice non opus est nostris nec iudice libris:
> stat contra dicitque tibi tua pagina 'fur es.'

[55] Laurentius Valla, *Opera Omnia*, facsimile of the 1560 Basel edition, foreword by Eugenio Garin, 2 vols. (Turin: Bottega d'Erasmo, 1962), I:42 [c_5^v]; my translation.
[56] One of the key *loci* in the history of this figure may be found in the *Nichomachean Ethics*, 9:7. Aristotle employs the figure of the poem as child to probe, not the relation of poet to poem – which, the context suggests, is familiar and uncomplicated and therefore a suitable instrument of illustrative comparison – but the relation of benefactor to benefitted.
[57] I have again adapted Bailey's translation: although his rendering of *nostris libellis* as "*my* little book" captures the basic sense, it misses the droll complacency with which Martial describes the plagiarism as a collaboration.

My books need no informer, no judge; your page confronts you and says, "You are a thief." (I:53, 1–3, and 11–12.)[58]

Once again, Martial transforms the literary system into a legal system, though this time the literary work is itself the complainant. It could not be so when it was personified as a slave, since the slave is disabled before the law – hence the comparative brilliance of the poem against the *plagiarius* which not only registers Martial's annoyance at the appropriation, but also by means of the particular choice of legal figure, insists on his own inability to do much to stop such misappropriations: he complains, in effect, that he can mount no complaint.[59] Heywood does similar work in his description of *The English Traveller*, of which "comming accidentally to the *Presse*, and I having Intelligence thereof, thought it not fit that it should passe as *filius populi*, a Bastard without a Father to acknowledge it": once again, the text is at once animated and disadvantaged. And, as we will see, when Jonson imports Martial's term, becoming, it seems, only the third author to speak of *plagiarism* in a modern European vernacular, it is just this sense of defenselessness that he wishes to convey.[60] The Renaissance revival of the classical vocabulary of intellectual theft or plagiarism bespeaks a sense, more or less obscure, of relative economic and legal disabilities; its English use adumbrates rights and protections that were as yet unavailable.

I do not mean to imply, however, that the figure does the same work, or expresses the same proprietary wishes, for Martial, nor to imply that Martial (or Vitruvius) is dimly seeking, by means of figure (or anecdote), the actual extension to literary works of rights of property. As Crook points out, reference to the law, both detailed and casual, is in no way remarkable in Latin literature, for legal thinking and the language of legal institutions seem to have permeated the normal consciousness of literate Romans.[61] Yet for all the energy with which Vitruvius, for example, wields the language of crime and punishment in the passage quoted above from the *De Architectura*, his call for "legal" redress is significantly shaded towards the moral – *qui impio more vixerunt, poena condemnandi:* the accusation of theft is devised to shame the plagiarist and to aggrandize the accuser, to manage, that is, the distribution of honor within a literary system utterly aristocratic in orientation, the economics of which were organized almost exclusively by patronage, and in most cases hidden by a language of otiose sociability. Vitruvius' vocabulary is unusually contentious

---

[58] For another poem on Fidentinus' literary thefts, see I.72.

[59] On the legal disability of slaves, see Watson, *The Law of Persons*, chapter 15, and particularly pp. 182–83.

[60] He is preceded by Joseph Hall, in *Virgidemiae* (1598); *Collected Poems of Joseph Hall*, ed. A. Davenport, *Liverpool English Texts & Studies* (Liverpool: Liverpool University Press, 1949), 57.

[61] *Law and Life of Rome*, 7–8 and 17–18.

compared to that of, say, Horace's third Epistle, in which the border between originality and dependent appropriation is patrolled with casual urbanity (and easy authority); writing to Julius Florus, on campaign in the East with Tiberius Claudius Nero, he asks after his friends and especially inquires into their literary activities – "*Quid studiosa cohors operum sumit?*"

> quid Titius, Romana brevi venturus in ora?
> ... fidibusne Latinis
> Tebanos aptare modos studet auspice Musa,
> an tragica desaevit et ampullatur in arte?

What of Titius, soon to be on the lips of Romans... does he essay under favor of the Muse, to fit Theban measures to the Latin lyre? Or does he storm and swell in the tragic art?

– then, moving from Titius's typical Greco-Roman appropriative version, he turns to another friend, the turn shaped by what we can recognize as a typical, a Roman, associative logic –

> quid mihi Celsus agit? monitus multumque monendus,
> privatas ut quaerat opes et tangere vitet
> scripta Palatinus quaecumque recepit Apollo,
> ne, si forte suas repetitum venerit olim
> grex avium plumas, moveat cornicula risum
> furtivis nudata coloribus. ipse quid audes?

What, pray, is Celsus doing? He was warned, and must often be warned to search for private treasures, and to shrink from touching the writings which Apollo on the Palatine has admitted: lest, if some day perchance the flocks of birds come to reclaim their plumage, the poor crow, stripped of his stolen colours, awake laughter. And yourself – what do you venture on? ... (*Epistles*, I.iii. 9, 12–20)[62]

Horace censures improper appropriation without the language of law or the threat of punitive damages, resorting instead to the sociable coercion of shaming – the threats of laughter and exposure; the monitory salt of beast-fable. The punishment fits the crime, which is, after all, little more than the misuse of the public library on the Palatine hill, founded only seven or eight years earlier.[63]

---

[62] I cite Fairclough's translation, having made a single adjustment of the translation. The cognate "private" seems to me to be a slightly more revealing rendering of *privatas* (line 16) than Fairclough's "home", and not significantly misleading. On the associative logic operating in another instance, see n. 66 below.

[63] The third-century commentator, Porphyrion, implies that Horace's oblique counsel was either ineffectual or too late, for he reports that Julius Florus wrote satires which were culled (*electae*) from the satires of Ennius Lucilius and Varro; Porphyrion is cited in the Kiessling-Heinze edition of Horace, *Vol 3: Briefe* (1914, 4th edition, repr., Berlin: Weidmansche Verlagsbuchhandlung, 1961), 36–37. Here, as in Epistle 20, Horace betrays – or, perhaps "discreetly displays" – misgivings that verge on disdain for the literary culture that operates outside the inner circle of connoisseurship.

Privatas ut quaerat opes: Horace endorses the cultivation of both individual resources and of those of the closed and *studiosa cohors*. This is, of course, a privacy of ethos and not of property.

The difference between Martial's idiom and that of Horace is obvious, although it is not so easy to explain. The sociology and economics of literature no doubt changed in the generations that separate them, but to claim this particular difference between Horace and Martial as the function of large changes in literary culture might be to claim too much.[64] Moreover, although Martial's idiom differs considerably from that of his predecessor, the difference ought not to be exaggerated: Horace's meditations on the proprieties of imitation were by no means uninflected by Roman law. In the crucial section of the *Ars Poetica* in which Horace squarely confronts the subject, and urges the ambitious poet to seek distinction by bold traditionality, he drifts easily into the language of the law of property

> Difficile est proprie communia dicere; tuque
> rectius Iliacum carmen deducis in actus,
> quam si proferres ignota indictaque primus.
> publica materies privati iuris erit, si
> non circa vilem patulumque moraberis orbem,

It is hard to treat in your own way what is common: and you do better to spin out into scenes a song of Troy than if, for the first time, you were giving the world something unheard of and unsung. In ground open to all you will win private rights, if you do not linger along the easy and open pathway. (lines 128–32)

Publica materies privati iuris erit: the full mystery of the cultural grammar of possession lingers in these lines. The private here is quasi-proprietary, for literary imitation is represented as a kind of cultural enclosure. The elitist ethos of the Epistle to Florus persists, plainly, in the withdrawal from the *vilem patulumque*

---

[64] Vitruvius, for example, a writer of Horace's own era, anticipates Martial's rhetoric in his criminalizing strictures on unacknowledged borrowing; Pliny, on the other hand, a writer of Martial's generation, exhorts the scholarly scientist to acknowledge his sources, and he is as gracefully committed to the language of courteous propriety as is Horace: "I have prefaced these volumes with the names of my authorities. I have done so because it is, in my opinion, a pleasant thing and one that shows an admirable modesty [*plenum ingenui pudoris – pudor*, the same affect that Martial wishes to arouse] to own up to those who were the means to one's own achievements, not to do as most of the authors to whom I referred. For you must know that when collating authorities I have found that the most professedly reliable and modern writers have copied the old authors word for word without acknowledgement, not in that valorous spirit of Virgil, for the purpose of rivalry, nor with the candour of Cicero who in his *Republic* declares himself a companion of Plato"; *Natural History* trans. H. Rackham, 10 vols. (Cambridge, Mass.: Harvard University Press, 1938–63), vol. I, Preface, 21–23. Modesty, valorous rivalry, candour, companionship: for Pliny, indebted literary practice is to be regulated by a patrician ethics not conspicuously different from that of Horace's *Epistles*.

orbem to the enclave of art, but that enclave, built from the loot of the common culture, is privatized by some figurative version of the law and not by coterie opinion. Horace imagines the enjoyment of no specific rights here and, unlike Martial, he refers to no particular area of the law of property. Indeed, this invocation of the Private Law is an amiably obscurantist feint, for the ensuing lines assert something very like a Kantian aesthetic sphere, governed by its own internal logic; an *ethos*, but not a law:

> publica materies privati iuris erit, si
> non circa vilem patulumque moraberis orbem,
> nec verbo verbum curabis reddere fidus
> interpres, nec desilies imitator in artum,
> unde pedem proferre pudor vetet aut operis lex.

In ground open to all you will win private rights, if you do not linger along the easy and open pathway, nor seek to render word for word like a dogged translator, nor, imitating, jam yourself into a corner from which you will be forbidden to budge by shame or by the laws of your craft. (lines 128–35)[65]

The triad of conditions is both vague and stipulative: the sentence paradoxically asserts that great imitative art is both governed by rules and mysterious.[66] The oblique legal references sustain this paradoxical effect. That there was no law of intellectual property in Horace's day serves his purpose, which is to inflate the stakes of imitative practice and to mystify its methods.

By the end of the Republic, then, and during the sway of the Empire, the law of property provided an important source of language and concept with which Latin authors could reflect upon literary relations. We cannot speak of a sustained tradition of such reflection, yet for Horace, the clarities of legal *dominium* offer a contrast to the mysteries of artistic distinction. For Martial, on the other hand, the language of theft provides a powerful means of branding those who might compromise his eminence, while the complex (indeed, nearly paradoxical) structure of legal slavery provides a nuanced analogue for the phenomenology of the literary *opus*. If Martial's distinguishing contentiousness seems traceable to the manners of the epigram, it is also true that we find nothing like the same fierce criminalization of close imitation in other Roman

---

[65] I have again adjusted Fairclough's translation. His "slavish" catches the mild snobbery of line 132, but it seems to me to be somewhat over-emphatic and certainly distorts the sense of *fidus* (line 133); I recognize that my own solution may also over-estimate the poet's dismissiveness in the interests of clarifying the logic of his lines.

[66] It may be worth remarking on the persistent prestige of *version* here, of Latin imitation of Greek models, as the leading case of all forms of traditional literary practice: in lines 133–4, unambitious imitation is figured as word-for-word *translation*. This is the same associative logic that enables the turn, in Epistle 1:3, from Titius's effort at Latinizing Theban meters to Celsus's light-fingered browsings at the Palatine library.

epigrammatists; to some extent, Martial's strenuous and curious literary possessiveness must be accepted as *sui generis*, a brilliant manifestation of the lambent grappling with necessity that pervades the *Epigrams*. The possessiveness would leave its bright impression, on Jonson; Horace's mystery would have drearier effects.

A vile phrase

It would be difficult to over-estimate the influence of Horace's *Art of Poetry*, the Epistle to the Pisos, on the literary culture of Renaissance England, but the epistle to Julius Florus had its own interested readers as well. Perhaps indirectly, perhaps not, it gave Robert Greene the vocabulary for the famous slap at Shakespeare administered sometime in the months just before Greene died, in September, 1592.[67] Greene addresses three of his fellow playwrights, all unnamed – two are certainly Peele and Marlowe; the third, almost certainly Nashe – and he speaks of the ingratitude of actors:

Unto none of you (like mee) sought those burres to cleave: those Puppets (I meane) that spake from our mouths, those Anticks garnisht in our colours. Is it not strange, that I, to whom they all have beene beholding: is it not like that you, to whome they all have been beholding, shall (were yee in that case as I am now) bee both at once of them forsaken?[68]

Not strange that Greene should have been forsaken by those burrs, not if "Cuthbert Cony-catcher" is to be trusted: recall the latter's accusation, in 1590, that Greene had been making double sale of his labors to acting companies that believed themselves to be acquiring exclusive use of his scripts.[69] But such provocation was hardly as specific as what follows here, when Greene notoriously sets himself against one particular actor, whose most recent role had been the impersonation of a playwright:

Yes trust them not: for there is an upstart Crow, beautified with our feathers, that with his *Tygers hart wrapt in a Players hyde*, supposes he is as well able to bombast out a blanke verse as the best of you: and being an absolute *Iohannes fac totum*, is in his owne conceit the onely Shake-scene in a countrey.

– a brutish layering of inauthenticities: the tiger's heart, the player's flesh, and finally Celsus' guise, the borrowed feathers of the plagiaristical

---

[67] J. Dover Wilson discusses the contemporary and classical background to the insult in "Malone and the Upstart Crow," *Shakespeare Survey*, 4 (1951), 61–65.

[68] Grosart, XII:143–4.

[69] This was not the only source of friction between Greene and the actors, for *Never Too Late* (1590) also makes passing attacks on the players.

poet.[70] Chettle and others hurried to Shakespeare's defense, provoking one of Greene's friends to reiterate the gibe:

> Greene, gave the ground, to all that wrote upon him.
> Nay more the men, that so Eclipst his fame:
> Purloynde his Plumes, can they deny the same?[71]

Literary historians have narrated this episode almost exclusively as part of Shakespeare's literary biography, but it's my purpose here to examine what it tells us about the *feel* of imitation at a moment at which commerce and competition threatened to convert that venerable practice into plagiarism. To understand the episode it will be useful to be clear about what Greene *meant* by his insult. He comes down as hard on bombast, blank verse, and the meanness of the actor's quality, as on plagiarism.[72] These had been the focus of the anti-theatrical moments in *Menaphon* (1589), where it is the "propheticall full mouth" of Marlowe ("a Coblers eldest sonne") that comes in for censure.[73] Greene treats the indulgence in blank-verse dramaturgy as a betrayal of gentility and a simplification of intellectual and artistic ambition; when he takes on Shakespeare, his focus is on misplaced, misjudged pretension. (Greene maintains some distance even from those whom Shakespeare clumsily emulates: they are "our feathers" but the blank verse is that of "the best of *you*.") In all these instances Greene casts himself as superior to fashionable theatrical practice, and this (quite unwarranted) self-conception shapes his attitude to plagiarism. In his attack on Shakespeare, as in his earlier floutings of Marlowe, Kyd, and the players, Greene is more condescending than he is proprietary; in a very limited but important sense, he is more Horace than Martial.

That this only slightly possessive snobbery anticipates and is continuous with the literary *ethics* of a Heywood is crucial to the history of intellectual property at this important juncture. A literary culture committed to imitation is undergoing a transformation into a culture fervently committed to such novelty as

---

[70] Peter Alexander supposed that no allegation of plagiarism is entailed in Greene's lines, but as Wilson observes there is more than the reference to Horace to counter Alexander's construction: in a pointed response to Greene in the preface to *Kind-Heart's Dream*, Chettle takes pains to testify to Shakespeare's "honesty" and "uprightnes of dealing"; "Malone and the Upstart Crow," 61–62. Wilson supplements this with a reference (68, n. 44) to the dedicatory epistle that Greene prefaced to *The Mirror of Modesty* (1584): "Your honor may thinke I play like *Ezops* Crowe, which deckt his selfe with others feathers, or like the proud Poet *Batyllus*, which subscribed his name to *Virgils* verses, and yet presented them to *Augustus*."

[71] *Greenes Funeralls*, ed. R. B. McKerrow (Stratford-Upon-Avon: Shakespeare Head Press, 1922), 81.

[72] Properly so for Greene himself was a blithe practitioner of what would now pass for plagiarism; see the introduction to "The Debate Between Pride and Lowliness," J. P. Collier, ed. (1841).

[73] Grosart, vi, 86; and cf. the important earlier swipe at Marlowe, in *Perimedes the Blacksmith* (1588); Grosart, vii, 7.

could be the object of proprietary protections, and, as this episode illustrates, the conventions of social discrimination – sumptuary rules, anti-theatricality, the stigma on mimickry of social superiors by social inferiors – function as powerful instruments of the transition. Close imitation becomes a Horatian impropriety on its way to becoming a crime. The formulation may seem to come dangerously close to trivializing the matter, but my purpose is to indicate the psychological valence of the transition, the transformation of imitation into an ethical problem, a problem of decorum in the nervous, modern sense of the term. The discussion of Shakespearean imitation that follows, together with the treatment of Jonsonian imitation in the next chapter are meant to expose the specifically ethical and psychological threshold to modern intellectual property.

It is hardly surprising that Greene's insult has been so important to Shakespeare scholars: the episode sheds light on a good deal more in that biography than the old question of whether Shakespeare began his career as a playwright as a botcher of others' plays. Much in the subsequent development of that career can be understood as a ramifying reaction to the sting of Greene's remarks. Shakespeare can be seen flouting Greene's remarks in the brazen, ranting extravaganza of *Titus Andronicus*, its fierce boldness focused precisely on the production of silence; the beastly bombast, the pretension (and self-transcendence) of Bottom *fac totum*, responds to Greene with slightly dryer wit. These are profound and ingenious responses, and they are only the earliest ones. Though Greene's insult is hardly some secret origin of all of Shakespeare's efforts at self-promotion and self-justification, many of those efforts sustain a particular responsiveness to Greene's terms and tone, a flyting dialogue with the dead. It is still faintly audible, I think, in 1596, when Shakespeare resumed his father's application for a coat-of-arms, deferred since 1568. The suit must have been costly, but the eventual grant of arms officially sanctions the family's transition to gentlemanly status. We have reason to suppose Shakespeare's pleasure in the event to have been complex; certainly he managed to endow it with lurking comedy. Consider the family crest. Its double design consists of a visual pun – a falcon beautified with wings argent, shaking a spear, a gesture of high astounding valor utterly impertinent to this family, whose most famous member had borne arms only on stage – and a verbal one – the motto, NON SANZ DROICT, at once claiming the family's *desert* and brandishing the writing and spending hand that had *earned* and *purchased* such eminence as the family now had. With a humor that Greene may be claimed partly to have provoked, the crest wryly acknowledges a degree of upstart imposture: the motto might just as well have been "Oh Bottom, thou art translated."

That Shakespeare continued to ruminate on Greene's insult is hardly surprising, if only because, in a single very efficient sentence, Greene had managed to impugn his profession as an actor, his ambition, his loyalty, his sincerity, and his taste; he had carried off the insult in a nicely classical idiom by means of the allusion to Horace; and he had, in the bargain, burlesqued a line which audiences had apparently especially admired or, at least, which other playwrights had particularly noticed, the description of Margaret in *3 Henry VI* as "a tiger's hart wrapt in a woman's hide" – perhaps an early signature line for Shakespeare, like Marlowe's "Holla, ye pampered jades of Asia and Inde" or Kyd's "Remember me." Shakespeare was still chewing on this remarkable insult at the end of the decade, long after Greene's death, indeed, after the deaths of all those (save Lyly) from whom he had learned the playwright's craft. As if it were still necessary to disprove Greene's insistence that the upstart plagiarist would forsake those whom he had imitated, Shakespeare gives us a hero, a passionate enthusiast of the theater, a hero whose reminiscences are conspicuously loyal and energetic. He is, also, conspicuously gentlemanly, and condescending in every sense, although, in his warm treatment of actors, he is condescending only in the best sense:

I heard thee speak me a speech once, but it was never acted, or if it was, not above once – for the play, I remember, pleased not the million, 'twas caviare to the general. But it was, as I received it – and others, whose judgement in such matters cried in the top of mine – an excellent play, well digested in the scenes, set down with as much modesty as cunning . . . (II.ii.430–37)[74]

Hamlet is remembering a play based on the *Aeneid*; with as much cunning as modesty, Shakespeare is also remembering *Dido, Queen of Carthage*, Marlowe's pioneering attempt to find a popular theatrical idiom for neo-classical imitation. This is an homage – an homage, as will be seen, of considerable complexity – to marlowe and his generation, Greene's own generation, which had made it the end of scholarism to adeqate a popular dramaturgy to the poetics of antique epic. Horace had given Greene the vocabulary with which to mock the admiring, imitative Shakespeare of the early 1590s, but he also gives Shakespeare terms for confirming the earlier admiration as well as a blueprint for resuming the imitative project:

> Difficile est proprie communia dicere; tuque
> rectius Iliacum carmen deducis in actus,
> quam si proferres ignota indictaque primus.
> publica materies privati iuris erit.

Greene had chosen the easier path of originality and novelty; from Marlowe a playwright could learn to copy, to privatize by copying. And from Marlowe one could more particularly learn to unfold in acts a song of Troy.[75] I do not mean to

---

[74] Except where otherwise indicated, I cite *Hamlet* from the new Arden edition of Harold Jenkins (New York: Methuen, 1982).

[75] Here and in what follows, I must disagree with Harold Bloom's allegation that Shakespeare is distinguished by the ease with which he absorbs influences. Greene constrains Shakespeare to

imply that Shakespeare's allusion to Marlowe in this play is unambivalent. When Hamlet tells us that "one speech in't I chiefly loved – 'twas Aeneas tale to Dido" he displays the generosity of Hamlet's memory, but he also shows us its uncertainty; "If it live in your memory, begin at this line – let me see, let me see –"

The rugged Pyrrhus, like th'Hyrcanian beast

This tentative line, this trial, recalls Marlowe's *Dido* ("And tigers of Hyrcania gave thee suck," 5.1.159), where Aeneas is the imposter with the tiger's heart; it recalls Shakespeare's own recursive elaboration of the line in *1 Henry VI*, in which York denounces Margaret ("But you are more inhuman, more inexorable – / O ten times more! – than tigers of Hyrcania," [I.iv.154–55]), in lines whose hexametrical stretch recalls the common source in Virgil; and above all it recalls Greene's reductive *un*elaboration of these complex acts of imitation.[76] All this is recalled, but as a misremembering –

'Tis not so.

– and then comes the macabre fantasia on the good son as fierce upstart, self-transformed into a coat-of-arms –

> It begins with Pyrrhus –
> *The rugged Pyrrhus, he whose sable arms,*
> *Black as his purpose, did the night resemble,*
> *When he lay couched in the ominous horse,*
> *Hath now this dread and black complexion smear'd*
> *With heraldry more dismal. Head to foot*
> *Now is he total gules, horridly trick'd*

(one last heraldic pun: to trick a crest is to sketch it, though usually with pen-and-ink, without colors, the penman's word or sign standing in for the actual colors)

> *horridly trick'd*
> *With blood of fathers, mothers, daughters, sons.*
>
> (II.ii.444–54)

Critics of the play have made sense of this passage by pointing to Pyrrhus as one of Hamlet's myriad self-projections. The oedipal character of Hamlet's project

apologia – or found in Shakespeare an aptitude for apologia – and *Hamlet* demonstrates that Shakespeare's experience of influence was not only oedipal, but willingly so. But perhaps this is only to refine Bloom's assertion: Shakespeare is distinguished by a volitional submission to the oedipal constitution of the poetic will – an astounding pre-emption.

[76] For a suggestive discussion of this passage, see David Scott Kastan, "'His semblable is his mirror': *Hamlet* and the Imitation of Revenge," *Shakespeare Studies*, 19 (1987), 111–24.

is flaunted in this figuring forth: though Pyrrhus acts on behalf of his own now-incapable but once-nearly-invincible father, he hesitates when his sense of duty brings him to the brink of unleashing a huge violence against an enfeebled patriarch. But a *ius privatus* operates on this most common cultural material. We can recognize the autobiographical charge that supplements and electrifies Shakespeare's rendering, for its bloody language recalls the poet's own suit, and points to the violence of its filial service – an application on behalf of his father, who had been himself insufficient to carry it through; an application for a crest in which the son flaunts the fact that the family claim is rightful because he himself has made it so.

Although the scene thus bears *tremendous* personal meanings, it is presented as a work of art, as an object of connoisseurship, and this no doubt effects a salutary psychological hygiene, containing and managing the poet's upstart sensations. Hamlet's self-correction shows him assessing what he speaks as he speaks it: he knows that this is a version of a tale that can be, and had been, told differently. We do well to remember the ancestry of this tale. Aeneas' tale to Dido, is Virgil's telling of Homer's tale, the archetype of literary genetics. Shakespeare's telling of this tale affiliates himself with this literary genealogy and, of course, the casual dismissal of the Marlovian mode amounts to a claim to a relatively direct affiliation with the antique singers of the *carmen Iliacum*. If bombast had offended, there was *Titus Andronicus*; if social pretension, there was the coat-of-arms; and if it was Shakespeare's literary ambition that had offended Greene, the dead arbiter hadn't known the half of it.

Shakespearean ascriptions

> what Players are they?
> ROSIN: Even those you were wont to take delight in the Tragedians of the City.
> HAM: How chances it they travaile? their residence both in reputation and profit was better both wayes.
> ROSIN: I thinke their Inhibition comes by the meanes of the late Innovation?
> *(The Tragedie of Hamlet*, F1, OO$_3^v$)[77]

Morey Amsterdam, unable to attend a testimonial dinner for Milton Berle: "I'll be there in material if not in spirit."

Alert to Greene's jealous configuration of literary property and condescension to an artistic ownership based on hoarding, the Shakespeare of this scene declines to stake his claim. This discussion will thus seem to have refurbished a rather old-fashioned picture of Shakespeare: here again is Shakespeare's Negative

---

[77] I cite the first Folio from Charlton Hinman's facsimile edition (New York: W. W. Norton, 1968), the second quarto from W. W. Greg's facsimile (Oxford: Clarendon, 1964). I silently adjust the facsimile texts to accord with modern typographic and orthographic norms in the use of *u* for *v*, *v* for *u*, *i* for *j*, *j* for *i*; long *s* is changed to short *s*.

Capability, discovered this time in the realm of material practice. I believe this to be an accurate picture, as far as it goes, of Shakespeare's relation to the proprietary groundswell that surrounded him. It may be usefully enriched, however, by taking into consideration the theatrical milieu in which Shakespeare found himself while he was writing *Hamlet*, the milieu in which he once more recalled Marlowe and Greene. Of course, that milieu crowds Aeneas' tale to Dido, which is, after all, part of a larger theatrical vignette.

In all editions of *Hamlet* with a complete textual apparatus, the actors approaching Elsinore get tangled in footnotes.[78] The Folio text includes some tart, but by no means straightforward comments on "the late Innovation" (happily, "the late Innovation?"). Many editors have found a reference here to the Essex rebellion or to the June 1600 Privy Council order for the restraint of the theater, but another critical tradition has settled on the rise of the children's companies, beginning in December 1600 with the performance of Jonson's *Cynthia's Revels*.[79] A few lines later in F comes an explicit reference to how this "ayrie of Children, little Yases . . . [who] have be-ratled the common Stages" (F1, OO$_3$^{v}–OO$_4$).[80] However the problem of glossing the innovation be solved – even if the fall of Essex impinges on the wanderings of this theatrical troupe – the passage, insofar as it dates the play, inevitably locates it within a primarily theatrical calendar. Rosencrantz bears news from a new *theatrical* world.

But there is a textual crux as well as a calendrical one to be dealt with, the fact that Q2 lacks the references to the little eyases and to a contentiousness specific to the London stage. The evidence here, both internal and external, has permitted a variety of textual hypotheses of which three general ones have commanded the greatest esteem.[81] The first and oldest hypothesis is simply that the play

---

[78] Much of this discussion of *Hamlet* is condensed from a discussion in "Plays Agonistic and Competitive: The Textual Approach to Elsinore," *Renaissance Drama*, n.s. 19 (1988), 63–96.

[79] This line of argument is usually bolstered by assertions that Gabriel Harvey knew the play, probably from having seen a performance, and probably before the fall of Essex in February of 1601; *Cynthia's Revels* was produced during the previous year. Another line of argument discounts the limitation *ad quem* of February 1601, and proposes that the topical moment in Hamlet refers to Jonson's *Poetaster*.

It should perhaps be noted that persuasive arguments *can* be marshalled on behalf of the Privy Council ruling as the "innovation": by virtue of its having limited the number of playhouses to two and the number of weekly performances at those theaters to two, the ruling could easily have inhibited theatrical business; see E. A. J. Honigmann, "The Date of *Hamlet*," *Shakespeare Survey*, 9 (1956), 24–34 and Kittredge's discussion of "innovation in his edition of *Hamlet* (Boston: Ginn, 1939).

[80] Roscoe A. Small, *The Stage-Quarrel between Ben Jonson and the So-Called Poetasters* (Breslau, 1899), may be recommended cautiously as an introduction to the subject of the War of the Theaters; see also Tom Cain's edition of *Poetaster* for *The Revels Plays* (Manchester: Manchester University Press, 1995), 30–36 and Harbage, *Shakespeare and the Rival Traditions* (New York: Macmillan, 1952), 90–119.

[81] For a useful introduction to how the theories of textual transmission evolved under the New Bibliography, see ch. 2 (and its appendices) of Honigmann, *The Stability of Shakespeare's Text* (London: Arnold, 1965), 7–21.

went into production without any allusion to the War of the Theaters and that the passage (roughly corresponding to 2.2.335–58 according to the lineation in the new Arden edition) was soon added but without affecting the copy text for the second quarto. Thus Q2 is held to be very close to the originally performed version of the play, and F is held to be very close to a later performance text. Though this hypothesis is now recovering a certain degree of prestige – and G. R. Hibbard's edition for the Oxford Shakespeare may have secured it even more – its adherents were a shrinking minority until fairly recently.[82]

One reason for the earlier loss of prestige is that some bibliographers, perhaps ambitious to penetrate the mysteries of Shakespearean creativity, sought to trace the state of these lines in Q2 to the vexed surface of the poet's own manuscript. According to a second hypothesis, Shakespeare added this passage late in the history of his composition of the play, before the promptbook was prepared or at least before the play went into production. This modification, which brings us closer to Shakespeare's study, comes in two versions: either the foul papers were supposed to make no mention of the child actors, or, more elaborately, the foul papers included such references but apparently as an afterthought. This latter version of the hypothesis provides that these lines *seemed* to be excrescences and were therefore passed over by either the compositor or the scribe who prepared copy for the compositor.[83]

---

[82] See Hibbard's introduction to *Hamlet* (Oxford: Clarendon, 1987): he displays not only the simplicity of this hypothesis, but also its explanatory power, for he argues that the unusual choice of copy-text for F – theatrical text instead of a quarto edition – may be *explained* by the inadequacy of Q2 to contemporary theatrical practice. But note that this argument might also be invoked in defense of the second hypothesis, discussed below.

It is worth noting that Fredson Bowers, in an important review of Jenkins, has implied that he holds this to be the best explanation, at least as far as this passage is concerned. He appears to recommend as the simplest explanation (though he offers this explanation entirely in the subjunctive) that the play went into production in late 1600 or early 1601 with this section of 2.2. more or less as Q2 gives it (i.e., with lines 335–58, according to the new Arden lineation, absent) and that these lines were added later in 1601 (*The Library*, ser. 6, 5 [1983], 284–88).

Bowers proposed this possibility less formally in 1962; see his "Established Texts and Definitive Editions," collected in *Essays in Bibliography, Text, and Editing* (Charlottesville: University Press of Virginia, 1975). He and Hibbard have not been alone in recent advocacy of this position. Steven Urkowitz has argued that Q1, Q2, and F *Hamlet* each represent distinct versions of the play, each with distinct Shakespearean authority, a position from which he has retreated to the extent that he no longer regards Q1 as authoritative ("'Well-sayd olde Mole': Burying Three Hamlets in Modern Editions," *Shakespeare Study Today: The Horace Howard Furness Memorial Lectures [1982]*, ed. Georgianna Ziegler (New York: AMS, 1986), 37–70.

[83] Here the difficulty will involve a supposition that authorial additions to an authorial manuscript appeared to lack authority. The hypothesis can be sophisticated – by supposing a fair copy to have intervened between the completion of a version prior to the "innovation" and the making up of the promptbook so that a subsequent authorial addition to that fair copy really seems an excrescence or the addition to have been written hastily, in another ink, or to have been dictated to someone writing another hand.

This version of the hypothesis has been magisterially adapted in Harold Jenkins's new Arden edition of the play, where he combines the first and second hypotheses, giving us early

But the variations of F and Q2 admit of a completely different sort of explanation. Instead of these theories of how the text of the play grew to include a certain amount of theatrical news, Bowers advanced a theory of how the play shrank, a hypothesis based on the idea of deliberate excision.[84] According to this third hypothesis, at some point, either during rehearsals or after the play had run for a while – suppositions concerning this moment will depend on how one weights the information regarding the date of the play – at some point, the company decided to cut some of the topical material preserved in F. That is, F is taken as reflecting a tentative production version prior to Q2; Q2 is taken to be a *subsequent* (and perhaps somewhat faulty) performance version.[85]

These, then, are the three essential textual arguments: (1) two performance versions of the play, one without, a second with the topical passage (this gives us a playwright eager to adjust this play to modulations in the theatrical conditions); (2) a draft without the passage, but an unbroken tradition of performance with the passage in (Shakespeare, the painstaking reviser); (3) rehearsals or early performances with the passage included, and its excision accomplished early in the theatrical history of the play (the copious poet and the pragmatic company). Versions of these hypotheses are legion; I have been condensing, summarizing, assimilating.[86] Yet it has been my purpose not to resolve the crux, but to construe

---

performances of *Hamlet* without the topical material, and a later version performed with the material inserted, but a text of Q2 that records only *some* of the insertions. In a sense this is a deep sophistication of the first hypothesis, with the distinction that Jenkins's Q2 is *not* a record of the early performances. Because his Q2 fails to reproduce a performance version, and fails because the foul papers record in confusing fashion the transition from the first to the second stage version, Jenkins may be situated in the tradition of the second hypothesis.

The tendency of Jenkins's arguments may be traced to Dover Wilson's influential *The Manuscript of Shakespeare's Hamlet and the Problems of its Transmission*, 2 vols. (Cambridge: Cambridge University Press, 1934); see especially, I:96ff. It was Wilson who first thinned out the ranks of those willing to entertain the first hypothesis.

[84] In his knotty review of Jenkins's edition, Bowers points out that the arguments here can be reversible (287–88): we can speak with comparable ease (or difficulty) of cuts or additions.

[85] This leaves one free to suppose that Q2 was printed from foul papers (or a copy of foul papers) marked up for preparation of the promptbook. To be sure, this third hypothesis has its difficulties. Although it enables us to describe a copy-text for Q2 that is both very close to foul papers and also proximate, with respect to the topical material, to the promptbook, it leaves us with a slight bibliographic embarrassment when we turn our attention to the copy-text for the Folio. Because of its particularly theatrical character, F is generally thought to be derived from the promptbook, yet F stands as our chief source for a passage supposed, according to this third hypothesis concerning the copy for Q2, to have been cut from performance. That is, the hypothesis proposes a theatrical cut in a copy-text close to foul papers in the case of Q2 and the absence of a theatrical cut in a copy-text close to the promptbook in the case of F. No wonder W. W. Greg remarked, "On the whole it seems to be a rather queer prompt-book, if prompt-book it is, that lies behind F" (*The Shakespeare First Folio*, 323).

[86] It is worth remembering in this context that Fredson Bowers distinguished some thirteen major categories of copy for the printed texts of Elizabethan plays; *On Editing Shakespeare and the Elizabethan Dramatists*, p. 11.

A fourth hypothesis might also be proposed as an elaborate, second-best alternative to the first hypothesis (which is not only the simplest but also, I think, still the best). We can suppose

the consensus to which it tends. Each of these hypotheses, and virtually every plausible version of them, explains the substantial variations in this portion of the text as deliberate products of theatrical intelligence, seriously concerned with whether and how to bring the pressures of the theatrical moment to bear on the play.[87] However difficult it is to date this play and to account for its text, this passage evidences a fussy creative responsiveness to contemporary theatrical fashion.

Whether this theatrical journalism was introduced into the text *Hamlet* before or after the play went into performance, whether this news was presented in early or later performances, or not at all, its affinities with the plot of the play are not difficult to discern.

ROSIN : . . . . there is Sir an ayrie of Children, little Yases, that crye out on the top of question; and are most tyrannically clap't for't: these are now the fashion, and so be-ratled the common Stages (so they call them) that many wearing Rapiers, are affraide of Goosequils, and dare scarse come thither.

HAM : What are they Children? Who maintains 'em? How are they escoted? Will they pursue the Quality no longer then they can sing? Will they not say afterwards if they should grow themselves to common Players (as it is like most if their meanes are not better) their Writers do them wrong, to make them exclaim against their owne Succession.

ROSIN : Faith there ha's bene much to do on both sides . . .

$$(F1, OO_3{}^v\text{--}OO_4)$$

The sudden rise to favor of London's child actors substantiates the hero's obsessive sense of the fickleness of human opinion; more important (insofar as it provides a context for the version of epic that ensues), the usurping children provide an image of the hero's own infantile rebelliousness. And insofar as the Danish past is here erased by an English present these lines rebel against mimesis itself, and so offer another instance of Shakespeare's own considerable rebelliousness. Finally, the passage obtrudes even more intransigent, more specifically anti-dramatic matter when Rosencrantz reports that economic

Shakespeare to have included a full version of the theatrical news in the text presented to the company. (We need not concern ourselves with the precise moment of their composition.) Again comes the decision to cut the passage. But suppose now that the cut was never, or seldom, actually observed in performance, that the decision to cut was reversed. Thus, one might surmise, these lines were marked for cutting in a messy, pre-promptbook theatrical text, which is why Q2 fails to print them; but they were actually performed when the play went into production – or back into production – which is why the Folio prints them.

For a similar theory, see J. M. Nosworthy, *Shakespeare's Occasional Plays: Their Origin and Transmission* (New York: Barnes, 1965): "the Q2 manuscript was very much an author's final draft which had been handed to the company in all its untidiness . . . [I]t is evident that the playhouse scribe recognized certain markings in the original manuscript (brackets in the left-hand margin) as deletions and that the Q2 compositors did not" (139). I have taken over this argument from illegible copy-text and simply relocated the origins of illegibility from author to acting company.

[87] See Wells and Taylor, *Textual Companion*, 401.

constraints have forced the players to their provincial tour in Denmark: "Faith, there has been much to do on both sides; and the nation holds it no sin to tar them to controversy. There was for a while no money bid for argument unless the poet and the player went to cuffs in the question" (2.2.350–54). Poets and players are laboring within a newly competitive economy: Rosencrantz brings news from the theatrical marketplace which was the front-lines of the War of the Theaters. One way of focusing the problem of dating *Hamlet*, the nature of its emergency, will involve determining how many skirmishes may be supposed to have been waged within this war, on where *Hamlet* comes in the sequence of theatrical skirmishes that culminate in Jonson's *Poetaster* (spring, 1601) and in Dekker's and Marston's *Satiromastix* (after *Poetaster*, with November 1601 as a *terminus ad quo*), a public squabbling that pits public theaters against private, Henslowe interests against Burbage, the Blackfriars' Jonson against the Paul's Marston. One play indisputably set Hamlet's favorite company on the road to Elsinore, and that is Jonson's *Cynthia's Revels* (December, 1600).

Cynthia's Revels comes early in the War of the Theaters. Hence, although it satirizes contemporary theatrical practice, it does so without much animus. It begins with an induction in which the brilliant boy-actor, Salamon Pavy, draws straws for the right to speak the Prologue with two equally ambitious fellow-actors. When he loses he seeks revenge on the Author – as if Jonson had abused his power by scripting Pavy's own bad luck. His revenge is to reveal Jonson's plot "and so stale his invention to the auditorie before it come forth" (*Ind.*, 36–37).[88] Not only does Jonson's Pavy play with the idea of competition between actor and author, he also begins a drift toward the representation of a dramatic script as a theatrical property, of drama as commerce. After the avenging plot summary, and some mild mockery – possibly aimed at Marston, possibly at Shakespeare – of playwrights who meddle in the operations of acting companies, Pavy undertakes to negotiate with the playwright on behalf of his audience. He encourages modesty of diction, ingenuity of sentence, and, above all, genuine originality. Speaking for the coterie audience, Pavy begs that playwrights "would not so penuriously gleane wit, from everie laundresse, or hackney-man, or derive their best grace (with servile imitation) from common stages" (Induction 180–82). Thriving on the energies of class competition invoked here, and brandishing the thematics of the *impoverished* imagination, the combatants of the War of the Theaters were using Greene's weapons.

Jonson makes plagiarism a central issue of Pavy's "revenge" in *Cynthia's Revels*. As the boy concludes, he modulates his attack on plagiarism with a figure that could not but have seized Shakespeare's attention:

---

[88] I cite Jonson from the eleven-volume edition of his works edited by C. H. Herford, P. Simpson, and E. Simpson (Oxford: Clarendon, 1925–52).

they say, the *umbrae*, or ghosts of some three or four playes, departed a dozen yeeres since, have bin seene walking on your stage heere: take heed, boy, if your house bee haunted with such *hobgoblins*, 'twill fright away all your spectators quickly. (Induction 194–98)

This may well be a specific reference to the Admiral's Men's 1597 revival of *The Spanish Tragedy*; though this particular revival was old news when *Cynthia's Revels* was staged, Jonson had some notoriety for his performances as Hieronymo, and he began a revision of the play for Henslowe within a year or so.[89] But Pavy's remarks take in more than a single play; instead, they gesture broadly toward the whole *fin-de-siècle* revenge play revival spearheaded by Marston. In the time between Henslowe's *Spanish Tragedy* and the opening of *Cynthia's Revels*, Jonson had done his stint of writing for the Lord Chamberlain's Men, and before he left off this association for a more up-scale relationship with the Children of the Chapel, he must have heard that they too were going to join in the move to revive the old revenge plays. Jonson may in fact have had more specific information – that Shakespeare was even considering reworking (Kyd's?) outmoded *Hamlet*-play of 1587, complete with its neo-Senecan ghost of the *Ur-Hamlet* and with some version of the play-within-a-play of Kyd's *Spanish Tragedy* – certainly this would explain the juxtaposition of an attack on "revivalism" to the the earlier attack on plagiarism.[90] It is pure Jonson to direct his most scathing attacks at versions of his own principles: the lapses that are here singled out for abuse (by the man who had already begun a career as the English theater's great imitative classicist) are plagiarism and slavish nostalgia. These issues resonate powerfully in *Hamlet*.[91] What Jonsonian psychopathology selects as the central vices of contemporary theatrical practice provide the essential conceptual framework for theatrical practice at Elsinore; indeed, the displacement of initiative by imitation and a lingering fixation on that which is past and gone provide the play's essential structures of plot and personality. Recognizing the framing context of the War of the Theatres thus enables us to say

[89] Moreover, Jonson may very well have played Hieronymo during the 1597 season – we know that he played the part at some point in his career – in which case we have another reason why the 1597 performances might have retained a hold on his imagination. The plagiaristical gull Mattheo quotes *The Spanish Tragedy* in *Every Man In His Humour* (1598).

[90] Jonson's Pavy goes on to attack precisely those theatrical nostalgias to which the Chamberlain's Men were catering, conjuring a satiric portrait of one who "prunes his musstaccio, lisps, and with some score of affected othes) sweares down all that sit about him; *That the old Hieronimo* (as it was first acted) *was the onely best, and judiciously pend play of Europe*" (lines 206–11).

[91] Dekker and Marston responded with a *tu quoque*: in *Satiromastix*, Jonson is mocked as an erstwhile actor of Hieronymo; in additions for the printed version of *Antonio and Mellida*, as a reviser of *The Spanish Tragedy*. One might specify a description of the War of the Theaters by describing it as a contest over the inheritance of Kyd's literary properties. The little eyases made their most pointed intervention in this contest sometime between 1599 and 1604 with *The First Part of Hieronimo*, "a full-blown theatrical burlesque of *The Spanish Tragedy*"; see John Reibetanz "Hieronymo in Decimosexto: A Private-Theater Burlesque," *Renaissance Drama*, n.s. 5 (1972), 89–121.

more articulately than ever that *Hamlet* is haunted by theatricality. Among the ghosts at Elsinore are *Cynthia's Revels, The Spanish Tragedy,* a *Hamlet* (Kyd's?) returning from oblivion, the Senecan mode, to say nothing of the Hyrcanian dramatists of the past, among them, perhaps, the upstart crow himself.

Jonson and his eyrie had criticized the imaginative penury that sent the adult companies back to their archives and, having alluded to this milieu, he has his hero call for a recitation from a very Jonsonian play, Jonsonian in its slavish neoclassicism: "one speech in't I chiefly loved," says Hamlet, " 'twas Aeneas' tale to Dido – and thereabout of it especially when he speaks of Priam's slaughter" (II.ii.442–44).[92] We can recognize it as a characteristic response, like the earlier responses to Greene: charged with the mindless revivalism of those who must penuriously glean, Shakespeare promptly displays the kinship between his revivalism and Jonson's neo-classicism, to recall the creative dearth that sent Virgil limping back to Homer, to demonstrate the way in which out-moded fictions uncannily possess the attentive present, while remaining irreducible to privatizing authorial possessiveness.

Of course the responsiveness to Jonson may be far deeper. The discussion of the little eyases – whether added to the version preserved in Q2 or subtracted from the version preserved in F – makes most sense as a response to *Poetaster,* by which point one can speak of "much to do on both sides" of the theatrical war. The argument that *Poetaster,* an aggressively censorious drama *à clef* which pits Horace and Virgil against the petty actors and poets of Augustan Rome, is the play that constituted diffuse competition as a genuine "innovation", converted it into a war, has its persuasive force; one other passage may be thought to have particularly startled Shakespeare, Tucca's not-altogether-comic censure of the actors of Rome, which raises the *umbra* of Greene:

They are growne licentious, the rogues; libertines, flat libertines. They forget they are i' the *statute* [Eliz. 39:4, making players, officially, vagabonds, *not* gentlemen], the rascals, they are *blazond* there [in the statute, not in the College of Heralds], there they are trickt, they and their pedigrees; they need no other *heralds,* I wisse. (*Poetaster,* I.ii.52–55)

Nearly five years after the event, the grant of the Shakespeare arms (and perhaps the similar grants to Heminges, Phillips, Pope, Marston, Burbage, and Cowley) is fresh in Jonson's consciousness.[93] (He may not have seen the crest; but even if he had seen it, he was not always responsive to others' wit and may have missed the lurking comedy of the coat-of-arms.) This will have

---

[92] Neoclassicism is not its only Jonsonian feature. Hamlet recalls a coterie play that discriminates against the undiscriminating, as Jonson aspired to do: " 'twas caviare to the general. But it was, as I received it – and others, whose judgments in such matters cried in the top of mine – an excellent play" (II.ii.431–35).

[93] These grants annoyed others besides Jonson: on grants of arms to players, see Chambers, *ES,* I:350.

stung.[94] If we suppose that the earliest versions of II.ii were written after Shakespeare had heard these lines, in the summer, say, of 1601, and so within a few weeks of John Shakespeare's death in early September, much coheres: *Poetaster* and the moribund father will have inspired the dismal heraldry; *Cynthia's Revels* and *Poetaster* both differently will have helped to conjure the spectre of Greene. (And this is to leave aside the family drama staged when Shakespeare impersonates his hero's dead father. Shakespeare may be said to exclaim against his own succession throughout the play: the little eyases parody his own long-standing professional usurpation of the roles of dignified old men.)[95] The "Flourish for the Players" at Elsinore is a concordance of discord; a sword-play of goose-quills; a suspension, not a solution, of competition.

Jonson, for his part, would aspire to a solution, if not an evasion, of competition, and he worked it out in ways quite different from Shakespeare's – retreating, on the one hand, to the private theaters, to Whitehall, and to the vagaries of noble patronage, and (as we shall see in the ensuing chapters) to the quiet confines of the Folio *Works* on the other.[96] Shakespeare works otherwise, seeking competition. During this fluctuant and heated cultural moment there will be many "constructions of Early Modern authorship," and an author's temperament will play an important part in the way authorship is construed. Shakespeare's construction involves *coordinating* the measured prestige of humanist imitation with the economic logic of popularity.

The coordination required a steady adaptation of script to circumstance, another version of editorial authorship. Of the three or four general explanations for the differing states of Q2 and F, only the second has recourse to a single performance version; the rest are theories of multiple "finished" states – that is, multiple versions each of which an acting company would regard as actable. If we are dealing in this case with multiple performance texts, it would not be idiosyncratic; revisions of popular plays were by no means unusual.[97]

---

[94] Jonson was apparently not alone in wishing to take Shakespeare down a peg. In 1602, Peter Brooke, the York Herald, accused William Dethick of elevating nobodies to the status of gentleman. Shakespeare stands fourth in Brooke's list of twenty-three cases of abuse.

[95] If Q2 is an early draft or performance version, and if it precedes *Poetaster*, then issues of canon and genealogy came up together, but without the stimulus of the slap from Jonson. If on the other hand the version in F precedes that of Q2, as Dover Wilson thought, and if both postdate *Poetaster*, then Jonson himself may have motivated the braid of meditations on theatrical, cultural, familial, and social competition.

The evidence for Shakespeare's "line" as an actor is not conclusive, but see Chambers, *William Shakespeare*, 2:214, 264, 265, 278.

[96] For a more detailed account of Jonson's response to competition, see my "Printing and the 'Multitudinous Presse': The Contentious Texts of Jonson's Masques," *Ben Jonson's 1616 Folio "Workes"*, eds. Jennifer Brady and Wyman Herendeen (Newark: University of Delaware Press, 1991), 168–91.

[97] For a superb introduction to theatrical revision, see Eric Rasmussen, "The Revision of Scripts," *New History of English Drama*, 441–60; theories of the revision of *Hamlet* are reviewed in Grace Ioppolo's *Revising Shakespeare*, (Cambridge, Mass.: Harvard University Press, 1991), 134–46.

G. E. Bentley has plausibly argued that *any* playwright who had a continuing relation with an acting company would normally have been expected to perform such revisions, whether of his own plays or of another's.[98] The record of Henslowe's payment to Jonson for revisions of *The Spanish Tragedy* is one of several such records; Chettle and, later, Massinger were specialists in such revising.[99] Revision was, in fact, understood to be essential to theatrical practice: we know from Campion that the phrase "Newly Revived with Additions" was a recognizable staple of players' bills.[100] Play texts partake of the mutabilities of manuscript texts and just as someone transcribing a poem might make a very large range of adjustments in his or her copy text – improving a rhyme or a rhythm, renaming a character, sharpening a metaphor, introducing a stanza – so a playwright might rearrange his own or a predecessor's text to accomodate a new character actor, to make up for a company's shrinking personnel, to avoid (or seek out) dangerous topicalities, to secure a censor's approval, to improve a rhyme or a rhythm, or sharpen a metaphor, or commemorate the death of a father.[101] At least some such adjustments have been discerned in *King Lear* and in several other plays by Shakespeare.[102] To speak of the early stages of his career as a reviser of his own plays (while conceding that editorial opinions differ on the extent of his revisions), there is reason to believe that around 1594 Shakespeare added a scene to the extant performance text of *Titus Andronicus*; Folio *2 Henry VI* seems to be based on a revision done in the late 1590s of an earlier performance version published (in garbled form) in 1594, and so forth.[103]

[98] *Profession*, 263 and see Ioppolo, *Revising Shakespeare*, 52–55.
[99] Henslowe's diaries record payments to Byrd, Dekker, Heywood, Middleton, and Rowley, as well as Chettle and some unnamed others.
[100] *Fourth Book of Ayres* (*c.* 1612); the datum is interesting if only in that it indicates that this form of innovation had drawing power. Massinger makes no effort to conceal that fact that his *Cleander* (1634) is a reworking of Fletcher's *The Lover's Progress*. On the other hand, not all theatrical companies treated such sameness-with-difference as something to be advertised. Bentley quotes, from 1632, a swipe against managers of acting companies who "are as crafty with an old play as bawds with old faces: the one puts on a new fresh color, the other a new face and name," (*Profession*, 238).
[101] In an admittedly extreme case, Robert Wilmot revised *Tancred and Gismond*, a play on which he had collaborated with several other Inner Templars in the mid-1560s, for publication in 1591, adding new scenes as well as dumb-shows. The printed play was advertised as "newly revived and polished according to the decorum of these daies."
[102] Despite an oddly entrenched contemporary myth according to which the editors of the past are supposed to have clung blindly to the idea that Renaissance plays have only a single form embued with absolute authorial intentions, Ioppolo has reminded us that there is in fact a continuous editorial tradition of explaining variants in Shakespeare's texts as authorial revisions; see chapter 1 of *Revising Shakespeare* (Cambridge, Mass: Harvard, 1991), 19–43.
[103] Eugene Waith, ed., *Titus Andronicus* (Oxford: Clarendon, 1984), 6–11 and 43; Ioppolo, *Revising Shakespeare*, 107–8. On the copy for F2 *Henry VI*, see Taylor and Wells, *Textual Companion*, 176. Here and in what follows, I recognize myself to be flying in the face of arguments by both Bowers and Jenkins – not a consensus of the bibliographic community, but an impressive pair nonetheless; see Bowers, "Review," 284.

It is not clear when revising became a recognizably normal theatrical practice – Campion's allusion to playbills advertising revivals with additions dates from around 1612 – but around the mid-nineties revising begins to emerge as a significant aspect of Shakespeare's professional identity. The first significant datum in this emergence may be the Thomas Creede's publication, in 1595, of *The Lamentable Tragedie of Locrine, the eldest sonne of Kinge Brutus, discoursing the warres of the Brittaines, and Hunnes ... Newly set foorth, overseene and corrected, By W. S.* Although this play was included in the third Shakespeare Folio of 1664, Shakespeare is not thought to have written the play, for which no particular authorial ascription is currently accepted. By 1595, Shakespeare had some reputation as the author of history plays, and Creede's ambiguous use of initials may simply exploit his prominence in the genre. But the title page is doubly ambiguous and may be construed as having claimed only that W. S. had revised the play, and not necessarily that he had written it; moreover, the phrase "overseene and corrected" seems to imply that W. S. had set forth the play specifically for print. As observed above, Shakespeare's name did not appear on a title page until 1598, authorial attribution of printed plays having only recently become a printer's norm, and at least one of the attributions of that year is notably editorial: Cuthbert Burby published *Loves Labors Lost* with a title page that advertises the play as "Newly corrected and augmented / *By W. Shakespere.*" These lines may be little more than a general puff, a rather approximate promise that the 1598 quarto was presenting an up-to-the-minute version of a play that, most likely, was first performed in 1594–95.[104] But the language is not insignificant. Burby's "corrected" is a trade term and it implies that a carelessly produced edition of the play is being displaced (though no external evidence of a prior, bad quarto has been discovered); "augmented" partners the argument for displacement. The title page thus claims for the new playtext an excellence specific to its print publication, a "printerly" authority derived from a doubled or augmentative authorship – an authorship both dramaturgic and editorial.[105]

In the following year, Burby repeated the claim for a textual authority augmented by the renewal of Shakespeare's attention in his title page for Q2 *Romeo and Juliet*, advertising it as "*Newly corrected, augmented, and amended.*" (In this case, with a prior quarto still surviving, we can assent to the truth of Burby's

---

[104] The line break may punctuate, of course: this may be one phrase or two. Yet even if these are separate claims about *Love's Labors Lost*, that this version is corrected and augmented, and that Shakespeare wrote it, the claims cannot be kept fully separate, for however casual the language of this title page (or unfounded its claims), we cannot but identify Shakespeare as the imputed author of the imputed "augmentations."

[105] Compare the claims of this title page to those of Barnabe Barnes's *The Divil's Charter* (1607), discussed in chapter 5 below: "As it was plaide before the Kings Majestie, /. . . by his / Majesties Servants. / But more exactly revewed, corrected and augmen- / ted since by the Author, for the more plea- / sure and profit of the Reader."

claim: Q1 is a reported text; Q2 is based on foul papers, though contaminated in places by Q1). Andrew Wise followed Burby when he published the second quarto of *1 Henry IV*, the first with an authorial attribution, which appeared early in 1599 "Newly corrected by William Shakespeare."[106] This quarto is in fact a reprint of the first, but there is a kind of half-truth to Wise's claim.[107] Copy for the *first* quarto had been quite carefully prepared, apparently in response to the censor's demand that the name of the vice-ridden character, Sir John Oldcastle, be changed to avoid offense to his modern descendants; the fat knight was "Oldcastle" in the first performances of the play, and his name was changed to "Falstaff" for subsequent ones, but the copy for the quarto seems to derive not from a playhouse manuscript, but from a scribal transcript of Shakespeare's foul papers, which not only revises "Oldcastle" to "Falstaff", but also changes several other names from historical to fictional ones.[108] Either Shakespeare or his fellows in the Chamberlain's Men took pains to provide Wise with a "corrected" text based on an authorial rather than a theatrical manuscript. It is often claimed that a professional man of the theater like Shakespeare would not have concerned himself with the printed versions of his plays, but some member of Shakespeare's company did so concern himself with the text of this play.[109] When we cease to ask merely how accurately Heminges's and Condell's letter prefatory to the Shakespeare Folio represents the author's editorial imagination, and ask instead what the letter tells us about Heminges's and Condell's editorial imaginations we discover that "professional men of the theater" had a considerable feel at least for the rhetoric of print publication. The plays are published as, finally, "cur'd, and perfect of their limbes," whereas earlier editions were described as "maimed, and deformed" and thus not so much published as "expos'd" to the harsh winds of opinion. To speak of the restored Folio editions as "absolute in their numbers" was not to speak the argot of the theater, but that of humanist philology, which had long been appropriated by the book trade.

---

[106] I should perhaps designate this "the (so-called) second quarto" and the first quarto similarly, since a fragment of a quarto prior to the "first," called "Q0," is preserved at the Folger Shakespeare Library; *Textual Companion*, 329.

[107] Q3 (1604) was also printed as "newly corrected", though it simply reprints Q2.

[108] Wells and Taylor, *Textual Companion*, 329–30.

[109] On the other hand, the foul copy for the quarto of *2 Henry IV* is based on a coherent and therefore "finished" authorial manuscript, but one which may well have been further revised prior to the completion of the first performance version. According to John Jowett and Gary Taylor ("The Three Texts of *2 Henry IV*," *Studies in Bibliography* 40 [1987], 31–50), the first issue misconstrues its copy, failing to insert III.i, a scene apparently inserted at a secondary stage of composition and interleaved in the manuscript copy; the second issue of Q corrects the misconstruction by inserting the scene. But the Folio text introduces even more scenes while consolidating others and its revisions carry forward the dramaturgic adjustment initiated with the introduction of III.i. The Chamberlain's Men may have performed a version of the play based on a transcript of the text that stands behind the second issue of Q, but Jowett and Taylor suppose that the play did not go into performance until Shakespeare had completed the revisions reflected in F.

If Heminges and Condell could think in these terms about Shakespearean texts, so, too, could Shakespeare; nor are such thoughts remarkable, for printing had become an aspect of stage business.

This is not to obscure the more general utility of claiming novelty for a printed play. Creede had printed the second quarto of *Richard III* for Wise in 1598, and when he printed Q3, again for Wise, he sought the gloss of renewed authorial attention, advertising the 1602 quarto as "Newly augmented, / By *William Shakespeare*", despite the fact that Q3 is a straight reprint of Q2.[110] When correction or augmentation could honestly be claimed, a printer would naturally make a great point of the matter, as in the case of Q2 *Romeo and Juliet*, Q4 *Richard II* ("*With new additions of the Parliament Sceane, / and the deposing of King / Richard*"; 1615), or Q2 *Hamlet* ("Newly imprinted and enlarged to almost as much / againe as it was, according to the true and perfect / Coppie"). This was by no means a procedure peculiar to the printing of Shakespeare's plays, as witnessed by the title page of one of Simmes' 1604 printings of "*The Malcontent. Augmented by Marston. With the Additions played by the Kings Majesties Servants. Written by Jhon Webster.*"[111] Not all such announcements specified an authorial source of the correction or augmentation offered by a printed book, but Shakespeare is so specified with some frequency, for plainly an editorial or revising Shakespeare was a useful figure, a printer's ornament, and never more ornamental than on the title pages of Q2 *Hamlet* – "*By William Shakespeare / Newly imprinted and enlarged to almost as much / againe as it was, according to the true and perfect / Coppie*" – or on the 1612 quarto of "*The Passionate Pilgrim Or Certaine Amorous Sonnets betweene Venus and Adonis, newly corrected and augmented. By W. Shakespeare*".[112]

Other aspects of theatrical culture conduced to the development of editorial dramatic authorship, of course. The actors at Elsinore flee from a competitive milieu: the detailed momentousness of their report on that milieu is clearly one of the products of that milieu. The author who attached this report to the playtext, or the author or actors who detached it from it, treats or treat the playtext as a malleable object made valuable by nodes of authorial definition. The various printed texts that derive from these nodes vary considerably – the quartos and folios reflecting foul papers, or fair copies of foul papers, or memorial reports of performance texts, or promptbooks, many of them in various stages of contamination – yet these various texts often reflect distinct,

---

[110] First performed in the early to mid nineties, the play perhaps needed some puffing in order to pass for current. The claim that a text has been revised or augmented is often pure puffery. Despite the claims of their title pages, the Q2 of *Soliman and Perseda*, the Q2 and Q3 of *The Faithful Shepherdess*, and the Q3 of *The Merry Wives of Windsor* vary from their predecessors only in trivial ways.

[111] For other contemporary examples of title pages advertising textual adjustment, see Bentley, *The Profession of Dramatist*, 243ff.

[112] See Ioppolo, *Revising Shakespeare*, 50.

stageworthy, and, hence, "completed" scripts: certainly this is the case with the various texts of, say, *Lear, Hamlet, Troilus and Cressida, Othello*. To say that by the turn of the seventeenth century Shakespeare was writing for an author's theater is therefore not to say enough. To specify: having seen the title pages of the most recent editions of *Love's Labors Lost, Romeo and Juliet,* and *1 Henry IV*, Shakespeare would be confirmed in understanding himself as an author who both revises and rectifies. The editorial playwright maintains a relation to the text that is always in some degree interrogative, seeking both a corrected completion and an improved augmentation.[113] We can recognize such an author in *Hamlet* as well as in Hamlet, for the hero, like his creator seems to experience textual adjustment as momentous and especially intimate. The rivalrous environment in which he finds himself teaches him to be vigilant against misremembering ("Tis not so") and to struggle against the unfashionable atavisms of bombast. He is a reviser and a reformer of plays and his campaign against clowning – which seems to disclose Shakespeare's good riddance to the improvising Kemp – bespeaks a new textualism: "let those that play your Clownes, speake no more then is set downe for them" (F1, OO₄v).[114]

And that textualism would continue to inflate the value of both authors and of printed plays – hence Moseley's letter prefacing the Beaumont and Fletcher Folio:

> When these Comedies and Tragedies were presented on the Stage, the Actours omitted some Scenes and Passages (with the Authour's consent) as occasion led them; and when private friends desir'd a Copy, they then (and justly too) transcribed what they Acted. But now you have both All that was Acted, and all that was not; even the perfect full Originalls without the least mutilation; So that were the Authours living, (and sure they can never dye) they themselves would challenge neither more nor lesse then what is here published; this Volume being now so compleate and finish'd, that the Reader must expect no further Alterations, (π 6).

The authors' prestige, borrowed for the text, is now secure. A tradition of performance, recalled with implicit nostalgia here in 1647, makes its contribution, but

---

[113] I am influenced here by Coghill's important argument about the revisions of *Othello* in *Shakespeare's Professional Skills* (Cambridge: Cambridge University Press, 1965), 197–201. Coghill argues that in the course of removing oaths from the play in response to the ban of 1606, Shakespeare became imaginatively engaged in the work of revising and began a series of adjustments in the play, the most obvious of which was the reworking of the role of Emilia.

[114] Notoriously, at this juncture in the faulty, reported text which is Q1, a text which may have been constructed by actors planning a provincial tour, Hamlet ambles into what seems to be an unauthorized augmentation; in the corrected Q2, on the other hand, a more laconic Hamlet represents the author more correctly.

It may be worth remarking on a powerful, but very different way of remarking the textualism of Q2: Giorgio Melchiori argues that Q2 *Hamlet* is a *literary* text, written for MS circulation, hence its length; "*Hamlet*: The Acting Version and the Wiser Sort," *The 'Hamlet' First Published*, ed. Thomas Clayton (Newark: University of Delaware Press, 1992), 195–201.

what Moseley advertises is the sort of author's text that Hamlet had endorsed almost half a century earlier. By promoting revision, the theatrical environment not only inflated the prestige of dramatic authorship, it transformed its nature. For Shakespeare, the editorial authorship is a useful professional development and an affecting imaginative stimulus. For Jonson, editorial authorship became one of the chief forms of self-experience, and one of the most powerful of imaginative stimuli.

4   Jonson, Martial, and the mechanics of plagiarism

> It is in the generall behalfe of this faire societie here, that I am to speake,
> at least the more judicious part of it, which seemes much distasted with the
> immodest and obscene writing of manie, in their playes. Besides, they could
> wish, your *Poets* would leave to bee promoters of other mens jests, and . . . that
> feeding their friends with nothing of their owne, but what they have twice or
> thrice cook'd, they should not wantonly give out, how soone they had drest it;
> nor how manie coaches came to carrie away the broken-meat, besides hobbie-
> horses, and foot-cloth nags.
>
> (Jonson, *Cynthia's Revels*, Induction, 173–78, 185–89)

Voluminous ambition

Heywood often tells us that playwrights who assist stationers are doing something vaguely improper. His allegation that those who profit by the arrangement
are making "a double sale of their labours" is interesting enough; his protesta-
tion "that it never was any great ambition in me, to bee in this kind Volumniously
read" is even more intriguing, since it brings us from the slight mysteries of
avarice to far more curious yearnings, to the emergent editorial imagination
of playwrights. Heywood was not the only playwright to brood disapprov-
ingly over this emergency. When William Cotton registered *Parasitaster, or
The Fawne* in the spring of 1606, Marston apparently had no hope of inhibiting
publication; the best he could hope for was to shape the publication – to approve
the printed text and to provide a prefatory epistle declaring his own distaste for
printing. Like Heywood, Marston is a curiously reactive figure in the changing
structure of media relations; the odd soundings and fissures of authorial self-
defense in the epistle to *Parasitaster* make it worth quoting at some length, as
a witness to the instabilities of the bibliographic ego:

> TO MY EQUAL READER
>
> I have ever more endevoured to know my selfe, than to be knowne of others: and rather
> to be unpartially beloved of all, than factiously to be admired of a few: yet so powerfully
> have I been enticed with the delights of Poetry, and (I must ingeniously confesse) above

better desert so fortunate in these stage-pleasings, that (let my resolutions be never so fixed to call mine eyes into my selfe,) I much feare that most lamentable death of him,

> *Qui nimis notus omnibus*
> *Ignotus moritur sibi.*   *Seneca.*

But since the over-vehement pursute of these delights hath bin the sicknesse of my youth, and now is growne to be the vice of my firmer age, since to satisfie others, I neglect my selfe, let it be the curtesie of my peruser, rather to pitie my selfe-hindring labours, than to malice me, and let him be pleased to be my reader, and not my interpreter, since I would faine reserve that office in my owne hands, it being my dayly prayer, *Absit à jocorum nostrorum simplicitate malignus interpres.*   *Martial.*

If any shall wonder why I print a Comedie, whose life rests much in the Actors voice: Let such know, that it cannot avoide publishing: let it therefore stand with good excuse; that I have been my owne setter out.

If any desire to understand the scope of my Comedie, *etc.* (A_2).

The self-regard is made tolerable and even a bit appealing by Marston's "ingeniously" disabused awareness of his self-betrayals. He leads us to expect a narrative of conversion – "since the over-vehement pursute of these delights hath been the sicknesse of my youth, and now..." – but no conversion comes, only the paradoxical deepening self-consciousness of self-neglect. To some extent, the knot of self-possession and self-loss is latent in the contradictory (Senecan, Stoic) ethical imperatives with which Marston and the epistle began; but the historical interest of the epistle lies in its oblique, almost off-handed concession that what rouses this contradiction from latency is the playwright's fascinated makings, that what maintains ethical contradiction as a permanent problem of Marston's firmer age is the theater. We have here an unusually nuanced instance of the anti-theatricality so firmly lodged in England's very theatrical Early Modernity, a description of stage-pleasings offered, unusually, from the point of view of an author, rather than from the usual place of the spectator.

Yet the theater is not the primary object of suspicion: Marston's purpose is not so much to confess himself an habituated and enervated playwright as to defend himself as an unaccustomed and unwilling editor. And although there seems to be a rhetorical gap between Marston's anti-theatrical quotation from Seneca and his less florid apology for printing, a veiled rationale of sequence may be found in the epistle. Marston tells us that he has been betrayed to publicity (*notus omnibus*) by stage-pleasings, but that loss of privacy can at least be lamented as a disruption of Stoic self-possession; it can be understood, that is, as a classical lapse. But now he is taken up into a more dissipating publicity, unprecedented and unclassical. (It is no accident, as this chapter will show, that Martial stands in the middle ground between publicities ancient and modern.) The play has been wrested from the stage, its speeches snatched from the actor's lips, but what is worse – and what is, again, most interesting for the cultural historian – the special publicity of the play-in-print instigates its own form of ethical chaos, quite distinguishable from that ascribed to the play-in-performance. The printed play seems utterly alienated, an automaton – "it cannot avoid publishing" – yet, at the same time, it seems to implicate Marston as if he were its subject, and it were his subjectivity – "let it therefore stand with good excuse that I have been my own setter out."

The mixture of involvement and dissociation turns out to be more than figurative. A second edition of *Parasitaster* was printed in the same year, its new title page indicating that the text was "now corrected of many faults, which by reason of the Author's absence were let slip in the first edition," yet the promise of the title page is partly rescinded in a new epistle: "Reader, know I have perused this copy, to make some satisfaction for the first faulty impression: yet so urgent hath been my businesse that some errors have styll passed, which thy discretion may amend." Marston then reasserts the priority of performance: "*Comedies* are writ to be spoken, not read: Remember the life of these things consists in action." Marston hovers over the presentation of his printed plays here, as he would elsewhere: William Sheares, who published the first collected edition of his plays in 1633, implies that Marston became an assiduous proof-reader, "more careful in revising the former impressions, and more circumspect about it than I can."[1] As the preface to *Parasitaster* suggests, the threshold of print could seem more dire than that of performance; editorial circumspection seems to have enabled Marston to manage, and so to transmute, the distaste with which he had contemplated dramatic publication early in his career.

In Marston's case, we can speak of distaste, a matter of temperament; Heywood's case is similar, but hardly identical, a matter of principle and of some pride. Of course, there are also playwrights who sought print with gusto, and not simply out of a desire to make what Heywood calls "a double sale of their labours." Marston's prefatory epistles to *Parasitaster* may be usefully measured against Richard Brome's letter to the readers of *The Antipodes*, published in 1640. The play had been written in 1636, during a hiatus in playing in which Brome believed – or hoped – that his initial contract with the Salisbury Court company had lapsed; the title page describes the play as "acted in the yeare 1638. by the Queenes Majesties Servants at *Salisbury* Court," which was in the period during which Brome was working under the terms of a second (but still unsigned) contract with that company. The letter both records the Queen's Men's claims on the play and discredits those claims:

[1] Cited in Albright, *Dramatic Publication*, 213. This develops an interest in dramatic reception already manifest at the beginning of Marston's career. In the prologue to *Antonio and Mellida*, for example, the anxious actors, who have just managed to learn their parts, fret over the speed with which a coherent performance must be assembled from their fragmented and uncertain preparation. Like prologue, like preface: Marston lingers at the threshold of publicity, registering its discomforts.

Courteous Reader: You shal find in this Booke more then was presented upon the *Stage*, and left out of the *Presentation*, for superfluous length (as some of the *Players* pretended) I thoght good al should be inserted according to the allowed *Original*; and as it was, at first, intended for the *Cock-pit Stage*, in the right of my most deserving Friend Mr. *William Beeston*, unto whom it properly appertained.

An important shift in urban literary culture has taken place between *Parasitaster* and *The Antipodes*. Marston's principle, that "the life of these things consists in action" still impinges on Brome, for he defends the nonconformity of the printed text to the performed text by arguing that the printed text represents the play as it would have been performed by others. He proposes, that is, no untheatrical (or anti-theatrical) ideal, for the ideal text is always a performance text. For Brome, print is not altogether an alternative, but insofar as it can correct for local inadequacies in the circumstances of performance it offers a special vantage on performance. Moreover, by means of print, Brome presents himself as a privileged arbiter of performance practices.

"Jonson's alive!" wrote "C. G." in the first of a pair of poems commendatory to *The Antipodes*. Although Brome's gift for fantasy exceeds even that evidenced in Jonson's anti-masques, and although the genial freedom of *his* hilarity is very different from the nervousness of Jonson's, Brome is very much a Son of Ben, and perhaps never more so than in the letter appended to *The Antipodes*. It had been Jonson's crucial contribution to literary culture to test print as an alternative to performance, to measure one publicity against the other, and to assert the advantage of the printed to the played. Brome learned to use the printing of a play to disown the accidents of performance from Jonson, learned the trick first-hand. He had been Jonson's man-servant while Jonson's Folio *Workes* were being prepared, and would have been party to whatever practical or theoretical reflections his master might have made on this important editorial project.[2] And Jonson taught the lesson again in the early thirties, in a way that

---

[2] Jonson professed to have encouraged Brome in his career as a playwright, though the encouragement was no doubt more than a little grudging. The commendatory poem, "To My Old Faithfull Servant, etc.," written for *The Northern Lass* (performed in 1629 and printed three years later) gives us Jonson at his least appealing, still smarting, it seems fair to suppose, from the failure of *The New Inn*:

> I had you for a Servant, once, *Dick Brome*;
>   And you perform'd a Servants faithfull parts:
> Now you are got into a nearer roome
>   *Of Fellowship*, professing my old Arts.
> And you doe doe them well, with good applause,
>   Which you have justly gained from the *Stage*,
> By observation of those Comick Lawes
>   Which I, your *Master*, first did teach the Age.
> You learn'd it well . . .

This is at least more temperate than the handling of Brome in the "Ode to Himself" drafted in 1629.

must have made an indelible impression. I am referring to the dreary lesson of *The New Inn*, performed in the first weeks of 1629 and printed in 1632. The premiere had been a disaster, and the shame of its failure was exacerbated by the enormous success of his ex-servant's play, *The Lovesick Maid*, which opened a few weeks later. Jonson wrote the notorious "Ode to Himself" ("Come leave the loathèd stage") shortly after these events and, in what is clearly a corrective mirror of contemporary critical gossip, invidious comparison is its central rhetorical principle: "Thou pour'st them wheat," he says to himself, "And they would acorns eat" (lines 11–12). (He is elaborating the culinary figure of the Prologue to the play, in which the actors welcome the audience to the new inn – "we ha' the same Cooke, / Still, and the fat, who says, you sha' not looke / Long for your bill of fare ... " (lines 3–5) – and counsel that "Before you judge, vouchsafe to understand, / Concoct, digest" (22–23).) In the course of wreaking the Ode's non-dramatic vengeance on the theater, Jonson not only made one of his several famous swipes at Shakespeare, but he also insured that his contemporaries would never forget the biographical connection between himself and Brome:

> No doubt a mouldy Tale
> Lyke *Pericles*, and Stale
> As the Shrives crusts, and nasty as his Fish,
> Scraps out of every Dish,
> Throwne forth and rak'd into the common Tub,
> May keep up the Play Club:
> Broomes sweepings doe as well
> There, as his Masters meale:
> For who the relish of these guests will fit,
> Needs set them but the Almes-basket of wit.
>
> (lines 20–30)

Writing and circulating the Ode was Jonson's first act of self-justifying revenge against this occasion; arranging for the printing of *The New Inn* in 1631, with the Ode as critical afterword, was his more fully meditated response.[3]

The whole episode must have been a landmark in Brome's professional biography, his old master humiliated by his servant's success and unable to keep himself from seeking Brome's humiliation. In the commendatory poem to *The Antipodes*, written several years after Jonson's death, C. G. implies the abiding memory of this awkward incident:

---

[3] He slightly veiled the specificity of the lines on Brome for the printed version of the poem (the original was printed in the 1640 *Poems*), tempering them to "there, sweepings doe as well / As the best order'd meale." (He would relent further, in the only slightly withholding commendatory verses for the print version of *The Northern Lass*.)

> Jonson's ghost
> Is not a tenant i'the Elysian coast
> But vext with too much scorn at your dispraise,
> Silently stole unto a grove of bays.[4]

Certainly, Brome must have been particularly interested in Jonson's printed monument to the episode. He would have found in the 1631 edition of *The New Inn*, Jonson's most furious attempt to use print to secure an advantage over the stage and so to project a transformation of the dramatic marketplace. Print as revenge against performers, print as the author's medium – we can see a muted version of this tactic in the printed *Antipodes* of 1640, more practical and more prudent.

Jonson's friends had rallied to him, levelling accusations against the servingman that are Jonsonian not only in allegiance, but in idiom. "J. C." very slightly adjusts the terms of Jonson's "Ode to Himself," shifting emphasis from the trashy character of Brome's sweepings to the willful criminality of the appropriation:

> Let him who daily steales
> From Thy most precious meales.
> (Since thy strange plenty findes no losse by it)
> Feed himselfe with the fragments of thy wit.

The explicit charge of theft exaggerates the more ambiguous insinuation of the phrase, "Broome's sweepings." Jonson's insinuation was perhaps strategically moderate, but he would have felt it especially appropriate insofar as it reflects the blur at the border between indebtedness and intellectual theft in Stuart England. Thomas Randolph's warm reply to Jonson's Ode maintains both the stern, general condescension –

> if they will have any of thy store,
> Give 'em some scraps, and send them from thy door.
> And let those things in plush
> Till they be taught to blush
> Like what they will . . .

– and also the particular insinuation –

> Like what they will, and more contented be
> With what Broome swept from thee.[5]

[4] C. G. concludes his endorsement of that play with the discovery of a Jonsonian spirit genially haunting Brome's book: "But stay, and let me tell you where he is: / He sojourns in his Brome's Antipodes"; ed. Ann Haaker, *Regents Renaissance Drama Series* (Lincoln: University of Nebraska Press, 1966), lines 7–10, 21–22.

[5] *Poetical and Dramatic Works of Thomas Randolph*, ed. W. Carew Hazlitt, 2 vols. (repr., New York: Benjamin Blom, 1968), II:58.

One contemplates this version of the insinuation with a special flicker of curiosity, for Randolph himself is "sweeping" here, reproducing the stanza of Jonson's Ode and drawing on its particular arguments and phrases. To remark this is not to catch Randolph out in some hypocrisy, but to discover an area of Stuart cultural practice, the practice of influence, in which differential valence is especially subtle. Randolph seems not to be brazening out his performance, yet we may wonder what enables it, how he can cast aspersions on Brome's indebtedness without betraying any uncertainty about the propriety of his own. Apparently, the simple psychological mechanisms of partisanship are adequate to maintain a distinction between plagiaristical and imitative indebtedness. But the distinction could not long remain a function merely of the secure and insulated disposition; it was historically doomed.[6]

In 1652, during the last year of Brome's life, John Hall would have to patrol the border between imitation and plagiarism; he explains the difference between culpable and justifiable indebtednesses as if he were explaining it to a very circumspect Brome, an apprentice dubious of the nature of his relation to his master –

> You do not invade;
> But by great *Johnson* were made free o' th' *Trade*.
> So, that we must in this your *Labour* finde
> Some Image and fair Relique of *his* Minde.[7]

The muddled figure of cult behavior in the latter couplet marks a mystification that is the abiding characteristic of post-Renaissance literary relations, but the preceding figure, the representation of Brome's relation to Jonson as an apprenticeship, is more particularly revealing and will bear some scrutiny. Hall is obviously reacting to the imputation of lawless invasion of property with a figurative counter-claim, that the relation between poets is formalized, regulated. With the exception of kinship relations, no association between two persons in Early Modern England was as fully articulated and comprehended as apprenticeship. One can say more of Hall's "argument" – that the reactive, fantastic work of figuration is deepened in this particular figure. As a consequence of the general weakening of guild structures apprenticeship was losing some degree of its institutional clarity and regularity, so part of the deep aptness of Randolph's explanatory figure has to do with the nostalgia with which it is seized: apprenticeship as it once had been (but was no longer) is used to figure a structure of

---

[6] That doom can be discerned as early as 1614, when a scholar in Thomas Tomkis's *Albumazar* alleges the ubiquity of literary theft: "This poet is that poet's plagiary. / And he a third's, till they all end in Homer" (W. C. Hazlitt, ed., *Dodsley's Select Collection of Old English Plays*, 15 vols. [London: Reeves and Turnerm, 1874–76], 11:302). For another approach to Early Modern plagiarism, see Stephen Orgel, "The Renaissance Artist as Plagiarist," ELH 48 (1981), 476–95.

[7] *A Joviall Crew* (London, 1652), A3.

unimpeachable indebtedness (that cannot remain above suspicion). The slight comedy (enriched for us by historical distance) of the situation, in which Hall pretends to instruct Brome on the nature of his own imitative practice, finds its motive in the embarassing historical emergence of imitation as a theoretical problem. As if faced with an opening seam, Hall and Brome must wonder how long this problem has been there, and whether anyone else had noticed.

Mimeography

Homer does not swell our purse with gold and silver, nor our stomach with gluttony, nor does he adorn our fingers with jewelled rings. But he surely fills, adorns, and endows the mind, which is more excellent, which is the immortal part of us, with enormous, and far more noble, and eternal riches. (Melancthon, *Praefatio in Homerum*)[8]

PUPILLUS: Pray what does she [Flavius] do with money?
MERCUTIO: Releeves poore Poets, that eats Oads, And Madrigalls.
 (Lewis Sharpe, *The Noble Stranger* (1640), G₄ᵛ)

Jonson had noticed. That the critique of Brome is carried on in a Jonsonian idiom is only fitting, since Jonson had long since made the ethics of imitation his own proper problematic. His unrivalled importance for the historiography of intellectual property stems from the centrality of this problematic not only to his professional and intellectual career, but also, it seems, to his very sense of self. This is a large claim, but I think it can be validated by concentrating attention upon a poem that, in many ways, anticipates the issues that eddy around *The New Inn* and the public flap over the ethics of Brome's debt to Jonson. Because "Inviting a Friend to Supper" is centrally concerned both with imitation and with the predicament of authorship in print, I wish to give it sustained treatment.[9] Moreover, the poem shares with Jonson's "Ode" a serious engagement with the culinary and I believe that this can be shown to be neither coincidental nor impertinent to the history of intellectual property.

Jonson invites the recipient of this poem to the "entertaynment perfect" of private festivity:

> your worth will dignifie our feast,
> With those that come; whose grace may make that seeme
> Something, which, else, could hope for no esteeme.

---

[8] *Liber selectarum declamationum*, 405, cited in Terence Cave, *The Cornucopian Text* (Oxford: Clarendon, 1979), 177.
[9] On *imitatio* in Jonson, see Richard S. Peterson, *Imitation and Praise in the Poems of Ben Jonson* (New Haven: Yale University Press, 1981), particularly 6–9 and Thomas M. Greene, *The Light in Troy: Imitation and Discovery in Renaissance Poetry*, Elizabethan Club Series, 7 (New Haven: Yale University Press, 1982), who offers a brilliant discussion of the poem on 278–84. In what follows, I am condensing and refocusing my argument in "The Jonsonian Corpulence; or, The Poet as Mouthpiece," *ELH*, 53 (Fall 1986), 491–518.

> It is the faire acceptance, Sir, creates
>> The entertaynment perfect: not the cates.

(lines 4–8)

For all their attractive gravity, these lines are not without their uncertainties: what the indicative of the last couplet affirms is, precisely, contingency. Although the meal proposed is sumptuous –

> An olive, capers, or some better sallade
> Ushring the mutton; with a short-leg'd hen,
>> If we can get her, full of egs, and then,
> Limons, and wine for sauce: to these, a coney
> Is not to be despair'd of, for our money.

(lines 10–14)

– it is a curiously soluble sumptuousness, like Ariel's feast. Jonson mocks invitation itself – "Ile tell you of more, and lye, so you will come: / Of partrich, pheasant, wood-cock" (lines 17–18) – but only after a squint of more rueful humor. "An olive" (perhaps the habitual litotes of polite invitation, perhaps something less) and "capers": the suggestion of Anacreontic piquancy and elegance is limited to Anacreontic *scale*. And the poem is rife with such tricks of parsimonious generosity. In the turn from line 11 to line 12 – "a short-leg'd hen, / If" – both rhythm and conditional grammar signal the inevitable drag of necessity on festivity. No matter how enticing the recipe, eggs cannot fill, nor wine and lemons sauce, a hen that won't materialize. More is less ("a coney / Is not to be despair'd of") and nominal detail comes to feel haunted by subjunction and condition: "partrich, pheasant, wood-cock, of which some / May yet be there; and godwit, if we can" (lines 18–19). Remarkably, this menu converts belly-hunger into an emptier emptiness, an appetite increasingly ontological.

This conversion is strategic; it readies us for a subsequent turn. With our appetites thus aroused and complicated, the sustenance that Jonson next promises betrays the habitual bias of the humanist:

> Knat, raile, and ruffe too. How so ere, my man
> Shall reade a piece of VIRGIL, TACITUS,
>> LIVIE, or of some better booke to us,
> Of which wee'll speake our minds, amidst our meate.

(lines 20–23)

Here the conversion of belly-hunger into more consuming appetites receives settled representation, for under the steadying influence of classical books, mind finds a place "amidst our meate."[10] Yet the attention to the uncertain

---

[10] The sway of the subjunctive thereby ends here, deliberately, at the very center of the poem; nothing could have more of the welcome, tonic certainty of line 26: "Digestive cheese, and fruit there sure will bee."

material – even creaturely – substrate of intellectual exchange and literary "entertaynment" gives a personal – even idiosyncratic – urgency to the poem's engagement with imitation – which engagement, implicit all along, is wryly announced in the poem's next line, when Jonson promises the purity of the proffered literary entertainment: "And Ile professe no verses to repeate" (line 24).

In a profound sense, the promise is breached even as it's made, for Jonson is here repeating Martial's verse, "plus ego polliceor: nil recitabo tibi" (I promise something more: I will recite nothing to you, *Epigrams*, XI.52, l.16). Indeed, "Inviting a Friend to Supper" is almost entirely a translation from Martial, a conflation of several such invitation poems:

> vinum tu facies bonum bibendo

[The wine you will make good by drinking it] (*Epigrams*, V.78, line 16)

> cetera nosse cupis?
> mentiar, ut venias: pisces, coloephia, sumen,
> et chortis saturas atque paludis aves

[Do you want to know the rest? I'll lie to make you come: fish, collops, sow's udder, and fat birds of the poultry yard and the marsh] (XI.52, lines 12–14)

It will be properly objected that the promise "no verses to repeate" means something else, that Jonson promises to recite no verses of his own. This is sensible enough, if unresponsive to the (slightly heavy) archness that gives contour to the poem. The host's promise of self-effacement should not be taken in isolation, for it joins a pervasive modesty voiced as a response to the careful contingency of the world; whenever individual will expands to express itself in festivity, it finds itself defined by dearth. Such measured and dispossessed ethics are the perfect analogue to an imitative poetics, with its lid on the individual poetic will. *Imitatio* makes possible a profoundly articulate poetic individuality, a voice made both quiet and personal by its knowing submission to others' voices.

Of course, Early Modern theories of imitation did not feature its submissiveness.[11] Though there are many variables in the theory and practice of

Although it would be pleasant to identify Richard Brome as the serving-man who reads to Jonson and his guest, there are too many uncertainties in play. The poem cannot be securely dated, though of course 1616, when it was printed in the Folio *Works* is a *terminus ad quem*. Like Riggs (*Ben Jonson: A Life* [Cambridge, Mass.: Harvard University Press, 1989], 230), I believe that the poem postdates the discovery of the Gunpowder Plot; Riggs argues from a sense that the poem concerns a specific dinner party which, he feels, would have been held while Jonson was living in St. Anne's in the Blackfriars. It is equally difficult to say just when Brome entered Jonson's service, though Jonson refers to "his man, Master *Broome*," in *Bartholomew Fair* in 1614.

[11] Thomas M. Greene, *The Light in Troy: Imitation and Discovery in Renaissance Poetry*, particularly chapter 9.

sixteenth-century education, imitation had been consistently understood as a means of acquiring symbolic capital, *copia*. It is therefore remarkable that Jonson should place imitative practice in "Inviting A Friend to Supper" under the aegis of scarcity, and not of *copia* – or rather that he should locate imitation between *copia* and scarcity, on a brink between largesse and insufficiency. The profession "no verses to repeete" is, then, the wry profession of a nostalgic, but peculiarly modern poet, peculiarly modern because self-consciously dispossessed.

The temperature of disabused wit continues to rise as the poem proceeds; and it rises to the precise occasion of an unpredictable literary market. Having promised that the meagre fare will be made copious with literary plenty, having bettered the promise with his gallant profession of further restraint, Jonson (again) submits that modern hospitality itself puts some things out of his control:

> And Ile professe no verses to repeate:
> To this, if aught appeare, which I not know of,
> That will the pastrie, not my paper show of.

>   (lines 24–26)

His verses may obtrude after all, because the evening's pastry – it is the first suggestion that pastry might enrich the moderate repast – the pastry will have come wrapped in printer's waste paper, sheets from unsold copies of Jonson's poetry.[12] The pastry would presumably have been unwrapped before being brought to the table, but because the shortening in baked goods made the ink on printed sheets fugitive, the pastry could still take an imprint from its wrapper, so that by an untidy miracle of chemistry Jonson's guests might apprehend too much of a feast of words. The publicity of print invades the private party.

One must be quite clear about the biographical timbre of this invasion. Jonson had a literary career distributed across several milieux, each more or less distinguishable by degree of publicity: plays for the private theaters, masques for the court, progress verses for the public streets, epistle, ode, and epigram for private consumption. (This latter medium is crucial: for all of his involvement with various publicities, Jonson was deeply enmeshed in the private culture of manuscript circulation, as widely transcribed a poet as any of his contemporaries, especially so, perhaps, because of his gifts as a lyricist.) Print cuts across all these milieux, complicating and sometimes disrupting the social logic of writing as it goes. In "Inviting a Friend to Supper" the imagined privacies of manuscript *vers de société*, the thoughtful iterations of *translatio*, are suddenly and specifically disrupted by the mindless repetitions of mechanical reproduction.

---

[12] I am indebted here to Roger A. Cognard's gloss, "Jonson's 'Inviting a Friend to Supper,' " *The Explicator*, 37:3 (1979): 3–4. The bemused imagining of writings transformed into waste paper is an ancient *topos*, at least as old as Horace (e.g., *Epistles*, II,1,267–70), and no doubt older.

The market in print serves up the printed pastry as the end of a history of imitation, its dessert. We may speak of the literary pastry as an instance of "automatic plagiarism," a term I used in an earlier chapter to describe how Heywood construes the conjunction of his translations and Shakespeare's name in Jaggard's *Passionate Pilgrim* (and so attempts to sort out the various meanings of the possessive constructions in this sentence, to distinguish and stabilize their meanings). Heywood defends against Jaggard and the press, seeking attributive justice; Jonson chuckles over the press, exposing the crude mechanics of its transmission, and measuring them against the delicacies of neo-classicist tradition. Their different responses, substantially but not exclusively determined by their different circumstances in the literary marketplace, manifest different authorial self-conceptions, different configurations of the bibliographic ego, selves both reflected and disarticulated in the unpolished mirror of the book-trade.

The automatism of the pastry, which mimics the automatism of the page, brings the iterability of the literary text to the point of parody; both page and pastry are presented as comic versions of literary imitation. This comic torsion prepares for a final turn which earlier commentators usually treat as little more than a tonal excrescence:

> But that, which most doth take my *Muse*, and mee,
> Is a pure cup of rich *Canary*-wine,
> Which is the *Mermaids*, now, but shall be mine
>
> . . .
>
> Of this we will sup free, but moderately,
> And we will have no *Pooly*, or *Parrot* by;
> Nor shall our cups make any guiltie men:
> But, at our parting, we will be, as when
> We innocently met. No simple word,
> That shall be utter'd at our mirthfull boord,
> Shall make us sad next morning: or affright
> The libertie, that wee'll enjoy to night.

(lines 28–30, 35–42)

The publicity from which private festivity here guards itself is the secretive violence of a repressive State: Poley and Parrat were professional informers.[13] As they make their non-presence felt, we are invited to recall that, sometimes, the iterability of the word has little to do with the automatisms of an amorphous

---

[13] Mark Eccles did the most authoritative detective work on the two men in 1937, though he was unable to determine whether Jonson was referring to Henry or William Parrat; "Jonson and the Spies," *Review of English Studies*, 13 (1937): 385–97. He did find reference to a prisoner at Newgate who filed complaints of bribery against one "Paratt."

Eerily, this is again a textual occasion for *imitatio*. Compare the (only slightly less topical) model in Martial's Epigram X.48; Horace's use of the topos (*Epistles*, I.5, lines 24–25) is extremely abstract.

marketplace. A Poll, a Parrot – these less-than-men give satisfaction to their keepers (Walsingham was one) by their distorted repetition of the words of others, a repetition neither mechanical, nor quite human. By virtue of his casual satiric play on their names, Jonson implies the slipperiness of their very being, their aptitude for the slide from human agency to mere instrumentality. "Inviting a Friend to Supper" thus resolves itself as a political poem, its final evocation of "libertie" reflecting upon the career of imitation in a commercial milieu apt to iterations both uncannily automatic and slavishly expedient. Recitation of verse; print publication that acquires, in the native English marketplace, its own comic extension into the bake-shop; and the fatal parrotings of government spies provide a steadily sinking sequence of analogues for the imitative composition of this invitation.

As is often the case in the work of this poet of relentless exposure and self-exposure, satire may redound upon the satirist. Jonson, it's now surmised, was not only spied upon in the nineties, but may have done a turn as an informant around the time of the Gunpowder Plot; whether or not Jonson spied on the embattled Catholic community in 1605, he dined in ordinaries with several of the key conspirators within four weeks of the discovery of the Plot. The dating of this poem remains uncertain – few scholars believe it to have been written before this time, and some believe it to have been written a good deal later – but even if we could confidently date the poem, we could not begin to assess the presence and relative proportions of self-consciousness, cynicism, false consciousness, rue, or innocence in the reassurance, "Nor shall our cups make any guiltie men." Whatever the psychological charge that hovers round the constellation of spy, parrot, printed pastry, all of these figures reflect gloomily on the work of imitation in the age of mechanical reproduction, exposing a fear that the imitative poet may be at best merely a cultural functionary, a plagiaristical mouthpiece and no more.

McLuhan's influential conception, Typographical Man, was, he believed, a species rapidly evolving into something else under the environmental pressure of new twentieth-century media, a species made identifiable *as* a species in the era of its passing. The taxonomic coherence of this historical species was produced by the long regime of print, which had selected for "typographical" traits during the early decades and centuries of printing. But early in the regime of print, the outward cultural praxis of printed books had not yet been thoroughly settled, and the same may be said of the inward disposition of typographical men: it was many years before the aptitudes and expectations that McLuhan described became established with all the security of a dominant historical strain. That is why we can observe a large range of responses to early English print culture, some more, and some less adaptive, some less intense, some – like Jonson's – very intense indeed. This is, as I suggested above, a matter of temperamental attunement to cultural conditions, an individual configuration of the bibliographic ego. For all his engagement with the various spheres of manuscript circulation, print had unusual resonance for Jonson, if only because it answered to his uneasy interest in all aspects and instruments of publicity. Since Jonson is such an important witness to institutional developments in print culture, I want to linger a bit longer over what "Inviting a Friend to Supper", together with some closely related Jonsonian texts, discloses about his idiosyncratic aptitude for such witness.

We can begin with a passage that has been quoted with perhaps stultifying frequency, a paragraph from Jonson's compendium of theoretical commonplaces, the *Discoveries*:

> The third requisite in our *Poet*, or Maker, is *Imitation*, to bee able to convert the substance, or Riches of an other *Poet*, to his owne use. To make choise of one excellent man above the rest, and so to follow him, till he grow very *Hee*: or, so like him, as the Copie may be mistaken for the Principall. Not, as a Creature, that swallowes, what it takes in, crude, raw, or indigested; but, that feedes with an Appetite, and hath a Stomacke to concoct, divide, and turne all into nourishment. (*Discoveries*, 2466–75)

The metaphor is traditional, but its special relevance to the culinary idiom of "Inviting a Friend to Supper," to central themes in Jonson's poems and plays, and to Jonson's vocation (what might now be designated "his incarnation as a poet") needs to be acknowledged.[14] Perhaps it is a small point to remark on the obtrusions of the bodily in the public career of one whom Francis Andrewes would commemorate as "a Bigg fatt man, that spake in Ryme."[15] On crucial poetic occasions, Jonson attends to matters of cuisine with special seriousness: in the mock-*paragone* of *Neptune's Triumph for the Return of Albion*, the eloquent Cook speaks for a half-serious Jonson when he says that "a good *Poet* differs nothing at all from a *Master-Cooke*. Eithers Art is the wisedome of the Mind" (lines 41–42).[16] As a masque-maker, Jonson was particularly concerned that his devices should have the rhetorical power to move their audiences to virtuous and heroic action, and he surely envied the Cook's authority over human bodily impulses.[17] By the same token, the characteristic choice of gourmandize as a special sign of vice betrays a curious aspect of Jonson's private mythology:

[14] The *locus classicus* of this metaphor is Quintilian (*Institutiones*, X.i.19), where it serves, significantly, as part of an argument about the superiority of reading to listening, but it is much older.
  Richard Peterson has discussed this passage from the *Discoveries* with particular shrewdness in "Poet as Vessel," in *Imitation and Praise*, 112–57. Jonson made a public matter of his corporeality. In "My Picture Left in Scotland" he complains that an unnamed beloved could already have "Told seven and fortie years, / Read so much wast, as she cannot imbrace / My mountaine belly, and my rockie face" (lines 14–17).

[15] From a poem by Francis Andrewes in Harley 4955, f. 166b, H&S, 11:388.

[16] The passage is itself an imitation, based on a commonplace from Athenaeus and appropriated later in Jonson's career, in *The Staple of Newes*.

[17] Jonson's defense of his decision to publish an annotated *Hymenaei*, one of the early maneuvers in the quarrel with Jones, ends with a sustained figure of obvious relevance here: "howsoever some may squemishly crie out, that all endevour of *learning*, and *sharpnesse* in these transitorie

for Comus in *Pleasure Reconciled to Virtue*, for Sir Epicure Mammon and Volpone, elaborately conceived gluttony is a central act of self-indulgence, which only confirms the sense one gets of the ideal Jonsonian Self as That Which Has Dined Appropriately.

The purposed seduction in *Volpone* (III.vii) is especially pertinent here, since mere lechery is nearly overwhelmed by the extravagance of the menu Sir Epicure proposes:

> The heads of parrats, tongues of nightingales,
> The braines of peacoks, and of estriches
> Shall be our food: and, could we get the phoenix,
> (Though nature lost her kind) shee were our dish
>
> (III.vii.202–05)

This Epicurean fantasy – on themes by Pliny and Lampridius – is placed within the attractive, though curious, context of Jonson's most famous and most melodious imitations, the adaptations of Catullus' "*Vivamus, mea Lesbia, atque amemus*," and "*Quaeris, quot mihi bassationes*" (*Carmina*, V and VII). What makes this such a curious context is that, however attractive, the imitations (as well as the imagined feasts) are specified as the work of an almost willfully unstable self. Volpone seems to rejoice in his own self-desertions, though Celia is blamed for that instability:

> applaud thy beauties miracle;
> 'Tis thy great worke: that hath, not now alone,
> But sundry times, rays'd me, in severall shapes,
> And, but this morning, like a mountebanke,
> To see thee at thy windore. I, before
> I would have left my practice, for thy love,
> In varying figures, I would have contended
> With the blue PROTEUS, or the horned *Floud*.
>
> (III.vii.146–53)

It is a commonplace of criticism that, for Jonson, such instability of self is the quintessence of vice. The commonplace can be stretched. An ethics of stability provides a strict context for the practice of imitation; it is this play's version of that critique of imitation implied by the imaginative intrusions of Poley and

---

devices especially, where it steps beyond their little, or (let me not wrong 'hem) no braine at all, is superfluous; I am contented, these fastidious *stomachs* should leave my full tables, and enjoy at home, their cleane emptie trenchers, fittest for such ayrie tasts: where perhaps a few *Italian* herbs, pick'd up, and made into a *sallade*, may find sweeter acceptance, than all, the most nourishing, and sound meates of the world" (lines 19–28). The analogy between poetry and cookery may have been with Jonson for some time, perhaps since *Every Man Out of His Humour*; see Terrance Dunford, "Consumption of the World: Reading, Eating and Imitation in *Every Man Out of His Humour*," *ELR* 14 (1984), 131–47.

Parrat in "Inviting a Friend To Supper."[18] Volpone here implicates both Jonson the actor and (more stringently) Jonson the imitative poet: recall that Jonson would lift Volpone's imitations of Catullus and claim them as his own by including them in *The Forest*, a collection of those poems most characteristically, most quintessentially, his own. As in "Inviting a Friend to Supper" morally over-coded cuisine haunts the practice of close imitation. The stable Jonsonian self must scruple over all forms of ingestion.[19]

Encouraging the imitative poet "so to follow" his model that "he grow very *Hee*: or, so like him, as the Copie may be mistaken for the Principall," Jonson significantly adjusts the classical figure of dietary imitation, representing the relation between *texts* as a nutritive relation between *poets* – that is, as a personal matter, one that serves the imitative artist more than the imitative art.[20] The terms of this description of an ideal *imitatio* suggest the uncertainties of identity that haunt imitation at this particular historical moment. As we saw in the previous chapter, Shakespeare connects those uncertainties with anxieties about his upstart social status, anxieties that seem to be oedipal in structure, albeit under a great deal of mature control; in the case of Jonson's more creaturely imagination and less settled temperament, imitation is a more unsettled practice. The blithe identifications of infantile feeding may be remembered with nostalgia – "till he grow very *Hee*" – but for the mature poet-critic identification must be corrected to similitude – "so like him." The correction traces the scruple that hovers over imitation in an age of emergent plagiarism, willful and automatic.[21] The shift argues for a differentiated self, warding off a nostalgia

---

[18] It may be no more than a wonderful coincidence that Henry Parrat published a sneering epigram against *Volpone* in his own satiric bird-book, *Laquei Ridiculosi, or Springes for Woodcocks* (1613); the epigram accuses Jonson, by means of the classic *topos*, of plagiarism:

> Put off thy Buskins (*Sophocles* the great,)
> And Morter tread with thy disdained shancks,
> Thou think'st thy skill hath done a wondrous feat,
> For which the world should give thee many thancks:
> > Alas, it seemes thy feathers are but loose,
> > Pluckt from a Swanne, and set upon a Goose.
>
> > (I:163; G₁ᵛ; cited H&S, XI:369)

[19] Haunting this conjunction of gourmandize, moral outrage, and imitation is not only Quintilian and Horace, but also a more ancient model of dieted imitation. In *The Frogs* (lines 937–43), Euripides explains to Aeschylus – although the explanation is really a self-advertisement for the benefit of Dionysus, who is also present – how he has received from Aeschylus a tradition of tragedy that is as over-ingenious, as over-elaborate as Volpone's cuisine; he boasts that his own quite critical creative practice has been a rigorous therapy of imitative diet.

[20] See G. W. Pigman, "Versions of Imitation in the Renaissance," *Renaissance Quarterly* 33 (1980), 1–32 and Greene, *The Light in Troy*, 74, 275–76. Greene remarks on how Jonson forsakes the conventional imitative goal, resemblance, for identification; neither Greene nor Pigman makes explicit Jonson's curiously emphatic shift from imitation of poems to imitation of poets.

[21] Much the same scruple haunts *Epigrams*, 112, "To a Weak Gamester in Poetry," in which Jonson describes a poetaster who steadily dogs Jonson's practice, shifting genres each time the poet does. The knowing reader will recognize that Jonson mirrors the mirroring, for the epigram is

available neither to adults nor to possessive individualists. Only at this point does Jonson elaborate the digestive metaphor, insisting that the modern poet fully internalizes, decomposes, and transforms the ancient, securing the poetic ego.

The development of this private defense began many years earlier; so did the process of incorporating Martial. Of course, in the late 1590s, the "one excellent man" whom Jonson vociferously chose to follow above the rest was Horace, yet even at this early date, the inappropriateness of this "choise" must have been as obvious to Jonson's colleagues as it seems to us: it hardly takes hindsight to alert one to the very un-Horatian fervor of Horace as Jonson portrays him in *Poetaster*. One way of mapping Jonson's creative development would be to follow the process by which other literary models – Aristophanes, Lucian, Cicero, but above all, Martial – jostle Horace, though this is perhaps to do little more than trace how asperity disabled mild cunning, how gravity is shaken by rage.[22] That Jonson was too bilious to digest Horace is, at any rate, clear enough in *Poetaster*, so it is more than a little ironic that the Jonsonian myth of a stabilizing imitative nutrition should have first shown itself in this play. It is not in the least ironic, however, that this play also provided Jonson the occasion to make his first serious imitative appropriation from Martial. When a lyric by the poetaster, Crispinus, is performed in Act IV, Jonson's Tibullus recognizes it and exclaims "Why the ditti's all borrowed; 'tis HORACES: hang him *plagiary*" (IV.iii.95–96). With the revival of Martial's legal metaphor, Jonson becomes the second European writer, to my knowledge, to use the term in a modern language.[23]

The reconstruction of of the Augustan cultural scene in *Poetaster* was one of Jonson's most audacious experiments in extreme neo-classicism, comparable to "Inviting a Friend to Supper" or *Catiline*: like those other curious achievements, it includes substantial passages (whole scenes in the case of the plays) translated or quite closely imitated from Latin originals. As in "Inviting a Friend to Supper," the work of rendering important Latin texts in the vernacular, a practice built into humanist educational discipline, is welded to a meditation on a range of imitative practices that do not have such institutional sanction. That meditation is given the juridical inflection that was already becoming one

itself a close imitation of Martial (XII.94); see Stella Revard "Classicism and Neo-Classicism in Jonson's *Epigrams* and *The Forrest*," *Ben Jonson's 1616 Folio*, 147.

[22] Even the free imitation of Horace's *Satires* II.i inserted into the Folio *Poetaster* as act III, scene v, is not brought to conclusion without an interpolation from Martial (*Epigrams*, X.33, lines 133–5). On Jonsonian rage, see William Kerrigan, "Ben Jonson Full of Shame and Scorn," *Ben Jonson: Quadricentennial Essays*, 199–217 and Ian Donaldson, "Jonson and Anger," *Yearbook of English Studies, Satire Special Number*, 14 (1984), 56–71.

[23] As noted above, Jonson follows Hall in *Virgidemiae*, follows him with nicely stinging cunning. As will be noted below, the poet apparently designated plagiarist in *Poetaster* is Marston, who had been nettled a few years earlier by Hall's claim, in *Virgidemiae*, to be the first to write classical satire in English. Marston had experienced secondarity as a stigma; Jonson announces that Marston's secondarity is more properly to be experienced as a crime.

of Jonson's signatures, hence the special appropriateness of appropriating Martial's criminalizing term. Like many of his plays, *Poetaster* ends with a trial, in this case the trial, for calumny, of two poets –

The one by the name of RUFUS LABERIUS CRISPINUS, *aliàs* CRISPINAS, Poetaster, *and* plagiary: *the other, by the name of* DEMETRIUS FANNIUS, play-dresser, *and* plagiary (V.iii.217–20)

– who seem to represent Marston and Dekker.[24] This accusation of plagiarism, quite secondary to that of calumny, is not directly prosecuted. (In the case of Crispinus, the justice of the accusation has already been demonstrated in III.iv.) But the poems attributed to the calumniators are given animated descriptions during the final trial, as bastards (V.iii.272, and cf. 266–68) – like slaves, disabled before the law and dubiously tethered to the poet. Moreover, plagiarism remains an issue throughout this scene, since it was one of the crimes that had been part of their own calumnies.[25] In his pasquil against Horace, read as evidence during the trial, Demetrius alleges with mock caution

> (but that I would not be thought a prater)
> I could tell you, he were a translater.
> I know the authors from whence ha's stole,
> And could trace him too, but that I understand 'hem not
>   full and whole
>
> (V.iii.310–13)

This not only probes the relation between sanctioned and unsanctioned imitation but, by exploiting the semantic range in English of "translation," neatly raises the question of the specific place of humanist inter-linguistic translation within a broad spectrum of imitative practices.

The poetasters' attack elicits a typically Jonsonian pair of responses: authoritative defense and humiliating punishment. Virgil responds to Demetrius on Horace's behalf, cooly advancing the strongest possible claims for *imitatio* –

> And, for his true use of translating men,
> It still hath bin a worke of as much palme
> In cleerest judgement, as t'invent, or make.
>
> (v.iii.365–67)

It may be noted that Virgil not only keeps alive the ambiguity of "translation," retaining inter-linguistic translation as a kind of leading case for a whole range

---

[24] Laberius was an author of mimes and Crispinus was a poet who once challenged Horace to a competition to see who could compose verse the most quickly; Demetrius was the carping musician, Fannius, the *ineptus* of Horace's *Satires*, I.x.79–80.

[25] It had also been a charge levelled against Crites, the Jonson-figure of *Cynthia's Revels*, III.ii.60–62.

of imitative practices, but that he also specifies the object of imitation as the emulable poets themselves, "very Hee." For Jonson, imitation is always gravely personal.[26]

Hoc volo

At first he made low shifts, would picke and gleane,
Buy the reversions of old playes; now growne
To 'a little wealth, and credit in the *scene*,
He takes up all, makes each mans wit his owne.
And, told of this, he slights it. Tut, such crimes
The sluggish gaping auditor devoures;
He markes not whose 'twas first: and after-times
May judge it to be his, as well as ours.
("On Poet-Ape," *Epigrams*, LVI, lines 5–12)

The final song in *Poetaster* concludes by stigmatizing unthinking imitation – "Apes are apes though clothed in scarlet." The sumptuary turn of the aphorism links the concerns of *Poetaster* with those of Jonson's other early plays. It is unnecessary to do more than allude here to Jonathan Haynes's wonderfully nuanced discussion of aping in Jonson's comical satires: as Haynes shows, Jonsonian realism is a hall of mirrors, for what it depicts is a social system of competitive copying, the glass of fashion.[27] At the earnest behest of the gull, the sharper reduces social behavior to iterable formulae of posture, gesture, and phrase. Imitation subsides into mirroring in a parody of humanist pedagogy as novices learn not only how to fence, but how to wear their clothes, how to take tobacco, how to insult. The revived use of the antique chorus in *Every Man Out Of His Humour* appears in this context as a good deal more than dutiful neo-classicism, for the persistent rhythm of public performance, observation, critically emulous commentary, and responsive performance is itself a representation of social reality in late Elizabethan London. By thus absorbing the theatrical convention of allowing gallant members of the audience a place on stage into the dramatic structure proper, Jonson indicates the place of the theater within a culture of copying, the indebtedness of realist comedy to a milieu of wit, and the mirroring indebtedness of wit to comedy. It is hardly surprising, therefore, that those whom Jonson would come to call *plagiaries* in *Poetaster*, should appear in these other comical satires. In *Cynthia's Revels*, Anaides

---

[26] Jonson more eerily adumbrates "Inviting a Friend to Supper" in the punishment served up to Crispinus. His libel had been read at the trial along with Demetrius-Dekker's, and his was full of such Marstonian terms as "glibberie," "magnificate," "cothurnall," "snotteries" and "bespawled." In a therapy imitated from Lucian's *Lexiphanes*, Horace and Virgil administer a purgative to Crispinus, a negative anticipation of Jonson's culinary epigram: he spends the balance of the scene vomiting up his glibbery vocabulary.

[27] Thus Asper in the opening "Chorus" of *Every Man Out of His Humour*: "Well I will scourge those apes; / And to these courteous eyes oppose a mirrour, / As large as is the stage, whereon we act" (lines 117–19).

determines to accuse Crites, the Jonson-figure of that play, of plagiarism and in terms almost identical to those of Demetrius's libel against Horace. In *Every Man In His Humour*, the poetaster, Matthew, first demonstrates his enthusiasm for poetry by reading from a copy of *The Spanish Tragedy* and then immediately thereafter, by reciting a pastiche of bits from Daniel and Marlowe. "Where's this?" asks Bobadill, to which Matthew proudly responds, "This sir, a toy of mine owne" (I.iii.149–50), convinced that his pastiche is virtually indistinguishable from *echt* Kyd. Later in the play he recites portions of "Hero and Leander," claiming them as his own, provoking Lorenzo/Knowell to splutter "Hang him filching rogue, steale from the deade? its worse then sacriledge" (III.iv.77–78).

The competitive atmosphere that led to the War of the Theaters is the same atmosphere that fostered the large achievements of Jonsonian realism, with its bristling ethics of imitation.[28] This atmosphere, this moment, was, I think, the most important single moment in Jonson's artistic life. He was still in his twenties when he wrote *Poetaster*, but was already recognizable as the most formally inventive playwright in England (with only one possible challenger). He had unwisely promoted himself in other terms, as a major critic of court and urban mores, and it was this self-promotion that was most provoking to the other combatants in the War of the Theaters. The War sputtered and flared at the end of a period of extraordinary personal ferment for Jonson: between 1597 and 1601, he was jailed three times – first for sedition, then for manslaughter, and finally for debt; he changed his profession twice and religion once; and he wrote and collaborated on his first plays. Waves of enthusiasm and fury will well up from this turbulent personal and professional *fons* throughout the rest of his career: while most careers can be mapped as a development, Jonson's may be distinctively mapped in terms of resurgences. The poems, the masques, and the "great" plays – *Volpone, The Alchemist, Bartholomew Fair* (to say nothing of the imperfectly brilliant *Sejanus, Epicoene*, and *The Staple of News*) – derive inspiration and energy from the early work as Jonson recalls and re-imagines the events of the late nineties and revises, edits, and reprints the writings of those years. His developing efforts to control all aspects of dissemination and reception (efforts occasionally remitted for quite local polemical purposes), his semio-tyranny, rehearse the attack on the misappropriation of texts and the uncritical replication of social routines that were his distinguishing concerns during the War of the Theaters. Such poems as "On Poet-Ape," "To Fine Grand," "To Prowl the Plagiary," or "On Playwright" (*Epigrams*, 56, 73, 81, and 100) are just such rehearsals, as is "Inviting a Friend to Supper."

I have already made much of the way in which that particular rehearsal – with its brilliant device of situating plagiarism in a comparative matrix with classical imitation, spying, and the automatic iterations of parrot and press – at

---

[28] This atmosphere was not merely a local, theatrical phenomenon. The efflorescence of non-dramatic satire at this time similarly contributed to exuberant reflection on what Marston calls "servile imitation" (attacking Joseph Hall in the ninth satire of his *Scourge of Villainie*, G7ᵛ).

once elaborates and specifies the earlier concerns. There is much to explain this elaboration: Jonson's experience of print publication, the specific effects of his work in new media and of his encounters with new competitors, new developments in the ways property in ideas was asserted under Elizabeth and James.[29] One other explanation may be usefully advanced here and that is the particular effect of Martial on Jonson's thinking.[30]

That influence is not reducible to his having offered Jonson the brilliant metaphor of plagiarism.[31] As Jonson developed as a non-dramatic poet and publishing writer, he would find in Martial's *Epigrams* an unabashed confession of authorial vanity, the writer exultant among a multitude of readers:

> *Laudat, amat, cantat nostros mea Roma libellos,*
> *meque sinus omnes, me manus omnis habet.*
> *ecce rubet quidam, pallet, stupet, oscitat, odit.*
> *hoc volo: nunc nobis carmina nostra placent.*

(Translation cannot do much justice to the chortle of Martial's consonantal clutter, the jostling crowd of verbs, the droll, self-pleasing shuttle from first person plural to singular to plural –)

[My Rome praises our little books, loves them, recites them; I am in every pocket, every hand. Look, somebody turns red, turns pale, is dazed, yawns, is disgusted. This I want. Now our poems please us.] [*Epigrams*, VI.60]

This bubbling egotism infuses a persistent attention to the social, commercial, and material circumstance of poetry unrivalled in Roman literature.[32]

---

[29] All but the last of these will be taken up in the next chapter; the new proprietary assertions are discussed in chapters 4 and 5 of *The Author's Due*.

[30] I shall concentrate here merely on the "bibliographic" influence of Martial, but the influence was wider and deeper. Martial inspired not only Jonson's poems but his conversation, and although Jonson's non-dramatic poetry eschews the obscenity that dominates Martial's *Epigrams*, he was eager to absorb Martial's achievements in the poetry of hospitality and generosity. For more general discussions of Martial's influence on Jonson's non-dramatic poetry, see Ann Baynes Coiro, *Robert Herrick's Hesperides and the Epigram Book Tradition* (Baltimore: Johns Hopkins University Press, 1988), 78–104 and Stella Revard, "Classicism and Neo-Classicism," 140–51.

[31] In fact, Jonson can hardly be claimed to have responded with particular sensitivity to Martial's term when he first made use of it. His earlier description of literary misappropriation as grave-robbing (in *Every Man In*) loosely anticipates the description of the revived play as a ghost (in the Induction to *Poetaster*) and both descriptions bear some resemblance to Martial's criminalizing metaphor of the misappropriated poem as kidnapped slave. Jonson's figure renders the offense a trifle more uncanny, "worse then sacriledge", though it is also somewhat less probing than Martial's.

Having surveyed Jonson's annotations in the various editions of Martial that he owned, David McPherson concludes, "The care with which he studied Martial is truly impressive" ("Ben Jonson's Library and Marginalia: An Annotated Catalogue," *Studies in Philology*, 71 (1974), 70.

[32] The other important record of the material culture of books (though not of poetry) is Cicero's *Atticus*.

Attunement to the sociable comedy of material life distinguishes Martial as much as the scabrous eroticism does. Imitating Horace, who had counselled his verses to preserve their pre-editorial modesty, Martial gives a rougher evocation of what lies in store for the book that dares to forsake his *scrinia* for the shops of Argiletum. He warns his poems of the "rhinocerote's nose" (I give Jonson's rendering, from *Epigrams*, 28.4) of Rome's typical critic, though he understands that the rhinoceran sneers of the Roman literati may seem preferable to the punishments inflicted by the author – his brutal scorings and rough erasures (I.iii). Martial's Augustan predecessors might frequently write fables on the fate of their lines or books, but when Martial speaks of his books, they are represented as objects, susceptible to vermin (VI.61, XI.1, *et al.*), rain (III.100), and fire (V.53). Our attention is turned to the labor of binding, scouring, and trimming the pages of a codex (I.117 and IV.10); to the size of various codices, tablets, and scrolls (I.2, II.1, II.6); to the purple covers that adorn cherished scrolls and the precious headpieces of their *umbilici* (III.2, V.6, VIII.72), and to the stains and fraying that the papyrus suffers when a scroll is frequently rolled and rerolled (X.93). We are alerted to the fit of poem to the page of a codex (X.1, X.59) and so encouraged to an attention to layout that would powerfully influence Jonsonian practice. But what was even more influential than Martial's attention to the shape, heft, texture, and material substance of books was his rendering of the social mechanics of Roman literary circulation – or, rather, of literary circulations, for Martial is particularly sensitive to the disarticulated systems of exchange in which the physical book participated.

Jonson would find the variable circumstance of Jacobean literature adumbrated in Martial's description of Roman book culture:

> Non urbana mea tantum Pipleide gaudent
>   otia nec vacuis auribus ista damus,
> sed meus in Geticis ad Martia signa pruinis
>   a rigidio teritur centurione liber,
> dicitur et nostros cantare Britannia versus.

[Not alone does Rome's leisure rejoice in my *Pipleis*, nor do I give these pieces only to empty ears. My book is thumbed by hard centurions beside Mars' standards in Getic frosts, and Britain is said to recite my verses] [*Epigrams*, XI.3.1–5]

The norms of Latin literary consumption were radically transformed by the simple fact of Rome's imperial expansion; a Renaissance English reader could reflect that English literary consumption had also changed, albeit by the more complex interaction of expanded and altered schooling, print publication, and subtly augmented physical and social mobility in the course of the preceding century. Martial's observations on the sheer geographical extent of his audience again recur to an Augustan *topos*, but he extends the observation in ways that would resonate in Early Modern England.[33] For Martial, the effect of expanded consumption is to unsettle an old image of the social relation of reader and writer; patronage relations based on direct contact were now felt to be incongruous with the reality of contemporary consumption.[34] He makes this the occasion of complaint: "*quid potest? nescit sacculus ista meus*" (What's the use? My purse knows nothing of all that; line 6). As Jonson's would be, Martial's response is conservative (although Martial's conservatism has a nice whiff of cynicism), for his purse gapes reverently for the advent of a new Maecenas (lines 7–10), a single patron to distill the poet's popularity into cash.[35] Here *exactly* is Jonson's straddling social posture, the dual presence in coterie and market, the poem as gift and as goods.

Despite such important studies as William V. Harris's *Ancient Literacy* it remains quite difficult to reconstruct the literary sociology and economics of Imperial Rome, but a good deal of what we know of this subject has been gleaned, as Jonson and his contemporaries would have gleaned it, from Martial's poems.[36] From the epigram cited above we gather that, by the first century CE, modest networks had been established for distributing contemporary literature to the imperial provinces – though this can also be inferred from Pliny the Younger, and from Horace, Ovid, and Propertius before them.[37] Although there is no reason to allege new norms of mass scriptorial book production (Atticus' effort on behalf of Cicero and Varro was almost certainly unusual), we can also learn from Martial's *Epigrams* (IV.72) that booksellers had begun stocking their shops with at least a certain number of exemplars so that a

---

[33] For other poems on provincial literary consumption, see IX.84 and X.78.

[34] On the transformation of literary fame in the imperial period, see Erich Auerbach, "The Western Public and its Language," from *Literary Language and Its Public in Late Latin Antiquity and in the Latin Middle Ages*, trans. Ralph Mannheim, *Bollingen Series*, 74 (New York: Random House, 1965), 237–47.

[35] But cf. IV.27. Martial describes the new instability of the poet's position as essentially aleatory in the obscure first poem of Book XIII. It is tempting, but it would be misleading to suppose that its conclusion – *haec mihi charta nuces, haec est mihi charta fritillus: / alea nec damnum nec facit ista lucrum* (This paper is my nuts, this paper my dice-box; such gambling brings neither loss nor gain; lines 7–8) – suggests the modern uncertainties specific to a retail market.

[36] Harris, *Ancient Literacy* (Cambridge, Mass.: Harvard University Press, 1989), and see also Starr, "Circulation" and E. J. Kenney, "Books and Readers in the Roman World," *The Cambridge History of Classical Literature, II: Latin Literature*, ed. E. J. Kenney (Cambridge: Cambridge University Press, 1982). Despite the fire that destroyed many of Jonson's books in 1623, three copies of Martial's poems known to have been owned by Jonson survive: the 1615 London edition of Farnaby, the 1617 Paris edition, and Scriverius' 1619 Leyden edition, the latter quite heavily annotated. Jonson is particularly fond of glossing allusions to oral sex – finds such allusions where many readers would not – and more than once defends Martial against the strictures of fastidious commentators. See McPherson, "Ben Jonson's Library," 67–70.

[37] Hence the story from Pliny in which Tacitus tells a stranger of equestrian status, "You know me by my writings" (*Epistles*, IX, 23:2); see Auerbach's gloss in *Literary Language*, 237–39, and Starr, "Circulation," 220, n. 58.

purchaser did not have to come up with a copy text himself. Martial is keenly aware that book acquisition no longer depended on a chain of more-or-less intimate social connections linking the purchaser to the author – a feeling that is refelt in the opening of Jonson's *Epigrams* and throughout that volume.[38] And although most Roman copying would still have been undertaken at the behest of an individual purchaser, some copying was now initiated by the bookseller himself, so that a book-buyer could occasionally make a purchase at the spur of the moment (I.117). Booksellers must therefore have concerned themselves with anticipating the taste of their clientele, thus providing some slight commercial focus and reinforcement to the more diffuse patterns of literary connoisseurship.[39]

Martial's own imagination plainly warmed to this small adjustment towards a *market* in books. An author would normally benefit only indirectly from his literary achievements, much as an amateur with a fine singing voice might benefit from that skill today. Such gifts attracted notice, confirm admiration, or otherwise consolidate social connections to those who could confer benefits, but Martial, whose own fame was built on ingenious insolence, contrived to flaunt the value that accrued to his poems in the booksellers's new, more impersonal system of exchange. He is amused by their cost: when an unpleasant acquaintance asks that Martial give him a copy of his poems – Martial employed a copyist to make such presentation copies – he refers him to the bookseller, Tryphon.[40] He refers his readers to Tryphon more than once:

> Omnis in hoc gracili Xeniorum turba libello
>   constabit nummis quattuor empta tibi.
> quattuor est nimium? poterit constare duobus,
>   et faciet lucrum bybliopola Tryphon.

[The entire assembly of Mottos in this slender little book will cost you four sesterces to buy. Is four too much? It could cost two, and bookseller Trypho still make a profit.] (XIII.3.1–4)

Scandalously, the volume declares itself to have been composed for sale. The book is a collection of texts to accompany gifts of delicacies – cheeses, young

---

[38] Classical scholars now speak with much more caution about antique book production than they did forty or fifty years ago. For a useful summary of the current literature on the subject, see Harris, *Ancient Literacy*, 223–25.

[39] Of course, booksellers could err in their anticipations. Kenney adduces Catullus, 95.8, and Horace, *Epistles*, 2.1.269–70, on the use of unsold, "pre-written" copies as wastepaper – of which I will have more to say in the next chapter – though he warns that "it is hazardous to press the significance of what was clearly a literary *topos*" ("Books and Readers," 22).

[40] "'*Aes dabo pro nugis et emam tua carmina sanus? / non,' inquis, 'faciam tam fatue.' nec ego*"; " 'Am I to give cash for rubbish?,' you say, 'and buy your verses in my right mind? I'll be no such fool.' No more will I" (IV.72.3–4). And cf. the more expansive I.117 in which the bookseller is Atrectus, not Tryphon.

peaches, fowl; a companion volume, the *Apophoreta*, provides texts to accompany miscellaneous trinkets. Both collections, compiled for disintegration and distribution, are guides to hospitable expenditure, but Martial undercuts the spirit of such largesse in a turn more insolent that Jonson could have dared, a turn obscurely ancestral to Jonson's withholding invitation to supper: "*hac licet hospitibus pro munere disticha mittas, / si tibi tam rarus quam mihi nummus erit*" (You can send these couplets to your guests instead of a gift, if sesterces are as scarce with you as with me; lines 5–6). This disruption of the niceties of gift-giving simply maintains the implicit force of the opening four lines from which the niceties of literary connoisseurship and community are banished, giving way to a culture of cheapening commerce.[41] Jonson might wish to rise above the smirking cleverness of such lines, but he could not but have found them arresting. In Jonson's copy of the Scriverius Martial, only book I of the *Epigrams* is as heavily annotated as are the *Xenia*: here is a volume that exposes the fragility of hospitality, that exposes hospitality to the market; here, too, is a verse that rivals food.[42]

Martial imagines the disintegrating book in other ways. Like Jonson, he enjoys referring to the fate of unpopular books, the papyrus reused to wrap fish, olives, pepper, or incense.[43] But the contrivance of the *Xenia* and *Apophoreta*, released quite early in Martial's writing career, in 85, suggested other market disintegrations, in this case the detachment of Martial's poems from Martial's name:

> Erras, meorum fur avare librorum,
> fieri poetam posse qui putas tanti,
> scriptura quanti constet et tomus vilis:
> non sex paratur aut decem sophos nummis.
> secreta quaere carmina et rudes curas
> quas novit unus scrinioque signatas
> custodit ipse virginis pater chartae,
> quae trita duo non inhorruit mento.
> mutare dominum non potest liber notus.

[You are mistaken, greedy purloiner of my books, in thinking that it costs no more to become a poet than the price of copying and a cheap length of papyrus. Applause is

[41] Cf. the brilliantly sharp couplet: "*Exigis ut nostros donem tibi, Tucca, libellos. / non faciam: nam vis vendere, non legere*" (You demand that I give you my little books, Tucca. I won't, for you want to sell them, not to read them; VII.77).
[42] McPherson, "Ben Jonson's Library," 69–70. Although the surviving copy of Jonson's Scriverius Martial dates from 1619, Farnaby tells us in the preface to his 1615 edition (A₄) that several of his emendations came from Scriverius through Jonson, who had been met the Dutch scholar in Leyden in 1613 (H&S, XI, 134–35). Since the first edition of Scriverius's Martial appeared in 1618, it seems that Jonson saw Scriverius's work in manuscript and made transcriptions from it. For Jonson's encounters in Leyden, see McPherson, "Ben Jonson Meets Daniel Heinsius," *English Language Notes*, 44 (1976), 105–9.
[43] III.2, IV.86, VI.61, XIII.1; cf. Jonson's Epigrams, 3

not to be had for six or ten sesterces. You must look for private, unpublished work, poems known only to the parent of the virgin sheet, which he keeps sealed up in his book-box, work not rubbed rough by hard chins. A well-known book cannot change author.] [I.66.1–9]

Here is the Martialian topic that most concerns us, the proprietary back-formation that a burgeoning and relatively indiscriminate market in books produces.

It should be insisted that Martial refers here to a figurative crime, since the poems are not authorial property, but it is not so clear that the poet is not proposing a real transaction.[44] As in the introduction to the *Xenia* the spirit of Tryphon's market insinuates itself into an older, non-commercial culture of writing and connoisseurship. Martial pre-empts Tryphon, having learned the lesson of his market: "*tales habeo; nec sciet quisquam*," "I have such poems, and nobody will be the wiser" (line 12). He is not simply offering his poems for sale. Martial proposes, rather, that the attributes of cultured personhood, his literary "gifts", can be put up for sale by the mere detachment of his name from his poems.[45] Of course, the quietly impudent subtext is that the purchaser will not be able to carry off the imposture, but, as always, Martial's impudence has an analytic, clarifying force:

> aliena quisquis recitat et petit famam,
> non emere librum, sed silentium debet.

[Whoever recites other men's productions and seeks fame thereby, ought to buy – not a book, but silence.] [lines 13–14]

With cheeky aplomb, Martial polices the market, insisting that skill is inaccessible to commerce, that poetic "gifts" cannot be made the object of sale. He casually denigrates the marketable book in order to emphasize and protect the value of those personal arrangements for which the book is only a vector; what Jonson could find clarified here is the incommensurability of two very different, but overlapping economies, the one of book-selling, the other of clientage, the one of personal property or goods, the other of the personal attributes or skills constitutive of reputation. So from Martial Jonson would learn to make

---

[44] Cf. I.29, one of the several poems addressed to the plagiarist, Fidentinus, which concludes, "*si mea vis dici, gratis tibi carmina mittam: / si dici tua vis, hoc eme, ne mea sint*" (If you want the poems called mine, I'll send you them for nothing. If you want them called yours, buy out my ownership; lines 3–4). See also I.38, I.53 (discussed above), I.72

[45] This may enable us to gloss the difficult passage in *Epigrams* IV.10 in which Martial instructs his servant to deliver a freshly completed book of his poems to a friend: "*comitetur Punica librum / spongea: muneribus convenit illa meis. / non possunt nostros multae, Faustine, liturae / emendare iocos: una litura potest*"; Let a Punic sponge accompany the book; it suits my gift. Many erasures cannot mend my jests, Faustinus, but one erasure can (lines 5–8). Will the crucial emendation be the removal of Martial's name?

poems about the buying and selling of poems; he would learn that one way in which the satirist can quickly penetrate the manners of a culture is to observe its commerce in books; he would learn to consider the effect of a burgeoning market in books on a fragile culture of clientage; and, to recur to the issues of the preceding chapter, he would learn to wonder – as Heywood, Marston, and the printers of their day had independently learned to wonder – what the market value of an authorial name and style might be.[46]

In 1612 John Stepneth registered for publication a collection of epigrams written by Jonson, but as far as we can tell the poems of Martial's most attentive English imitator did not appear in print until 1616, when the *Epigrams* were included in the folio *Workes* and offered to William Pembroke as "the ripest of my studies."[47] Jonson may have added to his collection or adjusted its shape during the same years in which his friend, Farnaby, was completing his edition of Martial. In 1615, in the preface to that edition, Farnaby gratefully records Jonson's assistance, and he knew Jonson well enough to know how pleased he would be to be praised as "*dignus . . . meliori theatro quam quo malevolo-rum invidiam pascat*" (deserving a better theater than that by which he feeds the envy of detractors).[48] Both non-dramatic poetry and print provided Jonson with just such a *melior theatrum*, and one might suppose him to have been referring directly to Farnaby's phrase when he concludes the dedication to his own *Epigrams* by referring to the collection as "my *Theater*, where *Cato*, if he liv'd, might enter without scandall" (lines 41–42). But Jonson is no doubt referring, not to Farnaby's *Martial*, but to Martial, whose own letter prefatory to the first book of *his Epigrams* concludes by banning Cato from *meum theatrum*. Instead of feeding his detractors in a public theater, Jonson, who has fed on Martial, will repossess his plays by revising them for presentation, like epigrams, in a theater more properly his.

It cannot be seriously proposed that Jonson derives the conception of the non-dramatic as a refuge from the theater, or the notion of print as an alternative to performance, exclusively from Martial. But it should not be supposed that Martial's influence on Jonson's thinking on these matters was trivial. The self-consciousness that dogs Jonson shaped his engagement with Martial; the strength of that engagement is evidenced by the depth of the self-consciousness it yielded – and by "self-consciousness" I mean both a consciousness of the self compounded of, at least, bodily hungers and the aspirations of the craftsman

---

[46] For Jonson's great improvisation on the Martialian theme of ghost-writing, see "To Fine Grand," *Epigrams*, 78.

[47] Drummond records having read Jonson's epigrams as one of the "bookes red be me anno 1612" (H&S, VIII:16). Unless there was a 1612 edition, of which no copy is known to survive, Drummond must have read the poems in manuscript.

[48] H&S, XI.134. Jonson and Farnaby had worked together before. Aside from assisting with the Martial edition, Jonson had written Latin commendatory poems to Farnaby's editions of Juvenal (1612), Persius (1612), and Seneca (1613).

and an awareness of those contemporary conditions least assimilable to the historical circumstances that Martial and his poems represent. In the course of reading Martial's *Epigrams*, Jonson sharpened his sense of contemporary literary conditions and conspicuously sharpened his sense of the various claims a poet might make on his readers, his publishers, his imitators, and his poems. To specify this further, re-reading and re-writing Martial as he does in "Inviting a Friend to Supper," Jonson discovered the book market as such.

Although the personal interests and urgencies in which "Inviting a Friend to Supper" participates are no doubt idiosyncratic, they are not disarticulated from the poem's historical milieu. This discussion – of Jonson's interest in "mechanical plagiarism" as a resurgence of excitations from the milieu of the late 1590s, of Jonsonian poetry as a cuisine, of Martial as an historian of Early Modern book culture – has delayed what might have been the first thing said of the imprinted pastry at the center of Jonson's poem, which is that this emblem of uncanny circulation adumbrates an analysis that would be undertaken later, by Marx, under the large rubric of reification. The analogy between the pastry and the commodity form in general, between the pastry's repetition of verses despite the professed will of the poet and the commodity's arrogation to itself of the personal energies of labor is impure, but significant nonetheless. To recall a passage more often-quoted than Jonson's sentences on imitation:

> The mysterious character of the commodity form consists simply in the fact that the commodity reflects the social characteristics of men's own labour as objective characteristics of the products of labour themselves, as the socio-natural properties of these things. Hence it also reflects the social relation of the producers to the sum total of labour as a social relation between objects. Through this substitution, the products of labour become commodities, sensuous things which are at the same time supra-sensible or social. . . . The definite social relation between men assumes here, for them, the fantastic form of a relation between things.[49]

It is not conceding much to submit that, however much the cultures of *Volpone* or of *The Staple of News* resemble those of, say, *Cousine Bette*, the realism of Jonson is not the high capitalist realism of Balzac, its human comedy entangled with, and sometimes experienced as, a "social relation between objects." Yet it is not too much to insist that Jonson's ban on the stool pigeons and his comic wariness of the pastry – oddly objectified persons and an oddly personal object – are defenses against the confusing obtrusions impending in the commodity form. Outside the confines of Jonsonian hospitality, but not securely outside them, the imitable word had gone on sale, and Martial's great modern reader (Marx's great Early Modern predecessor) was exquisitely alert to the threat this posed to human identity, as well as to the mere objectivity of both words and

---

[49] Karl Marx, *Capital*, 3 vols., trans. Ben Fowkes, *The Marx Library* (New York: Viking, 1977) I:164–65.

things.[50] Commodification, Jonson discovered, renders semantics the domain of the uncanny. Hence the energy, the busy zeal that (we will see) Jonson brings to the conversion of the written into the printed.

[50] Marx and Engels offer the neatest gloss on the staining of the poem: "private property *alienates* not only the individuality of men, but also of things" *Der Heilige Max, Collected Works*, 5 vols. (New York: International Publishers, 1976) I,vi,c, p. 230.

5   Scripts in the marketplace: Jonson and editorial repossession

LAPET: So, bring me the last proofe, this is corrected.
   [Lapet is correcting proof sheets for *The Uprising of the Kick*, his treatise on cudgelling]
CLOWN: I, y'are too full of your correction, sir.
LAPET: Look I have perfect Books within this half houre.
CLOWN: Yes sir.
LAPET: Bid him put all the Thumps in Pica Roman,
   And with great Tees, (you vermin) as Thumps should be.
CLOWN: Then in what Letter will you have your Kicks?
LAPET: All in Italica, your Backward blowes
   All in Italica, you Hermaphrodite
                    (Fletcher, *The Nice Valour* (1625?), IV.i.230–37)[1]

The instrumental view is closely associated with British political thinkers accustomed to a form of property law very different from that in the context of which Kant, Hegel, and Marx were writing. The English legal system discouraged a question which Roman law encouraged, namely, 'What is it to be the *owner* of something?' or 'How does a thing become Mine?' The English legal inclination to enquire what gave a man good title to possession and no more than that, seems to have diverted a certain psychological or metaphysical interest into other channels.[2]

On the other hand, for an Englishman deeply versed in Roman antiquities and jealous and exquisitely alert to the animations and depredations of commerce – for, say, Ben Jonson – such questions had import. Jonson could not formulate them, but he had his answers.

Martial's impress

As has already been observed in the history of the early publication of plays by Shakespeare, one of the novel features of publishing in the late 1590s (and, on the continent, at least half a century earlier) was the marketing of authorial

[1] *The Dramatic Works in the Beaumont and Fletcher Canon*, ed. Fredson Bowers, 7 vols. (Cambridge: Cambridge University Press, 1989), vol. 7; the full "title" of Lapet's book is given at IV.i.322–23).
[2] Alan Ryan, *Property and Political Theory* (Oxford: Blackwell, 1984), 7.

attention, the advertisement of books as newly revised by their authors. Even this source of value is anticipated in Martial's *Epigrams*:

> Festinata prius, decimi mihi cura libelli
>   elapsum manibus nunc revocavit opus.
> nota leges quaedam sed limi rasa recenti;
>   pars nova maior erit

[In composing my tenth little book, too hastily issued earlier, I have now recalled the work that then slipped from my hands. Some of the pieces you will read are already known, but polished with a recent file, the greater part will be new.] [X.2.1–4]

We cannot speak of *this* as advertisement: Martial provides a model here for countless Early Modern authors, who make a public display of their resistance to unauthorized circulation, to sale, and to the culture of advertisement. For Martial, revision is a plausible means of reclaiming the book from indiscriminate circulation. In the next line he therefore addresses his intended audience, a private and individual *lector*, as "*opes nostrae*," the author's wealth. Yet, despite the insistence that his reward is intimate social attention itself, Martial demonstrates that this intimacy is at best a salvage job, something recovered from a more public sphere of literary consumption. "*Quem cum mihi Roma dedisset / 'nil tibi quod demus maius habemus' ait*" (when Rome gave you to me, she said, "I have nothing greater to give you"; lines 5–6). In an earlier collection, Martial describes authorial revision in terms that make it seem even more ambiguously poised between social intimacy and the publicities of the market: to the library of an elegant country villa he commends seven slim volumes, hand-corrected – "*haec illis pretium facit litura*" (VII.17.8).[3] Bailey's rendering, "the corrections give them value," registers the crucial commercial flicker of *pretium*: the effect of autograph can only be described in terms of *pretium*, price, value added.

Martial did not provide the only classical model of assertive authorial revising. His contemporary, Quintilian, makes a point of retracting an earlier opinion, though he claims to regard the retraction as a threat to his fame; Quintilian alludes to similar publicized retractions by Hippocrates and Cicero in order to justify divulging the change in his views.[4] Such published adjustments are clearly related to those gestures by which writers like Virgil had configured their careers as *cursus* of linked texts, opening a work by recalling a prior text or concluding by anticipating a next one. The crucial difference is that Cicero, Quintilian, and Martial intensify the dialectical character of authorial development in a gesture that I will call *bibliographic authorship*, a gesture by which the author is presented as an editor of his own works, and thus as perhaps the pre-eminent reader of his works.

---

[3] And cf.VII:11.
[4] "*Et fortasse tutissimum erat famae modo studenti nihil ex eo mutare . . .*" (It would perhaps be safer for my reputation if I were to make no modification of [my] views; *Institutio Oratoria*, III.VI.63.) The entire passage, lines 63–65, is relevant.

Once again it may be useful to refer to Baudrillard's essay on "Gesture and Signature in Modern Art," since it offers such a deft consideration of the serial relation of works of art. Baudrillard asserts that artistic modernity begins in a triple shift, of which the first two aspects are simple to describe – "Meaning passes from the restitution of appearances to the act of inventing them. Value is transferred from an eminent, objective beauty to the singularity of the artist in his gesture."[5] The third is given a slightly more complex description, though one equally marked by a transfer of emphasis towards the author as conceptual center:

> And this new act is temporalized . . . The modern oeuvre is no longer a syntax of various fragments . . . The oeuvres no longer combine with one another to revive the model in its likeness (the world and its order) by means of their contiguity. They are only able to follow one another in order then to refer, by virtue of their difference and their discontinuity in time, to a quite different model, to the *subject-creator himself* in his unlikeness and repeated absence. (104)

Baudrillard finally summarizes this third aspect of modern artistic production as "the constraint of seriality," the constraint of audience and artist to construe the individual artifact as a constituent of a single and consecutive oeuvre; the oeuvre itself – the Work and not the individual works that are its mere instances – becomes the origin of aesthetic and market values.

It is the tedious habit of the historian to insist that something or other – plagiarism, say, or the constraint to seriality – is nothing new. Tedious or not, some version of such correction is in order here, since this particular aspect of modernist art is observable at earlier cultural moments, and not merely in pallid anticipatory forms. The various Early Modern manifestations of editorial authorship entail *at least* a compulsive attention to seriality. We can certainly say more: major transformations in reproductive technology – the shift to writing, the shift to writing on papyrus, the invention of the press, the invention of photography, phonography, or digital text encoding – unsettle the status of the persons involved in production, dissemination, and reproduction, and often excite renewed attention to seriality as a source of value.

As has been observed of other developments, a kind of feedback operated between commercial and artistic practice. When the book trade seized on specifically editorial authorship as a source of commercial value, the ancillary effect was to promote adjacent forms of authorial attention. Thus the market in *revision*, which responded to a commerce in novelty, produced a concomitant promotion of authorial attention to *correction*, whether of scribal or compositorial confusion. This is not produced solely and simply by the discovery of revision as a source of commercial value, of course. The alliance between printing and classical editorial scholarship was fairly mature by the end of the

---

[5] The second of these shifts, the implication of authorial personhood in the published text, is the principal subject of chapter 5 of *The Author's Due*.

sixteenth century, and although it must be insisted that scholarly publishing of ancient Greek, Latin, and Hebrew texts was still primarily a continental phenomenon, the philological interest in textual rectification, propagated in England by humanist university lecturing, must have made some small penetration in the consciousness of those who bought and sold books in England.[6] Although by the middle of the sixteenth century editors had developed a distinct preference for emendations founded on ancient manuscript sources, rather than on conjecture, one can nonetheless confidently generalize that the normal method for preparing a new printed edition, whether of a classical or a modern text, was to base copy on any available printed text – an ostensibly authoritative one, if one had a choice – which is why modern classical scholars lament the tyranny of Renaissance *editiones principes*. The hallmark of Renaissance editing is the adjustment of an earlier printed edition by recourse to a manuscript source; no climate of opinion forced the conscientious scholar to adopt a manuscript, no matter how ancient, as base text in preference to a printed text.[7] Jonson's brilliant friend, Heinsius, brings the veneration for manuscript authority to its zenith, yet he based his edition of Ovid on his father's printed edition, despite the availability of worthy manuscript exemplars.[8] And although there is evidence that such late fifteenth-century scholars as Merula and Sabellicus could muster a healthy skepticism about the quality of printed classical texts, the fact remains that well into the seventeenth century scholarly editors continued to manifest a (misplaced) faith in printing as a cultural bulwark, regarding the press as an instrument of clarification and preservation. And, more to the present point, authorial attention to the details of print publication seems to have carried a certain cachet associated with the ongoing work of classical editing, work which had re-energized the antique prestige of autograph and which also sustained the Erasmian cult of the scholarly press-corrector.[9]

---

[6] David Gants observes that serious involvement in printing the classics would also have been impractical for London stationers, who could import the relatively small number of classical printed books for which they had a market more cheaply than they could produce them (private correspondence, 2/19/01).

  As for editorial habits, it must also be insisted that paleographic and stemmatic insights from the late fifteenth century to the late sixteenth century do *not* much impinge on editorial practice. The humanist tradition of unsystematic emendation, originating in fourteenth-century Italy, continued more or less unimpeded through the Early Modern period, leaving its mark on the printed versions of classical texts. By the same token, readiness-to-hand almost always dictated the choice of copy text. E. J. Kenney takes on this problem in *The Classical Text: Aspects of Editing in the Age of the Printed Book* (Berkeley: University of California Press, 1974); his summary remark is a useful tonic – "It is indeed true that printing 'arrested textual corruption' [he is quoting Eisenstein]; but it also perpetuated and on occasion enhanced it" (17).

[7] Kenney, *The Classical Text*, 48–49, 54, and 68–69.

[8] Ibid., 62–63 and 67–68.

[9] Erasmus' classic statement on the subject is to be found in "Herakleioi Ponoi" in the *Adagia*, and particularly in the expanded version of this essay for the 1515 edition. That Erasmus *intended*

The data concerning the historical norms of authorial press-correction remain unfortunately sparse. Simpson's richly anecdotal but (perhaps inevitably) unsystematic study of Early Modern proof-reading documents a considerable range of practices and attitudes.[10] He makes much of the continental tradition of employing learned press-correctors, to whom authors were urged to defer, but claims that this practice was not taken up by the earliest English printers.[11] Yet Elizabethan and Jacobean printers occasionally profess great care in the reading of proof, and one frequently encounters a stationer's printed apology for an author who has been constrained by other business to neglect proof-reading. Thus Gabriel Cawood informs the public that an illness obliged George Gascoigne to turn the proof-reading of *The Droome of Doomes Day* (1576) over to a servant; similar apologies may be found from the mid-sixteenth century forward.[12] Yet the letter that John Beale appended to his issue of William Gouge's *The Whole-Armor of God* (1616), which also has any number of parallels, seems to imply a different norm:

Good Reader,

I have taken the best care that I could to set foorth this worke in the best manner that I could for true Printing: yet I cannot denie but that some faults have escaped in some copies: such diligence hath been used by the Author in correcting his worke, that so oft as his leasure permitted him, he came himselfe to the Presse, and as he found a fault amended it, so that there are very few faults but are amended in most of the Bookes. If therefore thou meete with any slippe that may make the sence obscure, compare thy Booke with some others, and thou maiest finde it amended.[13]

Gouge's proof-reading was remarkable in a strict sense of the term, but it was evidently not compulsive.[14] Beale seems to be telling us that *The Whole-Armor*

this as a classic statement is skillfully argued in Lisa Jardine, *Erasmus, Man of Letters: The Construction of Charisma in Print* (Princeton, Princeton University Press, 1993), 41–48.

[10] It is useful to read Greg's review of Simpson's study of *Proof-reading* ("From Manuscript to Print," *Review of English Studies* (1937), 190–205) in conjunction with Simpson's book itself.
   The following discussion of proof-reading does not distinguish between the reading of proof sheets pulled for the express purpose of enabling an author or press-corrector to correct composition preliminary to printing, and proof-reading in the midst of continuous presswork, of the sort that will yield stop-press correction. Pre-publication authorial participation in either form of press-correction is germane to the present discussion. The distinction is taken up in Greg's review, but is given even more searching discussion in McKenzie, "Printers of Mind," *Studies in Bibliography*, 22 (1969), 1–75 and in Bowers, "Elizabethan Proofing," first published in 1948 and revised for *Essays in Bibliography, Text, and Editing* (Charlottesville: University Press of Virginia, 1975), 240–53.

[11] *Proof-reading*, 136.

[12] For comparable examples, see Simpson, *Proof-reading*, 6, 8–10, 14, and 35.

[13] Cited in Simpson, *Proof-reading*, 18.

[14] Honigmann's observation is useful here: "Authors who proof-read their work frequently did so carelessly, and even when replacing a 'bad' text with a view to using it as printer's copy, and therefore conscious of the existence of errors, might allow hundreds of further errors to slip into their 'authorized' version – as, apparently, in the case of Browne's *Religio Medici*" (*Stability*, 191–92).

of God had been slightly more carefully prepared than many contemporary books and that it was the author's attention which had made the most appreciable contribution to the book's relatively high fidelity to copy.[15] Difficult as it is to generalize about sixteenth and early seventeenth-century practice, it seems fair to say that authorial proof-reading was neither an egregious exception nor a widely diffused norm.[16]

Where it occurs, authorial proof-reading blurs into – shapes and responds to – two other forms of attention. The first, as has already been suggested, is the author's critical reconsideration of a "copy," that textual formation which the printer was about to render fixed, but which remained for the author available to the sort of rolling adjustment characteristic of manuscript textual evolution. And proof-reading occasions wide-ranging authorial revision.[17] As Simpson observes, by the early seventeenth century, authors began to use the errata page to correct misconceptions: intellectual corrigenda sometimes threaten to swamp typographical ones.[18] Thus Edward Evans appended a list of "Faults of Omission and Comission; together with some Diversities of Reading" to his *Verba Dierum*. The religious language is not merely a sluggish instance of metaphysical wit. The moral vocabulary, which had long lurked within the language of text correction (Beale had spoken of *amending faults*), here grips revision as well.[19] As a text is about to be *locked* in the chase, revision acquires

[15] Simpson cites other examples of early proof-reading authors: Johannes Aepinus, Nashe, Marston, Sebastian Benefield, Foulke Robartes, Brathwaite, Massinger, Burton, Herrick, John Barnard, Drayton, Urquhart, Hume and, of course, Jonson.

[16] See Greg, "From Manuscript to Print," 191. There were occasions on which stationers and authors clashed over the standards of accuracy appropriate to print publication, and over who was ultimately responsible for maintaining those standards. See Simpson, *Proof-reading*, 16.

[17] The momentous attention of an author preparing a copy for its transformation into a printed text has its analogy in manuscript propagation whenever an author prepares a work for entrepreneurial publication or even for a particularly important presentation (to friend, patron, or some otherwise admired recipient). What unfixes the analogy is, obviously, the larger scale of print publication, the relative impersonality of such publication (since manuscript circulation, though irregular, was usually shaped by relatively high socio-cultural solidarities), and what I shall be calling "remediation," the technical (and cultural) discontinuity between composition-by-hand and reproduction-by-machine, a discontinuity obviously absent from manuscript publication. On the ethos of manuscript circulation in the Early Modern period see Marotti, *Manuscript, Print, and the English Renaissance Lyric* and Love, *Scribal Publication*, particularly chapter 2.

[18] *Proof–reading*, 116. "George Hakewill," he goes on, "took the bolder and more honest course of adding two fresh leaves to the end of the book," *An Apologie of the Power and Providence of God in the Government of the World*, "amplifying details and correcting misstatements, which he headed 'A Revise'."

[19] The verses that John Taylor prefixed to his sheet of errata go much further than does Beale's prose –

> *Faults*, but not *faults escap'd*, I would they were,
> If they were faults escap'd, they were not here
>
> . . .
>
> I will confesse my faults are 'scap'd, indeed,
> If they escape mens Censure when they read.

a punctual urgency that it does not carry within a predominately scribal culture; for more than a few authors this urgency had a moral cast.

But authorial proof-reading not only occasioned urgent rewritings; it also stimulated the development of what might be called compositorial authorship.[20] We can see a nascent form of this development in the paragraph that introduces the selective errata sheet for *The Anatomy of Melancholy*. Burton seems to have done no more proof-reading than, say, Gouge had done, yet the *idea* of proof-reading excites him to a characteristic imaginative nervousness:

> The Copie (as I have said) was once written and in hast, I could not always be there my selfe; or had I beene still present, *Non omnen molitor quae fluit unda videt.* The Miller sees not all the water goes by his Mill. Besides many letters mistaken, misplaced, added, omitted as *i* for *y*, or *a* for *e*, or *o*, false points, &c. which are in some copies onely, not throughout: (To point at each particular of which were to pick out the seedes of a foule bushell of corne) some of the chiefest, as thou shalt find them corrected, I desire thee to take notice of.

This is at best a glimmer of an author's compositorial imagination, an aspect of authorial imagination that burnt a good deal more brightly among at least a handful of Burton's contemporaries. The scene in *Nice Valour*, cited as epigraph to this chapter, assumes an audience familiar with authorial proof-reading. The rough humor of "Thumps in Pica Roman" and kicks "All in Italica" depends, if only in part, upon our registering that Lapet's engagement with the typography of violence is unusually detailed, *just* bordering on obsession.

Though Lapet's interest in format seems to be unusually pitched, the interest itself can be found in a number of Stuart authors. In the course of demonstrating that Webster read proof for *The White Devil* (1612), John Russell Brown adduced evidence that the author had stipulated cutting the frisket to make room for the printing of marginal stage directions.[21] The MS copy for Harrington's Ariosto demonstrates an even more meticulous concern with matters of page layout.[22] Webster, Harrington, and (as we shall see) Marston and Jonson put the cultural historian on the road towards the sort of fully developed compositorial authorship that Dr. Johnson found in Pope, who, he tells us, "first learned to write by imitating printed books; a species of penmanship on which he retained great excellence through his whole life, though his ordinary hand was not elegant."[23] The Stuart authors who anticipate Pope do not address the printed

---

[20] I take this up in "Spenser's Retrography."

[21] "The Printing of Webster's Plays," *Studies in Bibliography*, VI (1954) particularly pp. 125–27 and *SB* VIII (1956), particularly p. 117.

[22] This is preserved as BM Add. MS 18920, discussed in Greg, "An Elizabethan Printer and His Copy," *The Library*, 4th ser., 4 (1924). *Proof-reading*, 71–73. He also instances (p. 11) Sebastian Benefield's extraordinary insistence that a correction be hand stamped in the margin of *Doctrinae Christianae* (Oxford, 1610).

[23] *Lives of the Poets*, ed. George Birkbeck Hill, 3 vols. (Oxford: Clarendon, 1905), III:84.

page as if it were a transcript, a derivative reproduction: it is itself embraced as a literary intention.

This embrace was not always a willing one. As we have already seen, Marston was forced to take print publication seriously at least as early as the 1606 quartos of *Parasitaster*; "it cannot avoid publishing," as he put it. (And, in the preceding sentence of this same apologetical epistle, he had quoted the preface to Book I of Martial's *Epigrams – Absit a iocorum nostrorum simplicitate malignus interpres*.) Having acceded to publication, Marston took care over the proof-reading, at least over the proof-reading for the second quarto, hence the *second* letter to the reader prefixed to the play in that edition:

Reader, know I have perused this copy, to make some satisfaction for the first faulty impression: yet so urgent hath been my business, that some errors have styll passed, which thy discretion may amend.[24]

As if narrating a conversion, the ensuing sentence testifies to how fully Marston's creative intentions were split by competing media; the dicta already cited on the primacy of performance – "*Comedies* are writ to be spoken, not read: Remember the life of these things consists in action" – yield without transition to an assertion of the claims of (printed) writing – "and for such courteous survey of my pen, I will present a tragedy to you, which shall boldly abide the most curious perusal." A quarter of a century later, long after Marston had retired from theatrical life and from London, William Sheares brought out a collection of Marston's plays in which he advises the reader that the playwright, had he been living nearby, "would have beene more carefull in revising the former Impressions, and more circumspect about this than" Sheares himself could be (A₄). The remark seems more or less gratuitous; at least, it makes little obvious contribution to promoting the sales of Sheares's edition. Sheares may, of course be telling his potential readers something slightly piquant about Marston, as if it were somehow worth drawing attention to Marston's compositorial enthusiasms.[25] Or he may simply be confirming something that readers were coming to expect of the printed work of "serious" playwrights, that they could expect ambitious playwrights to wish to convert themselves into compositorial authors. Certainly this latter is what the editors of the first folio of Shakespeare mean when they assure us that "it had bene a thing . . . worthie to have bene wished, that the Author himselfe had liv'd to have set forth, and over-seen his owne writings," as if death were the only obstacle, as if Shakespeare,

---

[24] The title page corroborates Marston's claim, for it advertises the play as "now corrected of many faults, which by reason of the Author's absence were let slip in the first edition."

[25] These enthusiasms had, in fact, been shown before the grudging acquiescence to the press expressed in 1606. Marston prepared *Antonio and Mellida* (1601) for the press quite carefully, with latinate stage directions, and elaborate descriptions of entrances; that the layout may have been influenced by that of Jonson's *Every Man Out* (1600) seems worth entertaining.

had he been alive in 1623, would surely have wished to collect, *correct*, and publish them. If this authorial disposition was *de rigueur* by 1623, it is largely because of the influence of the likes of Marston, and particularly of Marston's old antagonist, whose compositorial imagination is perhaps the most curious of any of his contemporaries'.[26]

Discussion of Jonson's earliest involvement with print publication must proceed cautiously, however, for one of the truisms of twentieth-century scholarship on Jonson, that he "supervised the printing" of his plays has not been proven true – and may, in fact, be inaccessible to proof.[27] One must chose one's words carefully here: most of the quartos show signs of one sort or another that Jonson had adjusted the text at some point *after* having released the play to the players, had adjusted it in ways intended to influence the reception of the play in print.[28]

---

[26] The bibliographical study of Jonson's printed texts during the past sixty years has substantiated – and qualified hardly at all – Greg's summary characterization of Jonson's proofreading, that it "seems to have been more fussy than accurate" ("From Manuscript to Print," 193).

This will be the place to acknowledge my debts to Richard Newton's important work on Jonson and print publication, "Making Books From Leaves: Poets Become Editors," *Print and Culture in the Renaissance*, ed. Gerald P. Tyson and Sylvia S. Wagonheim (Newark: University of Delaware Press, 1980), 246–64 and "Jonson and the (Re-) Invention of the Book," *Classic and Cavalier: Essays on Jonson and the Sons of Ben*, eds. Claude J. Summers and Ted-Larry Pebworth (Pittsburgh: University of Pittsburgh Press, 1982), 31–55, and particularly pp. 44–46. The recent work of David Gants and Mark Bland enriches and advances Newton's work by their more detailed work on the press-work and commercial arrangements involved in publishing Jonson.

[27] I quote from Kirschbaum, *Shakespeare and the Stationers*, 174, who is making this claim of the six plays by Jonson that the King's Men performed: *Every Man Out, Every Man In, Sejanus, Volpone, Catiline*, and *The Alchemist*. This orthodoxy was promulgated by the H&S edition (on very weak evidence in the case of *Every Man In*, for which see the note following), though the Oxford editors' main purpose in bibliographical discussion was to defend the excellence of all Folio texts against the depredations of Henry De Vocht, an early proponent of the quartos. The Oxford editors could collate only a few copies of the quartos and could therefore secure very little data about press-correction, yet their assessment of Jonson's close attention to details of the quarto texts has been widely accepted. Simpson's most fully documented analysis of a quarto text appears in a discussion of *Cynthia's Revels*, H&S IV:5–17, which expands on several pages in *Proof-reading*. He examined five copies of one sheet of *Cynthia's Revels*, the second of Jonson's plays to be printed, and despite his not having performed the most exhaustive collation possible, the results of this small experiment seemed to him to be remarkable: he identified 89 alterations in the outer forme and 103 in the inner forme. He found initial capital letters lowered, roman points substituted for italic in portions of the text set otherwise in roman, and apostrophes inserted in words where the compositor had provided no marker of syllabic elision. But in a very damaging discussion of this argument, Greg demonstrated that the "corrections" are found in the *earlier* state of the forme, and that the imperfections of the "uncorrected" state derive from a hasty resetting (*RES* 14 [1938], 218).

One of the most disappointing effects of the Oxford edition was to divert bibliographical scholars from attending to the quartos, books which in some cases will have to be adopted as copy-texts for a truly modern critical edition.

[28] A summary may be useful here, though my purpose in what follows is to explore the forms of Jonson's engagement with his printed quartos in a less compressed, more careful way. The most obvious – but not all of the – signs of Jonson's post-performance involvements in quarto publication are:

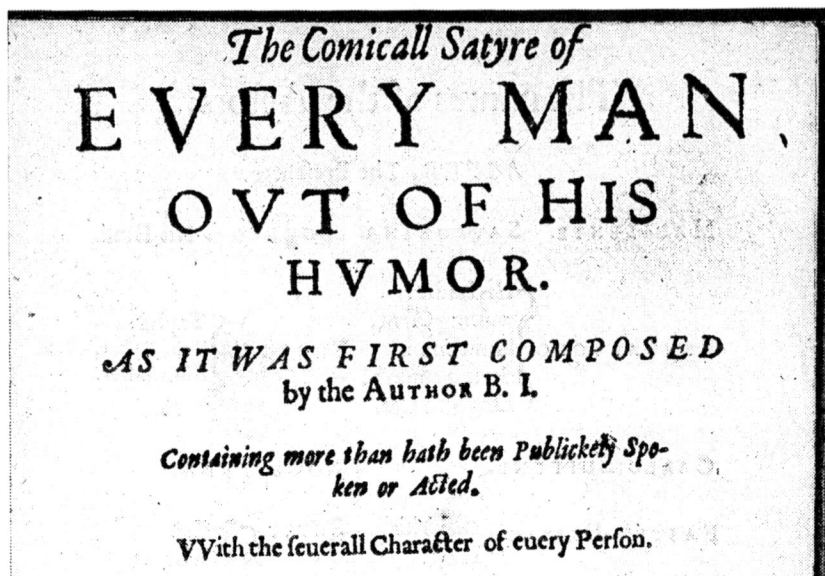

The Comicall Satyre of EVERY MAN, OVT OF HIS HVMOR.

AS IT WAS FIRST COMPOSED by the Author B. I.

Containing more than hath been Publickely Spo-ken or Acted.

VVith the feuerall Character of euery Perfon.

3   Title page of *The Comicall Satyre of Every Man out of His Humor*, 1600

In 1600, Jonson does seem to have provided William Holmes or his printer (probably Richard Bradock) with the copy for his first printed play, the great typographic ancestor of Brome's *Antipodes* (see figure 3):

EMO   Prose "characters," apologia for theatrically unconventional features of the play with comments on the reception of the play in performance, mottos from Horace.

EMI   (Of all the quartos, that of EMI shows the weakest signs of authorial attention, to wit:) Latin act-scene divisions, mottos from Juvenal. (The staying entry may suggest that when the play was finally printed it was by permission of the King's Men and that they, not Jonson, provided the copy.)

CR   Modal as well as theatrical text divisions, motto from Martial headed "Ad Lectorem" (on t.p. and A₂), dedicatory verses printed for presentation copies to Camden and Lucy, Countess of Bedford, concluding motto from Martial.

Poe   As with *CR*, motto from Martial repeated (and expanded) after list of characters with heading "Ad Lectorem," concluding apologetical dialogue described as suppressed in performance, marginalia indicating classical sources of poems rendered in translation.

Sej   Epistle to the readers claiming that the printed text revises the performance text, argument, marginal and interlineated annotation, "non-theatrical" typography, motto from Martial.

Vol   Acrostic verse argument, dedication to the two universities of Oxford and Cambridge, commendatory poem by Field apparently solicited by Jonson, stop-press corrections of punctuation.

Cat   Dedication to Pembroke, letters to readers "in ordinarie" and "extraordinarie," stop-press correction of fonts and punctuation.

Alc   Dedication to Mary Wroth, letter to the reader, acrostic verse argument.

The Comicall Satyre of

<u>Every Man</u>

<u>Out of His</u>

<u>Humor.</u>

<u>As It Was First Composed</u>

<u>by the Author B.I.</u>

<u>Containing more than hath been Publickely Spo-</u>

<u>ken or Acted.</u>

<u>With the severall Character of every Person.</u>

If there is no evidence that Jonson read proof for this play, the quarto text nonetheless has features that imply the specific influence of printing on the manuscript copy, a manuscript adjusted for print: "The Names of the Actors [i.e. characters]" are organized into a social diagram and this same analytic impulse is carried through in the list of character descriptions that follows the diagram.[29] These pages, the "more than" of the title-page, are only the first gestures in what would be a bibliography increasingly adversative to the play-wright's stage history. Although these "predictive" forms seem to be more or less at odds with specifically dramatic practice, it would be more accurate to say that they work out a conspicuously atavistic feature of Jonsonian dramatic practice. In a recollection of the old device of the presenter or Vice, Jonson makes a habit of prejudicing his audience by having those on stage offer de-scriptions of approaching characters and impending situations. The printed "characters," which Herford and Simpson shrewdly describe as inspired more by Martial than by Theophrastus, effectively reproduce one of Jonson's most cherished stage-effects. In this early case, then, the page is an homage to the stage. Other typographic devices (or "page-effects") work similarly. The half-title on B₁ and the heading, "*Inductio, sono secundo* / GREX", certainly affiliate the quarto with a tradition of humanist publishing, and the transliterated Greek name urges us to understand the not-quite-meta-dramatic Jonsonian Induc-tion as a modern reconception of a Greek chorus: the page applies – applies more than indicates – the tincture of an archly modified classicism.[30] But we are not thereby drawn away from a performance tradition, for even this small typographic obtrusion anticipates details of what the Chamberlain's Men had

---

[29] Riggs's case for Jonson's involvement in the publication of *Every Man Out* (*Ben Jonson*, 64–67) is not strenuously argued, though it is both plausible and consistent with the editorial tradition deriving from Herford and Simpson.

[30] The quarto gives Latin act and scene divisions throughout: sig. C₂ᵛ thus begins "Actus Primus. Scena Prima." The quarto makes fewer scene divisions than does the Folio and places some of the more-or-less common divisions differently. This is also true of Q *Cynthia's Revels*.

staged: in the induction to the play, the classical "lawes of *Com~ die*" that inform Jonson's play are expounded, including "the equall division of it into *Acts, and Scenes*" and "the furnishing of the *Scene* with GREX" (lines 235, 237, and 239). The induction as a whole, a dialogue between Mitis, Cordatus, and the fierce *satiromastix*, Asper, is hobbled by Asper's refusal to be constrained to dialogue: conversation collapses before the bursting fury of Asper's neo-Senecan rant. Asper's probity, fury, incivility, and hostility to the stage are specifically identified with his classicism; the slightly unsettling classicism of the quarto manifests a small typographic correlative of the dramatic device – a small anti-theatrical homage to the stage.

The quarto concludes, quite consistently, with a record of variant performances. In the stage version then current, the play concludes with an address to the audience by a composite Asper/Macilente, and the quarto faithfully records this, but Holmes also published, as an addendum, the text of the conclusion as originally performed. "Many seem'd not to rellish it" – the original performance version had concluded with praise of the reforming power of the queen's mere presence –

and therefore 'twas since alter'd: yet that a right-ei'd and solide *Reader* may perceive it was not so great a part of the Heaven awry, as they would make it; we request him but to looke downe upon these following Reasons.

The right-eyed reader can look down upon five "reasons," printed as a numbered list and thereafter, thus prejudiced, can read the original address to the queen. Since it entails a critique of popular reception, the quarto may be said to perform a playwright's homage to a *melior theatrum*, an idealized stage.

These small authorial engagements with typographic drama are themselves by no means anti-theatrical, nor do they embrace printing as an adversary alternative to performance, although Jonson would later employ these devices to adversative ends. The same might be said of the two plays that Walter Burre published in the following year: *Every Man In His Humour*, printed – after the attempt to restrain publication by means of a blocking registration – with a title page quite conventionally promising a text "as it hath beene sundry times / *publickly acted by the right* / Honorable the Lord Cham- / *berlaine his servants*," and *Cynthia's Revels*, "as it hath beene sundry times / *privately acted in the* Black- / Friers *by the* Children / *of her* Majesties / *Chappell*."[31] Yet *Cynthia's Revels*

---

[31] On each title page, Jonson's name is followed with the same mottos from Juvenal (Sat. VII: 90 and 93). The plays may well have been entrusted to the same printer, since the ornaments for each are identical. Both plays give a cast list, "The number and names of *the Actors*" and both give their act and scene divisions in Latin form, this latter not in itself a very remarkable feature. (It might be noted that Acts IV and V of *Every Man In* each contain only a single scene marking, whereas the revised Folio version subdivides the acts according to Jonson's customary practice. Since the quality of the text drops off at the end of Act III, it might be inferred that at this point Jonson gave over proof-reading, but other inferences might also be plausible.)

is conspicuously constructed as a reader's text. Instead of a half-title, the first page of the text proper (A₂) is headed "*AD LECTOREM.* / Nasutum volo, nolo polyposum" – it is from Martial (XII:37,2) – ". . . nolo polyposum. / Præludium." And unlike the quarto of *Every Man Out*, quarto *Cynthia's Revels* makes no reference to the "soundings" that introduce the play's *Praeludium* and, thereafter, its *Prologus*; in fact, there are very few stage directions in the quarto, very few references to the mechanics of performance. The pages are firmly organized, but sorted into modal units: *Praeludium, Prologus, Scena, Cant.* [for *cantus*], *Ode, Hymnus, Masque, Palinodia, Epilogus.*[32] This bookishness effectively extrapolates the privacies of Blackfriars performance to construct something like Martial's *melior* satiric *theatrum*. There is no colophon to this quarto, so its last words are authorial, and they cast the author as a privileged spectator:

> *Ecce rubet quidam, pallet, stupet, oscitat, odit.*
> *Hoc volo: nunc nobis carmina nostra placent.*

[Look, somebody turns red, turns pale, is dazed, yawns, is disgusted. This I want. Now my poems please me.] (Martial, *Epigrams*, VI.60, 3–4)

To some extent, the motto on the title page of *Poetaster*, the next of Jonson's plays to see print, will seem to retract this particular exultation, for there Martial is quoted in a moment of caution: "*Et mihi de nullo fama rubore placet*" (Nor do I desire fame from any man's blush; VII:12, 4). Yet there is no relinquishing of editorial authorship nor of the sense that this is a book fashioned by its author as a reader's text. The numbered cast list concludes with the final lines of that same epigram (addressed "Ad Lectorem") which provided the title-page motto, and they stake out a potent intimacy between author and reader:

> Ludimus innocuis verbis, hoc iuro potentis
>   Per Genium Famæ, Castalidumque gregem:
> Perque tuas aures, magni mihi numinis instar,
>   Lector, inhumana liber ab Invidia.

[I sport harmlessly with words: I swear it by the Genius of potent Fame and the Castalian troop and by your ears, Reader – a mighty divinity to me – free from inhuman Envy.][33]

The Wars of the Theaters had, in fact, embittered Jonson towards a number of his fellow-players as well as towards a small handful of poets and playwrights,

---

[32] The modal sorting is reinforced by typography: songs, the texts of masques, and even some instances of reported speech are printed in italics.

[33] Lines 9–12. Jonson has slightly altered Martial's text in lines 9 and 10, the original form of which is "Ludimus innocuis: scis hoc bene: iuro potentis / per genium Famae, Castaliumque gregem." *Poetaster* is a *cento* on envy, and texts from Martial shape it: after the final song of the play, the quarto quotes the final line from *Epigrams*, IX:97, "*Rumpatur, quisquis rumpitur invidia*"; let he who is bursting with envy burst.

and he had plainly begun to regard publication as a fortress from which self-defense could be mounted, though not the only such refuge. Jonson's humour plays had been warmly received in the theater, so it is hardly surprising that the quartos of those plays work out typographic devices that reinforce or replicate effects proper to the theater. *Cynthia's Revels*, however, seems not to have won such enthusiastic responses and *Poetaster* was even less well-received, and the texts of *these* plays solicit a readership conceived as an alternative to a theatrical audience.[34] Jonson wrote an "apologeticall Dialogue" as a *parabasis* for *Poetaster* and the Folio text preserves it, but it was performed only once and then, according to Jonson, suppressed. (It is a dialogue between the author and – no surprise – Nasutus and Polyposus, the alternative readers invoked from Martial on the title page of *Cynthia's Revels*.) Jonson tells us – he speaks of himself in the third person, in what might be taken as a stationer's voice or as the voice of the printed book itself – that he had intended to conclude the original quarto text with this dialogue, a longer address *ad Lectorem*, "but (since he is no lesse restrain'd, then thou depriv'd of it, by Authoritie) hee praies thee to think charitably of what thou hast read, till thou maist heare him speake what he hath written" (N_1^v). The imagined goal is unclear, perhaps an occasion of the play's revival at which Jonson could again perform the dialogue with Nasutus and Polyposus, or perhaps an occasion of intimate conversation with the ideal reader, unrestrained by Authoritie and even by publicity. In any event, that medium of unconstrained or unchallenged authorial expression which is imagined *here* is not print, not yet.

Sejanus

Lisa Jardine has recently offered a powerful account of how Erasmus used the press as an instrument of self-fashioning, but which I would slightly prefer to call self-composition (in moveable type and in engravings). This use of print as a medium of deliberate personal display has parallels among several later authors – Aretino, Montaigne, Harrington, Jonson, Congreve, Pope – and has important correlatives in the political sphere, since such figures as

---

[34] David Riggs offers an extremely useful account of this phase of Jonson's career, and particularly about Jonson's experience of himself in print and his vexed relation to the theater (*Ben Jonson: A Life*, 65–72). Like many scholars he alleges Jonson's immediate embrace of print and his virtually unqualified anti-theatricality; I believe the embrace of print and the recoil from the stage to be more complicated and, at this stage, somewhat less decisive. Riggs reads the very interesting evidence of Jonson's use of lines from Juvenal's Seventh Satire (lines 90 and 93) as title-page mottos for both *Every Man In* and *Cynthia's Revels* as proof of Jonson's determination to forsake theatrical activity as soon as possible, but the key line, "*Quod non dant Proceres, dant Histrio*" (What noblemen will not provide, the actors will), seems to me somewhat more than a simple reproach to the niggardliness of the English aristocracy, as Riggs would have it; I believe that the quotation carries with it some grudging appreciation of the players, as artists and sponsors and, above all, the vantage that any particular market could offer relative to another.

Maximilian, Elizabeth, and James were the objects of evolving, but coherent programs of print representation. Jardine's account of self-presentation in print slightly scants the interrogative or speculative character of this form of display. The compositorial author, with his absorption in detail, finds in print an instrument of self-discovery as well as of self-display, a form of self-display that entails the author's responsive adjustment of his type-set image. We can see this process work itself out in Montaigne's moveable self-typography: one of the great monuments of early print culture is the *exemplaire de Bordeaux*, Montaigne's "sixth edition" (as he put it) of the *Essays*. The *exemplaire de Bordeaux* is simply a copy of the fifth edition corrected and augmented in Montaigne's hand, a rewritten, reauthored printed book.[35] Of course, revision is not always an interrogative adjustment of *self*-presentation. When Jonson prepares a manuscript for print, or revises a quarto for folio presentation, he requires that the work and the medium adapt responsively each to the other; when he prepares a script for the press, the preparation explores and evaluates the theater, from which the script is wrested, and the press, to which it is entrusted. Edition is an essay in remediation.

It's worth keeping in mind that Jonson's early probings of print – as a surrogate for the stage, as a *melior theatrum*, or as an extra-theatrical fortress – all take place in a context of other negotiations of the relation of theatrical and printed texts. I have urged that we consider the print version of *Every Man Out*, with its promise of "more than hath been Publickely Spo-/ken or Acted," as an extra-theatrical and pro-theatrical rehearsal of the play, an artifact by which the author can supplement performance. But the quarto also reminds us that many regarded printed drama as a depredation of stage and author: just prior to the play's induction, the words of the stationer obtrude and confuse the impression of the play as an unmediated expression of Jonson's intentions. As if he needed to excuse the publication, Holmes piously protests that "It was not neere his thoughts that hath publisht this, either to traduce the Authour; or to make vulgar and cheape, any the peculiar and sufficient deserts of the Actors." We might seek an explanation for this piety by recalling that a few weeks after Holmes entered the play (on April 8, 1600) and thus around the time that *Every Man Out* was being printed, two other "my lord chemberlens menns plaies" were entered with the proviso that they "be not printed without further Aucthoritie"; by August, four more plays from the repertoire of the Chamberlain's Men, including *Every Man In His Humour*, were entered "to be staied." During the spring and summer of 1600 tensions between the stationers and this favored company of players had yielded new, experimental protocols and proprieties of interaction and the uncertainty of the situation is nicely expressed by Holmes's

[35] Richard I. Regosin, *The Matter of my Book: Montaigne's "Essais" as the Book of the Self* (Berkeley: University of California Press, 1977) and Barry Lydgate, "Mortgaging One's Work to the World: Publication and the Structure of Montaigne's *Essais*," *PMLA* 96 (1981), 210–23.

exaggerated deference. In this environment, in which players, stationers, and censorious "Authoritie" each claimed various rights to control when, if, and in what form, plays were to be printed, Jonson could hardly have come to think of print as a medium of uncontested representation. The book passes to a reading public through interfering fields of force.

Yet Holmes's apologetical sentence provides a map on which we may trace Jonson's progress towards the 1616 Folio. Holmes recognizes not only "the peculiar and sufficient deserts of the Actors," deserts given sketchy recognition in the Stationers' Register, but he also respects the possibility that an author could regard himself as traduced by publication. This possibility is not necessarily entailed by the competition recorded in the Register or, later, in the attack against the actors mounted in the prefatory epistle to *Troilus and Cressida*. It seems rather to be elaborated from a topos of Elizabethan prefatory matter, in which publication is puffed as a betrayal of secrets, a violation of privacies proper to the author and his circle. These are not violations of private property but rather of the proprieties of privacy – and thus affiliated less with Martialian jealousies than with those coterie proprieties eloquently evoked by a Horace. Still, what is *most* striking in Holmes's sentence is that it coordinates such proprieties with the actors' more richly institutionalized "deserts," an equilibration in which we can see authorial rights beginning to coalesce beneath the stationers' watchful gaze.

As has already been observed, the same equilibration, the same rhetorical constitution of literary property, takes place in contemporaneous non-dramatic publishing and we can see the antecedents of authorial property emerging from a rhetoric of propriety. The letter that Ling prefaced to *England's Helicon* (1600), adopts the language of scrupulous social distinction, lest publication be taken as a dangerously indiscriminate social event:

> If any man whatsoever, in prizing of his owne birth or fortune, shall take in scorne, that a far meaner man in the eye of the world, shal be placed by him: I tell him plainly whatsoever so excepting, that, that mans wit is set by his, not that man by him.

This vapid gallantry leads directly to the expression of attributive scruple discussed earlier, the apology lest "any man hath beene defrauded of any thing by him composed, by another mans title put to the same," and the promise that printing frees him "to challenge his owne in publique, where els he might be robd of his proper due" (along with the comical reassurance that if an author's decent anonymity be violated, well, others "in reputation every way equal with himselfe," will suffer alongside him). Though Ling begins with the language of honor, the violation soon appears as fraud, robbery, "more then theft." The legal force of the vocabulary is bolstered further in the very next sentence of the letter, its figurative character fading as Ling turns his face from the genteel author to his fellow tradesman:

Nowe, if any Stationer shall finde faulte, that his Coppies are robd by any thing in this Collection, let me aske him this question, Why more in this, then in any Divine or humaine Authour? From whence a man (writing of that argument) shal gather any saying, sentence, similie, or example, his name put to it who is the Author of the same. This is the simplest of many reasons that I could urdge, though perhaps the neerest his capacitie, but that I would be loth to trouble my selfe, to satisfie him.[36]

It will not suffice merely to remark here that the passage evidences disordered property relations within the book trade.[37] Ling seems to grasp at straws as he tries to place the protocols of scholarly manners and the regularities of stationers' copyright on a continuum of practice.[38]

The defenses of Ling and Holmes are landmarks. Both these men acknowledge that authors might feel "traduced" or "defrauded" by print publication, and both accept analogies between this indefinite sense of authorial infringement and forms of infringement – against actors and against other stationers – that had been articulated and proscribed by their own powerful trade association. Ling, indeed, is giving away the store: Daniel, Jonson, and, above all, Wither would learn to estimate the value of their names and of their writings by the proprietary standards of copyright and commodity. As modern authorial property here edges from rhetorical into institutional existence, it is hardly surprising that a writer like Jonson, formalist, domineering, and competitive, should manifest ingenious forms of literary possessiveness on the specific occasion of print publication.

Though I shall return shortly to *Cynthia's Revels* as a crucial document in the biography of Jonson as possessive author, it makes sense at this juncture to consider his fifth or sixth printed play, *Sejanus*, since so many of the various tendencies to which I have been directing attention are firmly manifested in that quarto of 1605; indeed, political exigencies intensified those tendencies.[39] Its title page is striking enough, although by now Jonson's choice of a motto from Martial cannot surprise us – it is from a poem in which the Roman poet denigrates practitioners of literary grotesquerie like Callimachus and exhorts

[36] *England's Helicon*, I:5–6.

[37] In 1606 Matthew Law was fined a pound for printing six pages from Chettle's *England's Mourning Garment* three years earlier, which had been duly registered and published that year by Thomas Millington.

[38] Under the commercial pressures of the moment, however, Ling clumsily misunderstands the force of attribution, which he treats as a kind of "royalty" or, rather, as the sole payment due to secure copyright. He is offering a genealogy of one of the key rights associated with modern intellectual property, the so-called "paternity right," the right to be identified as the author of a given work. Ling is amusing himself over the fact that this right conflicts with the right to anonymity claimed by contemporary poets.

[39] It has long been thought that *Sejanus* was printed before *Eastward Hoe*, but a good case can be made for the precedence of *Eastward Hoe*; see Thomas O. Calhoun and Thomas L. Gravell, "Paper and Printing in Ben Jonson's *Sejanus*," *Papers of the Bibliographical Society of America*, 87 (1993), 23–26.

the literate public to read *his* more verisimilar work.[40] What is startling about the title page is its austerity and, particularly, the absence of any reference to performance. It advertises an author's text.

SEJANUS
HIS FALL
Written
by
BEN. JONSON.

The details of the reception of *Sejanus* are better known than those of most of Jonson's plays: its performance at court during the Christmas season of 1603–4; its unsuccessful public performance by the Chamberlain's/King's Men either in early 1603 or in the summer of 1604 (the theaters having been closed for the year following Elizabeth's death); Jonson's report to Drummond that Northampton had him summoned before the Privy Council for this play; the deferral of its printing from late 1604, when Blount registered it, to late 1605, after a transfer to Thomas Thorpe; and the tangled coincidence of these delays with, first, the Privy Council interrogation, then Jonson's imprisonment for *Eastward Hoe* late in the summer of 1605, and, finally, the Gunpowder Plot, in which so many of Jonson's associates were implicated.[41] It would have been the politic thing for Jonson to emphasize the fact that the original performances dated from many months before the Plot, but he had no intention of adverting to the unsuccessful theatrical life of the play. This time, by an act of remediation, the quarto compensates for theatrical failure. And it does more: in performance the play had proven vulnerable to censorious responses and the printed text was charged with the burden of demonstrating the author's good faith and loyalty.[42]

Of course, the layout of the title page, which begins this remediation, may have been the decision of the printer, George Eld, but there is other evidence that Jonson himself wished to assert the quarto as an anti-theatrical, author's text. It includes commendatory verses by Chapman, Marston, Hugh Holland, and several others, unusual adjuncts to a printed play, and the last of these poems, by "EV.B.," describes printing as a recoil from the Globe, "that doubtfull Hell / From whence, this Publication setts thee free" (A3^v). In his foreword "To the

[40] Jonson does not quote the imperative, "*hoc lege*," but picks up the poem at the next lines, in which the matter of literary connoisseurship is reduced to a simple polarity: "*Non hic* Centauros, *non* Gorgonas, Harpyasque / *Invenies: Hominem pagina nostra sapit*" (You won't find centaurs, gorgons, or harpies here; my pages savor only of the human).

[41] The commendatory poem by *Philos* analyzes this split form of disapproval: "Yet some ther be, that are not moov'd thereby, / And others are so quick, that they will spy / Where later Times are in some speech enweav'd" (A3^v).

[42] My argument here closely parallels that of Evelyn Tribble in *Margins and Marginality: The Printed Page in Early Modern England* (Charlottesville: University Press of Virginia, 1993), 146–50.

Readers," Jonson expresses his gratitude to these poets, albeit on the curious grounds that their commendations are really apologia and have saved him a certain amount of explaining: "The following, and voluntary Labours of my Friends, prefixt to my Booke, have relieved me in much whereat (without them) I should necessarilie have touchd: Now I will onely use three or foure short, and needfull Notes, and so rest." He goes on to justify his violation of "the strict Lawes of Time" and elimination of a proper chorus, to defend his use of marginal notes and quotations against any imputation of pedantry, to excuse the fact that most of these marginalia are in Latin (he provides a full bibliographical reference to Lipsius' Tacitus and Etienne's Dio Cassius) and then,

> Lastly I would informe you, that this Booke, in all numbers, is not the same with that which was acted on the publike Stage, wherein a second Pen had good share: in place of which I have rather chosen, to put weaker (and no doubt lesse pleasing) of mine own, then to defraud so happy a *Genius* of his right, by my lothed usurpation.

Not at all surprisingly, translating a script into print occasions the clarification of property rights.

Granting the idiosyncratic zeal that Jonson could bring to dissociation, it must also be conceded that his protestations of scruple with respect to the second pen may be at least somewhat disingenuous, for it would be difficult not to accept the current scholarly consensus that Jonson undertook the revision chiefly in order to eliminate those passages in the stage version that had provoked his summons before the Privy Council.[43] Thus understood, the foreword to *Sejanus* offers a very sharp demonstration of Foucault's hypothesis that censorship constructs property, stapling, as it were, the author to his work: Jonson agrees to take the blame only for that form of the text over which he has total control, and such control – such mutual implication of author and book – can only be described in the language of property.[44] Still, it makes sense to remind ourselves of other mechanisms by which property is elaborated, recalling, for example, that Nicholas Ling used the *same* language, protested of the *same* scruple over defrauding the makers of books of their rights, in the editorial apologia to *England's Helicon*. In this very different case, Ling is attempting to restrict the property entailed by stationers' copyright, and he does so by pegging such rights to the traditional (and far less substantial) prerogatives of authors – an earlier case, in which competition, not censorship, breaks ideological ground.

Jonson's declaration of his scrupulous respect for the share of the second pen may be disingenuous in yet another sense. Not only does he obscure the anxious

---

[43] See H&S, II:3–5, where it is alleged that the revision was imperfect: the adjustment in the Folio at III.303, from "*Princes*" to "doubtfull Princes" is explained as a completion of the intended expurgation.

[44] For more sustained discussions of Foucault's assertions concerning the genetics of literary property, see *The Author's Due*, pp. 10–13.

motives of the revision by concentrating on authorial property, but he also turns attention away from other sharers who might regard themselves as having been defrauded by this publication. Jonson, that is, says nothing of having defrauded those "grand possessors," the King's Men, of *their* rights in *Sejanus*, though he does take pains to distance the printed play from the acting version. For this he is unapologetic and in this regard his foreword may be usefully contrasted with that which Marston wrote for *Parasitaster* a few months thereafter in which he insists that although the play belongs on the stage "it cannot avoid publishing." An earlier play, *The Malcontent*, published in 1604, is an even more telling foil for *Sejanus*, since in this instance Marston claims to have instigated printing. According to the foreword to this play, Marston sought print, as would Jonson, in the hope of regulating the reception of the play: "Some have been most advisedly over-cunning in mis-interpreting me, and & with subtlity (as deep as hell), have maliciously spread ill rumors" (A3ᵛ).[45] Although, unlike Jonson, Marston gestures with some slight nostalgia toward the stage, his argument anticipating that of the foreword to *Parasitaster* –

Onely one thing afflicts mee, to think that Scenes, invented meerely to be spoken, should be inforcively published to be read, & that the least hurt that I can receive, is to do my selfe the wrong...

– his motives for publication anticipate Jonson's:

...the least hurt that I can receive, is to do my selfe the wrong. But since others otherwise would do me more, the least inconvenience is to be accepted. I have my selfe therefore set forth this Comedy.

Marston is unashamed of the debt of his play to performance, whereas in the foreword to *Sejanus*, Jonson concedes such debt grudgingly.[46] When he makes his case for having written a play that lacks a chorus and trangresses the Unity of time, he admits the influence of contemporary theatrical taste on his dramaturgy, yet he promises to improve on the excuse: "but of this I shall take

---

[45] And cf. Lewes Machin's preface to the quarto of *The Dumb Knight* (1608), which also excuses print publication as a counter to envious misconstruction. Greg proposed interesting hypotheses on authorial involvement in the three early editions of *The Malcontent* in "Notes on Old Books," *The Library*, ser. 4, 3 (1921–22), 48–57.

[46] Though Marston's preface recalls theatrical origins, here, too, defensive publication seems to dissever the play from its theatrical origin, for the title page is as terse as that of *Sejanus*: it is, simply, "*THE MALCONTENT / By John Marston.*" It may be acknowledged that, although Marston and Jonson must have had occasional rapprochements, they develop in significant ways by defining themselves in contradistinction from each other. (As will be seen shortly, Jonson similarly defines himself *against* Daniel at important stages.) Marston is unquestionably reflecting on *Sejanus*, when he observes in the preface to *Sophonisba* (1606) that "to transcribe Authors, quote authorities, & translate Latin prose orations into English blak-verse [*sic*], hath in this subject beene the least aime of my studies" (A2). A reactive Jonson would find in this yet another inducement to the startling program for *Catiline*.

more seasonable cause to speake; in my Observations upon *Horace* his *Art of Poetry*, which (with the Text translated) I intend, shortly to publish." The logic of theatrical usage is offered merely as a place-holder for what he casts as genuine argument.[47]

It may be useful to sustain the comparison of *Sejanus* to *The Malcontent*, since at this historical juncture both Marston and Jonson seem to be attempting to ajudicate the claims of rival media, and to be situating authorial control above that rivalry. Marston's play was published in three editions in the course of 1604, with augmentations provided for both the second and third, though the second was at least partly printed from standing type, but each edition draws the printed closer to theatrical practice: the second adds a prologue and an epilogue and increases the number of stage directions; the third introduces a new induction, by Webster, and adjusts the title page (which had had a Jonsonian terseness in the first two editions) to accord with the more traditional formula: "*With the Additions played by the Kings / Majesties servants.*" If the King's Men tried to obstruct publication – and there is no evidence of an attempted obstruction – they were ineffectual. The same may be said of a Henslowe play, *The Honest Whore*, printed at almost exactly the same time by the same printer, Valentine Simmes, albeit for different publishers (*The Malcontent* was entered to Aspley and Thorpe; *The Honest Whore* was entered to Man). The title page makes no reference to the Prince's Men, who performed it at the Fortune, yet in this case there is nothing to suggest that Dekker was forced into print by censorious reception, and no evidence of Henslowe's approval or disapproval of these printings. What links it to the other plays is the evidence of authorial revising for print, or in response to it: as with *The Malcontent* several sheets of the second edition were printed from formes left standing in type from the first printing, but there are revisions throughout. *Parasitaster*, though printed over a year later, and not by Simmes, also went through two editions in rapid succession; again the second edition includes a number of authorial revisions (that is the gist of Marston's address to the reader for the second edition), but without entailing a full resetting of the text. However murky the pattern that emerges here, it is certainly interesting. Bowers supposed that the multiple issues-cum-editions of these three plays evidence an attempt to evade limits on the size of editions and the prohibition on books printed from standing type, old rules perhaps being newly enforced.[48] Authorial revision would thus be more

---

[47] There are other theatrical persistences in the quarto. Although Jonson did not add a classical chorus to the play in the course of his revisions, he contrived to make some reference to the form by marking the conclusion of each act with "MU. CHORUS." This marker alludes to the unevenly diffused practice of providing entr'acte music (common in the private theaters, less so in the public ones), but the allusion is almost entirely appropriative: Jonson remakes the theatrical novelty into a venerable textual form.

[48] "Standing Type in Elizabethan Printing," *Papers of the Bibliographical Society of America* 40 (1946), 214–24.

than a sign to the consumer of value added: the revisions would render colorable to fellow-stationers the assertion that each issue was a new one and would thus be a useful device for confirming some degree of industrial compliance. Bowers never reflected on how authors like Marston or Dekker might have responded to this sign of their usefulness in the regulatory dodge, or to the experience of remediating plays for the press. In the case of *Sejanus*, authorial response is perhaps more accessible to reconstruction.

He was in a convenient position to attend very closely to the details of printing. By the time Eld and his men finally began printing the play, Jonson had been living in the home of Esmé Stuart, Lord D'Aubigny, for at least several months (interrupted by his imprisonment for *Eastward Hoe*). D'Aubigny's mansion was situated in the Blackfriars district, near the private theaters, to be sure, but also near the center of English book production and, specifically, no more than a few streets away from Eld's shop. Although one can now no longer claim, as did Simpson and de Vocht, that Jonson took great care over all aspects of the printing, he evidently did pay fastidious attention to the layout.[49] Jonson's attention during printing was uneven: he seems to have checked the marginalia more carefully than the text, and he concerned himself more with page layout, capitalization, and pointing, than with spelling and letter spacing.[50] This is not

[49] Jonson's modern editors have made much of the fact that the book is generally well-printed and have usually attributed its excellence to Jonson; they ignored the fact that several formes preserve errors that argue against the most meticulous standards of correction, either by Jonson or by the men in Eld's shop. Greg's critique of Simpson's work on Jonsonian press correction in general, and on his correction of *Cynthia's Revels* in particular (see n. 27 above), together with Calhoun and Gravell's careful analysis of the variants in the *Sejanus* quarto ("Paper and Printing," 29–60) marshall a good deal of evidence against Simpson's claims, and until more meticulous work is done on the variants in Jonsonian texts published during his lifetime – and a good deal has already been done by David Gants (*A Descriptive Bibliography of the Works of Benjamin Jonson*, London, unpublished dissertation, University of Virginia [1997]), Mark Bland ("William Stansby and the Production of *The Workes of Beniamin Jonson, 1615–16*, *The Library*, 20 [1998], 1–33), and Kevin J. Donovan ("Jonson's Texts in the First Folio," *Ben Jonson's 1616 Folio*, eds. Jennifer Brady and W. H. Herendeen [Newark: University of Delaware Press, 1991], 23–37) – we should probably generalize from *their* work, rather than from Simpson's.
     Formes with the greatest density of stop-press corrections are identifiable by spelling evidence as the work of a particular compositor (Calhoun and Gravell, "Paper and Printing," 52). Thus it may be that the corrections owe more to a particular stationer's idiosyncratic working habits than to an author's capricious attention. To recur, as I believe one must, to McKenzie's skeptical principles in "Printers of the Mind," the extant record of stop-press corrections is a very small index of the total attention devoted to proof-reading, since proofs and revises that precede relatively printing were almost always discarded, leaving no record of early correction; see "Printers of the Mind," 42–49.
[50] There is good reason to believe that inner forme K was totally reset under Jonson's guidance (or at his insistence?) and primarily because the pages of its central opening (κ_2^v and κ_3) placed such unwonted demands on the compositor; Calhoun and Gravell, 57–58. This opening, which contains the scene of the sacrifice at Sejanus's home, is crowded with scholarly annotations, both marginal and interlineated. The resetting would have been Jonson's most serious intervention in the flow of printing, though he probably called for stop-press corrections to several other formes. Recent bibliographical work makes it reasonable to claim that he (or perhaps Chapman) called

to ignore the conspicuous classicism of the orthography, which probably derived from Jonson's manuscript, only to remark that stop-press corrections did not themselves do anything to enforce this feature. Certainly the spelling, as well as the styling of abbreviations and the typography of headings are idiosyncratic: they monumentalize the page, making steady reference to antique epigraphy.[51] But once Jonson had settled such matters of design, he gave only fitful attention to press-correction, for he was distracted by the task of providing the annotations in a timely fashion.[52] To secure the look he wanted for the page, Jonson needed to crowd it.

In his foreword, a defense of the book's unusual layout, he discusses the scholarly marginalia that clinch the remediation of the play. The eerie compulsion to self-exposure that makes Jonson so useful to the historian is in full force as he supposes that "in some nice nostrill, the *Quotations* might savour affected, I doe let you know, that I abhor nothing more; and have onely done it to shew my integrity in the *Story*." The turn is interesting: having asserted his unassisted, his integral authorship of the quarto (so as not to defraud his theatrical collaborator), Jonson argues his political integrity by disclaiming responsibility for the plot. Characteristically, he reclaims what he disowns, for his annotations are as much a stipulative guide to the reader as a deference to authorities: not content with singular title to *Sejanus*, Jonson nervously sought to control its reception. He had, after all, only recently been released from prison for an offensive line or two in *Eastward Hoe!* and, as we have seen, the stage version of *Sejanus* had already excited suspicion. Evelyn Tribble argues that Jonson contrived the annotations to protect himself from misconstruction: "marginal glosses, which function in Latin editions as a way of explicating the text, of making it available, are here a form of exclusion . . . 'none but the Learned' can have full access to the text."[53] It is a gambit that cemented Jonson's defensive attachment to print. Even the self-defense has anti-theatrical manifestations: such stage directions

for corrections to the first inner forme of the volume while it was in press and that he called for at least some of the stop-press corrections in four of the twenty-six other formes (outer formes B, F, H, and M) as well as perhaps one or two others.

Of course it is not a simple matter to distinguish an author's corrections from a print-shop worker's: Outer forme F was set by a compositor whom Calhoun and Gravell call Compositor C, prone to error in first settings and much given to stop-press corrections; heavy revisions on that forme may be his, not Jonson's. On the other hand, we can specify certain sites of authorial negligence, as when Jonson indicated that a word in $D_1{}^v$ should refer to a marginal gloss and then failed to provide the gloss before the entire forme was printed off.

[51] See, in particular, III.28–29, V.514–21, 523–24, 535 and 546–49.

[52] Hence there are a small handful of errors on the central opening of inner forme K: "scrupu' lous," "woe" (for "woo" or "wooe"), an inaccurate catchword.

[53] *Margins and Marginality*, 151; and see also Annabel Patterson, *Censorship and Interpretation: the Conditions of Writing and Reading in Early Modern England* (Madison: University of Wisconsin Press, 1984), 50–56, who argues that the marginalia emphasize the place of the play in the tradition of late Renaissance Taciteanism. Patterson sees the quarto as a somewhat more daring production than Tribble does.

as might aid a reader simply in making sense of the speeches find almost no place in the quarto, for the marginalia have squeezed most theatrical reference off the page.[54] In *Sejanus* the work of glossing, which shifts the focus of authorial control from the clarification of property rights to the clarification of meaning, is designed not only to specify certain meanings but also, and more urgently, to exclude other ones.

The quarto employs other devices to this end, one of which all but dates the printing and so explains the intensity of the defensive work. After his foreword to the reader, Jonson summarizes the play with an "Argument" – another anti-theatricalism – and its final sentence seems perfectly attuned to the atmosphere just after the discovery of the Gunpowder Plot: "This," the fate of Sejanus, "do we advance as a marke of Terror to all *Traytors, & Treasons*; to shewe how just the *Heavens* are in powring and thundring downe a weighty vengeance on their unnatural intents, even to the worst *Princes*: Much more to those, for guard of whose Piety and Vertue, the *Angels* are in continuall watch, and *God* himself miraculously working."[55] Jonson was no doubt eager to prove his loyalty and he may have already gone to greater lengths to do so – the reader will recall the theory that Jonson was recruited in September or October as part of the program of domestic espionage that led to the discovery of the Plot. Whether or not Jonson went so far to prove his loyalty to the crown after the trouble over his two most recent plays, it is no wonder that "The Argument" of *Sejanus* insists on the orthodox construction of the play. This semantic coercion is unabated throughout the book, carried on not only by the marginalia, but by the use of quotation marks to highlight *sententia* in the text.

We cannot be sure that Jonson chose which passages should be emphasized in this way: printers had long marked passages likely to appeal to a reader seeking new entries for his or her commonplace book. Yet even though the passages highlighted in Sejanus do not articulate a *particular* political ethics, there is reason to suspect this as authorial typography.[56] For though the sententia do not accumulate into partisanship, the pointing *is* slanted, for it emphasizes the highly topical problem of appropriate princely caution in the face of threat.

---

[54] A kind of stage direction is given, confusingly inter-lineated, at V. 172 and 183, to specify the ritual details of the sacrifice at Sejanus's house, a clarification more archaeological than dramatic; see the discussion of inner forme K above. One conventional stage direction ("Shoute Within") does persist, however, at V. 736. The Folio will reverse the typographical drift of the quarto, eliminating the bibliographic apparatus and inserting stage directions.

[55] The rest of the argument is printed in a font of reduced size, rendering this conclusion emphatic.

[56] The sententia reduce the play to an abstract struggle, with Machiavellian dicta (e.g. I.330, I.554–56, II.239–44, 273–78, 322–27, III.659–60, 735–43, IV.85–86, 91–92) battling statements of Ciceronian Stoicism (as II.257–59, IV.40–42, 67–70, 477–78, and, conclusively, V.733–35.) Debates between poles of political ethics are often carried out directly across page openings, a typographic rendering of opposition; see, in particular, the confrontation of maxims of the steadfast Agrippina and the servile Macro on the opening of H_2^v–H_3, which comprises IV.29–100.

In November 1605 Jonson or his printers could not but highlight Silius's rather banal maxim,

> There is nor losse, nor shame in providence:
> Few can, what all should doe, beware inough.
>
> (II.460–61)

If this seems merely dutiful, it significantly qualifies – perhaps even contradicts – the conclusion of Jonson's Argument, where he assures us that the angels themselves watch over pious and virtuous rulers. The highlighting focuses our attention on passages in which the question of *human* vigilance is raised. Thus,

> The way, to put
> A prince in bloud, is to present the shapes
> Of dangers, greater then they are (like late,
> Or early shadowes) and, sometimes, to faine
> Where there are none, onely, to make him feare;
> His feare will make him cruell.
>
> (II.383–89)

Jonson might have been taken to task for directing such remarks at the likes of Northampton, yet although the pointing goes far toward "absolutizing" this *sententia* and so extricating it from the narrative context, these lines are also merely the opinion of the shrewd and hapless Tiberius, and so perfectly deniable. The same ambiguity huddles round the highlighted sentence of the time-serving Silius, who speaks knowingly of "whisper ers [*sic*] . . . who have the time, / The place, the power, to make all men Offenders" [I.423–24].

I do not mean to suggest that Jonson adopts this highly ambiguous "voicing" with the simple intention that he might recast severe caution as dangerous paranoia and get away with it. Though Jonson no doubt felt abused by the suspicious reception of *Sejanus* and *Eastward Hoe*, the discovery of the Gunpowder Plot inevitably complicated his resentments, promoting the ethics of vigilance into a problem genuinely worth pondering. It eventually becomes, after all, the *central* problem of *Catiline* (1611). The events of 1605 had already made it urgent and so, by means of a fairly simple typographic device, *Sejanus* is transformed into a kind of proto-Catilinarian meditation. Heedless confidence is measured against repressive suspicion: in effect, the quarto provides a stern lesson in magnanimous interpretive prudence. In Act III, Cordus recalls how great men of earlier years responded to real and imagined attacks levelled against them, by Livy, Cicero, Catullus, and others:

> For such obloquies
> If they despised bee, they dye supprest,
> But, if they rage acknowledg'd, they are confest.
>
> (III.439–41)

Cordus promotes analytic poise as the ruler's greatest political tool, and he speaks for the typographer, whose highlighted *sententia* transform caution into the central problem of this printed play. This tranformation, the effect of a few emphatic quotation marks, is over-wrought, contrived, and, in its small way, impressively adroit.

Could we guarantee that Jonson chose the sententia for emphasis it would be quite enough to demonstrate that he had begun to assimilate the press as an instrument of poetic craft. But even more impressive contrivances may be found in other stationers' registers, also asserting both the author's loyalty and the foolish malice of those who might suspect him. Calhoun and Gravell have recently subjected the quarto to minute bibliographic analysis; they have determined that most of the surviving copies of the play are printed on a white paper manufactured in England around 1605 which bears the royal initials as its watermark. The paper is apparently very rare, appearing in no other books or manuscripts that these bibliographers managed to examine.[57] The use of this paper has a smug brilliance: readers like Northampton, disposed to "peer into" Jonson's printed play for hidden messages, would find only an insignia of utter patriotism. It is worth considering how Eld might have come by this paper. Calhoun and Gravell propose that the paper had originally been manufactured as a present to the king, intended perhaps as a private stock of writing paper, and that Aubigny, the king's cousin and a Gentleman of the Bedchamber, helped Jonson secure a supply of paper for the printing of the play.[58] It is easy to be distracted here by the impressive fact that Jonson contrived access to this precious material, but it is also worth remarking that it is quite unusual for an author to involve himself with the material stratum of book production in the first place. (Jonson and Aubigny are performing a function that would normally have fallen to Thorpe, the publisher: the cost of paper made up half of the normal expense of any given publication.) A motive of self-protection, of defensive pragmatism drives Jonson away from the theater and deep into the stationers' mystery, into an engagement with their materials, their methods, and the logic of their economy.

We can gauge Jonson's satisfaction with the printed *Sejanus* by his recurrence to its formal features and by his loyalty to Thorpe. A few months later, early in 1606, Thorpe published *Hymenaei*, and although this time the printer was Valentine Simmes, the format is profoundly indebted to that for *Sejanus*. It is hardly surprising that the same may be said for Jonson's next printed volume of masques, also published by Thorpe, but the formal influence of *Sejanus*

---

[57] "Paper and Printing," 18.

[58] The printer who almost certainly produced the paper, John Hans Spilman, had an English monopoly in the manufacture of white paper. The monopoly had been conferred in 1590 by Elizabeth, for whom he had produced white writing paper watermarked with her initials. James knighted Spilman when he visited his paper mill in 1605. See Calhoun and Gravel, "Paper and Printing," 18.

on *Volpone*, published by Thorpe sometime during the early months of either 1607 or 1608, also deserves to be remarked.[59] The quarto of *Sejanus* with its untheatrical title-page, its inner threshold of commendatory poems, its apologia and argument, and its scholarly marginalia, had been presented in ways that sharply distinguished it from contemporary play-texts, and the quarto of *Volpone*, though a plainer thing, was clearly modelled on its predecessor: again the untheatrical title page, again the commendatory poems; the prose argument of *Sejanus* is bettered in *Volpone* by an acrostic poem and the apologia is absorbed into a long dedicatory epistle addressed to the universities of Oxford and Cambridge.[60] The dedication, with its anxious attack on those "that professe to have a key for the decyphering of everything" is plainly fighting the previous year's battle (and serves to remind us what very particular business was on Jonson's mind when he conceived of Sir Politique Would-Bee), but the larger project of the dedication is to set the published play apart from a culture of performance; thus:

now, especially in *dramatick*, or (as they terme it) stage-*poetrie*, nothing but ribaldry, profanation, blasphemy, all licence of offence to god, and man, is practis'd . . .

For my particular, I can (and from a most cleare conscience) affirme, that I have ever trembled to thinke toward the least prophanenesse; have lothed the use of such foule, and un-washed baud'ry, as is now made the foode of the *scene* . . .

This it is, hath not only rap't me to present indignation, but made me studious heretofore; and, by all my actions, to stand off, from them . . .

– and his work on *Sejanus* has taught Jonson that print is a most effective instrument of such setting-apart – . . . "which may most appeare in this my latest worke" (lines 36–8, 43–7, 100–03). Although *Volpone* was a stage success, the quarto imitates and elaborates that of *Sejanus* in proposing itself as counter-theatrical. As he describes it in the dedication, the printed text is not at all derivative of performance; it is a proof-text, a distinguishing demonstration of who Jonson is. "My workes are *read*, allow'd, (I speake of those that are intirely mine) looke into them . . ." (lines 54–55; emphasis mine).

The compositorial authorship manifest in *Sejanus* was consequential in other ways as well – or perhaps it would be more accurate to say that the play is a leading instance of larger developments in the culture of English authorship. Many play-texts published in these years elaborate the themes of Jonson's early

[59] There are notorious difficulties in dating *Volpone*: most critics accept a performance date of 1606 and a publication date of 1607, based on a first-performance date of 1605 (on the Folio title page) construed as Old Style and a title page and dedicatory epistle dated February 11, 1607 construed as New Style – but this critical consensus was achieved without any decisive argument. For discussion of these issues, see Chambers, *Elizabethan Stage*, III:368–69 and Greg, "The Riddle of Jonson's Chronology," *Collected Papers*, 184–91.

[60] There are other resemblances of format: speakers' names in small caps, printed without indentation; continuous, columnar array of speeches.

quartos into *topoi*. Asserting the value of print as a medium of improved presentation, Barnes' *The Divil's Charter* (1607) is presented "as it was plaide before the Kings Majestie, upon Candlemasse night last: by his Majesties Servants. *But more exactly revewed, corrected, and augmented since by the Author, for the more pleasure and profit of the Reader.*" It was just such publication that nettled Heywood, provoking his pronouncements against playwrights who make "double sale of their labours" in the preface to *The Rape of Lucrece* (1608; A₂). No doubt he intends the allegation of venality to have a special sting, for when playwrights claim a preference for print, they often do so by condescending to theatrical audiences. Like *Sejanus*, Fletcher's *The Faithful Shepherdess* (printed *c.* 1608) is bulwarked by a string of commendatory poems by Fletcher's friends, together with several dedicatory poems and a letter to the reader by Fletcher, and the assemblage gives off a strong odor of coterie condescension. Fletcher's letter all but sneers at the vulgar misapprehension of tragicomedy in the theaters; Beaumont is less restrained:

> I not dislike
> This second publication, which may strike
> Their consciences, to see the thing they scornd,
> To be with so much will and art adornd.
> Bisides one vantage more in this I see,
> Your censurers must have the quallitie
> Of reading. (A₃ᵛ)

Webster's tone in the pages introductory to *The White Devil* is a bit more plaintive, and certainly less defiant, but his argument is similar: "ɪɴ publishing this Tragedy, I do but challenge to my selfe that liberty which other men have tane before mee . . . since it was acted, in so dull a time of Winter, presented in so open and blacke a Theater, that it wanted . . . a full and understanding Auditory."[61] As mentioned earlier, Webster also hovered over the layout of the printed play – a page from Jonsonian books.[62]

Client and owner

Sunt quidam qui me dicant non esse poetam
    sed qui me vendit bybliopola putat (Martial, *Epigrams*, VIV.194)

---

[61] *The Complete Works of John Webster*, ed. F. L. Lucas (London: Chatto & Windus, 1927), I:107. And cf. the title page of Webster's *The Duchess of Malfi*, printed in 1623, a decade after its original performance, "The perfect and exact Coppy, with diverse / *things Printed, that the length of the Play would* / not beare in the Presentment" (II: 29).

[62] Though hardly a Jonsonian play, *The White Devil* makes Jonsonian gestures. In his preface, for example, Webster defends his violation of classical rules in terms that seem closely indebted to the apologetics of *Sejanus*.

A sense that print achieves only an incomplete and therefore an unsatisfactory withdrawal from the theater may often be observed in Jonson's parerga. Thus the quarto of *Catiline* (1611) includes addresses to two groups of readers, "the Reader in Ordinarie" and "the Reader extraordinarie," which effectively translates Martial's distinction, invoked in *Cynthia's Revels*, between the *polyposum* and the *nasutum*: printing discriminates against the theatrical audience and now must further discriminate within the reading public. The famous preface to the quarto of *The Alchemist*, printed a few months later, pursues similar discriminations:

TO THE READER

IF thou beest more, thou art an Understander, and then I trust thee. If thou art one that tak'st up, and but a Pretender, beware at what hands thou receiv'st thy commoditie; for thou wert never more fair in the way to be cos'ned (then in this Age) in Poetry, *especially in Playes.*

Having thus divided the reading public, Jonson denigrates those readers who are not understanders by a rhetorical sleight-of-hand that identifies them, specifically, with theatrical spectators: ". . . *thou wert never more fair in the way to be cos'ned (then in this Age) in* Poetry, *especially in Playes: wherein, now, the Concupiscience of Daunces, and Antickes so raigneth, as to runne away from Nature, and be afraid of her, is the onely point of art that tickles the* Spectators" (A₃). Thus the distinction between theater and the press, spectatorship and reading, becomes illustrative, a *figure* for the more important distinction between good and bad reading. And there are other illustrations, other ways of marking this latter distinction, for as Jonson would have it the two readerships operate within different economies of consumption. The workings of the two economies is probably easiest to see in the preface to *Catiline*. Confronting "the Reader in Ordinarie," Jonson concedes that "the Muses forbid, that I should restrayne your medling, whom I see alreadie busie with the Title, and tricking over the leaves: It is your owne." "Your owne," like the text purchased by the pretending reader of *The Alchemist*, a "commoditie": Jonson finds his best figure for bad reading in the alienations of purchase, which divide producer and consumer. He sharpens the force of this description by contrast – hence his address to the reader extraordinary: "You I would understand to be the better Man, though Places in Court go otherwise: to you I submit my selfe, and worke" (A₃). The understanding of the extraordinary reader establishes a relation of intimate clientage between reader and writer.

For Jonson, then, committing a play to print has contradictory valences: he can experience publication both as a loss of control and as the recovery of a control earlier ceded to the stage. It is important to keep in mind that, in this context, "control" designates a variety of related forms of affect and effectivity, related but not identical.[63] In preparing his first plays for print, Jonson sought to affiliate them with a learned tradition and to stigmatize those who had not approved the work or might not approve it. In his more careful work on the typography of *Sejanus*, he pursued some new goals, ones that were specific to print: to redistribute semantic emphases by manipulating the medium of transmission and (for purposes both psychological and political) to eliminate the vagaries of theatrical transmission, the intercession of unreliable Others. But the 1611 quartos, of *The Alchemist* and of *Catiline*, throw into relief Jonson's pursuit of a specifically economic control. This pursuit manifests itself in two ways, each pointing in opposite historical directions, each of which may now be somewhat more carefully described.

Once again, Jonson's mature practices may be traced to the determining period of the late nineties, when he made his first aesthetic responses to his economic predicament. Jonson was virtually indentured to Henslowe in the late nineties and he began writing for other companies as a way of groping for his bootstraps. He might have felt that his prospects were improving in the winter of 1599/1600 when *Every Man Out Of His Humour* was selected for performance at Court, yet that performance also redounded directly only to the profit of the actors, and not to his. Whether or not Jonson could conceive of an alternative commercial arrangement, we can detect his nascent resistance to the disadvantaged situation of authorship in the conclusion he wrote for the version performed before Elizabeth. Macilente speaks the final lines of the play, but in a voice like that of the poet himself:

Marry, I will not doe as PLAUTUS, in his *Amphytrio*, for all this (*Summi Iovis causa, Plaudite:*) begge a *Plaudite* for gods sake; but if you (out of the bountie of your good liking) will bestow it; why, you may (in time) make leane MACILENTE as fat, as Sir IOHN FAL-STAFFE.

By means of this deft refusal of servility and its insistence on the poet's deter-mining choices, the critical character shoulders his way before the monarch, challenging her to spontaneous generosity, seeking royal patronage, though on his own resistant terms. The stiff-necked temperament that checks submission here is given economic articulation in the alternative conclusion. In the public performances of the play, Macilente addresses the audience as a spokesman for the actors, but something personal, something especially Jonsonian stirs in the lines in which Macilente addresses the "Kind *Patrons* of our sports (you that can judge, / And with discerning thoughts measure the pace / Of our strange Muse)" ("Revised Conclusion," lines 2–4). This is Jonsonian not only because of the fastidious distinguishing between the *nasutum* of these judicious patrons and the *polyposum* of the "vulgar Pallat" (11); in what would become a characteristic turn, Jonson imagines disabling the ignorant and scornful by quasi-legal means

---

[63] Love, *Scribal Publication*, 39–40.

> Such as these
> We pawne 'hem to your *censure*, till Time, Wit,
> Or Observation, set some stronger seale
> Of *judgement* on their judgements; and intreat
> The happier spirits in this faire-fild Globe
>
>   . . .
>
> That with their bounteous *Hands* they would confirme
> This, as their pleasures *Pattent*: which so sign'd
> Our leane and spent Endeavours shall renue
> Their beauties with the *Spring* to smile on you.

(lines 20–32)

Just as signature and seal confirms the patent, so applause confirms approving discrimination. The patent had long been the chief instrument of royal patronage, but under Elizabeth, this instrument had acquired an unprecedented liquidity; a source of crown revenue for the royal grantor, the patent was often quickly converted into cash by the recipient, the privileges it conferred to be exploited by the skillful capitalist. Jonson's figure is thus kept poised between the idiom of clientage and the idiom of commercial law, from which poised conjuncture the dual paths of Jonson's mature relation to the literary economy can be traced. Though he insists on the warm sociability of the relation instituted between the stage and its patrons, that rapport is figured in terms that imply the stipulative, regulated, and abstract nature of the relationship: the economy of literature is split between the ostensible ease and interest of clientage and the tensions and disaffections of a modern marketplace.

To choose the first path, towards patronage, is not remarkable in and of itself; what distinguishes Jonson's pursuit is its reactive and productive exorbitance. In the motto prefixed to *Poetaster*, Jonson follows Martial's lead in imagining the ideal reader as a super-patron, *magni mihi numinis instar*. Jonson's pursuit of clientage was both historically and psychologically atavistic: he never gave it up and it always had a fantastic character. The culling of readers which begins with Macilente's discriminatory seal of judgment continues in *The Alchemist* and *Catiline*, where the selection of a special class of extraordinary, understanding readers develops the earlier fantasy.[64] Such selection is at least a bit more than a fantasy, for Jonson *dedicated* these quartos – *Catiline*, "the first . . . that ever I dedicated to any person," to Pembroke; *The Alchemist*, to Lady Mary Wroth, making them among the first dedicated texts of *printed* drama in the history of the English theater.[65] He flatters Lady Wroth in terms that could also have

---

[64] Discrimination persists as a central concern for Jonson and the epigraph for the Folio *Workes* makes a motto of this concern. It is a thinly adapted line from Horace (*Satires*, I.x.73–74): "*neque, me ut miretur turba, laboro: Contentus paucis lectoribus*" (nor should I strive for the crowd's admiration, but will content myself with few readers).

[65] See Virgil B. Heltzel, "The Dedication of Tudor and Stuart Plays," *Studies in English Language and Literature*, ed. Siegfried Korninger, *Wiener Beiträge zur Englischen Philologie* Bd. 65 (Stuttgart: Braumüller, 1957), 74–86 and Franklin B. Williams, Jr., *Index of Dedications*

applied to Pembroke, as one whose "*judgement* (*which is a* SIDNEYS)" rendered her the leading member of the class of understanders, an ideal patron. Not surprisingly, Jonson sustains Martial's rhetoric in the devotional language of this dedication:

MADAME

IN the age of sacrifices, the truth of religion was not in the greatnesse, & fat of the offrings, but in the devotion, and zeale of the sacrificers: Else, what could a handfull of gummes have done in the sight of a hecatombe? *or, how might I appeare at this altar, except with those affections, that no lesse love the light and witnesse, then they have the conscience of your vertue.*

A sacrifice, a gift: thus described, the printed book is withdrawn, at least rhetorically, from the bookseller's stall. The pursuit of clientage in despite of a vulgar theater and a vulgar book trade radicalizes Jonson's relation to the media of publication and, on occasion, determines his plots, as if clientage were the very motive of genre. But Jonson's pursuit of clientage was complex and had been so since 1600, when he imagined himself as Crites in *Cynthia's Revels*. I have written elsewhere about the way in which this play anticipates Jonson's later career as a Jacobean masque-maker; here I need only point out that when he revised the play for the Folio, after years of masque making, he rewrote the fifth act so that that distinct and comprehensible unit took on the unmistakeable bipartite structure of Jonson's mature Jacobean masques.[66] It is also a biography. Crites begins the act as an actor, trapped within the constraints of public theatricality;

---

and Commendatory Verses in English Books Before 1641 (London: The Bibliographic Society, 1962), particularly p. 10. Honigmann (*Stability*, 180) makes the important observation that "very few early plays carried a proper dedication – very few, that is, in comparison with other pamphlets by the same authors." In 1607, Francis Burton claims to know of "but a singular President" for the practice of dedicating plays (*The Tragedy of Tiberius*). Excepting *Cynthia's Revels* (for which special dedicatory sheets were printed for presentation copies to Camden, and Lucy, Countess of Bedford, in addition to the general dedication of the play to "the Court"), Jonson first dedicated a quarto text, of *Volpone*, in that same year, the dedicatees being "The Two Most Noble and Most Equall Sisters, The Two Famous Universities." The single precedent was Marston's, whose earlier choices of dedicatee are as striking as Jonson's here: in 1602, he dedicated *Antonio and Mellida* to "Nobody" (a device imitated in John Day's *Humour out of Breath* [1608]) and, in 1604, he dedicated *The Malcontent* to Jonson himself. Chapman adjusted this procedure by initiating the crucial practice of dedicating plays to actual or potential *patrons*: in 1608, he dedicated *Byron's Tragedy* to Thomas Walsingham. (The dedication of *All Fools* [1605] to Walsingham is spurious, a forgery contrived by J. P. Collier for the 1825 *Dodsley's* edition of the play). The dedication of plays may be imitated from Italian practice, where it was not uncommon; either Marston, Jonson, or Chapman might have been influenced by such procedures.

Ironically, the practice of dedicating plays soon acquired a tinge of vulgarity, or so Massinger implied in the prefatory epistle to *The Unnatural Combat* (1639); appealing to Anthony Sentlinger, the son of one of Massinger's patrons, he begins, "SIR, *That the Patronage of trifles, in this kinde, hath long since rendred Dedications, and Inscriptions obsolete, and out of fashion, I perfectly understand*" (A$_2$).

[66] "The Script in the Marketplace," *Representations*, 12 (1985), 101–14.

he ends the act as patronized poet, a legislator of aestheticized morals. If *Cynthia's Revels* enacts Jonson's competition for a place in an older sector of the literary economy, the performance of the masques *allegorizes* the success of that attempt.[67] This structural autobiography is a wish-fulfillment, but the wish, or wishes, thus fulfilled are hardly simple and cannot be summed up as the extrication of the poet from a vulgar literary market and his secure relocation within the royal household. *Cynthia's Revels* and many of the masques that reproduce its paradigm place a poet-figure on stage, and dramatize his control by giving him extraordinary cohortative power, a power that not only reduces the actors to mediators but that also constrains the noble masquers. Insofar as the device of the main masque could be scripted it enables Jonson to retain that stiff-necked reserve that he brought even to the pursuit of patronage. "I will not . . . begge a *Plaudite*": the scripted revels express a desire not merely for patronage but for a patronage that would function as a controlled economy, and one in which poet, not the patron, determines the structure of exchange. Even in the masque, that most atavistic of forms, we become aware of Jonson's second economic path, the one that leads toward a regulated future in a public theatrical market.

It may be worth leaping ahead a decade and a half to consider Jonson's fullest and wittiest image of that future. In 1614, Jonson would hilariously usurp the company's rights, when a prompter intrudes upon a South Bank stage "Not for want of a *Prologue*, but by way of a new one," two literary agents, a Prompter and a Scrivener, intrude upon a South Bank stage and so shunt aside the erstwhile "grand possessors."[68] The Scrivener brings a contract from the author, "ARTICLES of Agreement, indented, between the *Spectators* or *Hearers*, at the *Hope* on the Bankside, in the County of *Surrey* on the one party; And the *Author*" (Ind., 64–66) which must be approved before the play can begin.

INPRIMIS, It is covenanted and agreed, by and betweene the parties abovesaid, and the said *Spectators*, and *Hearers*, aswell the curious and envious, as the favouring and judicious, as also the grounded Judgements and understandings, doe for themselves severally Covenant, and agree to remaine in the places, their money or friends have put them in, with patience, for the space of two houres and an halfe, and somewhat more. In which time the *Author* promiseth to present them by us, with a new sufficient Play called *BARTHOLMEW FAYRE*, merry, and as full of noise, as sport. (Induction, lines 73–82)

He drives a hard bargain: the extent of a spectator's right of censure is to be kept proportionate to the price of his seat; the spectator is entitled only to his

---

[67] See Richard C. Newton's pertinent remark on Jonson's presentation of his career in the 1616 Folio, "You might say that he presents his career not as a drama but as a masque"; "Jonson and the (Re-)Invention of the Book," 38.
[68] Induction to *Bartholomew Fair*, line 58.

own opinion, and none other's; he agrees to expect nothing more exciting than mimetic consistency allows; and he is to protect the play from topical construction and the playwright from the sort of punitive censure that had already twice landed Jonson in prison. The authorial obtrusion is, of course, an index of the eminence Jonson had obtained by 1614, but what is most remarkable is the form in which Jonson projects his aggrandized self, the legal articulation (fanciful, to be sure, and transient) of cultural authority. On the margins of less probing, more accurate dramatic representations – in non-Jonsonian inductions and epilogues – the Elizabethan play is usually represented by the speaking actor as "ours," the possession and, indeed, the product of the actors; where the playwright is mentioned, he is almost never "the Author" or "the Playwright," but instead "our poet," an adjunct to the proprietary group of performers. Yet in the revolutionary legal fiction of *Bartholomew Fair*, the playwright claims to be presenting the play through a subsidiary acting company – "by us," as the actor says. A development that we traced in some of the title-pages of the preceding decade, in which plays begin to be advertised, not "as played by" some particular acting company, but rather as "written by" some particular author, is now absorbed into the induction itself.[69] But what is most striking for my purposes about this contract is the agency of the author within the transaction, Jonson's claim to be presenting the play through a subsidiary acting company – "by us," as the actor says. Certainly the very idea of a market is under examination in *Bartholomew Fair*, but the induction is perhaps the most radical moment in the play's market analysis.[70] The induction purports to *change* the literary market contractually; further, it represents Jonson, and not the Lady Elizabeth's Servants, as the true publisher of the play.

Bartholomew Fair comes well along in Jonson's career, and it is by no means the first of his attempts to reshape literary market relations. Certainly the transformation of an acting company from proprietor into middleman – into middleman at best – had already been effectively achieved, if only at the Banqueting House at Whitehall. As masque-maker, Jonson had been compensated directly by his audience, and at a rate approximately three to four times that paid by an

---

[69] This assumption of printerliness into a performance text recalls the casual joking of the Induction which Webster wrote for the King's Men's production of *The Malcontent*. Marston's play was originally performed by the boys' company playing at the Blackfriars, probably in 1604, but the Induction suggests that the performance of the play by the King's Men was *quid pro quo* for the boys' appropriative performance of a play from the King's repertory: "Why not Malevole in folio with us," asks Condell during the Induction, "As Jeronimo in decimo-sexto with them?" and then, comparing this professional rivalry to the competitive tensions that fire revenge tragedy, "They taught us a name for our play; we call it *One for Another.*" This is light, but not likely to have escaped Jonson's notice: Marston dedicated the print version of *The Malcontent* – Malevole in quarto – which includes Webster's Induction, to Jonson, as a make-peace after their feuding at the turn of the the century.

[70] See the final chapter of Haynes, *Social Relations.*

acting company for one of his plays.[71] That experience of relative commercial autonomy was compounded and elaborated when Jonson prepared his masques for print. These were sensations that Jonson was reluctant to surrender as a public playwright. I take it that the induction to *Bartholomew Fair* spoofs that reluctance, though the spoofing is more than a little disruptive of the norms of dramatic induction, for the induction is Jonson's most unabashed fantasy of the playwright as masque-maker.[72]

The practice of semantic regulation

> He has the *monopoly* of sole-speaking. (Cymbal, of Penniboy Senior, in Jonson, *The Staple of News*, III.iv.69)

The publication of Jonson's royal masques and entertainments, which began in 1604 with the quarto that included *Part of King James Entertainment Through London*, the *Panegyre* on James's entry to the first Parliament of his reign, and the *Entertainment of the Queene and Prince their Highnesse to Althrope*, takes place at the forking of the path to clientage and the path towards monopolistic competition. To an important degree, the publication of Jonson's masques sustains his economic atavism, for it is one of those practices and fantasies by which Jonson sought to detach his scripts from their associations with a vulgar theater. And although this will seem paradoxical at first, this remediation, the turn to print, sustains Jonson's campaign for aristocratic patronage, for, despite the fact that publication in print is itself a vulgarizing gesture and one that removes the masque from the exclusive sphere of occasional consumption, Jonson took advantage of print to denigrate and so compete with the work of Samuel Daniel, whom he perceived as his chief competitor for the patronage of the Jacobean court.[73]

As a way of distinguishing his own practice as a deviser of court entertainments from Daniel's, Jonson fastened on their differing attitudes to explicitness and to the sociology of semantics, and he thereby sharpened his own sense of

---

[71] Jonson was usually paid 40 pounds for a masque; on expenditures for masques see Chambers, *Elizabethan Stage*, I:207–12.

[72] The complex feedback between Jonson's masque-making and his playwriting is a large topic and cannot be fully explored here. But it may be observed that colloquial prose, a form to which Jonson brought considerable attention during his early years as a playwright and which he no doubt associated with the satiric realism that flourished in the theatrical environment of the turn-of-the-century, was slowly eliminated from his plays, whereas it becomes more and more the distinctive feature of Jonson's masque-making, a verbal device for competing with the textural density of Jones's visual spectacles.

[73] I am here condensing a somewhat more ample argument in my "Printing and 'The Multitudinous Presse,'" from *Ben Jonson's 1616 Folio*, 168–91.

For a sensitive account of semantic regulation throughout Jonson's *corpus*, see George E. Rowe, "Author and Audience," chapter 2 of *Distinguishing Jonson: Imitation, Rivalry, and the Direction of a Dramatic Career* (Lincoln: University of Nebraska Press, 1988), 38–67.

the utility of print in the shaping of his own career. It had been Daniel's elegant compliment to the twelve aristocratic performers to assert how easily goddess and noble mortal interpersonate each other, yet Jonson alleges that it is simply tawdry to have the Countess of Bedford speak as if she were her own herald:

> Next holy Vesta in bright majesty
> Appears with mild aspect in dove-like hue:
> With th'all combining scarf of amity
> T'engird strange nations with affections true.[74]

According to Jonson, this explicitness amounts to semiotic bathos; he makes the point in a gloss to his text of the coronation pageant in 1604 and again in his printed annotations to *The Masque of Queenes* (1609): "to have made themselves, their owne decipherers, and each one to have told, upon their entrance, *what they were, and whether they would*, had bin a most piteous hearing, and utterly unworthy any quality of a *Poeme*: wherein a *Writer* should alwayes trust somewhat to the capacity of the *Spectator*, especially, at these *Spectacles*" (B_2–B_2^v).[75] This deference is certainly disingenuous, for the iconography of these early spectacles could be quite obscure, but it helps us make sense of the interpretive aids that crowd the pages of Jonson's printed masques from the very outset. *Queenes*, in particular, was full of the recondite demonological lore so dear to the king and Jonson probably supposed that even the noble participants in the masque would wish to have a souvenir program that would explain the devices and so ally the capacity of the spectator with the enthusiasms of the monarch. Jonson does all he can to produce a printed text that will function as a kind of pre-requisite supplement, the necessary adjunct to an ostensibly self-sufficient performance, one which will make up the gaps in the masquers' (again, ostensibly) total understanding, and which will provide the vulgar with the reference materials necessary for the imaginary reconstruction of a social and semantic event designed to exclude them. In essence, Jonson uses print to complete the event.

It is easy enough, then, to see the tactical continuity between the early printed entertainments and the printed *Sejanus*. His burgeoning reservations about theatrical performance and vulgar display spilled over to shape his attitudes to the coterie masquing of a court he longed to serve, with sometimes confusing effects. He felt the special pressure to celebrate the transitory magnificence of masquing, its conspicuous consumption, yet the texts of his masques are all

---

[74] *The Complete Works in Verse and Prose of Samuel Daniel*, A. B. Grosart, ed., 5 vols. (1885, repr. New York: Russell and Russell, 1963), III:200–01.

[75] Jonathan Goldberg was the first, to my knowledge, to have pointed out the implied attack on Daniel's procedures in these lines; see his *James I and the Politics of Literature* (Baltimore, Johns Hopkins University Press, 1983), 58. The relevant passage in the coronation volume is lines 253–67.

more or less anti-occasional in tendency.[76] With increasing regularity, Jonson's printed masques hint at the dependent insufficiencies of performance and generously compensate for them. Hence, for example, this glancing, perhaps slightly scolding comment in the quarto of *Hymenaei*, the wedding masque of 1606:

After them, the *musicians* with this song, of which, then, onely one *staffe* was sung; but because I made it both in *forme*, and *matter* to emulate that kind of *poeme*, which was call'd ... *Epithalamium*, and (by the ancients) us'd to be sung, when the *Bride* was led into her chamber, I have here set it downe whole: and doe heartily forgive their ignorance whom it chanceth not to please. (lines 435–41)[77]

In the quarto of *The Haddington Masque*, published two years later with the *Masques of Blacknesse and Beautie*, performance is even more invidiously compared to print, for at least a single moment in the performance is described as having been an actual obstacle to comprehension:

Here, the *musicians* . . . sung the first staffe of the following *Epithalamion*: which, because it was sung in pieces, betweene the *daunces*, shew'd to be so many severall *songs*; but was made to be read an intire *Poeme*" (lines 338–42)

Such corrigenda were a means to the kind of regulated expression towards which Jonson seems consistently to have been laboring. And there was a special fitness in this aspiration. The regularities of typography, the fact that print is a medium of far less density of information and thus far less susceptible to variation than is performance, were features that attracted Jonson. The typography of the Coronation entertainments (1604), the text of which is physically sectored and hedged both with Jonson's aesthetic pronouncements and with his scholarly notes, prepares for the anti-theatrical text of *Sejanus*, the typography of which inspired, in its turn, that of *Hymenaei* in 1606. But more important for the

---

[76] The early *Entertainment at Althrope* captures the contradiction in Jonson's attitude with some piquancy. The account of the event in the quarto concludes with a modest denigration of the mere text, "which was the least of the Entertainement in respect of the reality, abondance, delicacie, and order of all things else" (printed as a variant in H&S, which takes the Folio as copy-text), yet this deference to the event is printed after a speech of 24 lines that Jonson introduces thus: "There was also another parting Speech; which was to have beene presented in the person of a youth . . . but by reason of the multitudinous presse, was also hindred. And which we have here adjoyned."

For an important attempt to discriminate the various relations between text and performance implied or asserted in printed and manuscript accounts of masques, see Jerzy Limon, *The Masque of Stuart Culture* (Newark: University of Delaware Press, 1990).

[77] This is not an exclusively Jonsonian device. Dekker's account of the coronation entertainments for James concludes, "Reader, you must understand, that a regard, being had that his Majestie should not be wearied with teadious speeches: A great part of those which are in this Booke set downe, were left unspoken: So that thou doest here receive them as they should have bene delivered, not as they were"; Thomas Dekker, *Dramatic Works*, ed. Fredson Bowers, 4. vols (Cambridge: Cambridge University Press, 1953–61), II:lines. 1622–26. Note the difference between Dekker's tone and Jonson's.

historiography of property, the fact that no acting company could lay claim to the texts for Jonson's early entertainments meant that he could experience quite direct commercial and productive relations with the stationers who printed and published them. Masque-making changed Jonson's place in a variety of disseminative markets.

Here again the facts of industrial history impinge on those of literary history. James's accession provoked a flurry of competitive activity within the book trade and three books in particular leave obscure traces of this competition in the records of the Stationers' Company: Blount's edition of *B. Jonson's Part of King James' Entertainment Through London*, Man's edition of Dekker's *The Magnificent Entertainment*, and the architect Stephen Harrison's *Arches of Triumph Erected in Honor of James*. Rights to each of these publications were contested, though the details in the cases are obscure. Harrison, who was responsible for the construction of the several arches for the coronation procession and for the design of all but Jonson's for Fen-church and Temple-Bar, seems to have arranged publication with the printer, John Windet. The book was produced in two versions: one, with engravings only, which was sold by two company members, Sudbury and Humble, and a second, with engravings and accompanying text, which Harrison sold out of his own home. This is one of the rare but important instances in which someone from outside the Stationers' Company performed at least some of the functions of a publisher: the stationers involved must have been willing to forego exploitation of their monopoly rights in order to participate in a prestigious and perhaps lucrative venture, and Harrison thereby achieved considerable commercial control over the dissemination of "these fruites of my invention, which Time hath nowe at length brought foorth, and ripened to this perfection" (B_1). Yet because of the strictures on outsiders engaging in the book trade, it was Windet against whom Smethwicke complained before the Stationers' Court in October 1604 – whether over payment for job-work on this fairly elaborate production or over some matter relating to copyright is unclear at this remove. The book had never been registered, perhaps because Harrison wished to avoid vesting the copyright: those with whom he was working may have been willing to acquiesce in the arrangement. Ominously, an unusually firm assertion of authorial property could sharply disrupt trade.

A different conclusion may be drawn from the trade dispute excited by the other coronation volumes. Blount registered *Jonson's Part* four days after the coronation and Thomas Man, Jr. registered Dekker's *Magnificent Entertainment* two weeks later. Man no doubt planned a more or less comprehensive volume, whereas Blount's entrance is quite specific: "A part of the Kinges Majesties right royall and magnificent entertainment . . . so much as was presented in the first and last of their triumphall arches, with a speach made for the presentacion in the Strond." Controversy of some sort erupted, presumably concerning overlaps in the objects of protection: Blount may have attempted to print more of the coronation materials than he had specified in the entrance, or he may have challenged Man's right to print any mention of Jonson's part, or Man may have pulled strings to have Blount's registration voided – his father was Master and perhaps the most powerful member of the Stationers' Company.[78] Only the settlement that concluded the quarrel is recorded: on May 14, the Stationers' Court determined that Blount should turn over his remaining stock of four hundred copies to Man, who was to compensate him at the rate of 6s. per ream. By the time Man issued his second edition he would claim to be printing *The Whole Magnificent Entertainment* [my emphasis], though he did not integrate the full text of Jonson's contributions, which are mentioned only in sketchy summary.[79] Indeed, the Man–Dekker volume variously slights Jonson. Dekker acknowledges the architect, carpenters, painters, carvers, and city officials who collaborated on the event (lines 1591–1610), he carefully attributes the speech of Zeal at the Conduit in Fleet Street to Thomas Middleton (lines 1469–72), but Jonson goes unnamed, which strongly suggests that either Blount or Jonson, or perhaps both of them, had refused to participate in the preparation of a synthetic coronation book.[80] Moreover, Dekker keeps the description of "the *Genius* of the Cittie", the first of his allegorical speakers, ostentatiously brief:

To make a false florish here with the borrowed weapons of all the old Maisters of the noble Science of Poesie, and to keepe a tyrannical coyle, in Anatomizing *Genius*, from head to foote, (onely to shew how nimbly we can carve up the whole messe of the Poets) were to play the Executioner, and to lay our Cities houshold God on the rack, to make him confesse, how manie paire of Latin sheets, we have shaken and cut into shreds to make him a garment. (B₁)

Jonson, by contrast, had lavished many learned pages on the description of *his* Genius, of his attendants, his daughters, and his clothing: three years after *Poetaster* and *Satiromastix*, the War of the Theaters became a Battle of the Books. Whether or not the tensions between Dekker and Jonson impinged on those between Blount and Man, the two disputes are closely aligned.

This account does not exhaust the mysteries of *Jonson's Part*. Greg noticed that the bibliographic evidence suggests that the inclusion of Jonson's *Panegyre* and *Althrope Entertainment* in Blount's volume was an afterthought; these texts,

---

[78] See Greg's *Bibliography of English Printed Drama* (London: Printed for the Bibliographical Society at the University Press, Oxford, 1939–54), no. 200.

[79] Oddly, Harrison *does* give the text of Jonson's speeches for the declamations at Fen-Church and Temple Bar, another indication of the extraordinary privileges accorded Harrison and of Blount's lost claims to the Jonson volume.

[80] It might be noted that Dekker also speaks appreciatively of William Kip's illustrations for Harrison's forthcoming volume, deferring detailed verbal description of the arches: "your eye shall hereafter rather be delighted in beholding those Pictures, than now be wearied in looking upon mine" (260). At least to this extent, the Man-Dekker volume seems to have been coordinated with Harrison's *Arches*.

moreover, are not mentioned in the very specific description in Blount's registration entry.[81] By including them in the volume he eventually published, Blount
did exceed the terms of his registration, though the added material in no way
infringed Man's registration. It appears that, faced with the competition from
Man, Blount (or Jonson) decided to use these additions to reorient *Jonson's Part*,
making it a collection of Jonson's various devisings for the new king – more a
"Jonson" volume than a coronation book.[82] That is, if Man had somehow made
a colorable claim to the verbal representation of the coronation (with rights to
pictorial, or pictorial-and-verbal mimesis allocated to Harrison – an exceptional
arrangement, to be sure), then Blount could claim to be reproducing quite a different object, Jonson's royal devisings. The reference of Blount's text, like that
of Jonson's, is thus shifted away from the particular occasion. This rehearses a
development that we have already traced in contemporary dramatic publishing:
competition among "publishers" (whether within the book trade, among acting companies, or across trade lines) conduces to the heightened commercial
importance of "authorship" as an object of monopolistic protections.

Of course, if the reorientation of the volume had indeed been adopted to evade
Man's claims to the pageant text, the evasion was unsuccessful, for Blount was,
after all, still obliged to sell Man his remaining copies of *Jonson's Part*: this
episode amounts to no major development towards authorship as commercial
property.[83] Jonson prospered from the moment more than Blount, securing for
himself the commissions for *The Penates*, the royal entertainment at the home
of Sir William Cornwallis on May 1, 1604; for *The Masque of Blacknesse*
and *Hymenaei*, the Twelfth Night entertainments of 1605 and 1606; as well
as for entertainments at Theobalds in 1606 and 1607 – and all this despite the
momentous, if temporary, disfavor that he suffered for *Sejanus* and *Eastward
Hoe*.[84] Having staged a fantasy of his preferment in *Cynthia's Revels*, Jonson

---

[81] *Bibliography of English Printed Drama*, no. 200.
[82] The title makes a good deal of the argument: "*B. JON: / HIS PART OF / King James* his Royall
and Magnifi- / *cent Entertainement through his* / Honorable Cittie of London / . . . Also, a briefe
Panegyre of his Majesties first . . . *entrance to his High Court of Parliament,* / . . . With other
Additions. / Mart. *Quando magis dignos licuit spectare triumphos.*"
      Part I of the volume, consisting of Jonson's contributions to the coronation procession and
the "Panegyre," survives unaccompanied with Part II, the Althrope entertainment, in 3 copies;
2 copies of Part II unaccompanied with Part I, also survive. It may be that Blount delivered only
copies of Part I to Man, though there is no evidence that Man attempted to issue a composite
volume, Dekker's *Magnificent Entertainment* together with *Jonson's part* (i. e., Part I) – at least,
no contiguously bound copies of the two quartos survive.
[83] For the possibility that Blount turned over only a *portion* of his sheets, see n. 82 above. He
apparently still had hopes for his work with Jonson, for he registered *Sejanus* in November, but
he soon lost heart over that project for the reasons already discussed, and transferred his rights
to Thorpe, the stationer with whom Jonson would work most consistently during the next few
years.
[84] The commission for *Blacknesse* is particularly striking since Jonson *seems* to have contrived to
attend the performance of Daniel's *Vision* and to have been sufficiently disruptive to get himself

had turned to the press and, idiosyncratically, had made it an instrument of clientage. An inverse proportion: Blount may have sought to make the poet a modern instrument of press competition, but he thereby encouraged Jonson's considerable professional conservatism.

And yet, as has already been observed, the publication of the masques also put Jonson into direct contact with the controlled economy of Blount and Man. If masque-making seems to return Jonson to the circle of genteel clientage, his first text of a court masque proper indicates that, by 1606, he had developed a precise feel for attribution, for the proprieties of property in this form: a lesson he could have learned from the stationers with whom he had been working – though, as we have seen, the importance of attributive accuracy was undergoing a growth spurt in a variety of sectors. Not surprisingly, the attributive rhetoric of *Sejanus* reappears, cooler and more meticulous, in *Hymenaei*, as if precision in such things mattered a very great deal:

The *Designe*, and *Act* of all which, together with the *Device* of their *Habits*, belongs properly to the Merit, and Reputation of Maister YNYGO JONES; whom I take modest occasion, in this fit place, to remember, lest his owne worth might accuse mee of an ignorant neglect from my silence. (line 678, n.)[85]

He goes on in quite a different vein to name, praise, and pledge his friendship for Alphonso Ferrabosco, who wrote the music, and to acknowledge his own inability appropriately to assess or praise the dances of Thomas Giles: Jones is thus singled out as the proprietary stickler. But Jonson concludes these acknowledgments with a quotation from Martial that shows him to be as much the stickler: "What was my part, the Faults here, as well as the Vertues must speake. *Mutare dominum nec potest Liber notus*" – "a well-known book cannot change author" or, to render *dominum* more precisely, "cannot change its lord, its master." The quotation is taken from one of Martial's poems on literary theft and compensation, I.66, the epigram in which the aspiring *fur librorum* is advised to seek uncirculated work, *secreta carmina*, if he wishes to go undetected. The same *auctor*, the same concerns, and the same terms shape Jonson's commentary at the end of his next published masque:

The two latter [dances] *were made by* M. THO. GILES, *the two first by* M. HIE. HERNE . . . *The tunes were* M. ALPHONSO FERRABOSCO'S. *The device and act of the scene,* M. YNIGO JONES *his, with addition of the* Trophæes. *For the invention of the whole and the verses,* Assertor qui dicat esse meos, Imponet plagiario pudorem. (*Haddington*, lines 348–55)

ejected from the performance. (That this was the precise occasion of Jonson's ejection cannot be proven; see my "Printing and 'The Multitudinous Presse'", 170–72). Despite this and the trouble over *Sejanus*, Jonson was plainly (after Shakespeare) the most favored playwright of the early Jacobean court: two days after the performance of *Blacknesse*, the King's Men performed *Every Man Out* at court; they returned in less than a month with *Every Man In*.

[85] And cf. the remark in the dedicatory epistle of Volpone: "My workes are read, allow'd, (I speake of those that are intirely mine) . . ."

Adapting lines from the *locus classicus* of the proprietary concept, Jonson analyzes the objects of creative industry even more closely. As in *Hymenaei*, the *device* is attributed to Jones, but here *device* is distinguished from the more encompassing *invention* (here rendered, in what I take to be emphatic pleonasm, as "the invention of the whole"). The boundaries are being drawn, meticulously. As in Martial's day, as during the War of the Theaters, irregular competition for preferment and place is figured as theft, as plagiarism; this time the figure serves what Jonson was coming to regard as a crucial economic analysis.

Henslowe and the Chamberlain's Men, Blount, Man, Thorpe, and their fellows, Dekker, Daniel, Martial, and Jones – all variously taught Jonson to consider his literary works as property, and to imagine legal dominion over those works. In the early stages, this imagining of dominion grows out of a desire simply to control the reception of his work, to silence unappreciative critics and to encourage sympathetic "understanders": we can see its emergence in the conclusion to *Every Man Out*, in which Macilente seeks legal sanction against "rebelling Ignorance." A decade later, Jonson will specify the legal fantasy by associating semiotics with economics: understanding is an aspect of patronage, while misconstruction (that is, disapproval) is represented as a function of mere purchase. In *Queenes*, then, the client's deference to "the capacity of the [aristocratic] *Spectator*" partners a correlative dismissive gesture, the seller's forced indifference: "let the lookes and noses of Judges hover thick; so they bring the braines: or if they do not, I care not. When I suffer'd it to goe abroad, I departed with my right: And now, so secure an Interpreter I am of my chance, that neither praise, nor dispraise shal affect me" (E$_3$^{v}). (The autograph presentation manuscript that Jonson prepared for Prince Henry, to him Jonson dedicated the printed text of the masque, omits this brittle reflection: it is specified to the book trade.) Two years later Jonson will copy these lines into the front matter of the quarto of *Catiline*, where the dedication to Pembroke, and the submission to the understanding "Reader extraordinarie" is paired with a dismissal of the "Reader in Ordinarie", who is imagined just having completed his purchase and, now, fingering his goods. "It is your owne. I departed with my right, when I let it first abroad. And, now, so secure an Interpreter . . ." (H&S, V:432). The description of semiosis as an economy, of language as a system of exchange, is so much a staple of late twentieth-century literary theory (to say nothing of social theory), that it is easy to miss the imaginative force and historical pungency of Jonson's phrase. Among the greatest in a great generation of satirists, Jonson was especially alert to the nervous habits of commerce, and fascinated by the power of goods over social relations. He had witnessed an array of contested monopolistic practices traversing the theater and the book trade, attending with sometimes resentful imagination to the rules and regularities of the literary marketplace and toying with the idea of their extension and transfer. Thus, in *Sejanus*, he supposes that the rights of stationers' copyright might extend to his collaborator so that publication might effectively defraud that author; in *Queenes* and *Catiline*, he imagines the social fact of interpretive license as an economic law, a market invading what should be a social culture of intimate sympathy. Later, in the contractual prologue to *Bartholomew Fair* Jonson's invention once again springs from his longing to control reception, although this time he rouses himself to trim self-parody, so that, chastened, the passion appears as mere humour. As in *Queenes* and *Catiline* (for by now it is a signature ceremony) Jonson surrenders his authority, but this time the surrender is his part of a meticulous conveyance:

It is further agreed that every person here, have his or their free-will of censure, to like or dislike at their owne charge, the *Author* having departed with his right: It shall be lawfull for any man to judge his six pen'orth, his twelve pen'orth, so to his eighteene pence

– the sharp distinction between extraordinary and ordinary reader, between *nasutum* and *polyposum*, is temporarily dissolved by a radical and comic relativism –

so to his eighteene pence, 2. shillings, halfe a crowne, to the value of his place: Provided alwaies his place get not above his wit.[86]

Fantasy rescues Jonson's disabused intuition of his semiotic powerlessness: he has departed his right, but a legal fiction will constrain consumption, improbably extending the author's control of the text. In this inspired moment of knowing self-parody, Jonson imagines (constructs, yearns toward) nothing less than what modern law recognizes (constructs, imagines) as the moral rights of authorship.

Jonson, Jones, and the object of copyright

> "Well, what *is* the song, then?" said Alice. (Lewis Carroll, "It's My Own Invention," chapter 8 of *Through the Looking Glass*)

This fantasy of durable authorial rights naturally has its grounding in fact. That Harrison, the architect of James's coronation pageants, can take over the

---

[86] I think it difficult to over-estimate the arresting power of this moment for those most seriously involved in the Jacobean literary marketplace. When Heminge and Condell address "the great Variety of Readers" in the opening pages of the first Shakespeare Folio nine years later, they will adopt this same swagger on behalf of the departed Author: "And though you be a Magistrate of wit, and sit on the Stage at *Black-Friers*, or the *Cock-pit*, to arraigne Playes dailie, know, these Playes have had their triall alreadie, and stood out all Appeales; and do now come forth quitted by a Decree of Court, then any purchas'd Letters of commendation." Small wonder that Greg once toyed with the idea that Jonson, not Heminges and Condell, was the true author of this letter; *The Shakespeare First Folio*, 18–21.

functions of publisher and book-seller suggests occasional extensions of authorial power over the marketing of intellectual work.[87] But developments in the several spheres of dissemination that center roughly on the theater also gave Jonson's fantasy some warrant. Although the various wars of the theaters may have provoked Jonson's longing for a secure place at court, the mud-slinging skirmishes between playwrights, the subtler competition between players and stationers for control of the dissemination of plays, and the comings-to-cuffs between actor and author to which Rosencrantz attests – all this exuberant competition had happy consequences for playwrights: the war economy was inflationary. During the 1590s the prices that acting companies paid for plays hovered around six pounds, but by 1602 eight pounds was not uncommon, and by 1612, prices ranged from ten to twenty or twenty-five pounds.[88] During this crucial period, that is, a modest seller's market developed, and although these prices hardly compare with those paid for masques, they would have materially mitigated the distrust of theatrical business that Jonson might have felt at the very turn of the century. If his early professional career proceeds from the public theater to debtor's prison to private theaters to Whitehall, the period of his greatest achievement finds him shuttling between the professional theater and the Banqueting House. It would be easy to think of a Jonson repeatedly thwarted at court, thrown back again and again into the competitive milieu of the public theaters, but the emergence of an author's theater, in which a playwright might plausibly insist that "those that play your clowns speak no more than is set down for them," in which, moreover, players and printers had begun to compete for access to scripts would have substantially augmented Jonson's delight in what he could do with five acts and a professional cast.

The variety of markets in which Jonson willingly involved himself; the volatility of the specifically theatrical market, buoyed by the inflation in the value of plays; the instability of his reputation at court, also buoyed by frequent if uncertain invitations to collaborate in royal entertainments – this ferment gave point and force to the theoretical squabbling in which he engaged, elated, morose, and eager. Before I take up the nexus of professional and commercial concerns focused on the production of the Folio *Works*, it will be useful to return to his quarrel with Inigo Jones, which takes up and develops many of the polemical concerns of his earlier competitions, with Daniel, with Dekker, and, during the so-called War of the Theaters, with several of Dekker's fellows.[89]

[87] *The Author's Due* takes up a number of such extensions outside the sphere of dramatic publishing and performance.
[88] Chambers, *Elizabethan Stage*, I:373–74 and Greg, *Henslowe's Diary* (London: A. H. Bullen, 1904–8), 126–27.
[89] See D. J. Gordon, "Poet and Architect: The Intellectual Setting of the Quarrel between Ben Jonson and Inigo Jones" in *The Renaissance Imagination*, ed. Stephen Orgel (Berkeley: University of California Press, 1975), 77–101, and my *Responsive Readings* (New Haven: Yale University Press, 1984), 93–95 and 128–29.

This time rivalry provoked Jonson to pronouncements on the very ontology of the work of art and since Jonson's curious reflection on what constitutes the "soul" of the masque marks an important stage in the cultural history of literary artifacts, it may be worthwhile to cite passages with which students of the Jonsonian masque have long been familiar, such as this, the opening of the printed text of *Hymenaei*, published in 1606:

It is a noble and just advantage, that the things subjected to *understanding* have of those which are objected to *sense*, that the one sort are but momentarie, and meerely taking; the other impressing, and lasting: Else the glorie of all these *solemnities* had perish'd like a blaze, and gone out in the *beholders* eyes. So short-lived are the *bodies* of all things, in comparison of their *soules*. (lines 1–7)

Willful and not, I think, obtuse, Jonson slightly misrecognizes one of the eeriest features of these entertainments. It was, in fact, part of the ethos of expense to let these solemnities perish like a blaze, for after the aristocratic audience had retired from a performance the rabble was allowed in to strip the hall of the rich stuff of display.[90] From this institution of evanescence, part of the ongoing work of class distinction, Jonson abstracts a spiritual principle:

And, though *bodies* oft-times have the ill luck to be sensually preferr'd, they find afterwards, the good fortune (when *soules* live) to be utterly forgotten. This it is hath made the most royall *Princes*, and greatest *persons* (who are commonly the *personators* of these *actions*) not onely studious of riches, and magnificence in the outward celebration, or shew; (which rightly becomes them) but curious after the most high, and heartie *inventions*, to furnish the inward parts: (and those grounded upon *antiquitie*, and solide *learnings*) which, though their *voyce* be taught to sound to present occasions, their *sense*, or doth, or should alwayes lay hold on more remov'd mysteries.

This does not denigrate the material spectacle so much as put it in its place.[91] We are a long way from the sneering of "An Expostulation with Inigo Jones," with its mild ironies –

> You aske noe more then certeyne politique Eyes,
> Eyes that can pierce into the Misteryes
> Of many Coulors!

---

[90] See *Blacknesse*, lines 6–9 and Chambers, *Elizabethan Stage*, I:206.
[91] Denigration will come a few lines later in harsh words for those who "squemishly crie out, that all endevour of *learning*, and *sharpnesse* in these transitorie *devices* especially . . . is superfluous" (lines 19–22, and cf. l. 292, note e). It is a pointed slap at Daniel who had cast oblique but unmistakeable aspersions on Jonson's iconology in the second 1604 printing of his *Vision*: "and though these Images have oftentimes divers significations, yet it being not our purpose to represent them, with all those curious and superfluous observations, we took them onely to serve as Hieroglyphics for our present intention, . . . without observing other their mysticall interpretations" (Epistle to the Countess of Bedford, lines 44–52).
    On Jonson's slightly idiosyncratic use of the dyadic figure of body and soul, see Gordon, "Poet and Architect," 80–81.

– and its breath-taking sneer –

> O Showes! Showes! Mighty Showes!
> The Eloquence of Masques! What need of prose
> Or Verse, or Sense?

but even in this poem, written a quarter of a century after Jonson prepared *Hymenaei*, he recurs to the old vocabulary –

> Oh, to make Boardes to speake! There is a taske
> Painting & Carpentry are the Soule of Masque.

(lines 45–47, 39–41, and 49–50)

In the cool introductory passages of *Hymenaei* (as in the prefatory contract for *Bartholomew Fair*) Jonson is preoccupied with the idea of abstract endurance – that is the primary force of his emphasis on the "soul" of masque, which is anxiously poised to ascend from the moment of performance. But the Aristotelean tincture of the figure also carries a reminder of the metaphysical priority of idea to instantiation, as it does in the verse attack on Jones.[92] Later in the text of *Hymenaei*, when Jonson reuses this trope to describe a particular dance – "*which was so excellently performed, as it seemed to take away that* Spirit *from the* Invention, *which the* Invention *gave to it: and left it doubtfull, whether the* Formes *flow'd more perfectly from the* Authors *braine, or their feete*" (lines 311–15) – he does so with gallant condescension to those bodily "things . . . which are objected to *sense*," but which, of course, derive their actual form from authorial intention.

In Jonson's next published volume of masques, the polemical temperature rises towards that of the "Expostulation." *The Haddington Masque* tells us that work with Jones had further sharpened Jonson's attributive sense: hence his intention to shame any plagiarist who might challenge his claim to "the invention of the whole" and his differential use of the term, *device*, to describe Jones's contribution.[93] The volume opens with a courteous deference to "the honor, and splendor of these *spectacles* [which] was such in the performance, as could

---

[92] Stephen Orgel, *The Jonsonian Masque*, (Cambridge, Mass.: Harvard University Press, 1965), 61–67, as well as the works by Gordon and myself cited above.

[93] Gordon surveys several terms used to describe the contributions of poets and designers (see "Poet and Architect," 80–92 and "Appendix I: Poet and Architect," 269–71). *Device* and *invention* are often used interchangeably, as they are in *Queenes* (for which see the discussion below). But *device* can also be used, interchangeably with *argument*, in a subordinating sense, in which case it refers to a plot-summary, a teasing-out of some prior, more abstract concept for which the term, *invention*, is often used. Hence Gordon's summary statement on p. 81, that " 'Invention' is the most inclusive term"; he acutely cites Vasari later in the essay – "Invention always was and always will be considered the true mother of architecture, painting and poetry" (94). In *The Haddington Masque* Jonson applies *device* to Jones' contribution in the subordinating sense and, specifically, as if it were the visual correlative of a verbal argument, that is, of the narrative teasing-out of an invention. (*This* usage makes it interchangeable with the term "design," for which see note 94 below.)

those houres have lasted, this of mine, now, had been a most unprofitable worke"
(*Blacknesse*, 1–3), but honor and splendor turn out to be treated with exactly
the same respect accorded to the dancers' feet in *Hymenaei*. Jonson stakes his
claim: "the invention was derived by me, and presented thus" (lines 22–23)
after which come several paragraphs of scenic description that conclude, "So
much for the bodily part. Which was of master YNIGO JONES his designe, and
act" (lines 90–92).[94] So much indeed: with the exception of *Queenes*, the newly
published masque texts of the next dozen years make very little of the bodily
part and do not refer to Jones at all.[95]

Queenes is a crux. Elaborating the sketchy antimasque of *The Haddington
Masque*, *Queenes* gives us what has been accepted as the mature Jonsonian
form, a form which we can now recognize as staging a confrontation between
professional theatrical practice and courtly festivity, and this confrontation res-
onates with the polarities of Jonsonian aspiration and practice under discussion
here – between the economies of patronage and the market, between convivial
collaboration and scrupulous possessiveness. The introductory account of the
masque is full of attributive apportionment. "I chose the argument, to be, *A
Celebration of honorable, and true Fame, bred out of Vertue*," Jonson reports,
asserting his primacy in now characteristic fashion, but he attributes the formal
elaboration of the masque to Queen Anne herself – "her Majestie . . . had commanded me to think on some *Dance* or shew, that might præcede hers, & have
the place of a foile or false *Masque*." He then goes on fully to acknowledge
Jones's work, this time conferring the generally prestigious term "invention"
on his contribution, while at the same time circumscribing its scope – "the devise of their attire was M^r. *Jones* his, with the invention & *Architecture* of the
whole *Scene, & Machine*" – and allowing himself a final fillip of repossession –
"onely, I prescrib'd them their *Properties* of Vipers, Snakes, Bones, Hearbs,
Rootes . . ." (A$_4^v$).[96] This is the same author who dismisses the printed text a

---

[94] For *design*, see Gordon, "Poet and Architect," 94–95. Like *device, design* could be used to
mean the mental precursor to a derivative instantiation; it thus functions interchangeably with
invention. Hence, in *Queenes*, "the Scene, wch was the House of FAME" is said to be "intierly
Mr Jones his Invention and Designe" (lines 681–83). In Dolce and Vasari, however, *design* refers
to the visible expression of the *concetto* or *invention*. In general, when "invention" and "design"
are used together with any implied differentiation, the latter term is secondary; it is, therefore,
closely analogous to "device."

[95] After this long hiatus, in 1621, Jonson acknowledges that "*the invention*" of *The Masque of
Augurs* "*was divided betwixt Mr JONES and mee*." This is an after-thought – the acknowledgment
appears only in a second issue of the 1621 quarto – and it may be that Jonson had been forced
to mention Jones.
  Jonson was not the first to experience the publication of royal entertainments as a stimulus to reflection on literary ontology. As early as 1604, Harrison referred to his remediation
of the coronation pageants for James as conferring a "second more perfect beeing" on the
spectacle (sig. B$_1$).

[96] Cf. the concluding note on the second state of the 1622 quarto of *Lovers Made Men*: "*For the
expression of this, I must stand; The invention was divided betwixt M^r. JONES, and mee* . . ."
(H&S, 625). When Jonson published *Love's Triumph Through Callipolis* in 1631, the fact

few pages later: "when I suffer'd it to goe abroad, I departed with my right."
A crux: in one sense publication enables the precise distribution of authorial
claims; in another, it marks the surrender of those claims.

It will be useful to be very precise concerning what is crucial here. The author
who discharges the quarto edition onto a capricious semantic market represents
his editorial labor quite differently when he inscribes his presentation copy
for the queen: "The same zeale, that studied to make this Invention worthy of
yor Majestyes Name, hath since bene carefull to give it life, and authority."
Though printing exposes the invention to indiscriminate market forces and
vulgar misconstruction, it also serves to manifest the superiority of Jonson's
"part" to Jones's, for it enables the spirit of authorial invention to display its
transcendence of present occasions. Things being unequal, bodily shows are
thus subordinated to the material book (on the analogy of the subordination of
bodies to souls): annotation gives authority; print, life. It is as if, in quarto, the
soul of a masque could be raised a spiritual body.

I have cast this in an extreme form to emphasize the distinctiveness, if not the
singularity of Jonson's position. Heywood is uneasy about print publication and
casts aspersions on those who split their allegiances between stage and page
by making double sale of their labors; Marston, it will be recalled, claimed a
disinclination to see *The Malcontent* printed, and, as an apology for its textual blemishes, asked "that the unhandsome shape which this trifle in reading
presents, may be pardoned for the pleasure it once afforded you when it was
presented with the soul of lively action." Warmth of popular reception surely
bolstered Marston's sense that his plays were most perfectly animated on stage,
but when Beaumont, outraged at the hostile reception of Fletcher's *The Faithful
Shepherdess*, commended that play to a more discerning reading public, the
commendation is not only reserved, but back-handed: "I not dislike / This second publication" – a startling contrast to Jonson's attitude to print.[97] Beaumont
certainly makes no claims for the *essential* or metaphysical superiority of print
to performance.

Jonson is different. His growing allegiance to the page has temperamental
origins, which had rendered him especially alert to objective stimuli from a
variety of sources. And the competition with Jones, an artist of great intelligence, adaptability, and accomplishment, was also determining, for it forced
him to give a theoretical articulation to his typographic allegiances. Quarreling,
Jonson naturally insists on the old principle of the superiority of the mental

---

that Jones' name appeared only second on the title page precipitated a final explosion in their
sputtering relations: Jones refused to work with Jonson; Jonson wrote the "Expostulation."

[97] Later, in 1640, Thomas Nabbes published *The Unfortunate Mother*. The title page seems to
place him in Jonson's camp, since it advertises the play as "*A / TRAGEDIE. / Never acted; but
set downe / according to the intention / of the Author*," but the front matter of the volume allies
him with Marston, *et al.*, for it describes the play as "a piece that (undeservedly, I hope) hath
beene denied the credit which it might have gain'd from the stage" (A₂).

to the mechanical arts and asserts the essentially abstract nature of his own contribution. But because the printed book proved to be the most serviceable *index* of that abstraction, and because the book can be firmly differentiated from the blaze of performance, or from an arch hastily erected and left standing, gorgeous and vulnerable, in the street, Jonson begins to treat the (relatively) durable, (relatively) invariant printed book as if it verged, soulfully, on identity with his invention. Such assertions about the nature and location of the "object of art" activate concerns that had quietly unsettled turn-of-the-century title pages, making an issue of them. To have advertised *Every Man Out* as "Containing more than hath been Publickely Spoken or Acted" was perhaps something more than a mere insistence that all the theatrical cuts and corruptions had been restored; the same may be said of a sparer title page like "SEJANUS / HIS FALL. / Written / by / BEN: JONSON." That the formula, "as it hath been acted by . . ." appears neither on the title page of the quarto *Sejanus* (1606), nor on those of *Volpone* (1607), *Catiline* (1611), or *The Alchemist* (1612) may be somewhat more than a repudiation of performance, or of theatrical reception. These title pages seem to imply that the printed text *is* the play – or, at least, that is how Jonson would retrospectively have glossed these title pages from a very particular, but very important biographical vantage in 1631, when the tendency of his contentious aesthetics culminates in the title page of *The New Inne*:

> A COMOEDY.
> As it was never acted, but most
> negligently play'd, by some,
> the Kings Servants.
> And more squeamishly beheld, and censu-
> red by others, the Kings Subjects.
> 1629.
> Now, at last, set at liberty to the Readers, his Maties
> Servants, and Subjects, to be judg'd.
> 1631.
> By the Author, *B. Jonson.*

A quarter of a century earlier, *Sejanus* had also failed, and failure and censure would have made the King's Men willing enough to surrender whatever claims to that earlier play they might otherwise have sought to retain (whereas the censure had no doubt been expected to rouse the interest of book-purchasers); revision had simply secured Jonson's repossession. A later King's company was no doubt quite willing to give up its claim on *The New Inne*, but this time Jonson went out of his way to make its publication seem to flout the players: he undertakes no repossessive revision and he advertises the King's Men's dealings with the play as *mere* play. Peeved but deliberate, Jonson composed a title page that recalls Martial's figure, the object of art as manumitted slave, now to be set at liberty – as if players and censurers were kidnappers, plagiarists. He may have had another model in mind, one from a less distant past, for the phrasing also recalls the liberation of *Troilus and Cressida*, at which occasion the ever reader was exhorted to "thank fortune for the 'scape it hath made amongst you." The author of *The New Inne* presents the octavo as the realization of form; here, more than ever before, the force with which other realizations (blazing, mechanical, momentary, negligent) are repudiated redounds to enhance the credit of the printed book, a challenge to the boundary between the mental object of art and the typographic one.

Much has been made of Jonson's work in preparing the text for the Folio, perhaps too much. The fascination of this volume has led scholars to underestimate Jonson's earlier editorial engagements – so that we have missed the steady development of his career at press – and to over-estimate his involvement with the press-work of Stansby's folio – which has contributed to the long-standing uncritical acceptance of the folio as a model of Renaissance book-production.[98] Important as it is, Jonson's *Workes* is not quite a revolutionary book, though it will continue to bear scrutiny as a major event in English literary culture and in any historiography of authorship and book culture. In a deft article on the politics of the Jonson folio, Martin Butler offers a summary of the features that distinguish it as "the first important English book systematically to exploit the symbolic potential of typography and the technicalities of print."

The plays are presented less as scripts for performance than as reading texts that bear comparison with classic Latin literature. Stage directions are removed; speeches are digested into columns, and entrances and exits into massed headings; accidentals are scrupulously treated, with the punctuation being systematic rather than idiomatic, capitalization being regularized, and spellings preserving some evidence of etymology.[99]

This needs some adjustment. For example, although some stage directions are removed from the Folio, quite a few remain (in EMI and EMO) and a considerable number of new ones are added. The observation that these are reading texts is certainly correct, but not because of the effacement of theatrical markers. Such markers are, rather, elaborated – so that a mere disappearance, "*Exeunt*" in a quarto (*Poetaster*) becomes "*They withdraw to make themselves ready*" in the Folio (III.iv.269) – and displaced – stage directions, other than exits and entrances are usually shifted into a more obtrusive marginal position (though

---

[98] Greg knew better: his mature critical methods derive much of their nuance from the work of evaluating successive volumes of Herford's and the Simpsons' Jonson edition, which adopted the folio texts (or holograph) as copy wherever possible. De Vocht knew better: though hardly as theoretically consistent as Greg, he steadily opposed the Oxford editors by defending Jonson's quartos. For an excellent summary of the editorial lapses of the Oxford *Jonson*, see T. H. Howard-Hill, "Towards a Jonson Concordance: A Discussion of Texts and Problems," *Research Opportunities in Renaissance Drama*, 15 (1972), 17–32.

[99] "Jonson's Folio and the Politics of Patronage," *Criticism* 35 (1993), 378.

glossing marginalia are dropped from *Cynthia's Revels*).[100] With the gestural
sectored but not eliminated, the page is made both more articulate and self-
sufficient; the theater, on the other hand, returns as a referent.[101] Many of
the other features that Butler remarks – and many other related aspects, like
the dedication of *each* textual unit to a different personal patron or cultural
authority – were substantially anticipated in the quarto editions of Jonson's
plays.[102] While Butler is right to follow the Oxford editors in insisting on the
formal distinctiveness of the Folio, in many such instances – not only of spelling
and punctuation, but also of diction and capitalization – it "refamiliarizes"
features that had rendered the quartos even more distinctive. The Folio is a
remarkable book, but it is continuous with the remarkable quartos that provided
so many of its copy texts. The most striking feature of the volume – the grand
homogeneity it confers on its separate texts, written for separate occasions –
sustains the anti-theatrical, anti-occasional, and repossessive tendencies of the
quartos: the remediated texts now find their "proper" context and coherence
under the unifying rubric of the single author. The volume does not banish
the centrifugal forces of occasion and genre – each play has a separate title
page that commemorates the company that first performed it and the year of

[100] The Folio also adds a kind of "theatrical colophon" at the end of each play-text, a single
page indicating genre ("comoedie," "comicall satyre," "trag ˜die"), year of first performance,
the performing company, the principal actors ("com ˜dians," "trag ˜dians"), and the fact that
the performance had been officially "allowed" by the Master of the Revels. Little has been
made of the generic sorting, but it seems to have meant a good deal to Jonson: one of the two
mottos for the title page, "Locum teneant," is taken from the *Ars Poetica – Singula quaeque
locum teneant sortita decenter*; let each type cleave to its proper place (line 92).

[101] There are, however, some new anti-theatricalities of format, particularly the lightening of certain
forms of expressive typography – the use of blank spaces to indicate pauses and of italics to
indicate when a character is quoting or reading from a written text. More might be made of the
anti-theatricality of substantive variants. The long III.v. added to *Poetaster*, has no theatrical
value at all: a loose imitation of Horace's *Satires*, II:i, the scene contributes to the impression
that *Poetaster* is more an anthology than a play, a *livre vivant*.

[102] On the handling of entrances and exits, see H&S, IX:46–47. The Oxford editors indicate
Jonson's debt to Renaissance editions of classical dramatists, though they also attest to the fact
that this influence is manifest as early as the quartos of *Cynthia's Revels* and *Poetaster*. Indeed,
conspicuously classicizing page-effects had begun to appear as early as the quarto of *Every Man
Out* and were securely imposed on the format of *Sejanus*. In *Sejanus* one can also observe the
systematization of punctuation that Butler identifies with the Folio. The array of stops is more
finely graded in later quartos and in the Folio, this as part of Jonson's remarkable campaign to
dominate the rhythms of both prose and verse, yet he seems in fact to have begun relinquishing
some of the more idiosyncratic regularities of his pointing by 1616: many of the "sententious"
quotation marks that are so obtrusive in the quarto of *Sejanus* are pruned away in the Folio and
the presence of the peculiar metrical apostrophe that appears in that and other later quartos
is also reduced, so that we could claim a slight drift away from what Butler calls systematic
punctuation; see H&S IV:338–42. and IX:49–50. Similarly, Jonson's conspicuously classicized
spellings are more frequent in the quartos than in the Folio; see H&S, IV:337 and cf. V:278.
(A caveat should always accompany discussions of accidentals in the Folio: Simpson almost
certainly over-estimated the authority of its final state; see Kevin J. Donovan, "Jonson's Texts
in the First Folio," *Ben Jonson's 1616 Folio*, 25.)

that performance; the "Catalogue" (¶₃) provides a (heterogeneous) list of titles (*Poetaster, The Forrest*) and kinds (*Epigrammes, Panagyre, Barriers*) – but this heterogeneity is given a material coherence and a name, as *Workes of Benjamin Jonson*. If we focus on the production and not on the product, we observe the same various homogeneity, the same swarming authorial influence. Jonson revised, utterly transforming *Every Man In* and expanding the attack on actors in *Poetaster*, while leaving many of the masque texts largely unchanged but, paradoxically, one of the most intriguing aspects of the Folio has to do with the middle ground, with how densely variant the bulk of the book turns out to be – a cornucopia of minute variations.[103]

Recent scholarship by David Gants and Mark Bland, both drawing on slightly earlier work by Kevin Donovan, has addressed the *curve* of Jonson's attention to presswork on the Folio, the fact that stop-press corrections are generally heavier in Jonson's earlier plays than in his later ones.[104] Although many of these adjustments are probably traceable to professional press-correction, those that may be plausibly assigned to authorial intervention (expansions, fine adjustments of punctuation and capitalization, changes of font, changes not traceable to misreading of copy – that is, revisions) are fairly frequent in *Every Man Out, Cynthia's Revels, Poetaster*, and *Sejanus*, somewhat less frequent in *Volpone, Epicoene*, and *Every Man In*, very light in the *Alchemist, Catiline*, and the early masques, and negligible in all the later masques, with the exception of *Love Restored*.[105] It may indeed be true that his interest in production work subsided somewhat once he had finished preparing copy for *Every Man In*, but it now seems to be the case that Jonson was obliged to shift

---

[103] Herford and Simpson offer several useful summaries of variation: see I:358–70, III:412–17, IV:17–22, 190–95, 335–43, V:278–80 and 413–14, IX:45–51 and 72–73. See also Jonas Barish's discussion of the overhaul of *Every Man In His Humor, Ben Jonson and the Language of Prose Comedy* (Cambridge, Mass: Harvard University Press, 1960), 130–41.

[104] The Oxford editors had also discussed these variants (their summary assessment may be found at IX: 72), and the pattern they observed exposed the *rest* of their editorial theory to Bowers's devastating, but now largely forgotten, critique. Simpson clung to the belief that Jonson had not only made stop-press corrections, but had also read *proof* for the volume – i.e., that he had checked over those very first sheets pulled from the press that a compositor would normally examine as a means of correcting gross errors before printing might begin. In "Greg's 'Rationale of the Copy-Text' Revisited," *Studies in Bibliography*, 31 (1978), Bowers comments, "If Jonson had indeed read pre-printing proofs, this disparity [between heavy corrections in the early plays and light corrections in the later ones] need not have existed since then his in-press alterations should have shown light polishing and second thoughts plus the correction of compositorial failure to follow copy. Instead, the evidence suggests the serious correction and revision at the press that is to be expected if these were the only proofs he saw" (112).

[105] Stansby's was one of the largest printing establishments in London, probably second only to the royal printer, although the law printers (employed by the English Stock) would have had a larger output. (Indeed, he specialized in small runs of prestigious books, hence his appeal to Jonson.) According to Bland, Stansby kept three presses fairly busy during these years and always had a professional corrector on staff; he would therefore presumably have regarded Jonson's attendance on presswork as a voluntary matter.

his attention from press-correction to text preparation at the node marked by *Every Man In* and *Epicoene*.[106] The copy-texts for *The Alchemist, Catiline,* and many of the masques were quarto editions on which he had originally devoted a great deal of professional care, but the bulk of the latter half of the Folio – from *Epicoene* forward – is made up of previously unpublished texts. Confident in the skills of Stansby's press-corrector, whose abilities he had seen amply demonstrated as the first part of the volume went through the press, Jonson now concentrated his editorial energies on final work on the *copy* for those poems, entertainments, masques, and "barriers" that remained to be printed.[107]

---

[106] The simplest explanation for this pattern is generally flagging authorial interest in press correction, but the explanation will admit of some helpful sophistication. One plausible sophistication, which Simpson anticipates, is that, having developed what he believed to be increasingly nuanced skills as a compositorial dramatist, Jonson took special pains to bring his earliest printed texts up to the standard set by the quartos of *Catiline* (1611), *The Alchemist* (1612) and, above all, the masques, the printing of which had been so important to his professional identity and self-presentation – hence the meticulousness of his press-corrections to the early plays, to say nothing of the wholesale revision of *Every Man In His Humour*. But, as bibliographers since Simpson have shown, even this theory will benefit from further adjustment. Johan Gerritsen demonstrated that Stansby's men began printing with *Every Man Out*, proceeded through the volume to the end of *Volpone* and then began work on *both Epicoene* and *Every Man In*, presswork on each play interrupting presswork on the other; after both plays were completed, printing proceeded sequentially through the volume, with a couple of resettings required due either to faulty presswork or indecision concerning format; "Stansby and Jonson Produce a Folio," *English Studies* 40 (1959), 52–55. This account of the production *sequence* is not meant to imply that work on the Folio was otherwise steady and uninterrupted. Stansby had a good deal of other work in hand as well, as Bland has shown (see the following note). The deferred start on *Every Man In*, the play which opens the volume, implies that Jonson had not completed the revision when printing began; that it was printed in stages suggests that it came to the press piecemeal; that it was begun at that *particular* moment, interrupting work on *Epicoene*, suggests either that *Epicoene* presented some special problems in the printing house or that some other urgency, now inaccessible to reconstruction, forced this disruption in the sequential production of the volume. (Gerritsen argued [54] that the juggled presswork could be explained either by the piecemeal arrival of copy for *Every Man In or* by problems in the copy for *Epicoene* which, he surmised, required that the printers begin work on *Every Man In* while Jonson reworked the copy for *Epicoene*. But this version of the argument, which makes a difficulty with *Epicoene* into an independent explanation for the turn to *Every Man In* and not contingent on there also having been a problem in acquiring copy for that play, depends on the assumption that Stansby's printers were obliged to maintain more or less continuous work on Jonson's *Workes*, an assumption no longer tenable given the evidence that Stansby maintained attention to several overlapping projects.) It thus appears that as presswork proceeded toward *Epicoene*, Jonson fell under increased pressure, from Stansby or elsewhere, to finish the revision of *Every Man In* – which would explain, I hope not too neatly, the apparent relaxation of Jonson's attention to press-correction (which should therefore probably be described as a *distraction* of attention) as work proceeded from *Sejanus* through *Volpone* to *Epicoene*. This leads to what may account for Jonson's relative inattention to the printing of his non-dramatic poetry and previously unpublished masques.

[107] Bland adduces a good deal of contemporary evidence for the high quality of press-correction at Stansby's shop. Note that the shift from close attention to layout to a recurrence to essentially editorial labor recapitulates the pattern we have observed in the production of the *Sejanus* quarto.

This general reconstruction of Jonson's involvement in the production of the Folio differs from that of the Oxford editors (of Simpson, really), who established the orthodox view of Jonson as a meticulous press-corrector.[108] Jonson's apprenticeship as a maker of quartos had attuned him to the rhythms of production and to its latitudes and refined his ability to plan for print by the painstaking preparation of copy – and for this we *can* find textual evidence. Although he had taken great care over *Sejanus* a decade earlier, Jonson made some eighty changes in the folio text; he introduced many of these by annotating a quarto text which served as copy for Stansby's edition, but a surprising number of the substantive changes were introduced as press-corrections.[109] Analytical bibliography gives us a typographic poet and a printed page invested with many of the attributes of autograph. A central question now presents itself, whether print represents the typographic author as autograph represents the writing subject. To what extent is the printed book *his*?

And since such typographic writing also invests the author with many of the attributes of the stationer – in the case of *Sejanus*, Jonson not only supervised page layout, participated in press-correction, acquired paper stocks – another central question therefore presents itself, whether print profits the typographic author as it does the stationer? To what extent is the printed book *his*?

And in the case at hand, both sets of questions might even be reframed thus: what is the valence of the engraved italics, the typographic sign of personality and privilege, in

THE

WORKES

OF

Beniamin Jonson[110]

(see figure 4)

To resolve these questions requires a broader reconstruction of how the Folio was planned and produced, for this inevitably raises the difficult, if narrower question of when the project was conceived, and by whom.

---

[108] First Greg, then Bowers criticized Simpson's bibliographical reasoning; Bowers argued that Simpson had over-estimated Jonson's corrections of "compositorial transmissional error corrected in press" and had therefore missed "the amount of Jonson's independent revision to be found in the press-variants in the older plays." From this Bowers proceeded to a startling and attractive conclusion: "In turn this suggests that the original marking of setting copy may have been less extensive than usually thought in respect to the kind of details represented by his press-corrections since these would mainly be new changes"; "Greg's 'Rationale of the Copy-Text' Revisited," 112.

[109] H&S, IV:335–37.

[110] For more on italics as proprietary and personal figure, see *The Author's Due*, chapter III.

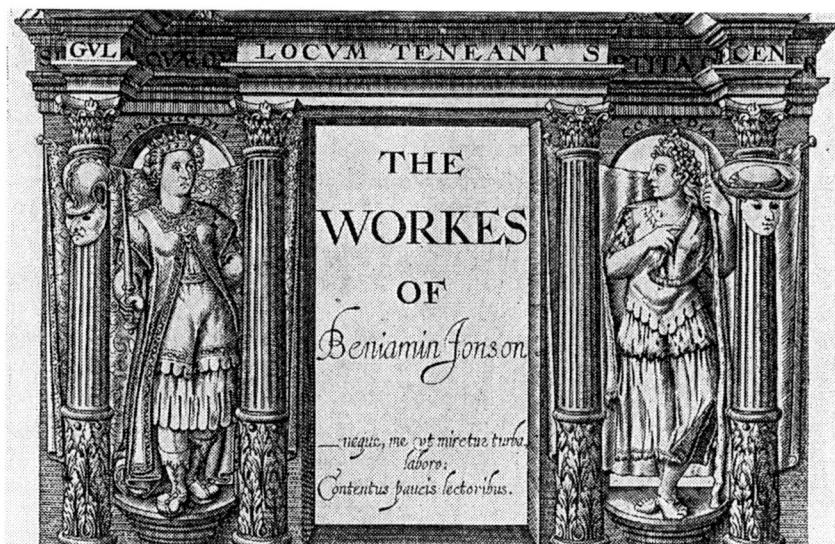

4   Title page of *The Workes of Beniamin Jonson*, 1616

Foliation: rights in the folio *Workes*

Musa nec insano syrmate nostra tumet. (Martial, IV:49)

The hypothesis that Jonson's attention was distracted from printed sheets to compositor's copy as the Folio moved from *Sejanus* through *Volpone* to *Epicoene* does more than explain the bibliographic facts; it has another very important resonance, since it reflects – inverted, as if in a magnifying mirror – the very professional developments that culminate in the Folio itself. To put this less gnomically – it was almost certainly in the period between the printing of *Sejanus* in quarto late in 1605 and the registration of *Epicoene* late in 1610 that Jonson came to think of himself as the inventor, the author, of Works. This was a period of great professional successes, during which he not only wrote *Volpone* and *The Alchemist* but also received a sequence of royal commissions sufficient to make him feel secure in the position of masque-maker to the court of James; this is the period in which Jonson sharpened his attributive practices and made theoretical sense of those practices; it is also the period in which the Jonson folio would have become practicable from the standpoint of intellectual property relations.

It is customary to refer to this not only as "the Jonson folio" but as "Stansby's folio." This is true, and remarkably so, if by "Stansby's" we mean that the folio was produced in his shop, no portion of it jobbed out. But it is by no means self-evident that Stansby handled all the business negotiations that led to the publication.[111] Rights in the work that had already been registered or published would have had to be negotiated, but we do not know that Stansby took the lead in these arrangements. The engraved title page informs us that the book was *"Imprinted at London by Will Stansby,"* and although this is the imprint we might expect for a book published and printed by a single stationer it is also the imprint that we should expect for a book printed in a single shop (or even a book predominantly printed in a single shop) for a loose syndicate of publishers. We cannot easily ascertain how the rights in the Folio were disposed and it will therefore be useful to review where copyrights were vested in those plays and masques that had been published prior to 1616. (I am setting aside *Eastward Hoe!*, which was widely recognized as a collaborative effort and, presumably for that reason, excluded from the Folio). The list implies a narrative:

Every Man Out   Entered to William Holme, April 8, 1600 (Arber, III:159); Nicholas Ling printed a third quarto, dubiously dated 1600, but no transfer from Holme to Ling is recorded. In 1607, Ling seems to have retired and he transferred a number of copies to John Smethwick, although *EMO* is not listed among them. Simpson infers that the transfer did take place, for *EMO* was transferred from Smethwick to Richard Bishop in 1638; moreover, in some copies of the folio the title page for *EMO* gives as imprint, "Printed by WILLIAM STANSBY / for *John Smithwicke.*"

Cynthia's Revels   Entered to Walter Burre on May 23, 1601 (III:185).

Every Man In   Entered "to be staied" along with *As You Like It, Henry V*, and *Much Ado About Nothing* on August 4, 1601 (III:37); entered to Cuthbert Burby and Walter Burre ten days later (III:139). Burby's widow transferred her share to William Welby in 1609 (III:169).

Poetaster   Entered to Matthew Lownes on December 21, 1601 (III:198).

Coronation Entertainment, Panegyre, Althrope   Entered to Edward Blount on March 19, 1604 (III:254). As has been discussed above, Thomas Man may have won control of this copyright.

Then come the traces of Jonson's three-year professional alliance with Thomas Thorpe:

Sejanus   Entered on November 2, 1604 to Blount (III:273); transferred to Thorpe on August 6, 1605 (III:297); and from Thorpe to Burre on October 3, 1610 (III:445).

Hymenaei   Printed, without registration, for Thorpe in 1606.

Volpone   Printed for Thorpe in 1607 or 1608, but without entry. His title was secure enough however to warrant an official transfer to Burre, along with *Sejanus*, on October 3, 1610 (III:445).[112]

---

[111] For an active printer, Stansby did an unusually small amount of publishing: he published only about 3 per cent of his printed output, compared to Jaggard's nearly 80 per cent (Gants, private correspondence).

[112] This is quite normal. Other instances of unentered plays that were later formally transferred by the original publisher include Marlowe's *Dido, Queen of Carthage* (published by Woodcock and assigned to Lynlay); Dekker's *The Shoemaker's Holiday* (Simmes to Wright); Dekker and

Masques of Blacknesse and Beautie; Lord Haddington's Masque   Entered to Thorpe, April 28, 1608 (III:375), but without mention of *LHM*.

The transfers of *Sejanus* and *Volpone* point towards a professional relationship that would be even more important than Jonson's relationship with Thorpe: following on the success of *The Alchemist*, Walter Burre must have felt that his properties in *Cynthia's Revels* and *Every Man In* were genuinely valuable and he reinvested in Jonson. As will be seen, October 1610 marks the beginning of his steady campaign to secure copyrights in Jonson's plays.

The Case is Altered   Entered on January 26, 1609 to Richard Bonion and Henry Walley (two days before their entry of *Troilus and Cressida*, which would be printed shortly thereafter with boasts of its having been wrested from the grand possessors); a revised entry was made, on July 20, adding Bartholomew Sutton's name as a third registrant. The play was printed "for Bartholomew Sutton," with no mention of Bonion or Walley; a new version of the title page added William Barrenger's name as publisher, for Sutton and Barrenger became partners at this time, and removed Jonson's name from the title-page; that new title page was in turn replaced with a version that restored Jonson's name.

Masque of Queenes   Entered to Bonion and Walley, on February 20, 1609.

Epicoene   Entered on September 20, 1610 to John Browne and John Busby (III:444); the play was not printed at this time and was possibly suppressed.[113] Browne's share was transferred to Burre on September 28, 1612 (III:498).

Alchemist   Entered to Burre on October 3, 1610 (III:445), the same day that he effected the transfers of *Volpone* and *Sejanus* from Thorpe.

Catiline   Published by Burre, though without entry, in 1611.[114]

Burre was hoarding Jonson. In 1612, he acquired his sixth copyright in a play by Jonson, and he had long controlled a half share in a seventh, *Every Man In*, of which Welby owned the other half. His partner, John Stepneth, entered the *Epigrams* on May 5, 1612; since he died later that year and no records survive

Middleton's *The Roaring Girl*, Webster's *The White Devil*, and Marston and Barksted's *The Instatiate Countess* (all Archer to Perry); Greene's *Tu Quoque* and Middleton and Rowley's *A Fair Quarrel* (both Trundle to Dewe); and so forth.

[113] Greg makes a good case that either a projected quarto was not printed or a printed quarto was suppressed because of application to Arabella Stuart; see his "Was There a 1612 Quarto of *Epicoene*," *Collected Papers*, 314–21.

[114] The absence of entry here perhaps requires an explanation. The play was very unsuccessful in the theater and there can have been little hope that the quarto would attract enough readers, extraordinary or ordinary, to warrant a second quarto; certainly, none seems to have been printed. There would have been very little risk, therefore, if Burre made a formal presentation of copy at Stationers Hall without then proceeding to the expense of registration. Moreover, whether or not he had made such a presentation – and lack of entry is no proof that a work had not been formally presented – if the work were published and Burre's claim went unchallenged within a few weeks of that publication, it would have been very difficult for another stationer to mount a successful attack on his rights to the work at a later date. Certainly no stationer would have disputed his title in, say, 1614.

of a posthumous assignment of that copy, it seems clear that Burre effectively controlled that copyright as well. He had made no attempt to acquire copyrights in any of the masques and entertainments, of which Thorpe owned copyrights in two quartos, Blount in one, and Bonion and Walley one (though Bonion drops out of sight *c.* 1611 and his share in the copy *may* have passed to Walley). Aside from these, Lownes controlled the copyright in one play and Smethwicke almost certainly controlled another; rights in *The Case is Altered* belonged certainly to Sutton and Barrengar, who may have shared them with Bonion and Walley, or perhaps with Walley only.

It will bear remarking here that these rights seem to have been vested without much contest. With the exception of the staying entry of *Every Man In* in 1601, there are no clear signs of direct competition between players and stationers for rights to disseminate Jonson's plays, and much evidence that these plays were being hurried into print. *Every Man Out, Cynthia's Revels, Poetaster, Sejanus,* and *Catiline* were printed, or at least registered for printing, within six months of their first performances (as best can be determined, given the slight uncertainties of dating). Still, we cannot always discern an uninterrupted sequence from composition-for-performance to performance to preparation-for-printing to print publication. From *Sejanus* forward Jonson's plays seem to have slowed their progress to the press. *Epicoene* was first performed late in 1609 or in the first months of 1610; it was entered in September of 1610, transferred two years later and *possibly* published before the end of 1612.[115] *The Alchemist* was first performed in the first half of 1610, entered that October, but not printed until 1612. *Bartholomew Fair* was first performed in 1614, but it was not printed – in quarto or in folio – before 1631 (and it was never entered). *Catiline* is the exception: performed in the first half of 1611, it was ill-received and published before the end of the year – hurried into print, perhaps, because Jonson was seeking approval from readers, having been once again disappointed by spectators. As for the other plays of this period, there is some reason to suppose that Jonson himself slowed publication in order to take the opportunity to polish a text for the press: this would explain why *Bartholomew Fair,* performed in 1614, was not included in the 1616 folio, i.e., for the simple reason that Jonson did not consider it ready for publication yet.[116] It may be that Jonson or his publishers agreed to defer publication of the other plays as part of some arrangement with the King's Men in the cases of *Sejanus, Volpone,* and *The Alchemist* (of course, we have other explanations for the delayed publication of

---

[115] On the uncertainties hovering around the reputed 1612 quarto of *Epicoene* see n. 106 above.

[116] It must be granted of course, that masques performed in 1614, 1615, and even, in the case of *The Golden Age Restored,* on January 1, 1616 *were* included in the Folio. These later masques are less elaborately annotated than the *Coronation Entertainment, Hymenaei,* or *Queenes,* and, being of smaller scale than a play such as *Bartholomew Fair,* may be supposed to have placed relatively modest demands on Jonson's skills at polishing and revision.

Sejanus), with the Lady Elizabeth's Servants in the case of *Bartholomew Fair*, and with the masters of the Revels Children in the case of *Epicoene* (although the delayed publication of *Epicoene* may be a special case).[117]

In fact, when we compare *Sejanus*, *Volpone*, and *The Alchemist* with other plays written for the King's Men, we find that it is *speed* of publication (within a few years of first performance), and not *delay* of publication that calls for explanation. Beaumont and Fletcher began their careers as playwrights just around the time of the publication of *Sejanus*: of the plays in their canon first performed by the King's Men before, say, 1613 – *Philaster*, *The Maid's Tragedy*, *A King and No King*, *The Captain*, *Bonduca*, *Valentinian*, and possibly *Thierry and Theodoret* – none saw print before 1619.[118] *The Two Noble Kinsmen*, the collaborative project of Shakespeare and Fletcher, was not printed until two decades after its first performance. With the exception of *King Lear* and *Pericles*, Shakespeare's other plays of these years (*Lear*, *Macbeth*, *Timon*, *Pericles*, *Antony and Cleopatra*, *Coriolanus*, *Cymbeline*, *The Winter's Tale*, and *The Tempest*) were not printed until 1623. Quarto publication of *Lear* and *Pericles* lagged their first performances by over two years, and the 1609 *Pericles* may well have been published against the wishes of the King's Men, a publication in some sense comparable to that of *Troilus and Cressida* in the same year.[119] Of course, this company had very special relations with Shakespeare, Beaumont, and Fletcher; moreover, they were, after all, the *King's* Men and, as we have seen, mustered unusual forms of disseminative control in the course of their corporate history, so it is unsurprising that very few of the other plays that survive from their repertory saw print during these years. If Jonson's plays generally came more slowly to the press after 1604 than they did before, they were, at least, printed.[120] The King's Men may have granted permission to

---

[117] Chambers, *The Elizabethan Stage*, III:370–71 and n. 113 above.

[118] It may well be that the restraint on publication was part of a deliberate strategy on the part of the King's Men to create and control a small but steady market in manuscript copies of those plays. When Moseley published the Beaumont and Fletcher Folio in 1647, he observes in his prefatory epistle that the printed book finally provides a cheaper alternative: "Heretofore when Gentlemen desired but a Copy of any of these *Playes*, the meanest piece here (if any may be called Meane where every one is Best) cost them more then foure times the price you pay for the whole *Volume*" (A4ᵛ).

[119] Blount entered both *Pericles* and *Antony and Cleopatra* on May 20, 1608 and, since he made no move to publish either work, it has been supposed that this was a blocking entry. *Pericles* was published by Henry Gosson a year later, without transfer, and the poor quality of the text, probably traceable to reported copy, sorts very well with Hemminges and Condell's descriptions of the "stolne and surreptitious copies" in which some of Shakespeare's plays appear. (They excluded the play from the 1623 Folio.)

I have excluded *The London Prodigal* and *The Yorkshire Tragedy* from the list of plays relevant to this discussion of "Shakespearean" publication.

[120] If we try to put *Epicoene* into a similar context we get a similar perspective. The Queen's Revels Children regularly performed Chapman's plays and with the exception of *Eastward Hoe* (significantly, a collaboration with Jonson) and *Charles, Duke of Byron*, first performances during these years precede publication by at least two years.

publish on the proviso that he somewhat delay publication of those that flourished in performance, although no record of such agreements survives, but they either did not, or could not, bar him or his stationers from publishing *Sejanus*, *Volpone*, *The Alchemist*, or *Catiline* – more King's Men's plays than any other single playwright published during the years 1605–1611, an impressive record of publication.

It has the look of a special arrangement, engineered perhaps by Thorpe or Burre (though neither man had conspicuous ties to the King's Men), perhaps – and more likely – worked out by Jonson, who had long-standing ties to the King's Men and whose reputation at court was at its height. The arrangement need not have been a formal one. This record suggests that by about 1607 both the players and those stationers who involved themselves in dramatic publishing would have been aware of Jonson's unusual concern with the printing of his works and were persuaded to respect it. The stationers were rewarded for indulging him by a small measure of professional loyalty, for it may be noted that his dealings with particular publishers are clustered into brief periods – work with Blunt, then Thorpe, then Burre, and, eventually Stansby. This accords with one's sense of Jonson's temperament: one can imagine the intensity of his commitment to these professional alliances, the furies, and the exasperated fallings-out.[121]

---

[121] *The Case is Altered* does not conform to the patterns noted here and thus does not seem to reflect the professional understandings just inferred. The poor quality of the text of this long-unpublished play and the absence of the usual signs of Jonson's involvement in text preparation *may* suggest some sort of irregularity in the acquisition of copy. Unlike the other Jonson quartos, which seem to have been based on texts provided by Jonson himself, the printed version of *The Case is Altered* seems to have been based on a playhouse manuscript. (It is one of six plays in the repertory of the Revels Children that came into various stationers' hands in 1608 and 1609, a period in which plague, royal disfavor, and organizational upheaval at least slightly disrupted their playing; of these six plays Bonion acquired three. But even if Bonion acquired his texts from the players, we cannot assume that he intended to bring these plays to print without at least consulting their authors: as we have seen, one of the three, Fletcher's *The Faithful Shepherdess*, was an elaborate print production, with an epistle to the reader and commendatory poems, including not only Beaumont's fierce attack on the theatrical audience, but a poem by Jonson in a similar vein.) Yet the fact that Jonson turned to Bonion and Walley with the exceedingly complex manuscript of *Queenes* within a few weeks after their entrance of *The Case is Altered* certainly complicates the suspicion that they had sought to publish the play against Jonson's wishes, complicates suspicion if it does not confound it: Jonson is not likely to have turned a masque over to stationers who had annoyed him. On the other hand, Jonson may not have heard about their entry of *The Case is Altered* when he entrusted them with *Queenes*; that their names appear nowhere on the various title pages of the play suggests that they may have been trying to conceal their involvement with the publication. Finally, it must be noted that Jonson never worked with these stationers again and that *The Case is Altered* was not published in either the 1616 or 1640 folio *Workes*, making it the only one of his plays not known to be a collaboration that was thus excluded. It is thus difficult to dispel the impression of irregularity: either Stansby (or Burre or the folio syndicate) failed to come to an accommodation with whomever held the copyright, or Jonson repudiated the play on aesthetic grounds – or Jonson repudiated the play because of persistent annoyance over the original circumstances of its publication. It may be observed, however, that the Folio does include a version of *Queenes*

This sketch of shifting property in Jonson's plays and masques makes it possible to surmise how the idea of publishing Jonson's *Workes* evolved. We cannot determine the moment at which the project was conceived, nor by whom it was conceived, but as Jonson would have been somewhat painfully aware, it would not have been an unprecedented venture to publish such a collection by a poet in mid-career. In 1601, Simon Waterson published *The Works of Samuel Daniel*, Jonson's great Jacobean rival-to-be.[122] Early in 1605, George Eld printed a new closet drama, *Philotas*, together with *Cleopatra*, and a selection of poems for Waterson: the volume, *Certain Small Poems Lately Printed: With the Tragedie of Philotas* would presumably have been printed and distributed to the booksellers before Jonson began making his presence felt during the printing of *Sejanus*. But at the precise time of the press-work on *Sejanus*, Waterson entered Daniel's tragicomedy, *The Queenes Arcadia*, and turned the copy over to Eld; in 1607, it was reprinted as part of still another collection, *Certaine Small Workes*, modelled on the collection of 1605. During the same period, then, and in the same printshop in which Jonson was undergoing his transformation into an editorial author, Daniel was thriving as the author of printed Works.

Daniel's collections hardly created the splash that Jonson's folio did. The anonymous poet who praised Jonson's volume in *Wits Recreation* fastened on the startling difference:

> The authors friend thus for the author sayes,
> *Bens* plays are works, when others works are plaies.[123]

The epigram implies the crucial distinction between Daniel's *Works* of 1601 and Jonson's 1616 *Workes*, even as it singles out the scandal of the Jonson folio – the publication of *dramatic* texts as Works. Here again is the historical irony that haunts the prologue to a play like *Bartholomew Fair* (an irony of mass culture that history has now rendered commonplace) which is that drama, that contested form of intellectual property – the object of various monopolistic practices, including sputtering, but energetic campaigns against plagiarism – was at the same time systematically denigrated.[124] Jonson's own acute sense

although no record is preserved of how the rights of copy were secured, a circumstance that is, in itself, unusual.

[122] Waterson had been producing agglomerative volumes of Daniel's work since the early nineties: *Delia* and the *Complaint of Rosamund* in 1592, to which he added Daniel's closet drama, *The Tragedy of Cleopatra* in 1594; in 1599, he published Daniel's *Poeticall Essayes*, containing five books of *The Civil Wars*, *Musophilis*, *Cleopatra*, and some miscellaneous verse; the 1601 *Works*, a collection in folio, adds another book of *The Civil Wars* and cumulates the previously published texts. Thereafter Waterson produced selective collections.

[123] H&S, IX:13, cited from *Wits Recreations* (1640), though the epigram is surely of a substantially earlier date.

[124] Even one of the commendatory poems prefaced to *Volpone* fashions praise out of the obligatory reservation: "thy last work's best:/Pase, gently on; thy worth, yet higher, raise;/Till thou write best, as well as the best PLAYES (IC, "To the ingenious Poet," H&S, XI:321).

of the low status of dramatic writing is what makes his efforts to dignify his printed drama particularly fervid. He is still fighting this battle in 1631 on the title page of *The New Inne*, where the stigmatizing term, "play," is peeled from the printed text and affixed to performance. But the battle had begun a quarter of a century earlier: as Simpson pointed out, the 1605 quarto of *Sejanus* affiliates the play with classical drama by imitating the layout of Renaissance editions of Plautus, Terence, and Aristophanes, venerated authors of *opera* whose plays lay outside a tradition of commercial performance.[125] Not coincidentally, this is the format that had already been adopted for Daniel's *Cleopatra* and *Philotas*, ready-to-hand models of plays that are works.

Nonetheless, a fundamental, or deeply internalized, anti-theatricality seems also to have inhibited Jonson's imaginings for publication: although the collections of Daniel's works provide a galling and proximate model, it is unlikely that in 1605 Jonson could have proposed imitating it with a collection of work that he himself felt had been clapper-clawed with the palms of the vulgar. Still his aspirations tend in this direction. His emulation of Daniel may be discerned in more than typography: with *Sejanus*, Jonson begins to imitate Daniel's professional loyalty by allying himself with the publisher, Thorpe. That alliance (and the later ones, with Burre, or with Stansby) is fleeting compared to that between Waterson and Daniel, which had begun in 1585, when Waterson printed Daniel's translation of Paulus Jovius' treatise on *imprese*, and continued until Daniel's death and beyond, for his will names Waterson as co-executor. Such a sustained alliance between author and stationer is hardly a novelty: Daniel's ties to Waterson are comparable to the personal and professional bonds between Erasmus and Froben, or between More and Rastell. One measure of the economic transformation of authorship, the decay of literary feudalism, is the increasing importance of such alliances. Late in the sixteenth century the possibility of sustained relations between a playwright and an acting company began to refashion the status of dramatic authorship and Jonson elaborated this decisive transformation by attempting a parallel alliance with a publisher. Of course, life-long professional relationships were well beyond Jonson's capacity; work with Thorpe lasted about three and a half years.

Thus, if Jonson and Thorpe – or, a less likely possibility, if Thorpe alone – had begun planning for a collected works during those years, the plans were fragile, and would have been very substantially disrupted when Jonson turned to Bonion and Walley with the text of *Queenes* in 1609. The exclusive relationship between Thorpe and Jonson collapsed with the publications of *Queenes* and *The Case is Altered* and the registration of *Epicoene*; thereafter, Jonson's relations with the book trade went through a briefly unsettled period of a year or so, for his relations with Bonion, Walley, Browne, and Busby show no signs of stability. But the record changes decisively in October of 1610, when Burre acquired control of

---

[125] H&S, IX:46.

The Alchemist, *Volpone*, and *Sejanus* in addition to the copyrights he already controlled.[126] That he purchased Thorpe's rights in *Volpone* and *Sejanus* without reissuing them is not an unprecedented procedure (though usually such transfers do anticipate an imminent printing, unless the transfer disposes of a deceased stationer's property or resolves a dispute over copy), but it nonetheless suggests a long-range plan towards an enterprise more substantial than mere reissue in the format of previous editions. This is not conclusive evidence, but the weight of it suggests that by October of 1610, Burre was preparing for some sort of collection.[127] By 1611 Jonson and Burre seem to be cooperating fully: *Catiline* is turned over to Burre for swift publication – printed, apparently, by William Stansby – after its cool reception in the theater, and the meticulous attention to accidentals in the stop-press corrections accords with the habits Jonson had developed during his "compositorial" apprenticeship; *The Alchemist* is printed the following year. Burre continued securing copyrights in other texts – *The Epigrams* and *Epicoene* – and Jonson, for his part begins withholding masques from print – *Oberon* and *Love Freed From Ignorance and Folly* (performed in 1611), *Love Restored* (in 1612), and so forth, all the masques through *The Golden Age Restored* in 1616.[128] In January of 1615, shortly before he must have begun printing the Folio, Stansby registered "*Certayne Masques at Court*

---

[126] Thorpe's apprenticeship with Richard Watkins had overlapped Burre's during the late 1580s and early nineties and they had occasionally collaborated since then: the transfer was presumably amicable.

[127] Complicating this hypothesis is Browne and Busby's registration of *Epicoene* only a few weeks earlier. This registration may, of course, pinpoint the moment at which Jonson and Burre together projected the collection – after Jonson turned over a manuscript of *Epicoene* to Browne and Busby and before Burre registered *The Alchemist*. But the record may be plausibly construed otherwise. Browne and Busby could have acquired their copy of *Epicoene* surreptitiously, perhaps from the players who, inhibited from acting the play, hoped to make back at least some of what they had paid for the script. (That Browne and Busby did not proceed to publish *Epicoene* quickly does not argue against surreptitious acquisition of copy. Registrations were seldom challenged because of scruple over the source of copy – and this registration went uncontested: the transfer from Browne to Burre two years later is quite regular, casting no shadow over the original entrance. We may suppose either that Browne and Busby hoped to print the play, but were inhibited from doing so, as the Children of the Revels were inhibited from playing it; or we may suppose that they acquired the copy from the managers of the Revels company hoping to secure Jonson's cooperation in preparing a copy for print, only to be frustrated. But I think it very improbable that, having heard of his interest in other plays by Jonson, Browne and Busby had acquired the copy of *Epicoene* in hopes of reselling it to him. What disconfirms the hypothesis of such slightly sharp practice is the mere fact that Burre printed *Catiline* the following year without entrance: he would not have foregone the available protections had he been frustrated by Browne and Busby's registration of *Epicoene* a few months earlier.) Surreptitious acquisition of *Epicoene* may explain why Burre moved so swiftly to secure rights in *The Alchemist*, *Sejanus*, and *Volpone*; if so, we need not imagine that Burre and Jonson only began planning the Folio after the registration of *Epicoene*. But one must also entertain the possibility that Burre is ahead of Jonson, that, unbeknownst to the playwright, the publisher had conceived of a collection of Jonson's plays, but was slightly thwarted when he found that Jonson (or those in charge of the Revel's Children) had turned *Epicoene* over to Browne and Busby.

[128] *Prince Henry's Barriers* also went unpublished. If the string of unpublished masques marks a period of preparation for the Folio, then this scripted joust, performed in January 1610, months

never yet printed" (III:562), the first sign that Stansby was to be a major figure in the production of the Folio.[129]

From 1611 forward, he had published and printed the work of a number of Jonson's associates and, in a few cases, Jonson had involved himself in the production of these volumes. He provided some of the front matter for Stansby's edition of *Coryats Crudities* (1611), including a series of distichs keyed to vignettes on the title-page, which had been engraved by William Hole, who would later engrave the title-page for Jonson's folio; later, in 1614, he contributed commendatory poems for Selden's *Titles of Honor* and Ralegh's *History of the World*, which latter Stansby printed for Burre.[130] Like the distichs for *Coryats Crudities*, Jonson's poem for the *History* interprets the engraved title-page, versifying its elaborate allegorical program. These small engagements with Burre and Stansby would have encouraged Jonson to imagine the folio form as a product of unusual semantic and aesthetic coherence.

The title-page for the *History* does not mention Stansby, advertising the book as "printed for WALTER BURRE," which contrasts with the engraved imprint for the *Workes* and so seems to suggest Stansby's greater leadership in this second enterprise, yet as has already been suggested, his status in the enterprise remains a bit blurred.[131] In order to account for the absence of any record of copyrights transferred to Stansby, Kirschbaum supposes him to have negotiated temporary rights from Burre and the other holders of copyright, though there is no compelling reason to believe that Stansby was the prime mover in the complex arrangements for this venture. There is good reason to suspect contest over the business arrangements for on August 21, 1615, Burre received official permission from Stationers' Company to proceed against Stansby at law.[132] The

---

before Browne and Busby registered *Epicoene* might be taken as reinforcing the hypotheses both that Jonson, or Jonson and Burre, had already begun those preparations and that the copy that Browne and Busby registered in September had been procured surreptitiously. But Jonson had not published several texts of relatively unspectacular entertainments, *The Entertainment at Highgate* and the two entertainments at Theobalds, and the reservation of the *Barriers* from print may conform to this pattern.

[129] Bland has established that printing would have taken about 86 weeks and must have begun, therefore, early in 1615. When planning for the second Jonson folio began many years later, Stansby may have believed himself able to claim copyrights in *all* the masques published in 1616 by virtue of this entry, though the qualifying phrase, "never before printed," would have vitiated the claim were it looked into. Still, neither Thorpe, Bonion, nor Walley ever assigned their copies in masques they had registered earlier.

[130] These were later printed as *Underwood* XIV and XXIV. Jonson had been on the continent as tutor to Raleigh's son while Raleigh's book was in production, but he returned in time to write this poem, "The Mind of the Front."

[131] James K. Bracken undertakes to clarify the relation between Burre and Stansby in "Books from William Stansby's Printing House, and Jonson's Folio of 1616," *The Library*, ser. 6, 10 (1988), 20–21.

[132] The disagreement erupted despite their having worked together frequently in the then recent past. Since 1610, Stansby had printed ten books "for" or "to be sold by" Burre, including not only Raleigh's *History*, but also Donne's *Pseudo-Martyr* and Rathbone's *Surveyor*, this

terms of the dispute are not recorded, yet the documentary record implies that, in terms of stationers' copyrights, the 1616 folio was far less "his" than Burre's.[133] Indeed, it would be best to think of the Folio as the production of a loose and perhaps slightly unstable syndicate. In 1618, when Burre's sharer in the rights to *Every Man In*, William Welby, died, his widow transferred her rights neither to Stansby nor Burre, but to Thomas Snodham.[134]

If Stansby did not secure permanent control of the copyrights in Jonson's works in 1616, the record of subsequent transfers suggests that he continued to work in that direction. When Snodham died in 1626, his widow transferred his share in *Every Man In* to Stansby, but as part of one of the largest mass transfers of copyright in Arber's *Transcripts of the Stationers' Registers*

last, like Raleigh's book, a project of considerable scope. Stansby conducted his business a bit more recklessly than most stationers and he was not infrequently fined for violating company rules – for swearing, for irregular binding of apprentices, and, most frequently, for infringing other men's copies. Greg supposed that the suit concerned an edition of Raleigh's *History* that Stansby had printed for Burre, but his theory is based somewhat illogically on the fact that the *History* caused a certain amount of trouble in subsequent years – James called in the book in 1616 and, in 1621, Burre, Stansby, and Pollard were caught up in an obscure dispute about the finances for a new edition of the work – but these later disturbances hardly explain a trade dispute in 1615; see Greg, *Companion to Arber* (Oxford: Clarendon, 1967), 52, and Jackson, *Records* (Court Book C), 134. The timing rather suggests a struggle over the Jonson folio and certainly the aftermath of their negotiations for the Folio has the look of slight irregularity (see the following note). Bland has recently arrived at the same conclusion, that the suit concerned Jonson's book and not Raleigh's; see his "Invisible Dangers: Censorship and the Subversion of Authority in Early Modern England," *Papers of the Bibliographical Society of America* (1996), 187–88.

[133] I venture this despite Bracken's assertion that "we must assume that Stansby negotiated successfully with Burre" ("William Stansby," 20); I believe Bracken to be under the sway of the Oxford editors, who consistently refer to Stansby as the organizer of the enterprise. See Kirschbaum, "The Copyright of Elizabethan Plays," *The Library*, ser. 5, 14 (1959), 231–50, especially 246–49.

Much later, on July 4, 1635, Stansby "entred for his Copies by vertue of a note under the Hand of Walter Burre and master Mathew Lownes warden bearing date the 10th of June 1621" all seven of the titles in which Burre had held rights – a cautious formality undertaken perhaps in anticipation of the end of his career, or perhaps in preparation for the forthcoming second folio edition of the *Workes*. The unusual back-dating was necessary in order to authenticate the note, for Burre had died sometime between December 1621 and December 1622. (The entry is in fact doubly eccentirc: around the end of 1631 the phrase, "assigned over unto him by [or, later, 'by virtue of'] a note under the hand of ," became the normal formula for transfer of copies (it had been used sporadically before that time), but the key term is always "assigned"; "entered" in the context at hand may be an insignificant variation, or it may have been chosen to stipulate that Burre's note corroborates Stansby's right, while at the same time denying the security of Burre's prior claims – denying, that is, that the titles were Burre's to "assign.") What forced Stansby to the 1635 entrance is quite clear: in 1630 Burre's widow had transferred *Cynthia's Revels*, *The Alchemist*, and *Epicoene* to John Spencer and, in 1635, Spencer brought out a new quarto of *Catiline*, perhaps hoping that he could also make a claim on that text, which had never been registered: Stansby made his 1635 entry in order to fend off any further challenge from Burre's heirs or assigns. At any rate, the 1621 note on which that entrance was based established what were then new rights for Stansby, rights that he did not have when the original Folio was being produced.

[134] Arber, III:621.

(see frontispiece).[135] For decades copyrights had been singly acquired and sold (challenged and contested, too); thus accumulated they were assigned, inherited, and, occasionally, transferred to the use of the Company (this was particularly the fate of the copies of deceased stationers whose widows failed to marry company members). More and more, the governance of the Stationers' Company was taken up with supervising such transfers and with regulating such corporations as the various English and Latin Stocks, all in such a way as to maintain the internal stability of the trade and to preserve its public reputation. This was the destiny of the remarkable political coup of the mid-sixteenth century, when the London Stationers secured their monopoly and of the regular reassertions of Company's limits on its own numbers – political events that functioned to convert writing into a cumulable form of stationers' working capital. The production of composite volumes, of collected works, is the *bibliographical* correlative of these accumulations.

How does the author participate in such developments?

The author as publisher, I: Hayward and Jonson

Contentus paucis lectoribus. (Horace, *Satires*, I.x.74)[136]

On August 21, 1615, the day that Burre got permission from the Stationers' Court to proceed against Stansby, Ambrose Garbrand got permission to bring suit against him as well. We can be no more sure of the subject of Ambrose's complaint than we can of Burre's, but it seems to have developed out of a joint venture with Stansby, the publication in 1614 of Sir John Hayward's *Sanctuary of a Troubled Soul*. This would have been perhaps the ninth edition; Stansby had printed the eighth for Garbrand and Edgar in 1610. The 1614 edition was never completed, for Hayward had complained to the Stationers' Court that Stansby and Garbrand were printing the book "wth [out] his privitie." The Court decreed that Stansby should turn over all the sheets he had printed to Hayward and that "Garbrand whose Coppie it is shall print it in that volume m^r do^r Haward shall thinke fitt and no other"; a moment later, the Court also fined Garbrand "for using unfitting speeches to w^m Stansbey."[137]

This is one of a small number of intriguing records of authors' formal complaints to the Stationers' Company: the complaint itself is as remarkable as the official sympathy it elicited. Here is one more sign of a decisive transformation

[135] Arber, IV:153.
[136] The line was used with an adapted version of the preceding line as the epigraph for Jonson's 1616 *Workes*. Jonson's version, "*neque, me ut miretur turba, laboro*," switches the Horatian exhortation (*te . . . labores*) to self-command. With what would become an increasingly characteristic privacy the page "addresses" the poet himself, and in a voice more emphatically "first-personal" than that of Horace's original.
[137] Jackson, 70 (*Court Book C*, 36^b).

of literary clientage. Although nothing resembling modern royalties had yet come into existence, the stationers sporadically recognized that an author might maintain a continuing interest in the conditions of publication, an interest that survives the provision of copy or the supervision of presswork in first or revised editions. Haward calls it his "privitie." Part of the ancient mythology of mimesis is that the text (or painting or sculpture) confers immortality on its author, as well as on the patron and the mimetic subject, a common immortality which the act of mimesis makes dependent upon the durability of the mimetic medium; the stationers' response to Hayward's complaint shows us how the old idea that the author is immortal in the work is reinflected within a capital-intensive disseminative industry, developing into a principle of durable and not-quite-alienable authorial interest.

Yet we have already seen that, after his relationship with Thorpe had subsided and before his relation with Burre had begun, Jonson had seized upon an idea and a phrase that was to haunt him: "when I suffer'd it to goe abroad, I *departed with my right.*" The phrase, from *Queenes*, witnesses Jonson's morbid sense of the fragility of an author's *semantic* control over published work. Given the professional developments between 1609 and 1614, it is hardly surprising that when Jonson adapts the phrase in *Bartholomew Fair* this statement of professional misgiving takes on both a more comic tone and a more specifically legal inflection, for with help from Burre and Stansby the "right" of semantic control was being partly recovered. This development constitutes a tentative and ambiguous assertion of authorial "right": in the interim between *Queenes* and *Bartholomew Fair* Jonson "asserts" himself by printing dedications to his plays, an attempt to re-inscribe clientage within a medium the economics of which are ultimately inimical to it; he also "asserts" himself by *not* departing his right, that is, by deferring the moment of publication and so dislocating each of these masques of his middle period from the historical moments in which its semantic charge was at its height.[138] Hayward's complaint can help us keep Jonson's "assertion" in perspective. Jonson slightly stretches customary authorial rights by aligning his interests with those of Walter Burre and William Stansby; Hayward probes the structure of stationers' copyright and finds out its fissures, asserting his own rights in competition with Walter Burre and William Stansby, and, effectively, to their disadvantage. Yet Jonson was hardly aloof from the commercial transformations more vividly instanced in Hayward's still unusual complaint: after the publication of the Folio, Jonson's bibliographic career continues to drift in Hayward's direction.

We gain a useful perspective on that career and on its commercial impact by considering the Folio from the later vantage of *The New Inne*. A fifteen-year

[138] This may have enabled Jonson to control a small market in manuscript copies on the lines of that which Moseley describes in his preface to the 1647 folio edition of Beaumont and Fletcher's *Works*; see above, n. 118.

interim separates them, which is remarkable in itself: between 1616 and 1631, Jonson offered no new play to the press. He was writing very little for the theater, however; only a single play written between 1616 and 1631 has come down to us, though he may have written a few others.[139] But, as if there had been no break in continuity, the printing of *The New Inne* recovers and exaggerates professional themes that had developed early in Jonson's print career. Whereas several of the early quartos had detached Jonson's plays and masques from the theater or banqueting hall and remediated them within an erudite culture, *The New Inne* furiously repudiates performance. Jonson re-enacts the discriminations of the Jacobean quartos, sneering at those "*impertinents*, who were there present the first day" and who came only "to see, and to bee seene" and dedicating the play "to the Reader" – "I make thee my Patron" ("Dedication", 1–9). But *The New Inne* also makes use of the professional devices of the Folio. Jonson's *Workes* had carried the anti-occasional relocations in the Jacobean quartos forward by placing individual works within the coherence of a personal *oeuvre*, and had vindicated "plays" by associating them with non-dramatic poetry and ennobling both by associating them with royal culture; as if it were an epitome of the Folio, *The New Inne* seeks to vindicate its theatrical text by appending two verse epilogues (the second singled out as never having been performed) and a final pindaric ode to the play, "Come leave the lothèd stage" (with its severe culinary poetics), so that the volume concludes non-dramatically, with the poet's self-dedication to royalist work of "tuning forth the acts of his sweet raigne: / And raising *Charles* his chariot, 'bove his *Waine*" (lines 59–60). As in the Folio, Jonson has here refashioned his materials into more than a royalist plot. In the Folio, print impresses a personal coherence on disparate public materials and into a personal whole and *The New Inne* takes a similar, if narrower conception: its finale is an "*Ode* to himselfe", as if the repudiation of the stage has collapsed into a wholesale repudiation of publicity. The title page of the volume initiates the saving and stifling authorial embrace with the odd redundancy of its ascription –

By the Author, *B. Jonson*

The peculiar phrase makes some sense, actually, as part of the bitter repossessive wit of this page.[140] We have already taken in some of its angry humor – "*THE NEW INNE ... As it was never acted, but most / negligently play'd ...*" – but the dim recollection of Martial, the fantasy of the remediated and so liberated work, deserves a second glance. "*Most negligently play'd, by some, / the Kings Servants.*," we are told (see figure 5),

---

[139] *The Devil is an Ass* was first performed in 1616, too late to be included in the Folio; Jonson's next surviving play was *The Staple of News* of 1626, which was followed by *The New Inne*. Stansby did publish a quarto *Epicoene* in 1620, but he merely reprinted the folio text and Jonson seems not to have been involved in its production. On plays that may not survive, see n. 151 below.

[140] "The Author B. J." is the usual title-page formula in the 1616 folio; the anomaly here is "By."

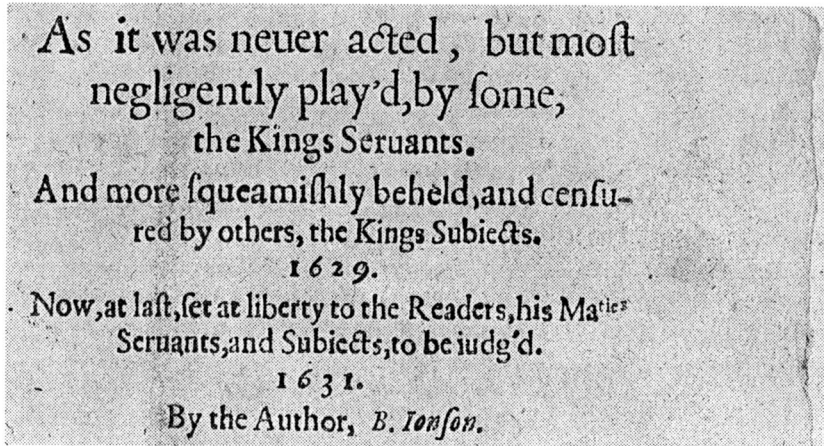

As it was neuer acted, but most
negligently play'd,by some,
the Kings Seruants.
And more squeamishly beheld,and censu-
red by others, the Kings Subiects.
1 6 2 9.
Now,at last,set at liberty to the Readers,his Maties
Seruants,and Subiects,to be iudg'd.
1 6 3 1.
By the Author, *B. Ionson.*

5   Title page of *The New Inne*, 1631

And more squeamishly beheld, and censu
red by others, the Kings Subjects.
1629.
Now, at last, set at liberty to the Readers, his Maties
Servants, and Subjects, to be judg'd.
1631.
By the Author, *B. Jonson.*

The last line does not simply tell us who wrote *The New Inne*; it tells us that the author, Ben Jonson, has set the work at liberty, the mocking hero of this mock-heroic fantasy. If it does more, if the syntax ambiguously introduces the idea that the author has not only set the work at liberty but now also competes with the readers as ultimate judge of the work, that is entirely consistent with the introversion of the volume. Having snatched the work from the theater, Jonson is feverishly, but imperfectly, committed to privatizing republication.

To this extravagantly repossessive title page and the imperious dedication – it concludes with the exhortation, "fall too. Read" – Jonson appends an "Argument" after the manner of *Sejanus*. This summary of the action performs a triple function. First, it pre-empts and thus partly disables the power of specifically theatrical suspense; second, by dividing the plot into a Beginning, an "Epitasis", and a "Catastrophe", it classicizes the play, modelling a form of analysis aloof from popular censure; and finally, it draws attention to the several stages of authorial production – the argument as authorial blueprint to a construction.[141]

[141] Jonson published only one argument, other than those provided for *Sejanus* and *The New Inne*, the brief acrostic plot summary to the *Alchemist*, which seems more a small, non-dramatic *tour de force attached* to the script than an anti-dramatic assertion or exposure of the subtending form of the work.

All this may seem unremarkable, but at least one of Jonson's peers examined the book with rigorous attention, determining that remarks were in order; once again, Heywood proves to be a particularly useful commentator. Although not usually very rivalrous, he was acutely sensitive to the evolving relations of page and stage. We have no record of Heywood's contemporary response to Jonson's folio – it did not, for example, provoke a reiteration of his strictures from 1608 on those who "have used a double sale of their labours, first to the Stage, and after to the presse" – but *The New Inne* plainly annoyed him. Both parts of Heywood's *The Fair Maid of the West* were published in the same year as was *The New Inne* and the brief letter to the reader – a brief explanatory letter and not a dedicatory one – measures his own theatrical manners against what he saw as Jonson's egregious bibliophilia:

These Comedies, bearing the title of, *The fair Maid of the West*: if they prove but as gratious in thy private reading, as they were plausible in the publick acting, I shall not much doubt of their successe . . . I hold it no necessity to trouble thee with the Argument of the story, the matter it selfe lying so plainly before thee in Acts and Scenes, without any deviations, or winding indents

– two swipes at Jonson. Yet a first, from the opening of the letter, is perhaps the harshest: "Curteous Reader, my Plaies have not beene exposed to the pub-like view of the world in numerous sheets, and a large volume, but singly (as thou seest) with great modesty, and small noise." The anti-theatrical vanities of *The New Inne* recalled the earlier enormity of the *Workes*, which had continued to reverberate through the literary scene, dominating Jonson's public reputation. In 1631, after all, he was the only living playwright with such a volume: Shakespeare had died in the year when Jonson's folio had appeared, and Shakespeare's own folio works would not appear until 1623 (though the collection of "Pavier" quartos was issued by Jaggard in 1619); Daniel, whose largely *non*-dramatic *Works* appeared in 1601, had died in 1623; the Folio Lyly would not appear until 1632, a quarter of a century after his death and the year of the second Shakespeare folio. The Marston folio was published in 1633, in the year before his death. Jonson's works stood ostentatiously alone.

Perhaps Heywood bristled at this juncture because he had heard that a second folio was in the offing. A few months after *The New Inne* appeared, Robert Allot secured the rights to *The Staple of News*, which had been entered but not printed early in 1626; shortly after Allot registered the transfer, John Beale began printing the "second volume" of *The Workes of Benjamin Jonson*.[142] Once

---

[142] The phrase, "the second volume," is taken from the title-page of 1640, which was applied after the fact to the texts Beale printed in 1631. We have no way of knowing what sort of encompassing title was originally planned for the volume, or even whether it was to receive a summary title page: that there was to be a single volume is evidenced by the fact that collation is continuous between *Bartholomew Fair* and *The Devil is an Ass*. As will be observed below,

again, it is difficult to know whether it was the stationer or the author who made the first move. Allot had already shown an interest in this sort of book, for in November of 1630 he had purchased Blount's rights to sixteen plays by Shakespeare, making him the major sharer in the syndicate that would produce the second Shakespeare folio in 1632.[143] That Jonson had seen fit to return to print with *The New Inne* may have emboldened Allot to make his approach; or perhaps what happened was that Jonson heard of Allot's interest in a second Shakespeare Folio, and he himself made overtures to this enterprising literary capitalist: certainly, the failure of *The New Inne* and the furious editorial engagement it provoked seem to have renewed what Heywood would have called Jonson's "ambition . . . to be in this kind Voluminously read." Had Heywood known better, he might have recognized the ambivalence of that ambition.

Along with *The Staple of Newes*, *The Second Volume* was to include Jonson's two other unprinted plays, *Bartholomew Fair* and *The Devil is an Ass*. It is at least slightly intriguing that the latter two plays had gone unpublished for so long: no stationer had secured the rights to these plays, nor did Allot confirm his own rights in 1631 by registration.[144] Such evidence cannot cumulate to proof, of course, but it seems to suggest that even when he *was* ready for the publication of a second folio collection of his works, he was unwilling permanently to relinquish his control of the two unregistered plays and so denied Allot permission to make a formal entry of these titles in the Stationers' Register. If these conclusions are apt, then in his own way Jonson was becoming a Hayward. Less equivocal signs of such proprietary assertion may be found if we take a wider view of Jonsonian publication since the Folio. Although Jonson was involved in the publication of no plays between the printing of the *Workes* and that of *The New Inne*, he nonetheless continued to supervise the preparation and publication of printed masques – seven, in fact, during these years, five of which were printed without imprints. These five – *Lovers Made Men* (1617), *The Masque of Augurs* (1622), *Time Vindicated* (1623), *Neptune's Triumph* (1624), and *The Fortunate Isles* (1625) – all share the same fairly spare layout, although *Augurs* and *Neptune's Triumph* employ the scholarly marginalia that had the been the hallmarks of Jonson's early masque texts. Jonson's name appears nowhere on these quartos, yet three have one of Jonson's typographic

---

Jonson himself would refer to the several texts being printed as "my Booke" in a letter to Newcastle (Harl. 4955, 202ᵛ, printed in H&S I:211). In what follows I shall continue to refer to this projected book as *The Second Volume*.

[143] Thomas and Richard Cotes had purchased Jaggard's share from his widow in 1627; they are the likely initiators of the project.

[144] The Lady Elizabeth's Men, the very unstable troupe which had first performed *Bartholomew Fair* in 1614, was not likely ever to have been able to constrain publication. As for *The Devil is an Ass*, first performed around the time that the first Jonson folio was released, it could not have been particularly important to the King's Men; as we have seen, moreover, there is no sign that the King's Men ever inhibited publication of his plays for more than a year or two, if at all.

signatures, a title-page quotation from Martial; a fourth carries a quotation from Tibullus; and a variant state of the fifth, *Augurs* (the second state, surely) contains an attributive note signed "B.I." claiming the "expression" and *half* the "invention" as "mine." So if their similarities justify the generalization, these five quartos represent a small but important editorial breakthrough: all appearances suggest that these five masques were privately printed, that Jonson was the publisher, that they were printed for use as presentation copies, perhaps for distribution on the occasion of the performance, that they were not to be offered for public sale. The names of stationers could therefore be banished from the title pages: certainly there was no reason to direct a bookseller to the wholesaler where copies of these books might be purchased. And, of course, none of these five masques was entered as any stationer's copy.

In fact, all seven of the masques published between the Folio and *The New Inne* went unregistered. I have proposed that this implies Jonson's will to control the circulation of his texts, his will to authorial dominion. It may be construed in negative terms, as a reaction against publicity; here is an old Jonsonian phenomenon, at worst a reaction in many ways self-destructive for a poet, and at (neo-feudal) best, a repudiation of the marketplace.[145] Jonson's bibliographic career since the Folio makes some sense as one more of his jealous rejections of collaborators, only this time the denigrated collaborator would be William Stansby. After 1616, Stansby worked steadily to take over from Burre as the central producer of Jonson's public, printed face. He reprinted the folio text of *Epicoene* in a quarto of 1620, he bought Burre's accumulated copyrights in 1621 and, in February of 1625, he secured the half share in *Every Man In* that had descended from Cuthbert Burby. May not that last assignment explain why John Waterson (the son of Daniel's devoted publisher), should have acquired and registered *The Staple of Newes*, though he never published it – as a quite pointed form of blocking registration, designed to thwart Stansby's accumulations of copy? No new text by Jonson had been registered since Stansby entered "Certayne Masques at Court" in 1615; no other would be registered during Jonson's lifetime. Anyone but the far-too-richly vested Stansby.

Things began to change around 1631, thanks, no doubt, to the theatrical failure of *The New Inne*, which renewed Jonson's allegiance to the press as a weapon against the theater, making it seem a lesser disseminative evil. Yet *The*

---

[145] Yet this and the related data may be construed otherwise, as the market's repudiation of Jonson. The non-registrations, the delayed publication of plays, the absence of wholesalers' names on the imprints of masques – it might be argued that all of this is evidence of Jonson's mere unpopularity and, more specifically, the traces of stationers' practical assessment of the playwright's marketability. This reading of the evidence would not necessarily contradict the case for Jonson's will for authorial dominion; it would only lend it irony. Whatever their merchantability, Jonson still concerned himself with what was "his" in the masques and, as will be seen, Stansby continued to behave as if the plays were valuable commodities.

Second Volume must have presented Jonson with its own frustrations: even if he had managed to dictate a few terms to Allot, that is, even if he denied Allot the prerogative of registration, Beale was plainly a disappointment. Jonson sent a copy of Beale's *Bartholomew Fair* to the Earl of Newcastle, the patron on whom he relied during his last years, and, later, when he sent *The Devil is an Ass*, he complained, "It is the Lewd Printers fault, that I can send yo[ur] Lo[rdship] no more of my Booke done." Although he had been much disabled by a stroke in 1628, Jonson had closely attended to the presswork on *The New Inne* and had made a considerable effort to do the same in Beale's shop, but "w[ith] his delayes and vexation, I am almost become blinde."[146] The two plays that Jonson sent to the Earl of Newcastle are, in fact, very badly printed and *The Staple of Newes* is in no better shape. Production stopped with these three plays: no title page seems to have been printed, nor apparently was the book supplied to the booksellers – the only extant title page for *The Second Volume* was printed in 1640. Moreover, there was a good deal more that might have been included in a second volume. Chambers once proposed that Jonson had planned to produce the second volume by installments, a plan that Jonson might plausibly have worked out with Allot, and although this is hard to reconcile with Jonson's extreme vexation over the sluggish pace of Beale's presswork, Jonson and Allot might have deferred publication in order to include *The Magnetic Lady*, which Jonson seems not to have completed before mid-1632.[147] Of course, if a larger volume were wanted, the five masques printed between 1617 and 1625 were available: they had apparently been kept off the open market and, unentered and printed without imprint, they were unquestionably available for folio issue.[148] But no such efforts were made. Simpson supposes that the enterprise collapsed simply because Jonson and Allot were disgusted with Beale – but one more hypothesis, an hypothesis more telling for the history of intellectual property, may be entertained.

The Second Volume was not issued to the public until 1640, when it could be presented together with the "first" volume, a reprint of the folio of 1616. As it finally appeared, the second volume augmented with the texts mentioned above – the masques and *The Magnetic Lady* – along with *The Underwoods*, several other plays, and some substantial pieces of non-dramatic prose – but the conjunction with the texts of the 1616 folio was crucial to the logic of the volume. In 1631 this conjunction was not yet possible. By that time Stansby had quietly assembled many of the copyrights in the texts of 1616, but he

---

[146] H&S, I:211.

[147] *Elizabethan Stage*, III: 355.

[148] There would have been no point in negotiating for reprintings of *The New Inne* or for the two masques of 1631, stocks of which would not yet have sold. It would have been impossible to accomodate Alchorne, who had entered the play; although Walkley had not entered the masques, Allot could hardly have hoped to challenge his copyright before the Stationers' Court.

had by no means completed the project. It was a small matter that George Cole and George Latham had sold the copyright in *Poetaster* to Robert Young in December 1630.[149] The entry of the previous July, when Mrs. Burre sold three of her dead husband's most valuable copyrights to John Spencer, was rather more unsettling. As has already been mentioned, Stansby would claim the rights in these copies, yet in the absence of a recorded assignment from Burre, Stansby's consolidation was vulnerable to challenge.[150] Allot or Allot and Jonson might have hoped to come to an understanding with Stansby, but if they approached him Stansby was apparently unwilling to extend himself. "It is the Lewd Printers fault . . ."

I have been giving this account more or less from the author's perspective – from the outset I have been concerned with the place of authors in that historical aggregate of private fantasies and trade practices which was the precondition of modern intellectual property – but Stansby's vantage is at least as instructive and has as much to tell us about those preconditions. Literary scholars must remind themselves that Early Modern authorship remains a negotiated social form; in the period under discussion, authorial property evolved rapidly, but many of its most decisive developments take place, not in the minds of authors or in the pages of books, but in the commercial arrangements and legal struggles that unite and disrupt the Stationers' Company. Authorial property continued to advance in the name of Jonson, but it advanced in property battles among

[149] This turns out actually to have simplified property in *Poetaster*. Since Young already owned a half-share in *Poetaster* (though Cole and Latham were probably unaware of his "rival" claim), the sale consolidated his claim; see Kirschbaum, "Copyright," 249–50.

[150] The shifts, by 1631, in the disposition of copyrights in texts assembled for publication in Jonson's *Workes* (1616) may be summarized thus:

Every Man Out   Smethwick
Cynthia's Revels   Spencer (?); Stansby (?)
Every Man In   Stansby (half by recorded assignment; half by unrecorded assignment.
Poetaster   Young
Coronation Entertainment, Panegyre, Althrope   As before, either Blount or the assigns of Man, or, by virtue of his 1615 entry, Stansby. See n. 129 above.
Sejanus   Stansby
Hymenaei   Thorpe had retired without assigning the masque; Stansby might have been able to claim copyright by virtue of his 1615 entry.
Volpone   Stansby
Masques of Blacknesse and Beautie; Lord Haddington's Masque   B&B had been entered to Thorpe; *LHM* had been printed with them. Presumably their status resembles that of other masques.
Masque of Queenes   Walley and assigns of Bonion.
Epicoene   Stansby (?); Spencer (?)
Alchemist   Stansby (?); Spencer (?)
Catiline   Stansby; though Spencer published the book in 1635, on the basis perhaps of an unrecorded assignment by Mrs. Burre.
Epigrams   Stansby
Other Masques   Stansby.

stationers, their widows, and their heirs, which is to say that the preconditions of modern intellectual property are to be found in the aggregate of private fantasies, articulated imaginings, trade practices, and acts of consumption. From Stansby's point of view, at any rate, the months following the performance of *The New Inne* presented nothing but obstacles to the publication of an expanded edition of Jonson's *Workes*, for his own steady accumulation of copyrights was being undermined. A number of works by Jonson had recently been published for the first time, but their production had been handled by other publishers – by Alchorne, Walkley, and, most formidably, Allot; copyrights in a number of older works had recently been transferred – but to Young and, most annoyingly (although perhaps least securely), to Spencer. This slight dispersal was hardly an insuperable obstacle to the production of a second Jonson Folio: the second folio of Shakespeare appeared in 1632, the joint production of a syndicate of five publishers, Allot among them. But Jonson himself would seem to have presented a problem. I must again stipulate that I am working here with an accumulation of negative evidence, yet the fact that only two of the eleven plays and masques printed since the Folio had been entered (and there were also perhaps a small handful of completed plays that had never been printed), suggests a significant shift.[151] Before 1616, a very high proportion of Jonson's plays had been entered in the Stationers' Register, either prior to publication, as they were supposed to have been, or on the occasion of a subsequent transfer: only *Hymenaei* and *Catiline* violate this pattern. After the appearance of the Folio, however, Jonson's texts are decisively withdrawn from the formal control of London's book producers, the printed texts reserved from those monopolistic protections that the Stationers' Company afforded its brethren, protections that Stansby had habitually sought in Jonson's plays. Yet we can hardly suppose Jonson to have been uninterested in the subsequent printing of his work: *The Fortunate Isles*, one of the masques published without entrance or imprint, appeared in 1625, and Henry Herbert's office-book records the fact that Jonson himself had brought in the manuscript, which was duly "allowed of for the press." Involved and obstructive, possessed by what we could call the spirit of possessiveness, or the spirit of Hayward, Jonson would not have been an appealing partner for Stansby, if tolerable for Allot. Small wonder that Stansby chose to bide his time.

[151] Shortly after the first folio was published, Jonson told Drummond "that the half of his comedies were not in Print" (H&S, I:143). The accents of boasting exaggeration are hard to miss in Drummond's notes on his conversations with Jonson, but Jonson must have spoken in some detail about the pastoral play, *The May Lord*: it sounds like a completed play. Even if there were not another dozen or so plays (or another eight or nine *comedies*), a few other plays are not unlikely. There is, of course, a long list of plays in which Jonson collaborated to which his remarks to Drummond might refer. Henslowe records one loan to Jonson in 1602 in earnest of a *Richard Crookback*; he mentions no collaborator (*Diary*, ed. Foakes & Rickert, 203).

Stansby's perspective offers a useful view in other ways. His successes at accumulating Jonson's copyrights alert us to the amassing of intellectual property by the still-exclusive company of stationers, a process that would achieve historically determining force later in the century, in the publishing house of Jacob Tonson. Yet Stansby also witnesses the appearance of fissures in the edifice of stationers' property. The competition from authors, from Haywards and Jonsons, is the most obvious, but the competition from Mrs. Burre and her assigns is also interesting and consequential. As in most guilds, company rules provided for regulated forms of spousal inheritance, for this was a traditional aspect of guild fellowship. Wives could inherit their husbands' businesses, despite not having served formal apprenticeships, and they could transmit copyrights, by transfer or by remarriage, as long as the recipients were members of the company. By encouraging guild endogamy, these arrangements generally served as a means of stabilizing the trade, but things could go awry. From an economic point of view, a widow – like any member of an informal partnership – was potentially a loose cannon. Whether out of misunderstanding or cunning, stationers' widows or their second husbands occasionally printed or transferred texts that the first husbands had already transferred or in which they had had only contingent rights. We cannot know if Mrs. Burre had been privy to her deceased husband's understandings with Stansby, but she proceeded as if Walter Burre's copyrights were unencumbered, as if they were hers. As a result, stationers' property in some of Jonson's most valuable plays was rendered unstable. In the last stages of the progress towards the second Jonson folio, stationer's property is fissured and shaken both by nascent authorial property and what we may call widow's property.

To an extent, indeed, authorial property and widow's property *themselves* compete in 1637. As has already been observed, the two new plays that Beale printed for Allot in 1631 went unregistered, the third having been transferred from John Waterson. I have proposed that Jonson was himself unwilling to allow such registration, though, of course, by long-standing convention, copyright in unregistered, but uncontested publications was usually vested with the stationer "for whom" the work was printed, according to its imprint. Thus it is not entirely remarkable that Allot transferred two of these plays, along with 59 others, to John Legatt and Andrew Crooke on July 1, 1637. Mary Allot still had a stock of these three plays, which seem never to have been put on general sale, and whatever the understanding that had obtained between Jonson and her husband, it was natural for her to suppose that she had inherited the "Right Title and Interest in these Copies" along with the stock of unsold folio plays.[152] Whatever

---

[152] Simpson's proposal that the omission of *The Devil is an Ass* from Mrs. Allot's transfer to Crooke was simply an oversight is probably correct. He cites (H&S, IX:95) a manuscript note on the play in one of the surviving copies of the 1631 *Second Volume* as evidence of a belated attempt to correct it: "June 6 1640. Let this be entered for Andrew Crooke but not printed till I give further directions. John Hansley."

the propriety of this transfer, it was obviously in the interests of the company to endorse it, which brought these copies into their records and brought them into nominal conformity to their customs: their jurisdiction was, if not confirmed, at least bolstered. And Jonson was hardly fit to protest the transaction, for he died after a wasting illness six weeks after the transfer was recorded.

But the story does not end here, for property in Jonson's works provoked a lawsuit. It seems that shortly before his death Jonson gave his unpublished works to Sir Kenelm Digby "to whose care & trust the said Benjamin left the publishing and printing of them." And shortly *after* Jonson's death, Digby in turn "delivered the same Copies to" Thomas Walkley, "to have them published and printed according to the intencon of the said Benjamin Johnson freely bestowing the benefitt of the printing thereof on yor Orator" – this according to Walkley's bill in Chancery, dated January 20, 1640[1].[153] Elsewhere Walkley claims to have paid Digby £40 for the parcel, which must have included *Underwood*, Jonson's translation of Horace's *Art of Poetry*, *Timber*, *The English Grammar*, *The Magnetic Lady*, *A Tale of a Tub*, *The Sad Shepherd*, and several masques and entertainments – a large quantity of material, including a number of older plays and poems that might have been printed in 1631, but were not.[154] Walkley did not register these texts, somewhat foolishly assuming, perhaps, that he had unique copies. During the winter of 1639–40, John Benson registered several poems, the Horace, and *The Masque of Gypsies* – in "false & imperfect Copies," as Walkley put it in his later bill – and he swiftly published them in two small volumes, a quarto of poetry and an omnibus duodecimo. Then, in March, Richard Seirger and Andrew Crooke (the latter the beneficiary of Mary Allot's assignment two years earlier) registered four masques and a collection of Jonson's poems, again overlapping the Digby materials. Realizing that he could not hope for company support against other stationers who had duly registered their copies, Walkley petitioned one of the Secretaries of State, on whose authority he secured an injunction against Benson and Crooke – Seirger is not mentioned – prohibiting them from printing or publishing the works that Walkley himself already had in press. Benson's books had already been printed; but Crooke's had not. Walkley links Benson and Crooke in all his complaints and he no doubt believed that they were acting in concert. In any event, Walkley plausibly claims that they retaliated, and if his account is to be trusted, they retaliated brilliantly. According to Walkley, John Parker, a printer, "p^{r}tending the said Benson to be greatly indebted to him," and knowing that titles that had

---

[153] H&S, IX: 98–99. Simpson summarizes these events on pp. 95–98, guided by discussions in *The Library*, ser. 4, 11 (1930–31), by Frank Marcham, 225–29, and Greg, 461–65, both titled "Thomas Walkley and the Ben Jonson *Works* of 1640."

[154] Walkley names the sum of £40 in a petition to the House of Lords from 1648, part of the stationers' appeal for the appointment of more press licensers. According to a related petition, the inefficiency of the current licensers was such that "divers books lye unprinted that would be beneficiall to ye Common Wealth, and trade is much hindred." Both petitions are cited in H&S, IX:100.

been entered to Benson were being printed for Walkley, "did . . . cause the said bookes wch yor Orato^r had soe caused to be printed to be attached in London as the wares of him the said Benson" (H&S, IX:99). Presswork on Walkley's volume stopped and the printed sheets were indeed seized by order of a judgment at the London Guildhall, and Walkley was forced to proceed in Chancery. The trail of legal documentation ends here, but Walkley eventually completed his edition of the Digby manuscripts, although two sections of the volume bear imprints dated 1641.

Both Greg and Simpson are disposed to assist in judging the case and they take Walkley's part: he almost certainly possessed autograph copies – it is a New Bibliographical habit to treat autograph as endowed with a kind of intrinsic moral goodness – and he claimed to derive publication from authorial intention.[155] Yet there is no reason to suppose that Benson and Crooke had doubted their right to print the previously unpublished manuscript texts of a deceased poet. And, in fact, by the middle of 1640, Crooke was in a fair way to becoming a major figure in the production of a coherent collection of Jonson's works. In June he had entered *The Devil is an Ass*, missed in Mary Allot's general transfer of copyrights three years earlier, and so had fully documented title to three plays, four masques, and "sundry Elegies and other Poems" (Arber, IV:503). He was plainly hoping to participate in a consortium for the Second Jonson Folio; the uncooperative Walkley, full of the disruptive spirit of the author, had deprived him of the masques and poems that Jonson had long regarded as most idiosyncratically his. The confrontation was imperfectly articulated, but it is not difficult to discern the fact that author's intellectual property and moral rights are here pitted against stationer's copyright. More may be discerned as well, since the jurisdiction of the Stationers' Court is also pitted against the court of Chancery, the Stationers' Warden against the Secretary of State. Here on the eve of a national upheaval over licensing, during which the relation between guild self-regulation and state control of the press was given an epochal scrutiny, that relation is given a quick, but telling going-over. Property in books could no longer be regarded as a guild matter; for authors had now to be reckoned with. We might cautiously refer to this conjuncture as Jonson's legacy.

---

[155] To his credit, I think, Greg is at least tepid: "there seems no reason to suppose that Walkley's assertions are not in the main true, especially as the absence of any reply from the other parties makes it probable that they preferred not to bring their case before the Court," "Thomas Walkley," 461.

The bibliographical history of the Second Folio is confusing, not only because of its complexity, but also because of our unfamiliarity *with* such complexities. We are unaccustomed to construing bibliography as cultural history or, more narrowly, as literary history and that is because bibliography, so granular and composite, is quite often presented as a kind of impediment to other forms of historical narrative. But the three volumes of the Second Folio tell a complex story of proprietary negotiation, and it will be useful to review it: they mark the Jonsonian moment in this history of authorship as both a threshold and a flux.

Volume one

Stansby had bided his time and was dead. Just before he retired he made formal entrance of the Jonson copyrights he claimed to have received from Walter Burre in 1621; he thus settled a key property before he sold his business to Richard Bishop, for £700.

Bishop was a publisher for a new age, a cautious book-keeper, recipient not only of Stansby's goods but of his cumulative experience. We see his caution in the language of an entry in the Stationers' Register for March 4, 1639, which records the transfer of a long list of books

by vertue of a deed of bargaine and sale under the hand and seale of William Stansby lately deceased and alsoe by vertue of a note under the hande and seale of Elizabeth Stansby the widdow of the said William these Copies and partes of Coppies following which were the Copies of the said William.

By 1639 Bishop had actually already begun preparing for a second edition of the texts in the original *Workes*: in 1638, he had purchased Smethwick's copyright in *Every Man Out Of His Humor* in 1638, so the 1639 transfer from Stansby left him a clear documentary record of every copyright in the 1616 volume save that in *Poetaster*. That play had been transferred to Young in 1630 – and Young's name therefore appears, slightly misleadingly, as printer on the title-page of volume one of the 1640 *Works*, a sign that his interest had been acknowledged and, presumably, accommodated.

The title-page for the entire first volume is printed from the reworked plate for the 1616 *Workes*, but the new phrase, "*LONDON. Printed by* Richard Bishop," has a very different meaning from that of the original "*Imprinted at London by Wi~~ Stansby.*" In 1616, Stansby was little more than a printer; his proprietary campaign was to come, and Bishop would pay to acquire its fruits.

Volumes one and two

"*Printed by* Richard Bishop, *and are to be sold by Andrew Crooke*": clearly when Bishop had the 1616 plate reworked, he intended it for a coherent augmented collection of *Workes*, not a mere "first volume." He must have made an accommodation with Crooke, for Crooke controlled the three plays printed for Allot in 1631, and had, together with Benson, secured rights in a great number of Jonson's unpublished works, presumably all they could get their hands on. But Walkley, as the agent and beneficiary of authorial intellectual property and moral rights, destroyed this plan. Whatever happened in Chancery, Crooke seems to have been routed for, at the last moment, he must have sold his rights in the plays of 1631 to Richard Meighen, hence the new, rather paltry title page (see figure 6):

THE

WORKES

OF

BENJAMIN JONSON.

The second Volume.

CONTAINING

THESE PLAYES,

Viz.

1 Bartholomew Fayre.

2 The Staple of Newes.

3 The Divell is an Asse.

LONDON,

Printed for RICHARD MEIGHEN.

1640

This page may have been all the printing Meighen intended, for he had acquired a substantial stock of Allot's original edition. But the 1640 *Workes* was itself

THE
VVORKES
OF

BENJAMIN JONSON.

The second Volume.

CONTAINING

THESE PLAYES.
Viz.

1 Bartholomew Fayre.
2 The Staple of Newes.
3 The Divell is an Affe.

LONDON,
Printed for RICHARD MEIGHEN,
1640.

6 Title page of Volume 2 of *The Workes of Benjamin Jonson*, 1640

a large production, and Meighen was obliged to hire Thomas Harper to reprint *The Devil is an Ass*.

Jonson's volume

Walkley's portion of the collection followed, the texts he claimed, through Digby, by virtue of possessive authorial intention. Paradoxically, this intention, this volumnious ambition is still so disruptive that it undermines cumulation: Walkley's portion of the collection was issued without general title page and, in many cases without title pages for the several sections; there is no imprint, the collations are discontinuous, and Walkley's name is nowhere to be seen. It has become customary to refer to that portion of the 1640 edition which follows *The Devil is an Ass* as "The Third Volume", but the phrase first appears in the Stationers' Register in 1658, when Walkley belatedly registered these texts, preliminary to a transfer to Humphrey Moseley.[1]

Volumes one, two, and three

It has also become customary for bibliographers and cautious literary scholars to disparage the textual quality of the 1640 folio.[2] But the book is a marvelous index of the heterogeneous proprietary forces bearing down on the Stationers' Company on the eve of the Licensing Acts: Bishop's *Workes*, a monument to stationers' copyright; Meighen's *Second Volume*, testifying to the minor disruptions produced by widow's property; and Walkley's portion, unnamed and oddly dispossessed, in which authorial "privitie" – Jonson's legacy – stakes its posthumous claim. A weak claim, but not merely because posthumous: such privitie is opportunistic, cobbled together out of neoclassical fantasy, friendship and patronage, commercial convention and inadvertent concession – opportunistic and so, at once, an achievement and an anticipation.

---

[1] G. E. Briscoe Eyre, H. R. Plomer, and C. R. Rivington, *A Transcript of the Registers of the Worshipful Company of Stationers from 1640 to 1708*, 3 vols. (London: Roxburghe Club, 1913–14), II:196 and 206.

[2] For Simpson's summary remarks on the Bishop's text, see H&S, IX:91–92; of the rest of the book, he observed succinctly that "the utmost that could be said of Walkley's printer is that, after all, he was a better workman than John Beale" (H&S, IX:107).

Index

intellectual (*cont.*)

57–59, 80, 82–84; and exclusive contract, 53–55; and imitation, 73–75, 85–87; and Jonson, 2, 199; and promptbooks, 30–31; and Roman Law, 74, 78, 83; violation of, 50–53; and Vitruvius, 73–74

invention, 8, 20, 135, 174–75, 179, 180–81

Jaggard, William, 58–60, 64–68, 115, 188n. 111, 202
James I, 175
Jardine, Lisa, 136–37n. 9, 146–47
Jeffes, Abel, 28
Jeffes, Humphrey, 18
Jeronimo, see Kyd, Thomas, *The Spanish Tragedy*
Johnson, Samuel, 139
Jones, Inigo, 173–75, 176n. 89, 177–80
Jones, Richard, 30–31
Jonson, Ben: as actor, 95n. 89; and attitudes toward the theater, 146n. 34, 183n. 101; and authorship, 2–3, 8–9; classicism of, 143–44, 183n. 102; and commodification, 131–32; and the culinary, 108, 109, 111–13, 117–18, and Horace, 120, 121–22, 198n. 136; and instability of the self, 118–19; and intrigue, 115–16, 152, 158–59; and Juvenal, 142n. 28, 146n. 34; and the literary economy, 131–32, 160–67, 170–76, 181, 204n. 145; and manuscript circulation, 2n. 5; marginalia of, 151, 154–56; and Martial, 113, 120–21, 124–34, 140, 143, 145–46, 148, 161, 163–64, 173–74, 181, 200, 204; and the masque, 158, 164–65, 167–70, 172–80, 184–85; and patronage, 126, 162–65, 167, 174, 179, 183, 200, 205, 214; and plagiarism, 9, 80, 84, 94–95, 115–16, 119–24, 131, 173–74, 178; and print publication, 114–17, 124–25, 127–32, 141–64, 167–70, 172–73, 179–96, 199–207; proof-reading by, 141n. 26–27, 144n. 31, 154n.49, 184n. 104, 185n. 106, 186n. 108; and property, 111, 151–52, 170–71, 173–74; and revision, 98, 103, 147, 150–52, 162–63, 185n. 106, 107n. 108; and semiotic coercion, 156–59, 174–75, 199, 201–202; and stationers' copyright, 188–98, 204, 206–14.; and the war of the theaters, 23, 122–23, 145–46, 171, 174, 176

Works: *The Alchemist*, 123, 141n. 127, 161–63, 181, 184–85, 187, 189–92, 195, 197n. 133, 201n. 141, 206n. 150; *Art of*

Poetry (from Horace), 84, 153, 209; *Bartholomew Fair*, 113n. 10, 123, 165n. 68, 166–67, 175, 178, 190–93, 199, 202n. 142, 203, 205; *The Case is Altered*, 188–90, 192n. 121, 194; *Catiline*, 72n. 42, 120, 128n. 27, 152n. 46, 157, 161–63, 174–75, 181, 184–5, 189–90, 192, 195, 197n 133, 206n. 150, 207; *Certayne Masques at Court*, 195–204; "Come Leave the Loathed Stage," 108; *Cynthia's Revels*, 90, 94–97, 104, 121n. 75, 122, 141n. 27, 143n. 30, 144–46, 149, 154n. 49, 161, 164–65, 172, 183n. 102, 184, 188–89, 197n. 133, 206n. 150; *Coronation Entertainment*, 169, 188, 190n. 115, 206n. 150; *The Devil is an Ass*, 200n. 139, 202n. 142, 203, 205, 208n. 152, 210, 214; *Discoveries*, 117; *Eastward Ho*, 149n. 39, 150, 154–57, 188, 191n. 120; *The English Grammar*, 209; *Entertainment at Althrope*, 169n. 76; *Epicoene*, 123, 184–87, 189n. 113, 190–91, 194, 195n. 115, 191, 194, 195n. 127, 197n. 133, 200n. 139, 204, 206n. 150; *Epigrams*, 125, 127–28, 130, 206n. 150; *Every Man in His Humour*, 42, 47, 95n. 89, 123, 142, 144, 146n. 34, 147, 184–85, 188–90, 197, 204, 206n. 150; *Every Man Out of His Humour*, 118, 122, 142–45, 147, 162–63, 174, 181, 184, 188, 190, 206n. 150, 211; "An Expostulation with Inigo Jones," 177; *The Forest*, 119, 183; *The Fortunate Isles*, 203, 207; *The Golden Age Restored*, 190n. 116, 195; *Haddington's Masque*, 169, 173–74, 178–79, 189, 206n. 150 ; *Hymenaei*, 117n. 17, 158, 169, 173–74, 177–79, 188, 190n. 116, 206–07; "Inviting a Friend to Supper," 2n. 5, 111, 113–14, 116–17, 119–20, 122n. 76, 123, 131; *The Isle of Dogs*, 22; *Love Freed from Ignorance and Folly*, 195; *Love Restored*, 184, 195; *Lovers Made Men*, 179n. 96, 203; *Love's Triumph Through Callipolis*, 179–80n. 96; *The Masque of Queenes*, 168, 174–75, 179–80, 189, 192n. 121, 194, 199, 206n. 150; *The Magnetic Lady*, 205, 209; *Masque of Augurs*, 179n. 95, 203; *Masque of Gypsies*, 209; *Masques of Blacknesse and Beautie*, 169, 172–73, 177n. 90, 178–79, 189, 206n. 150; *The May Lord*, 206n. 151; *Neptune's Triumph*, 117, 203; *The New Inne*, 107n. 2, 108–09, 111, 182, 194, 199, 200–05, 207; *Oberon*, 195; "Ode to Himself," 107–11, 200; "On

Cambridge Studies in Renaissance Literature and Culture

General Editor
STEPHEN ORGEL
Jackson Eli Reynolds Professor of Humanities, Stanford University

Lightning Source UK Ltd.
Milton Keynes UK
UKOW042101061112

201732UK00002B/76/A